INDEX OF BACKPACKING TOURS AN

CHAPTER	COUNTRY AND T(	
	INTRODUCTION	
	THE FIRST BACKPACKIN...	
1	ENGLAND	7
3	**FRANCE**	25
4	SWITZERLAND	27
5	AUSTRIA	29
6	GERMANY	57
7	AUSTRIA	65
8	ITALY	103
9	SWITZERLAND	120
10	FRANCE	166
11	ENGLAND	169
12	THE SECOND BACKPACKING TOUR	179
	Minehead-Lynton-Exeter	
13	THE THIRD BACKPACKING TOUR	211
	The isle of Wight	
14	THE FOURTH BACKPACKING TOUR	246
15	SCOTLAND	248
16	NORWAY	280
17	SWEDEN	301
18	DENMARK	310
19	GERMANY	319
20	AUSTRIA	339
21	SWITZERLAND	348
22	GERMANY	351
23	HOLLAND	357
24	ENGLAND	363
25	THE FIFTH BACKPACKING TOUR	364
26	FRANCE	366
27	ITALY	408
	EPILOGUE	439
	TRAVEL GUIDE INDEX	441
	ABOUT AUTHOR	450

INTRODUCTION

Backpacking by Train is based on a book I wrote with the title *An Australian Backpacker Abroad 1951-1953*, which tells the complete story of the two years I spent away from Australia. Portions of this book and others I have written have been published with various titles on Smashwords and they are still able to be downloaded from this EBook format. *Backpacking by Train* varies from the original books in that the theme is about the years 1952 and 1953, travelling by train to many destinations in western Europe, Scandinavia and the UK, with most of my accommodation in Youth Hostels, of the world wide Youth Hostel Association (YHA), of which I am a life member.

Tuesday 1st January 1952: On board my ship the *TSS Moreton Bay* just four days away from reaching Southampton, I began keeping a daily diary supplemented by notes in various notebooks for every day during the two years I was abroad. It is from these that this book is being written. Besides telling the story of my two years abroad, this book has another important function. That of a *Travel Guide* for the present day backpacker and tourist. I will explain more about this later in the introduction.

My love of trains began from my early childhood and being an ardent reader of railway books, it was my motivation for joining the Victorian Railways (VR) as an apprentice fitter and turner. I completed my apprenticeship with the VR in 1949 and became a qualified tradesman. I was earning a full wage and was very happy working in the railways which I fully expected would be my lifetime career. In 1946 I began skiing with the Rover Scouts and later joined

2

YHA to ski with them, never imagining how significant that move would be in determining the exciting path my life would take me in future years.

Leon Langley, a member of YHA asked me in 1950 if I would be interested in accompanying him on a working holiday to the UK in 1951. I was surprised that Leon asked me because, although we had both been members of YHA for some time, I was not amongst his group of YHA friends. I was aware too that Leon had asked other members of YHA to join him with no success. I said that I would have to think about it and would let him know as soon as I had made up my mind.

For some time I had been dating Judy, YHA member and our relationship was getting serious. However, Judy decided to go abroad, and in 1950 she sailed away to the UK. I was very sad, but Judy promised to keep in touch while she was away. Judy did, our letters taking five weeks to be delivered each way. What the hell I thought. Why not follow Judy to London and go to the UK with Leon? I phoned Leon and told him I would like to go with him, but I did not have enough money. I told Leon that if Tom Webb, another YHA member who had been pestering me to leave the railways and work for him and make a lot of money, still had work for me I would probably be able to earn enough money to go abroad. I rang Tom and yes, the job was still available.

Somewhat sadly, I resigned from the VR, another big decision, because the VR would not give me leave. I commenced working for Tom right away on parts for the new Holden car. I worked in a shed at the rear of our house in Rosanna. The work was on a piecework basis and I was soon earning more money than I ever dreamed possible, about £40 each week, compared to about £6 a week as a fitter and turner with the VR. Now that I was sure I had enough money to go abroad, Leon and I straightway went to a shipping agent in the city, where we paid a deposit and reserved our passages to Southampton on the *T.S.S.* *(*turbine steam ship) *Moreton Bay* of the

Aberdeen and Commonwealth Line. They said the intended sailing date was the on 25th November in 1951. This suited me well because it gave me time to earn much more money for the voyage, and travel to various countries in Europe. I wrote to Judy and told her the news. Judy replied writing that she was really looking forward to seeing me in London in about a year's time.

This was a huge adventure I was about to embark on, and it was a surprise of course to my parents, but they quickly accepted that they would not be seeing their 23 year old son for about two years, which was how long Leon had suggested we would be away. My mother certainly got a lot of pleasure telling all her friends that her eldest son Gordon was going abroad to the UK. Leon and I had vaccinations against smallpox and other diseases, because we could not get our passports until we had a doctor's certificate confirming we had the injections. In November 1950 the shipping agent advised us that the *Moreton Bay,* would, as scheduled, be leaving Port Melbourne on 25th November 1951 at 9:30 p.m. He asked us to come in and pay the balance and pick up our tickets. We did and the total fare was £68 Sterling.

Leon had relatives who lived in Hitchin about 30 miles north of London. He said we would be staying with them for about three weeks until we commenced our first tour, which he said would be to Austria, where we would hitchhike and stay in youth hostels (YHs). I had no particular destination that I wished to visit except to go to Scotland and see my mother's Auntie Ruby, see the mountains and perhaps ski in Austria and Switzerland, about which I had read so much. I was content to go along with Leon wherever he wished to go. However, one week into our tour of Austria, Leon suddenly said he was leaving me and did so with a quick handshake.

I discovered later that unbeknown to me, Leon had made arrangements with friends to leave me and join them during this Austrian tour. I was now on my own and I managed brilliantly, relishing in the freedom of deciding when, where and how I travelled

4

from then on. It was the best thing that happened, because it was the way I travelled for the rest of my tours (except one short English tour with a YHA friend).

I worked for Tom for seven months and earned just over £600, ending up with only £400 to take away with me. I spent a lot on clothes and golf equipment, because I had taken up golf as a sport while working for Tom.

A week before 25th November, I was packed and said farewells to most of my friends and relations. I also visited the Newport railway workshops, to see my former apprentice mates and tell them that I was going abroad. They all wished me luck. Leon and I went to the YHA club night in the city to say goodbye to all our friends there. Everybody wished us well, some saying they were already booked on ships to follow us early in the New Year. Many addresses were exchanged for meetings in the UK. In fact, while I was working and living in London, seventeen YHA Mt Buller ski club members were in London and thereabouts. I have listed all their names in one of my books.

During my two years abroad I embarked on three long backpacking tours, the first two being of two months duration and the last one month, together with two short tours in the south of England, which I took during the three months I worked in England at my trade between my first and second backpacking tours. I began my third and last backpacking tour in September 1953, through France and Italy to board the T.S.S. *Orion* in Naples, to take me back to Australia, reaching Port Melbourne on 30th October 1953.

The 1950 decade was I believe, the best ever years for backpacking, tourism and travel abroad, especially if you possessed a British passport. The term 'backpacking' was not in the Australian vocabulary at this time, and young Aussies had only just commenced travelling abroad on what were termed 'working holidays'. Later in the fifties, rucksacks evolved into one that still used a frame, but which supported a large rectangular pack that covered the whole of the wearer's back. These were called 'backpacks', which I believe is where the term 'backpacker' originated.

Back in London after my second long backpacking tour in Europe, I easily found work again in my trade and affordable full board. I lived and worked in London for an exciting eleven months, but during that period I did not undertake any backpacking tours or related activities. For this reason the story of those eleven months are not included in this book, nor is the narrative of my two voyages from Port Melbourne and return from Naples.

However, the story of my two years abroad would not be complete without these two enthralling times being told. Two books published by Tale publishing fill this gap. *Come on Board* describes my fabulous voyage from Port Melbourne to Southampton, and the rather troubling voyage back home from Naples to Port Melbourne on board the *Orion. An Aussie Backpacking Londoner* 1952-1953, describes the wonderful, event filled eleven months I lived and worked in London, culminating in the most important event of all, the crowning of Queen Elizabeth II on June 2nd 1953.

As well as telling the story of my two years abroad, I believe that this book can serve as a valid *Travel Guide* for the present day backpacker and tourist, planning a holiday in Europe, the UK and Scandinavia. Because in telling the story of my travels I have used various headings, icons, maps and a large, index to give the reader valuable information about the method of travel to towns, cities and localities and items of interest therein. This together with accommodation available, especially that of the world wide Youth Hostels Association of (YHs), as it was for me over 70 years ago, and many of these hostels are still in operation.

There have been many changes since then in these countries however, the main historical sights are still virtually intact. Churches, famous buildings, museums, city scapes, beautiful landscapes, mountains, lakes, fjords and forests, and sadly receding glaciers. Railway routes between principal cities and towns are still mostly as

6

they were, but there have been changes and additions, both in rail routes, new highways, autobahns and roads. Fantastic road and rail infrastructure has been constructed. Many, railway tunnels, and extra long base tunnels, together with a new age of concrete highways with huge bridges, tunnels, snow sheds and long viaducts, traversing country along routes that hitherto would have been thought impossible. All of these have produced a spider web of travel options which allow much faster, direct travel between main and more out of way destinations. Especially now with the advent of the EU

The trains are hauled by large, electric or diesel electric locomotives and the carriages are of many types, single and double decker, all resplendent in colourful liveries. Most are air conditioned so it is no longer possible to take photos from a train as I took, such as the portals of the Simplon Tunnel and many others. This book contains descriptions of travelling on three classic railways of the world–Bergen to Oslo–Glasgow to Fort William and the Semmering Railway to Vienna. I skied for three weeks in Switzerland using fantastic, rack railways as my principle means of transport and all are described in this book.

It is over 70 years since I travelled abroad. However, during my retirement in the last 5 years or so I have acquired the use of You Tube and KAYO. One of my greatest viewing pleasures beside watching, Aussie rules football, American baseball, golf and world event programmes, is nearly every day, travelling in the cab of a railway locomotive, or beside the driver in a car on journeys through Europe, the UK and Scandinavia, some of which I have travelled, and are described in this book. This has given me a very comprehensive knowledge of these countries as they are as I write, particularly Austria, Switzerland and Germany

This book contains many photos, all of which were taken with Kodak cameras that only had eight exposures to a roll of film.

7

CHAPTER 1

ENGLAND

Friday 4th January 1952: The *Moreton Bay* arrived in Southampton at 9 a.m. After a welter of hugs and hand shaking all round, Leon and I disembarked. Walking down the gangway of the *Moreton Bay* at Southampton brought to a conclusion one of the most enjoyable, and certainly the most relaxing and interesting five weeks of my life. Sailing to England on a one class, medium sized ship was a true, voyage of discovery. Sadly, this mode of travel is no longer an option for the tourist or backpacker. Leon and I disembarked to find that our first step in England was on the platform of the Southampton railway station adjacent to the wharf. We were directed to board a special boat train that was waiting to take us to London. At the head of our train, it was a great thrill for me to see my first English locomotive, a *School's* class, its olive green livery accentuating its clean, simple lines. It was an object of my childhood admiration having seen many photos of this locomotive class and others of the Southern Railway in my railway books.

iiiiiiiiiiiiiiiiiiiiiii

SOUTHAMPTON TO LONDON

I took one last look back at our wonderful ship the *Moreton Bay* as I began the next stage of my grand adventure, climbing aboard the train with only our hand luggage. We were told that our large luggage items in the ship's hold would be put on the train to be collected when we arrived at Waterloo Station in London. Very soon

8

with a high pitched whistle, the train began moving slowly at first then wound up to quite a high speed. It was music to my ears to hear the engine chugging away, but not so much the tinny whistle that was sounded frequently on the journey. The carriage seats were upholstered in a dark pattern and the interior of the swing door compartment, a 'dog box' as we would call it back in Australia, was quite warm. We didn't see much of the English countryside on the way because the windows were fogged up and it was quite misty outside. The train stopped a couple of times on the 70 mile journey and took about an hour and a half to reach Waterloo station.

LONDON

When we alighted from the train at Waterloo station we found that the luggage from the ship had been brought to a central point on the station platform, for us to identify and collect. We couldn't believe our eyes. Standing on the platform beside the luggage to welcome us was Netta Higgins, an attractive young lady that Leon and I had skied with in YHA. It was a wonderful surprise and a little puzzling, because we didn't know that Netta was in London. She told us that one of her YHA friends had written to her about our voyage. The last time I saw Netta, was at the end of a function for the Victorian skiing fraternity in Melbourne. I had had a little too much to drink, and went and lay down on a sofa and listened to some rather beautiful background music. After a short while Netta came over and knelt down beside me and asked me if I was OK. I said I was. I asked her if she knew the name of the music that was being played. She said it was "The Peer Gynt Suite by Grieg". Whenever I hear that music of Peer Gynt being played it always reminds me of Netta and that exciting meeting with her on Waterloo Station.

We made a note of Netta's address and telephone number, said goodbye and gathered up all our luggage. We hired a taxi outside Waterloo Station to take us to King's Cross Station on the opposite side of the city. On the way across London in the taxi, the only London landmarks we recognised were the Thames River, which we crossed over on Waterloo Bridge, very exciting, because I remembered seeing the movie *Waterloo Bridge* some years earlier. London taxis were mostly Austins, all of the same design and colour, black. There was a space beside the driver where our luggage was placed while we sat in the rather voluminous back seat, which was separated from the driver by a glass screen. King's Cross Station with its central clock tower was very familiar to me, as I had seen the station's photo in my railway books many times.

iiiiiiiiiiiiiiiiiiii

LONDON TO HITCHIN

We caught a steam hauled train to Hitchin 30 miles or so north of London in the County of Hertfordshire. I had never heard of Hitchin and strangely had never looked up any information about the town where Leon's relations Mr. and Mrs. Baker lived, and who we were going to stay with for three weeks before commencing our first backpacking tour across the English Channel to Austria. The journey to Hitchin took about 30 minutes, but once again we didn't see much from the windows because of a heavy mist. England it appeared was a little reluctant to show itself to us. It was a stopping train, but I only remember seeing two stations the train stopped at, Hatfield and Welwyn Garden City.

There was a long bridge the train crossed before stopping at Welwyn Garden City and there was also a tunnel the train bored through near there. The carriage was warm and the upholstery was the same as the train to Waterloo, a dull pattern which wouldn't show the dirt too much, a wise choice I thought. The doors were all swing type, which I found out later were referred to as 'slam doors.'

HITCHIN

We left the train at Hitchin with our luggage and took a taxi through the mist and cold to Mr. and Mrs. Baker's house, arriving there a short time after noon. Their house at 3 Hillcrest Avenue was not very far from the station. Mr. and Mrs. Baker were a lovely middle aged couple, and they immediately made us very welcome. Mr. and Mrs. Baker are Leon's brother in law's parents. Their son Howard immigrated to Melbourne where he married Leon's sister. That was a great surprise, as I had heard Howard Baker many times in Melbourne reading the news on radio stations 3AR and 3LO.

When we commenced unpacking, I suddenly I realised with dread that I had not collected my rucksack with the rest of my luggage at Waterloo station! Leon said he didn't remember seeing my rucksack there. I was devastated. My rucksack contained all my skiing clothes, sleeping bag, hike tent, golf shoes and jacket, and many other items of clothing and ski gear.

We wondered if my rucksack had actually been taken on the train, or indeed if it had been taken off the *Moreton Bay*. What to do? I suppose I should have rung Waterloo station, but I didn't want to impose on their welcoming for both of us, particularly Leon, their close relation. My problem could wait. The rest of the day passed with stories of our travels and with Leon telling the Bakers about their son Howard's life in Australia.

Another shock awaited me on that first day at the Bakers. I was beginning to feel a little hungry as I waited for the evening meal to be served, but it never eventuated. All we had were scones and tea. I discovered later that this was the English custom of 'high tea,' the main meal being at lunchtime. I wondered if this was the custom in all English households or just a convenience that was adopted by retired couples like the Bakers, and the gentry.

I could not imagine how a working man could live with this strange eating arrangement. After a supper of tea and cake we went to our beds. It had been a long exciting day spoiled only by the loss of my rucksack. Even though I was very tired I couldn't sleep for a while worrying about my rucksack, and what it was going to cost me to replace it all, but with the hope that my rucksack must be somewhere and will be eventually found, I dropped off to sleep.

HITCHIN TO LONDON

Saturday 5th January: I travelled from Hitchin to London by train in search of my rucksack. I had time to have a good look at Hitchin station. There were four tracks between the platforms, and as I waited for my train a passenger train sped through at an amazingly high speed towards London, its high pitched whistle heralding its approach. The journey to London King's Cross was very enjoyable because this time the sun shone feebly and the mist had mostly gone. I could at last see the green farming country separated by hedges. The mist I discovered was a predominate feature of sunny days in winter in England. As the train ambled along I was surprised by the number of trains that passed us by on adjacent tracks going both to and from London.

The train stopped at each station on the way and every time when it stopped at a station, just before the train started up again, the noise of the closing doors, bang, bang, banged all along the train. Then after quietness reigned, the guard waved his green flag, blew his whistle and with a pathetic answering peep from the locomotive we were on our way again. Some of our early Victorian Railways (VR) trains in Melbourne that I travelled in to work each day were also swing door carriages, but I was never conscious of the doors closing loudly as I was on English trains. The term 'slam door carriages' was very appropriate for these carriages. The locomotive that hauled my King's Cross-Hitchin train I discovered was a Thompson B1 4-6-0 painted black, but nowhere near as impressive as the green *Schools* class locomotive, I saw in Southampton station.

LONDON

Arriving at King's Cross Station I took the tube to Waterloo Station lost property office, but my rucksack was not there. I left them with all my particulars and then decided to try and ring Judy my girl friend back in Australia, who was really responsible for me making the big decision to go abroad. In the last letter I got from Judy before I left Australia, she gave me her phone number FRO

12

2300. I rang the number. Judy was home and excitedly invited me out to her boarding house, or 'digs' in English slang. After hugs and kisses, we had a lot to talk about, but there was no hint of us getting back together again. We were both enjoying being on a great adventure far from home. Judy had a good job at the Argentine Embassy. I told her about Leon and our plans to go backpacking in Austria in a couple of weeks' time. She was very interested, but had no plans to go backpacking. I said I would ring her again soon and take her to a show. With that I left her with a hug and kiss and took the train back to Hitchin.

During the next couple of days I made many phone calls to the British Railways (BR) lost property, and travelled up to London in search of my rucksack. While I was in London, I explored the great city and became familiar with the London Transport System, which includes the underground railway (the Tube) and all the red, double decker buses, as well as other forms of London based transport. I was amazed at how close a fit the tube carriages were to the sides of the tunnels. Standing on a platform waiting for a tube train, it was always possible to know when a train was about to appear from the tunnel mouth, even before its lights could be seen, by the rush of air as it advanced along the tunnel. I later read that this was a feature of the design, it helped ventilate the tunnels. I loved the brilliant red, double decker buses, they were fun to use and quite fast. Riding in the top deck of a double decker bus was a great thrill, because it provided a very good view of the streets and buildings as the bus passed by. It was not the first time I had sat in the top deck of a double decker bus, because Melbourne had double decker buses running to Northcote for a short time. Riding in a double decker bus in London however, was much more thrilling than riding down High Street Northcote. One of the differences that I had to become familiar with compared to buses in Melbourne, was that the place names were not changed when the bus reached its destination and reversed direction. The first time I travelled on a London bus, I found I was going the wrong way. I learned to check with the conductor as soon as I boarded the bus if it was going the right way. Another difference I noticed was that the London policeman, affectionately referred to as 'bobbies'. Their black helmets were a matt finish, whereas ours were gloss black, which I thought were easier to see in a crowd. It was already nearly dark by 4 p.m., which like 'high tea' will take a bit of getting used to. I used the tube a lot, and the more I got to know London, the more I liked it. It was so big, so exciting and busy, although I would hesitate to call it beautiful. I saw some peculiar sights in London, a chauffeur driven Roils Royce with only poodles on the back seat. Then there were the young, well-dressed lads who I imagined were office boys in well-tailored dark suits wearing bowler hats, but with pimply faces, which looked rather incongruous.

Hitchin is 32 miles (51 km) from London on the main railway line to Edinburgh in Scotland. It was also an important rail junction, with lines going to Cambridge, Peterborough, King's Lynn and many other places. I learned too that it is the route of the famous *Flying Scotsman,* so I was really looking forward to seeing this famous locomotive and train. The junction was very busy, high speed steam trains roared through at all times of the day and night. As a rail fan, the Bakers could not have lived in a better locality in all of England, for my love of railways. From my railway books, I knew quite a lot about this famous railway line the London and North Eastern Railway (LNER), and the trains that ran on it.

Monday 7th January: We were visited by two Australians, Ralph Bateman and his wife Gladys. They came from Sydney in 1949 on a voyage to the UK, intending to stay for about a year and tour around. They liked England so much that Ralph a dentist, set himself up in a dental practice in Hitchin. I imagined that there must be many more Australian professionals like Ralph and Gladys in the UK. Ralph told Leon and me that if we needed to see a doctor, dentist, or an optician while we were in the UK, we would not have to pay anything. The day we set foot on English soil at Southampton, we qualified for

14

National Health. I decided to waste no time. I needed a new pair of glasses. I would have an eye test and new glasses all for free, simply because I am British! I went into Hitchin and found an optician. I showed him my passport and he said he could give me a test in an hour, so I went and watched the trains go by on Hitchin station. The eye test showed I did need new glasses, and from the limited choice of frames supplied by the National Health, I chose black horn rims, which were quite popular and fashionable at the time. The optician assured me there would be no charge. How wonderful is the British National Health.

Tuesday 8th January: Mrs. Baker took Leon and me into Hitchin to show us around. The shopping centre was not very large and most of the shops were built in quaint old style, Tudor architecture, with white walls criss-crossed with black wooden slats. Some too had thatched rooves. At one end of the town there was a big Church of England church with a graveyard in its grounds, which Mrs. Baker said was quite usual for churches in England.

Wednesday 9th January: It snowed overnight, leaving only about an inch still on the ground, which for me was nothing exciting compared to the snow that I was used to seeing, skiing in the alps back in Victoria. In the evening we went to a pub with the Bakers and the Batemans. The pub walls were dark timber, as were the tables and seats. The bar was quite small. Draught beer was pulled with long handled taps. We had a beer, but it is served at room temperature, which made it less enjoyable than cold, Aussie beer. Otherwise it was a nice drop. Although it was freezing cold outside, it was lovely and warm inside the pub as we sat drinking and talking, while a game of darts was being played at one side of the bar.

Thursday 10th January: Leon and I took the train to London. We went to Australia House where we caught up on news from Australia. It was really great to meet a few people from the *Moreton Bay,* and we swapped experiences about our time in England. Some had found digs and jobs. Some like us, were about to travel to various places in England and across the English Channel. Once again, I enquired at British Railways lost property office about my rucksack, but to no avail. As the days went by, I became less optimistic about it turning up. Leon and I enquired about the cost of a train journey to Salzburg in Austria. The price seemed quite reasonable. We then split up. I went to the Bank of New South Wales in Berkeley Square, but no nightingale sang for me. I drew £110 in a combination of cash, traveller's cheques and Austrian shillings. This left me with a balance of £190 in the bank. One strange unit of English currency that I did not want to carry in my wallet was the huge, white, £10 Sterling note, about eight by five inches. I changed these back to singles.

Leon made his way back to Hitchin and by now it was nearly dark. I rang Netta who had just got home from work. She said she would love to see me. We had a bite to eat together at a cafe nearby. Netta told me that she had no trouble getting a good job as a stenographer, but the pay was not very good. She was about to book a place for two weeks in Grindelwald, a ski resort in Switzerland. Netta asked me if we would like to join her. I said I was certainly interested, but would have to ask Leon. I said I would let her know before the end of the week.

Netta then took me to visit two Australian friends of hers living in digs close by, Nellie Hobern and her daughter Jan, both on working holidays. Nellie, I guessed, was in her mid-thirties and Jan was about 18. Nellie was not a skier, but was going to go with Netta to Switzerland. I stayed too late and missed the last London Transport bus back to Hitchin. After some frenzied enquiries, I was directed to the Green Line bus, which went on a more roundabout route. About halfway back to Hitchin I realised I had lost my wallet, containing £60 in odd notes from my back pocket! I went to bed that night wondering what was going to be the next disaster. Life in

England was certainly not as relaxing as it was aboard the *Moreton Bay*.

Friday 11th January: Early the next morning I rang the Hoberns and was very relieved to find my wallet was there, and decided to go to London straight away to pick it up and do some shopping. I was going to go by train, but Mr. Baker told me about the double decker bus that went from Hitchin to London, so I decided to try it. The journey was a little cheaper than the train and slower. The view of the passing countryside and towns from the bus were much more interesting than from the train, because the bus passed through the centre of all the towns along the way on the Great North Road. The bus took me directly into the West End, so reluctantly on most occasions after that ride I went into London on the double decker bus. As soon as I arrived in London I went straight to the Hoberns and picked up my wallet, which was a great relief. They told me to be more careful and I certainly will in future. I then went to Lillywhites, a large store that sold all manner of outdoor equipment. I finally settled on a framed rucksack, much like my missing one, but a little larger. It had quick release tabs on both shoulder straps and the waistband, which I thought was an excellent safety feature, allowing the wearer to quickly release the rucksack, in the event of a bad fall on skis. I also bought a sleeping bag, small stove and a bum bag. Next at a golf shop I bought a navy blue, gabardine golf jacket, with a shot silk lining. It was expensive, but well worth the money, because I wore it skiing and golfing on and off for over forty years.

Saturday 12th January: I was beginning to get a little sick of Leon, as he was always trying to take rises out of me, making me look a fool in front of the Bakers and their friends. He acted sometimes as though he resented my company. I told him about Netta's ski holiday in Switzerland, and said I was going with her, but Leon didn't seem to be too keen. I suggested we should both go to London soon and see Netta.

Sunday 13th January: Back in Hitchin In the evening after high tea, I had my first English bath, as the Baker's house didn't have a shower. Hitchin is situated in a limestone area and the reticulated town water supply is not crystal clear, but a light green colour. Soap provided an acceptable lather, but left a large white scum around the bath, which was quite tiresome to remove. Kettles we were told, had a limited life. Over time, a hard chalky deposit, built up on the inside, and they eventually had to be discarded. Quite a change from living in Melbourne, said to have purist, water supply in the world.

Monday 14th January: Early morning I went by double decker bus to Luton, about 13 km from Hitchin. It is a large, dirty, industrial town in the county of Hertfordshire as is Hitchin. It is also the home of the famous Luton Girls' Choir, renowned for their beautiful singing. I shopped and bought some corduroy trousers. I was delighted when I returned to Hitchin, to find that there was mail from home. I read the letters over and over again, soaking up every word my mother wrote in her beautiful handwriting. A YHA friend, Maurice Spanger who was backpacking in Austria, wrote a letter to Leon saying that the cost of everything had gone up in Austria. On learning this, Leon took fright. He said, he didn't want to go skiing, but wanted to go to Italy, alone. Strangely, I didn't attach too much importance to Leon's statement about going alone to Italy. Perhaps I should have asked him about it, but didn't. I rang Netta and told her I would go skiing with her in Switzerland, but not Leon. Netta was delighted. Now I really had something exciting to look forward to.

Tuesday 15th January: After lunch I decided to have a game of golf. I caught a bus to Letchworth, a Garden City about 10 km north of Hitchin. I had no trouble getting a game on the private course. It was very cold, but I was wearing my new golf jacket, which was very comfortable and warm. I had a good game and enjoyed the relatively flat course. Golf in Great Britain is not a game for the working class. The green fees for the round were 10 shillings, which

18

was very expensive. However, it was an interesting experience, and made me very pleased that I had brought my golf clubs with me.

When Leon made that criticism of me, I didn't retaliate with what I considered were Leon's shortcomings, although I thought he was more than a trifle immature. The remark he made about going to Italy alone, and he didn't want to go skiing, was when I think, we both realised we were not compatible as travelling companions, even though we had enjoyed ourselves together on the voyage. This didn't look too good for our Austrian tour together, but I thought, 'time will tell.' Leon didn't mention my failings anymore, so I left it at that, but watched my table manners, which I thought were OK. It was not the custom in England to have a daily bath or shower, not surprising I thought if all the water in England is like it is here at the Bakers. Both men and women made extensive use of deodorants. I bought a bottle of some sort of deodorant, and tried to make myself more presentable, if in fact I did have BO.

Thursday 17th January: Leon and I took the bus to London where we split up, planning to meet at Netta's digs after she came home from work. First of all I enquired about my rucksack, but it had not been found. Then I wandered along Oxford and Regent Streets, each with a character of their own. Regent Street with its long curve and many large shops, Oxford Street lined with shops including Selfridges, a large emporium that reminded me of Myer in Bourke Street Melbourne. Flakes of snow were falling as I travelled out to Netta's place. Leon was already there, as was Gil Rowe another YHA member, who had just landed in England. Gil was a great bloke, tall, dark and handsome. It was good to see him again.

Netta had booked us into a Friends of Nature Hostel in Grindelwald for two weeks in March. It is a famous Swiss alpine skiing and climbing resort. Netta said we couldn't stay at a YHA hostel there, because she was over 24, the age limit for staying with YHA in Switzerland. Netta was wrong about the age limit in YHs, because there is none. I was 23 at the time, but it didn't matter. Leon was still not interested in skiing, but Gil said he might join us there.

We all went off to see *South Pacific* at the Theatre Royal in Drury Lane. I enjoyed the show, Mary Martin was the star and Larry Hagman and June Whitfield were also in the cast. My favourite tunes were; *'Some Enchanted Evening'* and *'I'm in Love with a Wonderful Guy'*. It was very exciting to be seeing a show in the legendary West End. Before we parted we made a date to go to the opera at Saddler's Wells.

Friday 18th January: I had a morning at home with the Bakers and wrote letters, one to Auntie Ruby, my mother's cousin in Scotland. I was always aware of the relatives my mother had in Scotland, particularly Auntie Ruby. They wrote to each other regularly, and exchanged calendars of countryside scenes in Scotland and Australia. There was also Bob, Ruby's husband, and John, Greta, May and Heather, other relations all of whom I expected I would meet later in the year.

Leon had gone to London and in the afternoon I helped Mr. Baker cut and stack wood. I then went in to Hitchin and picked up my new, free glasses, which looked good on me, then up to the Hitchin railway station to watch the trains go by, and test out my new glasses, which earned a pass. The English locomotives have high pitched, shrill whistles, so unlike our VR locos, with their loud chime whistles that can be heard for miles. Mr. and Mrs. Baker were looking after us very well, with nice, filling meals at lunch time whenever I was home with them, but I still couldn't get used to high tea in the evening. Every now and again Leon and I helped Mr. Baker chop wood and do other odd jobs around the house.

Monday 21st January: After lunch Leon and I went to London by double decker bus, where we purchased our train tickets and cross channel tickets for Salzburg in Austria, which Leon said would be the first leg of our trip on the Continent. I was prepared to go where he wanted to for a start, as I imagined we would work out our route

20

when we arrived in Salzburg. We met Gil at Netta's digs and off we went to the Saddler's Wells theatre at Angel, which was not in the West End, but north of London's central districts. I thought the theatre was quite ordinary.

We saw two short operas, *Cavalleria Rusticana*, by Mascagni, and *Pagliacci*, by Leon Cavallo, which I believe are usually always performed together. I enjoyed both operas. The stage sets and the costumes were very colourful. Both operas are short and have uncomplicated stories. This was the second time I had been to the opera the first time being in Melbourne. I found I quite enjoy going to the opera. After the opera, Leon went back to Hitchin, but I stayed with Gil and Netta, to have a drink at a rather noisy pub in Angel. Gil invited me to sleep at his boarding house, so we continued drinking for a while, before making our way back to Clapham, where we said goodnight to Netta We were both looking forward to meeting her in a month's time in Grindelwald.

On the way to Gill's digs, we caught the tube to Clapham South station, where I foolishly accepted Gill's challenge, of running up a descending escalator. Maybe because of my condition and the fact that I had a belly full of beer, I did not realise how difficult it would be. The first half was very easy, the next quarter much harder, but the last quarter was extremely difficult—and those last two steps, were virtually impossible. It was only later, that I discovered that Clapham South had the longest escalators in the London Underground! When we arrived at Gill's digs he brought out a couple of small bottles of English beer, which helped to bring my blood pressure and heart rate back to normal.

Gill told me he planned to ski in Austria, then to hitchhike down to southern Italy and France where it was warmer, before returning to England to find a job. I was now getting quite excited about crossing the Channel to the Continent, and couldn't wait for the journey to begin. I slept 'the sleep of the dead' on the couch, in my clothes.

Leon and the author on board just before the Moreton Bay sailed

A last look back at our wonderful ship the Moreton Bay

Netta Higgins a YHA friend who met us on Waterloo station

The larger rucksack that the author purchased and used to replace the smaller one that was lost and then found

A street in Hitchin with the C of E church at the end of the street

A Thompson B1 locomotive with a slam door carriage train at Hitchin

Tuesday 22nd January: The next morning I caught the bus back to Hitchin. As soon as the front door was opened, I saw that everyone including Leon, had a big smile on their faces.They led me into the lounge room where, surprise, surprise, on the floor was my rucksack! There was also a letter from my mother, but I left that unread, until I checked the contents of my rucksack, Thank goodness it was all there. How my rucksack came to be delivered to the Bakers was a bit of a mystery. Mr. and Mrs. Baker seemed to think a railway official brought it. I never did find out the story of where it had been. There were no tags on it, which might have given us all a clue as to its whereabouts since it arrived at Southampton. Everything comes to those who hope, even though in the last week I had really given up all hope of ever seeing my rucksack and its contents again.

After settling down from that pleasant shock, I read my mother's letter, telling me how the family missed me and how hot it was, as they prepared to go on their annual holidays at Edithvale on Port Phillip Bay, I went to sleep that night very relieved, feeling like a millionaire. Now that I had my lost rucksack back, I remembered what joy it had given me as a Boy Scout, when I purchased the rucksack at Andy Broad's skiing and hiking shop in Melbourne nearly ten years ago. Our framed rucksacks were in the shape of an 'A' tapering to the top with large pockets on each side, the normal type of rucksack used at the time for hiking, skiing and most other outdoor activities. They were excellent rucksacks and mine served me well. We were both madly packing. Now I had two of everything, I had to decide which of every duplicated item I would keep.

Wednesday 23rd January: Still packing, I picked out the best to take with me, mostly it was the new items because they were better than my originals. I was fairly sure that at some later date I could sell a few of these items, especially the rucksack. The new rucksack was better and larger than my other one and that was the first choice. We will both be carrying a rucksack and secured inside its zipped pockets are our valuables, traveller's cheques, extra money and other such valuable items. Because we will be mostly staying in Youth Hostels, our rucksacks will only contain our sleeping bags, changes of clothes, underwear, toilet gear and pyjamas. They will be light to carry, and our bum bags strapped around our wastes will hold all the small things we need day to day, some money, sunglasses, maps, Youth Hostel (YH) guide books and most importantly my diary. I will wear my ski boots and keep my golf shoes in my rucksack. Leon is wearing his hiking boots.

Thursday 24th January 1952: Early in the morning we thanked Mr. and Mrs. Baker for looking after us wonderfully for nearly a month. They wished us good luck, and with a few hugs we began our journey. Leon said he would write to them of his whereabouts and tell them when he would be returning to Hitchin. I said that they could expect me back on or about 10th March. As soon as I returned I would look for a job and board.

CHAPTER 2

THE FIRST BACKPACKING TOUR

ENGLAND
HITCHIN

HITCHIN TO DOVER

Our tour really began when we went by train to London and took the Circle Line train to Victoria Station, where the train for Dover left promptly at 1 p.m. (1300 hours). From now on we would have to get used to International Time, because all train times on the Continent are shown in this manner. We didn't see much from the train window for most of the way to Dover, because of the mist and fog, but at Dover it had cleared enabling us to see a short way across the famous English Channel. We went through customs without any problems

DOVER TO CALAIS

We crossed the English Channel in a large, cross channel ferry. It was a smooth crossing in fine weather.

CHAPTER 3
FRANCE

At 5 p.m. the ferry tied up at the wharf in Calais. The harbour and some buildings still showed many signs of war damage, The most evidence I had seen of the war even in England, since landing in Malta from the *Moreton Bay* and seeing the war damage there. My first look at France was quite a dreary experience, especially as it was dark. Without much ado we followed a motley lot of people from the ferry along the wharf to the ground level platform where a train to Salzburg was waiting. We climbed aboard, sat down and waited with anticipation for the train to begin our long journey.

iiiiiiiiiiiiiiiiiiiii

CALAIS TO BASEL

With a long beep from its whistle, a much higher note than from an English locomotive, our steam train moved off into the gloom. Our compartment in the corridor type carriage was drab, but clean and warm. A middle aged French couple joined us and they were a little drab too. Leon and I both had maps and we followed the route as best we could. From Calais the train travelled east through Lille and Strasbourg, which were the only two stations we were able to recognise. The French couple left us with an "Au revoir" in Strasbourg, where we noticed that there was snow on the ground. It was great now because we had the compartment to ourselves.

26

CHAPTER 4
SWITZERLAND

From Strasbourg the train turned south and I slept on and off in my seat. Many miles later the train crossed the French–Swiss border at les Verrieres, in Switzerland, where there was a customs check of our passports.

LES **VERRIERES**

We did not require visas for France, Switzerland, Austria or Italy, except if we intended to go to Vienna we needed a Grey Card, which we had obtained in London.

We felt nothing, but there had been a very smooth change of locomotives to our train, while our passports were being checked in our compartment, by Swiss customs officials in their well-tailored uniforms who spoke excellent English with little accent.

Very soon the train moved off again heading for Basel in the north. After going a few miles, I realised by the sound that our train was being hauled by a Swiss electric locomotive, which was not surprising, because I was aware that virtually all Swiss railway lines were electrified. We were getting hungry, but the meals in the dining car were 12 shillings Stirling. Much too dear, so we had the chocolate and some other food we had packed in our rucksacks. From then on I slept a bit until the train after about 80 km, came to a halt in Basel where dawn was breaking.

BASEL

Friday 25th January: Our train arrived in Basel in Switzerland at 6 a.m. on a very cold snowy morning. There was a quick customs check. Then a porter showed us the platform where our train would leave for Salzburg, but not until 8.30 a.m. We had two hours to fill in so we had a breakfast of fried eggs and bacon at a cafe on the platform, which filled a rather large void in my stomach. We then took a short walk around Basel, the second largest city in Switzerland, and an international railway junction. Basel is close to the borders of France and Germany, as well as being a large port on the Rhine River.

My first impression was that Basel was very 'Americanised' as most of the cars we saw were American. The shops displayed many beautiful, but expensive products, clothes, jewellery and furs, while the other impression I had, was that everything was spick and span, even with 15 cm of snow on the ground. I was delighted to see all the large, American cars of many makes and colours on the streets and discovered that they belonged to American Occupation Force soldiers.

Back at the Basel station we decided it would be a good idea to change our pound Sterling notes into Austrian money. Swiss currency was very good compared with Austrian, so by changing our money in Basel, we received a better deal. 72 Austrian Shillings (Asch) for £1 Sterling, better we thought than if we had waited and changed it in Salzburg.

iiiiiiiiiiiiiiiiiiiiiii

BASEL TO SALZBURG

With its many platforms and a mixture of steam and electric trains arriving and leaving all the time, we found that our train, which was to be hauled by an electric locomotive was already in the platform, so very quickly we climbed aboard and settled back in our seats looking forward to enjoying the long 409 km journey to Salzburg. Although the fog was not apparent during our walk through the city, it was a pity that the weather was foggy leaving Basel, because we saw very little from the train. The comfortably filled train sped along stopping first at Aarau, then after some twenty

28

kilometres suddenly the mist and fog was replaced by darkness except for our carriage lights, because the train entered a tunnel longer by far than any railway tunnel we had ever been through. Emerging from the tunnel into the mist and fog once again, the very large city of Zurich was our next stop where we caught a glimpse of Lake Zurich on which the city is located.

Leaving Zurich, the train headed in an easterly direction skirting around the edge of the calm, misty waters of Lake Zurich for many kilometres, then began climbing through a hilly, forested landscape passing through a couple of stations before coming to a stop at Buchs. This was the last Swiss station before the train crossed over a big long bridge over the Rhine River that defines the western border between Switzerland and the small Principality of Liechtenstein, which is only 41 km long and 24 km wide.

29

CHAPTER 5
AUSTRIA

AUSTRIA AND NORTH ITALY

A map showing the railway lines and location of towns and cities the author visited in Austria, Germany and Italy. Youth Hostels where the author stayed are shown in bold type with the letters YH after the name.

Our train crossed the border into Austria and slowed down as it climbed through mist and cloud. This again was very frustrating because we knew that there was marvellous mountain scenery hidden from us, because the train was now in the western most province of Austria, the Vorarlberg. Very soon the train came to a stop in Feldkirch our first Austrian town, but there were no border checks.

30

The train continued on wending its way around many curves and along benches cut into the side of mountains, but the only part we could see because of the low cloud, were where the mountains began their steep climb from the snow covered valley floor. Sometimes we could only see the black walls of mostly short tunnels of around 500 metres that our train passed through every now and again, where a forested spur of the mountain range jutted out extending right down into the valley floor. Then suddenly we were plunged into darkness except for the carriage lighting, as we entered the 10.5 km Arlberg Tunnel, which burrowed under the Arlberg Pass.

When our train eventually emerged from this long tunnel, surprise, surprise! The clouds had lifted and at last we could see the mountains in all their glory. What a revelation it was. It was really wonderful to at last see the sun shining on the high, snow covered mountains, complete with ski lifts and skiers skiing down. It may have been the light, or perhaps the type of snow, but the texture of the snow looked different, softer maybe, than any snow on the mountains back home.

The train stopped at St Anton to let passengers on and off, many dressed in various coloured ski clothes and carrying skis. Both names St Anton and Arlberg were very familiar to me. I was at a very significant place with respect to the sport of skiing. It was here that the famous 'Arlberg School' technique of skiing was first taught by the Austrian, Hannes Schneider, the founder of the school. I learned to ski by this technique taught by Austrian ski instructors with the Rover Scouts, a technique that served me faithfully all my long skiing life.

Leaving St Anton the train entered another tunnel at the end of which, a short way further on the weather closed in again. I thought to myself, while the train was stopped in St Anton and I was admiring the sunlit, snow covered mountains that the ski Gods had lifted the veil of cloud and mist just for us. "This is really living!"

We exclaimed, as the train continued on its way to Salzburg, burrowing through more tunnels and gradually losing altitude as it wound its way along a steep sided valley to Landeck. There were passing tracks at Landeck and we hardly had to wait before a train passed through. From then on it was single track through rather dense forest, the railway clinging to the right hand side of narrow deep valleys.

There were more passing loops situated at a few stations where it was relatively flat and open for a short stretch to accommodate the loop. One of these stations was called Schonwies. Our train was quite long and had some sort of café or restaurant car in its consist, but we didn't walk along the corridor style carriages to investigate. We had bought ham rolls, chocolate, cheese and drinks in Basel and had been consuming these ever since we crossed into Austria. Soon the cloud a fog began to thin and we could see a few hundred metres up the sides of the steep mountains that enclosed the narrow valley on both sides.

The next big towns were Ostel and Haiming and it was after these stations that the train really sped up. I noted that we were now running on the right had side of double tracks. The electric locomotive's truck type horn whistle sounding many times as it approached boom gated level crossings. The next stop was at a really large town with a large name to suit, called Pfaffenhoven. The snow covered valley here was much wider and flatter. The train passed by a number of small towns, but I was not able to read their names as we were going very fast and it was getting dark.

At 7 p.m. our train came to stop in the brightly lit city of Innsbruck, but we couldn't see much past the colourful lights of the station and the city. We still had another 130 km to go to Salzburg and we had eaten all our food. I dozed on and off and looked out the window from time to time seeing the snow on the ground flash by in dazzling white lit by the carriage lights. At last our long, but very interesting train journey came to an end and at 9 10 p.m. our train

32

pulled into the Salzburg railway station. Tired and hungry after the long journey, we climbed down from the train.

⚠

SALZBURG

We began looking for the youth hostel *(Jugendherberge)* in the snow covered, busy streets of the city. Although it was night the street lights and the headlights from the many cars reflected back from the snow made it easy to move along the icy pavements. We soon found the YH in Hellbrunner Strasse where we were welcomed by Franz the warden, who arranged a quick meal for us, which was most enjoyable and sorely needed. The YH was very warm and comfortable with good bunks to sleep on. Meals could be purchased if ordered. There were not many in the YH beside us, so after talking for a while with Franz over a warming cup of tea, we climbed into our sleeping bags. It had been an exciting day and before long I was fast asleep.

Saturday 26th January: Breakfast the next morning was provided by the warden at a very low cost. Leon said the next place he wanted to visit was Bad Ischl about 80 km away by rail. By now from what we had seen of the snow covered countryside from the train and here in Salzburg, there was no possibility that we would be able to hitch hike to Bad Ischl. Looking at our maps, the train seemed the best way to get there. Maybe there was a bus going there, but we never thought to enquire. Leon suggested we have a look around Salzburg today and go there early the next morning. I agreed.

Consulting our YH guidebook, we decided first to see Mozart's birthplace. Emerging from the warm, snug interior of the YH on to the snow covered street, we were met with sights and sounds that were completely unfamiliar to us. There was about 15 to 20 cm of snow on the rather narrow streets on which cream, trolley buses with trailers attached, ran around the city churning up the mushie snow, the first trolley buses I had ever seen. The buses were fitted with tyre chains and the sound of the tyre chains clinking on cars and buses were I thought, musical and enjoyable, coupled with the melodious sound of church bells that rang from time to time. There were many large American cars of all models, makes and colours. I am a great admirer of American cars, so different from the monotonous black of virtually all the taxis and cars in England. Franz told us that Austria was divided into four occupation zones, administered by the armed forces of France, Britain, Russia and America. Salzburg was the headquarters of the American army of occupation in Austria, which was the reason we saw so many American cars being driven by soldiers in uniform.

We paid a small fee to visit the Mozart Museum situated in a narrow, snowy street. We entered the house where Mozart was born in 1756, and where he lived and composed many of his works. His violin, piano, and clavichord were on view in a small room with a very low ceiling. There were also many photos and sketches of Mozart on the walls. In a room on the floor above, lots of manuscripts and books were on view, but the museum was so terribly cold that we didn't linger after we had seen the main exhibits. How Mozart ever played his instruments and wrote music in that cold house in winter I was not quite sure, but I supposed that being a genius made him impervious to the cold. However, we learned that most of his music was composed in Vienna and other Austrian towns and cities.

I wanted to buy skis and boots so that I could soon go skiing. Along the street from the Mozart Museum I saw a sports shop. Leon didn't want to come with me, so we agreed to meet back at the YH. I had a look at a lot of fantastic skis and boots in the shop, the like of which I had never seen back home. I finally purchased a pair of magnificent, Kneisel, laminated skis for about 800 Austrian Schillings (Asch), as well as bindings, ski stocks, boots and socks. I was absolutely thrilled with my purchases, especially as they were so cheap compared to what they would have cost in Australia. The

34

exchange rate was 72 Asch to £1 Sterling. The total bill for the whole lot was about £11. After purchasing all the gear, I walked down the street with the skis over my shoulder, and was taken by surprise when Austrians passing by stroked and admired the skis, saying: *"schon, schon"* (beautiful, beautiful). I told Franz the warden about the reaction of the Austrians to my new skis. He said that was not surprising, as the average Austrian wage is only about 900 Asch. per month, so Austrians had very little hope of owning skis such as mine. He added that having the Yanks in Austria had caused a rise in price of many goods.

I decided to try out my new skis somewhere close by. I ended up on the snow covered slopes running down a wall of the Salzburg castle where some Austrians were skiing and tobogganing. It was great to be on skis again. I skied for a while and returned to the YH for a meal of soup and a form of stew. Salzburg castle is a large castle dominating the city of Salzburg, overlooking the Salzach River, a wide river that runs through the city. Salzburg we knew is overlooked by a range of rugged, high mountains, but we could not see them because of the lingering fog and cloud.

Franz the warden suggested that we go and have a look at a game of ice hockey played under lights, so we rugged up and off we went. We managed somehow to get in without paying, and sat in a grandstand to watch the game played between two Austrian provinces, Styria and Salzburg. All the time the game was on it was snowing heavily, but this did not dampen the spirits of the spectators, who cheered madly all through the game, which looked very spectacular in the floodlights.

As we sat there, with the falling snow covering us from head to toe, I tried to imagine watching a football game at home under these conditions. The snow however, was quite dry so we didn't get wet through. In fact it was more comfortable than watching a football game in the pouring rain back home. I was not sure who won, but ice hockey I thought was a very rough, fast game as well as requiring loads of skill.

Sunday 27th January: We didn't wake up until 11 a.m. I suppose we were still suffering from a form or jet lag or rail lag after the long journey from Basel. Leon wanted to go to Bad Ischl today, which surprised me because it was so late. We could have stayed another day in this very comfortable YH and gone to Bad Ischl the next day.

||||||||||||||||||||||

SALZBURG TO BAD ISCHL

I reluctantly agreed, and off we went after a very late breakfast. We had difficulty finding the right platform for the train at the large Salzburg bahnhof, and it wasn't until I 30 p.m. that we boarded a steam train to take us to Bad Ischl, just under 90 km by rail through Attnang to the north east of Salzburg The train was crowded and my new quick release, framed rucksack was an absolute boon. All I had to do was pull the quick release tabs and I was freed from the rucksack, which just dropped to the floor with no need to swing it around my shoulders. I think in some respects it was not so bad that I lost my rucksack, because some of the replacement items I had to purchase were better, especially the rucksack which was larger.

I couldn't get near a window so I didn't see much, but there was a tunnel the train went through. It was still snowing heavily and I reckon there was about 20 cm of snow on the ground. It was a delight to hear the puff-puff of the locomotive and its high pitched whistle. I thought the locomotive's wedge plough blades, where the cow catcher is normally located, could easily deal with this amount of dry snow on the track.

ATTNANG

The train reached Attnang an important railway junction with lines going to Bad Ischl, *Linz* and then on to Vienna. This railway line through Attnang opens up the mountains and lakes of the

Salzkammergut region of Austria for travellers from Vienna. We had to change trains in Attnang for Bad Ischl, and once again confusion reigned, mainly because it was snowing and there was snow everywhere on the partly open low platforms. In the dusk trying to find the right platform, which in Austria are just concrete strips a little above ground level was a big hassle. I noticed it is usual for passengers to walk from one platform to another by just walking across the tracks, watching out for trains of course. The PA was only being broadcast in *Deutsch,* which made it rather difficult to say the least, and this caused us to miss the connecting train to Bad Ischl. It was freezing cold, but the waiting room on this large station was quite warm.

At last at around 5 p.m. a train for Bad Ischl came along and we were able to resume our journey. All the way from Salzburg passengers had been getting on and off the train at various stations and this continued as we progressed towards Bad Ischl. Stopping at the big town of Gmunden, many passengers left the train and from then on we had a seat all the way to Bad Ischl. After burrowing through a couple of short tunnels we arrived in Bad Ischl at 7 p.m.

⚓

BAD ISCHL

We asked directions to the YH from a kind Austrian couple and they took us to a large comfortable hotel, the Golden Ox in the town, which we discovered was used as a YH during the winter months when there weren't many guests. It was extremely comfortable with lovely eiderdowns on the beds and excellent washing facilities. After a filling hot meal, we washed ourselves and our clothes, hanging them in the drying room before we went to bed. I was very tired, which was not surprising as it had been another long, exciting day that came to an end travelling by train through a very snowy landscape. So far it had all been very cheap.

Monday 28th January: We woke late again, I suppose because the beds were so comfortable. The warden or hotel manager put on a good breakfast for us, and then we went around the town buying postcards. Bad Ischl on first appearances is a small town, the main buildings being located between the *Traun Fluss* (river) and its tributary the *Ischl Fluss.* By our maps we knew that surrounding Bad Ischl, there is a range of high mountains, but again they were covered by cloud. Leon left me saying he was going to look up an address he had in Bad Ischl. It was obvious that he didn't want me with him, because he asked me to meet him in the afternoon at a small inn he pointed to across the street. I returned to the YH, wrote cards and studied my maps of Austria and Bad Ischl. After a light lunch at the YH, I took my skis, posted the cards, and skied on a hill at the back of a large hospital. My new cheap skis and boots went really well.

I then skied over to the inn to meet Leon. I bought myself a beer, a very nice cold drop while I waited. I sipped my beer while trying to make sense of some Austrian magazines and enjoying the woody atmosphere and warmth of the inn. Some Austrian men were playing cards, accompanied by many loud remarks in German *(Deutsch)* on a table nearby.

Soon, Leon entered the inn and came over to where I was sitting. Before I had time to ask him if he was going to have a beer, he said: "I am leaving you. I am going to stay with friends." I was shocked! He held out his hand, which I shook and we wished each other good luck. Without either of us saying another word, Leon turned around and quickly left the inn, leaving me alone with my beer! Now that I was 'left to my own devices' as the saying goes, I had to decide what to do next. I remembered the remark that Leon made back in England about going to Italy *alone,* and not wanting to go skiing. I had expected however, that he would warn me when he would soon be taking off, and that we would have some discussion about our plans, but I was very wrong. I was not really critical of Leon for leaving, as I should have realised that sooner or later we

38

would be going our own ways. I was however, very disappointed in the manner he chose to make the break. I decided to enjoy my beer and have another, before I returned to the YH to plan my next move. I imagined that my thoughts, would be enhanced by consuming another of the excellent tasting, cold Austrian beers, and that my decision making processes would be further enhanced by having another one after that.

I scarcely had time to do much thinking or drinking before a young, plump pleasant looking Austrian girl of about 16 or 17 years of age, came over to my table and spoke to me in excellent English. We talked together for a while, and I told her I was touring through Austria. She said her name was Helga and I told her mine. Helga asked me if I would like to come up to her house and meet her parents. "Yes thank you, I would" I replied. Helga said she would first have to get permission from her father, one of the men playing cards. While we waited for him to finish his game we kept talking. Helga spoke English with a delightful accent. She said her surname was Wagner and her mother used to work for the American occupation forces. As soon as her father rose from the table, Helga went over and they had a short conversation. Helga brought her father over to me and introduced him and we shook hands. Helga's father was a short, well rounded man, with a deep voice. The three of us left the inn first crossing a bridge over the Ischl Fluss, and then we climbed up a slippery icy slope to their house, a typical natural wood walled house of two storeys with a sloping roof and extended eaves. The house was in a street called Jainzendorf Strasse in the village of Jainzendorf on rising ground above Bad Ischl.

I was introduced by Helga to Mrs. Wagner, an attractive, middle aged lady, with red hair. She welcomed me warmly in English, which she spoke with an American accent. We all sat down and I told them about my travels leaving out any mention of Leon. I was introduced to their son Heinrich, a fair headed, young man, who I thought was about 22 years old. I was invited to have dinner with them, which I readily accepted with thanks. We sat down to a dinner of macaroni and meat, which was very nice and filling. After dinner we sat and talked until late. Mrs. Wagner invited me for lunch the next day, which I again gladly accepted. After thanking them for their kind hospitality I returned to the YH, where there was no sign of Leon or his belongings.

I climbed into bed marvelling at the unbelievable events of the day. I believe that the meeting Leon's friends in Austria had been loosely planned even before we left Australia. There were no mobile phones and the only communication was by mail, and once Leon was in England without my knowledge, he must have made contact with his friends, either by phone or personally.

Tuesday 29th January: I woke up late again. After breakfast I decided to stay in Bad Ischl for a few days and then probably move on east towards Vienna. But first I had to take stock of my finances. It was most important that I knew how much I could spend each day until I met Netta in Grindelwald on 17th March, ski with her for two weeks and then return to Hitchin. I worked out that it would be 65 days which really surprised me that it was so long. I still had £50 in traveller's cheques, about 100 Asch and about £10 in notes. I converted all this to Austrian Schillings and divided it by 65, which came to 97 Asch. This was to be my daily budget to cover accommodation, food, entertainment and travel, mainly by train because this was not the season for hitchhiking, because the roads and countryside were covered by around a foot of snow. Based on the costs so far I was confident that a budget of 97 Asch/day would be adequate. Time would tell.

I went up to the Wagners for lunch, a pie filled with macaroni. The Wagners told me a little about Bad Ischl, a spa and health resort in the heart of the Salzkammergut, an old salt mining region and Lake District east of Salzburg. Spas in Austria and Germany could be recognised by the prefix 'Bad' (bath) before the town name. It was claimed that spa treatments provided many benefits and cures

40

for a host of human ailments, upper respiratory tract diseases, glandular and blood circulation disorders. I read later that treatments in the kurhauses (sanatoriums) included salt and sulphur spring baths and allergen free chambers. These were a few of the vast range of treatments available for anaemia, sclerosis, gout, asthma and emphysema, together with convalescence from the effects of a stroke. Each spa or resort specialised in a varying range of treatments depending on its locality and type of spring. It all sounded very good, but of course I had enjoyed this every day when I had the 'treatment' of a salt water shower on board the *'Bad' Moreton Bay*.

I was just about to leave to do a little skiing in the beautiful sunshine, when Mrs. Wagner asked if I would like to stay with them. I couldn't believe it. Here I was, a day after Leon left me, being asked to stay with this lovely Austrian family. Of course I accepted with thanks. It gave my ego a huge boost to find that I had no need of any prearranged list of addresses to help me on my way like Leon had. I was free to go and do whatever I wished, without making any compromises with a travelling companion.

I asked Helga if she would like to go skiing with me? Helga said she would love to and off we went, but as soon as we began to climb up the hill behind the house, I found to my surprise that Helga was not far removed from being a beginner on skis. I realised I would have to teach her how to traverse across the slope and kick turn. It was sill snowing lightly as we slowly made our way up on lovely powder snow some 30 cm deep towards some houses further up.

Teaching a beginner to learn the basics of skiing in deep untracked powder snow is not the ideal snow surface. Helga was doing very well considering the snow conditions. The weather appeared to be getting better, but I still couldn't see the high peaks. By now it was late afternoon so we gave skiing away for the day. Helga went back home, and I returned to the Golden Ochse (Ox) and booked out. The cost was only 30 Asch for two nights and meals, which was really, really cheap.

BAD ISCHL

I moved in with the Wagners before the evening meal, and spent the night playing cards and learning German (*Deutsch*). One of the important aspects of learning *Deutsch* was the pronunciation of many words which contain an 'I' and 'E' together. The rule was that the last in the pair determines the sound. If 'E' is the last letter, as in the word 'vier' (four), it is pronounced like 'fear'. But if 'I' is last, as in 'stein' (stone), it is pronounced like 'time'. The Wagner's house was quite large and I slept in a comfortable bed in the same room as Heinrich.

Wednesday 30th January: I took a walk around the town, but the mountains were still covered in fog. I saw the Kaiser Villa, the summer residence of Franz Joseph, the last Emperor of Austria. The building was not very impressive in wintertime, although I imagined it would look much grander in summer. From a tourist brochure I learned that another famous person the Austrian composer Franz Lehar, had a villa in Bad Ischl, where he spent his summers. He died only a couple of years ago in 1948. He composed the popular operettas *The Merry Widow* and *The Count of Luxembourg* as well as many other works. Franz Lehar wrote this about Bad Ischl: *'I must frankly admit that I have always had the best ideas in Bad Ischl. That must surely have something or other to do with the air.*

Bad Ischl is certainly an enchanting town with many styles of buildings. I noticed that all the statues were boarded over. Mrs. Wagner told me it was to protect them from cracking with the frost– 'frost heave' as it is called. There were also horse drawn sleds with tinkling bells moving through the snow covered streets and people pulling small sleds and a baby in a sled pram.

There was another new sight that struck me as being very different to anything like I had ever seen. I saw people walking around Bad Ischl wearing armbands of different colours. Mrs. Wagner told me that black armbands were worn for one year after a

42

family death. Yellow with three black dots was for people with poor sight, and those with five black spots were for deaf and dumb persons. The armbands were very conspicuous, which of course they were meant to be, just as I had seen them.

Thursday 31st January: I woke up to a lovely sunny day. From the window I could see some of the lower tree clad mountains surrounding the town. I couldn't wait to get out on my skis on the slopes above the town. Helga wanted to come with me again and we made our way uphill to where we had skied yesterday. As we herringboned upwards, I gave Helga more advice on the kick turn and traversing across the slope. She was doing much better today as the snow had packed down a little making it much easier for her.

Suddenly, turning around I beheld a superb panorama of high, snow clad mountains through a gap in the lower mountains of Bad Ischl. A high range of mountains rose in breathtaking beauty. A large snowfield could be seen glistening among the higher peaks. Helga said that the mountains were the Dachstein (stone roof) mountains. I looked at my map later and found that the Hoher Dachstein was the highest mountain in the Salzkammergut at 2.996 m (9,280 ft). I stood with Helga feasting my eyes on the majestic scene of Bad Ischl below, and the snow covered Dachstein in the distance through a slight mountain haze.

As we stood there Helga told me about her family. She said that Mrs. Wagner was really her and Heinrich's stepmother. When their father came home from the war, he found his wife was living with another man. He divorced and married again. I thought today must be the day for revelations, first the beautiful mountains then the family history of the Wagners, but that wasn't all. Helga told me she was 17 years of age, and then blurted out that she loved me! With that last revelation I felt it was time to move on, so we skied back home for lunch. On the way we passed three Bad Ischl children gleefully building a snowman. It was a delightful scene, made all the more so by the snow covered Dachstein mountains behind them.

43

St Anton's mountains a quick photo from the train

Salzburg Castle and Salzach River

Mozart's birthplace. The entrance is below the white canopy

The Wagner family L to R Mrs Wagner Mr Wagner, Helga and Heinrich from a summer photo sent to me by Mrs Wagner a year or so later

My ski tracks in Jainzendorf above the Wagner's house

A photo of Bad Ischl and the Dachstein from a Christmas card sent to me by the Wagner family

44

After dinner the Wagners said they were going to the movies. I said I would like to shout them. I had to explain the meaning of the word 'shout' (to pay for them) as we walked down to the picture theatre. The tickets were only 6 Asch each. The movie was *Der Ratte von Soho* (The Rat from Soho) with Harry Fabian, Gene Tierney and Richard Widmark. The words were originally spoken in English, but so well dubbed into *Deutsch* that it was extremely hard to tell the difference because the lip movements are much the same. Mrs. Wagner translated the important parts to me during the movie. The movies were a great source of entertainment for the Wagners and I imagined also for many other people in Bad Ischl during the winter. There were various radio programs to choose from, the best from my point of view, was the American Occupation Forces radio station. I had a nice bath before I went to bed, and thankfully there was no scum left around the bath like at the Bakers.

Friday 1st February: Helga and I went skiing again. There were many other people skiing on the lovely dry snow. After climbing above the trees and admiring the view of the Dachstein, which wasn't quite as clear as yesterday but still as majestic. Helga wanted to hold my hand all the time when we weren't actually skiing. I tried to ignore her and carried on with the ski lessons. We skied back home for dinner, which was mostly macaroni based. I had not eaten macaroni much before, but I found it quite enjoyable and filling. I noticed that when Mrs. Wagner made the tea, she never boiled the water. I suggested that she should make the tea with boiling water as we did in Australia and see the difference. She said she would give it a try and promptly made a new pot of tea, this time with boiling water. All the Wagners thought the tea tasted much better, but more importantly they were surprised by the number of extra cups they could get out of one teaspoon of tea. There were no tea bags then, of course.

Saturday 2nd February: It snowed all day. Mr Wagner was not as outgoing as Mrs. Wagner, perhaps because his English was not very good, but at no time did he make me feel I wasn't welcome, on the contrary, they were all very nice and pleased to have me stay with them. However, I didn't want to wear out my welcome and besides I was getting itchy feet. In the evening we went to the movies again and Mrs. Wagner said she would 'shout us' happy that she had learned an Aussie slang word. We saw the movie *Intimidation* a comedy but it wasn't dubbed and I just sat there and did the best I could to enjoy it while Mrs. Wagner told me about the plot.

That night while we were lying in bed, Heinrich asked me to explain how a democratic government operated. I wasn't sure of the type of government in Austria at the time except that it was a republic. I suppose I should have first asked Heinrich to describe it. The conversation took place in the darkened room, from bed to bed. Using Australia as an example, I explained the principles of a democratic government. I said every citizen had freedom of speech, religion, association, and there was also freedom of the press and other forms of communication. Every citizen charged with a criminal offence is presumed innocent until proven guilty, by a lawfully assembled jury, which is selected at random.

I told him that our government was elected by popular vote, about once every three years. In Australia voting was compulsory, each vote having equal value. There are usually two or three parties contesting elections, each claiming that their policies were the very best for all Australians. Whichever party received the most votes formed a government, and elected the Prime Minister. In democratic countries there are usually two government bodies, called the upper and the lower houses, both elected by majority vote. To enact a law, the law has to be passed by both upper and lower houses of parliament. Australia, I said, had a Liberal government and Robert Menzies was our Prime Minister.

He thanked me and said he understood, and we both fell asleep. Heinrich was about 20 years of age so I imagined that his formative

46

years would have been during the rise of Hitler and the Third Reich. To this day I don't know why I didn't ask him to tell me about his boyhood.

Sunday 3rd February: I wanted to get in some skiing where there were ski lifts. I mentioned this to Mrs. Wagner and she suggested I go to Bad Aussee for a few days as there was a chair lift there and it was not very far away. I was intrigued by the name and thought, ski lift or not, I must go and see Bad Aussee.

When Helga heard where I was going she was very sad, saying she wanted me to stay in Bad Ischl. I said I would go the next morning, stay and ski in Bad Aussee and then come back and spend a few more days with her in Bad Ischl before I had to leave, which seemed to satisfy her. Helga was becoming a nuisance, wanting to hold my hand at every opportunity. I decided to tell Mrs. Wagner how her stepdaughter had developed a 'crush' on me, and I didn't want to hurt her. I asked Mrs Wagner to explain to her that I was only passing through and to tell her not to be stupid and leave me alone. Mrs. Wagner said she understood completely, saying I was not to worry, she would have a word to her. Mrs. Wagner must have said something to Helga, because she sulked all night. Mrs. Wagner said to just ignore her.

With that issue somewhat settled and with the weather not that good I went walking around the town. I bought a delicious chocolate covered cake from a vending machine. They were very tasty and only cost 1 Asch each. I had seen these vending machines in Basel and thought they were a great idea for dispensing food and other small articles. Mrs. Wagner told me that there were a lot of Co-operative stores in Austria and recently prices were cut 5% by order of the Premier Dr. Leopold Figl.

!!!!!!!!!!!!!!!!!!!!!!!

BAD ISCHL TO BAD AUSSEE

Monday 4th February: With my skis and light rucksack over my back I said goodbye to the Wagners, and made my way down the snowy street to the Bad Ischl bahnhof. I bought a return ticket that only cost 6 Asch for the 63 km return journey. The line had been cleared of snow by the locomotive's wedge plough and its wedge plough and boiler front were plastered with snow. I really should have taken a picture of it, and certainly would have if I had known that I would be writing this book. The snowy journey was very beautiful, first along the valley of the Taurn River stopping at many stations along the way. As the train puffed along I saw high, snow clad mountains where we were heading and soon the river gave way to the end of a lake the Hallstattsee, which grew larger and more beautiful as the train approached Hallstatt.

Only the first 100 m of the mountains were visible as they rose from the depths of the lake, a pity because I am sure they rose to great heights, but it was all very impressive in grey scale. Large icicles, some over two metres long were hanging over the side of some of the railway cuttings. The train continued along the snow covered track around the side of a mountain range and came to a stop at the Hallstatt bahnhof, which is on one side of the lake and the town of Hallstatt is on the other, but there were not many passengers getting on or off to take the boat journey across the lake to Hallstatt.

Leaving Hallstatt the train ran on along the lake for a few kilometres before turning to the left to begin a slow climb with the locomotive puffing loudly as it lifted the train up the valley of the Traun River with high, snowy mountains on both sides, and after a journey of about half an hour the train arrived at the snow laden Bad Aussee bahnhof.

▲
BAD AUSSEE

I found the town to be quite small. There was a lot of snow on the ground and I put on my skis and poled along following the directions in the YH Guide book to the Bad Aussee YH, a three story building, on the brow of a hill, a magnificent example of domestic,

48

alpine architecture. This style of building is not called a house, but a chalet. Chalets of this style I have seen in most alpine areas since leaving France. Most are constructed of large pine timbers and there is no cladding covering the outside walls. The overhanging, sloped rooves keep the snow that slides off the roof away from the building.

When I booked in the warden told me that it was 7 Asch per night and meals were 4 Asch each. I was rather hungry so he prepared a very welcome meal of spaghetti and sauce for me. He said that there was a chairlift about 2 km away, so after I consumed my meal I didn't waste any time and skied over to the lift station and bought a ticket for 3 Asch. The length of the lift was 1.300 m, with a vertical drop of 300 m. This was the first time I had been on a chairlift and it was a big thrill. The journey to the top took about 15 minutes and although they put a blanket over my knees it was a bitterly cold ride.

When I reached the top of the lift there was no view at all, but there was a restaurant at the top where I indulged myself in a cup of tea laced with rum and a sandwich, which cost 8 Asch, too dear, but nice and warming. Suitably recharged, I made ready for my first true downhill skiing in Austria. The snow was dry powder, a snow type I rarely if ever encountered in Australia and being unused to those conditions, I fell a couple of times. That too was a new experience, being covered from head to foot in dry powder snow. The dry powder snow was very slow and balling up under on my skis. I did not have any ski wax for the running surfaces of my skis to make them slide better so I will have to buy some.

It was very cold and my skiing was so bad that I went back to the YH. I wrote a few letters and had a bit of a snooze, then had a look in the visitor's book. The entries by some Aussies, showed that there were Aussie backpackers abroad even before us, who left Australia only a couple of months or so after the end of WWII. I should have copied more of their entries. Why I didn't I do not know, because I had plenty of time.

49

However, below are some amusing entries I did copy

Bonzer hospitality in a beaut place. Whacko!! From a Dinkum Aussee

Benje Blare

Newcastle Australia Sept 1950

This is a champion hostel Aussies. The sheila in charge is fair dinkum she laced our morning tea with plenty of over proof rum. Why do the Aussies come to Bad Aussee? Cos they think it's right on here. 22-4-51. Eric B. Denneisten South Yarra

There was also another undated entry:

Four Australians found typical Melbourne weather (wet) and in contrast to the weather, very good hospitality.

J.B. Koschade L.J. Langley

I hoped that Leon was enjoying his friends and tour as much as I was, but his undated entry in the visitors book and the reference to Melbourne's weather was gratuitous, but typical of Leon's outlook on life.

Tuesday 5th February: It was blowing a blizzard, so I didn't get out of my sleeping bag until late, but instead I spent the day working out my itinerary. I decided that I would move on towards Vienna after I left the Wagners. I had a whacking great meal of rice, and retired early as it was still snowing heavily. I didn't know much about Vienna, except that it was a big historic city and the capital of Austria. I would be able see too, if Vienna bread was as delicious when baked in its namesake city as it is back in Australia. The weather showed no signs of clearing up, which would have enabled me to do a little more skiing. The YH was quite good one and after I had a nice lunch, I paid the fees to the warden and booked out. The cost of 16 Asch. was well within my budget.

iiiiiiiiiiiiiiiiiiiiiii

BAD AUSSIE TO BAD ISCHL

On the train journey back to Bad Ischl the cloud lifted a little as the train ran along the shore of the *Hallstattersee,* again revealing a

50

beautiful scene across the lake and the surrounding snow clad hills and villages in greyscale. I arrived back at the Wagners in the late afternoon.

BAD ISCHL

Wednesday 6th February: I told the Wagner family before dinner that I would leave in the morning and return to Salzburg. They said I was welcome to stay longer, but I felt it was time for me to move on. Mrs. Wagner told me about a narrow gauge steam train that went from Bad Ischl to Salzburg, passing by the lakes of the Salzkammergutt on the way. I thought that would be wonderful, so I decided to take this train instead of going back the way I had come.

On the radio after dinner we heard the unexpected and sad news of the death of King George VI in Sandringham. Princess Elizabeth was holidaying in Kenya when she heard the news of her father's death. I found that I was touched deeply by the King's death. I quickly realised how fortuitous it was for me that the death of King George VI occurred during this period of my time abroad. I was sure that next year (1953) in the spring, our new Queen, Queen Elizabeth II would be crowned, so I would definitely plan to be in London for that marvellous, once in a lifetime occasion.

I explained to the Wagners what the British Royal Family meant to me, an Australian. I told them that as an Australian I was a member of a large family called the 'British Empire' composed of many kinds of people from countries all over the world, who work together for the common good. There are many times as I write this book that I have wished that I was as inquisitive then as I am now. I did, however, talk with Mrs. Wagner about the war. She said she served in the German Army, but had no love for the Hitler regime, and that the Americans were too lenient with the Russians to a point of stupidity.

Thursday 7th February: I had a breakfast of scrambled eggs with the Wagners and prepared to catch the train, which left at 12 noon. I was very sad to leave, but I considered myself very fortunate to be offered their hospitality, especially as it happened immediately after Leon left me. During the eight days I spent with them, I learnt a lot from the Wagners about the Austrian way of life in Bad Ischl and a little from Mrs. Wagner about her experiences when she worked for the Americans. I corresponded with Mrs. Wagner for some years afterwards until I lost her address.

iiiiiiiiiiiiiiiiiiiii

BAD ISCHL TO SALZBURG

Mrs. Wagner insisted on coaching me in the use of correct *Deutsch* to buy a ticket for the train journey from Bad Ischl to Salzburg. After we said our farewells, and I had thanked them for their wonderful hospitality, I walked down to the station, repeating these *Deutsch* words over and over again. *'Eine fahrkarten dritter klasse nach Salzburg bitte'* (a ticket, third class to Salzburg please). The train was steam hauled and ran on a narrow gauge 76 cm (25 inch) track. The locomotive was very like our own narrow gauge tank VR locos, as too were the carriages. The 0-6-2 locomotive was coal fired and I noticed when we stopped at various stations along the way, coal in baskets was taken aboard as the tank engine didn't have much space for a lot of coal in its bunker.

Leaving Bad Ischl the line began its journey along a snow covered valley and surprisingly after another couple of kilometres the train passed through a short tunnel. I was a beautiful day and I rode some of the way on the rear platform of the observation car. It was a wonderful experience to see the rails recede into the snowy landscape behind the train, the only part of the railway line above the snow. The train passed through snow covered fields and through very short tunnels, which I hardly noticed, although I counted six in all. Sometimes the train hovered on narrow ledges above a valley, over bridges and alongside lakes. The first of these was along the shores of the *Wolfgang see*. On the opposite side of this large

52

beautiful lake, which reflected the snowy mountains above, I could see the village of St Wolfgang, and rising 1.738 m above it, the *Schafberg* mountain peak, which has a rack railway to its summit.

The whole area around this lake has become famous as the setting for the operetta, *The White Horse Inn,* with music by Benatzky, songs by Stolz. There are two film versions, one of which starred Richard Tauber. I put St Wolfgang on my list to visit sometime in the future, because even in winter it seemed such a beautiful area. The train puffed along slowly, stopping every now and again at small, snowy, picturesque villages, the largest of these being St Giligen at the western end of Wolfgangsee where at Huttenstein the train passed through a gap in the mountains. It then ran along the shore of another lovely lake, Mondsee, equally as beautiful as Wolfgangsee. At St. Lorenz, a town by the Mondsee a branch line went to the town of Mondsee where as I write, an Ischl Localbahn museum is now located.

From then on the train made its way through various valleys on the way to Salzburg. I read later that this was the area where some scenes of the movie *The Sound of Music* was filmed. The train arrived in Salzburg at 3 p.m. after a delightful 63 km journey full of scenic and railway interest.

My mind went back to the summer of 1944 the first time I rode our VR narrow gauge railway from Ferntree Gully to Gembrook, it was the same gauge as the Lokalbahn, but only half the distance, 34 km on its winding route to its destination of Gembrook in the Dandenong Ranges of Melbourne. This train is still operating, but sadly the train I was travelling on, the Ischl Lokalbahn, ran for the last time in 1957.

SALZBURG

Having arrived at back at Salzburg after that most enjoyable train trip, the cloud had lifted and it was so great to be able to see the mountains surrounding the city for the first time, however, they were

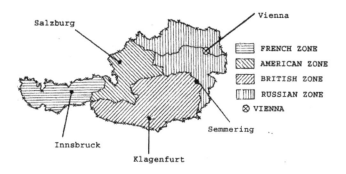

Allied Occupation Zones in Austria

The Hallstattsee and the town of Hallstatt across on the other side of the lake

The Bad Aussee Youth Hostel

The Ischl Lokalbahn 0-6-2 locomotive and train

A view from the train of Wolfgangsee and the Schaftberg mountain

54

not at all like the Dachstein mountains I had seen in Bad Ischl, but more like 'foot mountains' (as distinct from foothills, to coin a word). It was good to be back in Salzburg, the home of the famous Salzburg Music Festival, which I had heard about back in Australia. I went straight to the YH where Franz welcomed me back with open arms. I went shopping and bought some Toko ski wax, so the next time I go skiing I hoped my skis would run better whatever the type of snow. I also bought my first copy of *Time* magazine to enable me to read and keep abreast of all the important events happening around the world, the most important event was of course, being the death of our King.

I found a good restaurant on the other side of a bridge across the Salzach River. There were many Americans soldiers in the restaurant. I bought a beer, sat down and watched the American soldiers, some of relatively high rank chatting up some well dressed Austrian girls (frauleins). Very instructive, I thought. I decided to lash out and buy a steak and vegetable dinner for 9 Asch, as I was well within my budget. There is nothing like a great piece of succulent steak with vegetables to make one feel happy, especially as I was free to go and do as I pleased.

Completely satisfied with a full stomach I went back to the YH and washed my clothes. I then sat down with Franz and a couple of others to have a talk over a cup of tea (coffee is too expensive). I said I was on my way to Vienna, but would spend a couple of days in Salzburg first. Franz said: "That would be good, but why don't you take a trip to Berchtesgaden? Berchtesgaden in Bavaria, Germany is only 25 km across the border from Salzburg, and is a US Army Recreation Area. US Army buses run a regular service between the two towns for army personnel." Franz said he had a bus timetable and there was no problem getting a ride in a bus, just climb aboard.

There was no youth hostel in Berchtesgaden, he said, but there was a very good one in Strub just outside the town. I asked Franz whether I could ski there? He said: "Yes, there are lifts and good

55

runs too." I decided I would go the next day on the bus leaving at 10 a.m. from the Salzburg Bahnhof. I went off to bed, and as I lay in my sleeping bag I tried to recall everything I knew about Berchtesgaden, which was frequently mentioned in news reports. I remembered that it was the place where Hitler had a large villa. I had seen photos of him there with Eva Braun, his mistress. Then off I went to sleep.

SALZBURG TO BERCHTESGADEN

Friday 8th February: Breakfast over, I made my way down to the bahnhof and climbed aboard the bus with my skis without saying a word, as I didn't want to let anyone on the bus, including the driver, hear my Australian accent. There were a few uniformed army personnel in the bus, so I kept to myself and went and sat in the back of the bus. It wasn't snowing but the clouds were covering the high peaks as the bus moved off through Salzburg and onto a snow covered road. After travelling about 20 km along the snow covered road bounded by forested mountains, the bus arrived at the border between Austria and Germany and stopped at the barrier gate.

AUSTRIAN–GERMAN BORDER

A couple of German customs officer came aboard and I showed one of them my passport. He asked to see my visa. Not bothering about speaking in my Aussie accent, I said that I didn't have one. He was very polite and told me that I would have to get off the bus and return to Salzburg to get a visa. He said I should be able to get one from the US Occupation Force Headquarters in Salzburg. I imagined that he took me to be an American. I got off the bus with my skis and waited at the border for a US Army bus to take me back to Salzburg,

A–G BORDER TO SALZBURG

I didn't have long to wait. A US soldier in a US Army sedan came along going to Salzburg, and the border guards asked him if he would give me a lift. OK he said, so I climbed aboard a big army Dodge with my rucksack and skis. The soldier drove very fast along the mostly straight road. It was an exciting experience, but I felt quite safe, as the snow covering the road was at such a low temperature that the surface was as hard as bitumen. I told him about the visa, and he said he was going straight to Headquarters anyway. We talked a little about ourselves and in a very short time we were in Salzburg.

SALZBURG

I thanked him for the ride, my first success at true hitchhiking– no not really–an assist. The soldier directed me to the American Customs office in a square. They sent me to the British office, which thankfully was in the same large building. Within 15 minutes I had my visa, valid for three days at a cost of 30 ASch. I had a quick look at the magnificent big American cars, Buicks, Oldsmobiles, Pontiacs, Chevs and Fords of all colours as well as khaki, parked outside the building, and also a large statue of Mozart. The square was called Mozart Platz. I then hurried back to the bahnhof and just managed to catch an army bus back to Berchtesgaden at 12 noon.

SALZBURG TO BERCHTESGADEN

I sat in the back seat again of the bus and didn't speak to anyone but I don't think anyone cared who I was. When the bus arrived at the border, the guards welcomed me as I showed then my newly acquired Visa. I thanked them for their help and the border barriers were raised, and I was on my way to Berchtesgaden in Bavaria. The diversion had really been a lot of fun and allowed me to see a historic square in Salzburg.

57

CHAPTER 6
GERMANY

BERCHTESGADEN

The bus arrived in Berchtesgaden at 1.30 p.m. Berchtesgaden was like little America, alive with American army personnel and American cars on the snow covered main street. Both sides of the street were lined with bowling alleys, fast food cafes, amusement venues and shops displaying a vast range of wares, jewellery, furs, ski clothes, cameras and the like. Most of the goods on display I imagined were for the consumption of American servicemen, because ordinary Austrians would not have the money to purchase them. I found an American Express office and changed some Austrian schillings into *Deutsch* (German) marks. The exchange rate was not very good, 15 *Deutsch* marks (Dm.) for 72 Asch.

STRUB

The YH was in the village of Strub, a kilometre or so above Berchtesgaden. I walked up the snow covered road, skis over my shoulder to the YH. The Strub YH was a large cream painted building more like a hotel than a hostel. The interior was in keeping with my first impression. It was large, spick and span, and had good washing facilities. It also had large dormitory and dining room. After a filling meal I talked with a couple of young Bavarians, who said they were going to a masked dance nearby. They invited me to accompany them: "Would it be OK to just wear my ski clothes?" I

58

asked: "Yes" they said. We trudged through deep snow in darkness to a nearby dance hall, which would have been impossible to miss as there were bright lights and lots of noisy music coming from inside. I enjoyed myself sitting at a table watching the dancers in their costumes. We ordered beers that came in half litre *steins* with the name Berchtesgaden glazed on to the side. Because I was wearing ski boots I didn't dance, but I thoroughly enjoyed myself sitting and watching the goings on while drinking Bavarian beer, which was quite sweet compared to Austrian beer. I hadn't changed into my shoes because we had to walk through the snow to the dance hall.

A man of about 30 years of age, with his wife and two children, came and sat down beside me, but there were no introductions by my two Bavarian friends, I think however, they must have told him that I was an Australian, because the man turned towards me and straight away asked me if I knew whether Australia allowed former SS men to emigrate. He said it was not allowed by other British Empire countries and the USA. He went on to give me a long drawn out explanation about not being a true SS soldier, but an SS physical training instructor. He said that he was not responsible for any SS atrocities. I was finding this all very amusing and unconvincing when one of the Bavarian boys started to argue with him.

I butted in and told him I did not know if Australia prohibited SS members from coming to Australia, but did remember reading about some who had got through the screening process. I told him to write to the Australian Department of Immigration. He was not finished yet, and went on to tell me and the others listening how mighty the Russians were, and thankfully concluded by saying: "In this world all the people are the same except a few with the money, they are the people who start the wars." I knew of course that he was referring to the Jews.

At the end of the night he shook my hand vigorously. As he left the hall I could easily picture him as a typical brutal member of the SS in an awesome black shirted uniform, even though he tried so hard to convince me that he was not such a man. His wife by this time was becoming a little agitated as she had not had a dance for nearly an hour and it was time to go home. As we got up to leave, I asked my Bavarian friends where I could get a stein like the one I was drinking from. One of them quickly said: "Just take one and put it down the front of your vorlagers (ski pants) and pull your parka over the top." Making sure no one was looking I did as he suggested, thinking to myself that no one would question the appearance of a protuberance in that part of my body. Then disaster struck! As I walked across the dance floor the dam beer mug slid down the leg of my ski pants. That was as far as it got however, because the trouser leg was tucked into my ski boot. I was certainly glad I hadn't changed into my shoes. The stein mug is still one of my prized possessions. Strangely I never did, nor do I now, have a guilty conscience about taking it. I looked upon it as small part of the German's reparations they paid after the war.

Sunday 10th February: It was snowing heavily so I spent the morning writing in the spacious warm interior of the YH. When I went down to the dining room for dinner I got involved in a drinking party with the warden Hans and his mates. The warden's wife was not very pleased because drinking alcohol in a YH was against the rules. After a satisfying dinner of rice and meat, a discussion began with the warden and his mates, with me in the centre of the group. We were now only drinking cups of tea, so I assumed that the warden's wife had read the riot act to him and said; "No more beer!"

The long discussion was all about the war. For my benefit, most of it was spoken in English, some of which was not very good. I was enjoying it all immensely and gleaned many pieces of war information. What more appropriate place for a discussion such as this I thought, than in this area of Berchtesgaden, which had played such a significant role in the history of the war, and of Hitler in particular. Later that night, the warden's wife must have gone to bed because out came some beer and Beinwacher, a white wine like gin.

60

Hans began talking again and I listened intently. Over our drinks he said he was 50 years of age, and confessed he was a Nazi. He said that Adolf Hitler was a good man for the working people of Germany, but there were many traitors among the upper classes. He looked at me sternly saying: "The Russians were a very formidable enemy and I had great respect for their strength." He proceeded to draw me a series of diagrams, which I copied in my notebook. He was attempting to explain what he believed were the differences between the various armies. Russian armies he said concentrated on soldiers who were very good, but no comforts; anything in the way of food and luxuries they acquired from the conquered enemy. The German armies on the other hand, had a good blend of soldiers, munitions and comforts. The American armies however, had a minimum number of soldiers, who weren't very good, and a maximum of comforts. Munitions were looked on as a necessary encumbrance!

Hans went on to say that he hated the American Occupation Forces because he didn't regard them as soldiers. He believed in the United States of Europe minus Russia, but was adamant that Berlin for economic reasons must be the capital of the Federation, because of the farming in the north and industry in the south. He had a definite hate too of the Jews, whom he said, thought they were 'Lords of the Earth.' He said he was trying to get his children away from Europe in case of another war.

His main delight he said, thumping the table with a big fist, was that if another war happens, unlike the last two wars: "They will not be able to blame us!" He wasn't finished yet: "At the end of the last war the world had a chance, which it would never have again, of putting a finish to the Reds. The defeated German Army would have only been too pleased to fight beside the Allies to rid the world of the Russians."

Beside me, listening in to all the warden was saying to me was a young Austrian student. He was 21 years of age and spoke very good

English. He added to the conversation saying that he thought that democracy was the best form of government. He said he was in the Hitler Youth (*Hitler Jugend*), which was good at first, but very bad at the end. The Americans treated him all right now. He had no complaints, but just after the war, things were a bit tough for a while. I assumed that he did not agree with the ideas of the warden. At last at 11 p.m. we all decided it was time for bed.

Monday 11th February: I took my skis and followed the directions of the warden to a cable railway *(bergbahn)*. The weather was clearing and I was able to see the mountains surrounding Berchtesgaden. They were not very high, but were heavily forested with many clearings showing vast areas of snow. I found the *Obersalzbergbahn* (cable railway), a short distance from the centre of the town. I rode up in a cabin with other skiers to the top station called Sonneck. I guessed it was a lift of about 300 m, but the map I had did not show any heights at all. What it did show was that not very far away at the about same height as Sonneck, there was the locality called the Obersalzberg. I wondered if Hitler's retreat the Berghof, which I knew was in the Obersalzberg was nearby. I couldn't take any photos because I had forgotten to bring my camera, but I did have the Toko ski wax to make my skis run better. The snow was again, deep powder snow, so I selected the correct wax for powder snow and waxed the running surfaces of my skis, which made my skis run more freely, but I skied horribly.

I returned to the YH for lunch, a huge meal of potatoes and fried cabbage, something I have never had, but it tasted OK. I think the tea was laced because it was very sweet. I was told I must see Konigsee (King's Lake) and that a US Army bus ran on the hour there. Hardly able to walk, I picked up my camera and waddled down to the city centre. There were only a couple of others beside me on the bus and after a twenty minute journey, I alighted from the bus and walked along a snow covered path with a sign *Nach Konigsee*. I walked about a kilometer along the snow covered path on the water's edge,

62

then the path turned a corner, and there before my eyes I saw a very beautiful lake frozen at the edges, bounded by steep, snow covered mountain slopes on all sides. This was Konigsee, a lake 8 km long, 6 km wide 182 m deep. It looked like a Norwegian fjord that I had seen in photographs. Konigsee was a scene of beautiful tranquillity in black and white, with very little other colour evident, and not a breath of wind to disturb the surface of the water, which reflected the mountains rising high above. I had never seen such a beautiful lake as this before, not even at Hallstatt. I walked along a little further and was able to see what lay beyond the first corner of the lake. The scene was the same, a study in tranquil beauty.

Suddenly, there was a thunder-like noise, which destroyed the serene silence. It seemed to come from far away over the high snow covered mountains behind the lake. I looked at the sky, but the clouds were not those indicating a likely thunderstorm. I was puzzled and returned back along the track to catch the bus back to Berchtesgaden. Near the bus stop there was a slope with people skiing down. At the top of the slope a portable rope, ski tow was operating. It consisted of a diesel engine driving a rope about 200 m long, capable of lifting about 10 skiers. It was the first portable ski tow I had ever seen and had been set up by the US Army, but I didn't have my skis with me. I went back to the YH and booked out, once again paying only a small sum for accommodation and food. The warden wished me good luck on my travels. I told him I was grateful for the talks we had together because I learned so much about the war.

BERCHTESGADEN TO SALZBURG

I caught a late afternoon bus back to Salzburg. On the way I thought about the three days I spent in Berchtesgaden, thanks to the US Army and Franz for telling me about it, which really put into perspective all I had previously known about the war. More so than

63

Looking from Austria across the border to Bavaria

American cars parked outside the US Occupation Forces Headquarters and the statue of Mozart in Mozart Platz

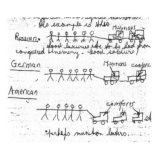

The author's sketches of the differences in the armies as told to him by Hans the warden

The Strub Youth Hostel

A view of beautiful tranquil Konigsee at the end of my walk

The Stein I acquired.

the physical facts of the events, it gave an insight into the thoughts of the men who served in Hitler's army. Each night I wrote up in my notebook the conversations we had, before they escaped my memory. I would venture to say that no other city in Europe after WWII, in so short a time, had undergone such a metamorphosis from being the meeting place of the German war hierarchy, to a recreation centre for the German US Occupation Forces!

It was said that many of the top SA 'Brownshirt' leaders were homosexual, while others were viewed as 'undesirables'. Because they quarrelled amongst themselves, Hitler required a more dependable organisation, so he created the SS and dressed them in black uniforms. He made them swear a special oath of loyalty to himself. He then searched for an ideal leader of the SS, eventually finding one by the name of Heinrich Himmler. The SS was assigned to be first and foremost a bodyguard for Hitler, but grew into a feared organisation of men under Himmler's leadership.

65

CHAPTER 7

AUSTRIA

⚠

SALZBURG

I returned from Berchtesgaden at 5.15 p.m. and found it had been raining in Salzburg, which made an awful mess of the roads. Back at the YH, I talked a while with Franz and then went to bed.

Wednesday 13th February: After a tasty breakfast of fried eggs and toast, I said goodbye to Franz at the YH and thanked him for his advice and hospitality. Salzburg had been a convenient base for my journeys to Bad Ischl and Berchtesgaden, but now it was time to move on. Salzburg was still wreathed in fog and cloud and snow was falling as I made my way to the bahnhof. Although my final destination was Vienna, I bought a ticket only as far as Klagenfurt 180 km distant, because the train journey of just on 500 km to Vienna was too long for one day. Besides I would have arrived in Vienna very late at night. By only going as far as Klagenfurt, I could stay overnight in the YH there, or longer if there was anything worthwhile to see and do in Klagenfurt and its environs. The ticket cost 45 Asch, quite cheap I thought for such a long distance even if it was third class.

Just before I boarded the train to Klagenfurt, I saw a report in an English language newspaper that a large avalanche had come down the previous day and caused extensive damage, killing several people in a village in Bavaria just beyond *Konigsee*. This must have been

66

the thunder like noise I heard as I was walking around the beautiful lake.

||||||||||||||||||||||

SALZBURG TO KLAGENFURT

My train hauled by a big electric locomotive, left Salzburg at 10 55 a.m. It seemed like a slow journey at first as the fog didn't allow me to see anything much of the snow laden countryside. Apart from that the corridor type carriage was warm and comfortable, but certainly not conducive to seeing the scenery go past, especially if passengers in the compartment wished to have the sliding door closed. I had overcame this problem on many occasions by moving into the corridor and watching many kilometres of wonderful scenery pass by, standing and looking through an open corridor window. My train passed around the mountains behind Salzburg on double tracks and along the floor of a valley, only stopping at a few stations on the way. Very soon high snow covered mountains began to appear in the south, where the line reverted to a single track and the train began climbing. A couple of a trains were passed by at stations with loops. As the high mountains drew closer I expected the train to go through another one of the ubiquitous railway tunnels of the Swiss and Austrian railways, but the train found other passages along narrow valleys, with the track being cut into the right hand side of one valley and the next on the left hand side.

.This was not to last however, because after a while the train came to Bad Gastein a very popular high class ski resort at the foot of high mountains. It looked like a big and beautiful town, 1.086 m above sea level. It was one of the principal venues for the World Cup Ski Championships. I knew that there was a YH near Bad Gastein at a place called Sonnblick. If the weather had been good and I could have seen the tops of the mountains, I would have been tempted to break my journey there and go skiing. I noticed many leaving the train with skis over their shoulders, but I was not one of them.

Leaving Bad Gastein, I thought we must be going to encounter a tunnel soon because there appeared no other way to get out of Bad Gastein, because behind the town there was a huge mountain wall. The train however, didn't give up, but turned to the right and began to climb along a bench cut into a steep sided valley. A little further on the line turned away from the valley and changed from single to double track along which the train sped up. It then slowed to negotiate a sharp curve and then suddenly dived into a tunnel.

My train had at last succumbed to the inevitable, which it had dodged for so many kilometers. This was the Tauern Tunnel, 8.56 km long, which burrows under the Tauern Alps, a large mountain chain sometimes referred to as the 'Backbone of Austria.' These Alps contain Austria's highest mountain, the Gross Glockner (Great Bell), 3.798 m (12,454 feet) high. Leaving the tunnel, the train travelled high above the floor of a wide valley until we arrived at Ober-Villach, a large town. Most of the houses could not be seen because they were surrounded by snow with only a church spire standing out. The line then travelled along the Drau River valley, to the town of Spittal on the left hand side of the fast flowing river, which the train followed all the way to Villach a large rail junction.

VILLACH

Villach is only about 16 km from the Italian and Yugoslavian borders, and railway lines branched from here to these two countries. The train appeared to be in no hurry to get moving again, so I stuck my head out the window to see what was going on. I saw a railway employee walking along the side of the train tapping each wheel with a hammer. I had read about wheel tapping in my railway books. Now I was seeing it happen before my very eyes. Wheel tapping is a test carried out by a railway safety inspector with a good pair of ears. His job was to walk the length of the train on both sides tapping each wheel in turn with a hammer. By the sound it made, the inspector was able to tell if there were cracks in the steel wheel or tyre, or any

68

other defects. I suppose the inspector was the railway version of a piano tuner.

The motive power of my train was changed here from electric to steam. Electric traction was used on most lines that run through long tunnels, such as the Tauern Tunnel because of the problem of exhaust smoke from the locomotives. All our wheels must have been OK, because the train finally moved off.

At Villach a middle-aged Austrian couple came and sat down in my compartment. They immediately began a conversation with me in English with their delightful Austrian accent, which I very much enjoyed hearing. They thought I was English because they had seen the Union Jack on the Australian flag on my rucksack. I told them I was Australian and they asked me many questions about Australia, where I had been and where I was going. They said many people travelled by train, not only in the winter, but all year round because very few had cars. They said they were going to visit friends in Klagenfurt. They told me how beautiful the countryside was and that I should come back to visit in the spring or summer

Although I still couldn't see the mountain tops as they were still under cloud cover, I was able to view the villages and countryside with a good scattering of isolated houses in between the main villages and towns. Seeing my skis and stocks in the rack above the seats, and I suppose noticing that I was dressed in ski clothes, they asked if I had being skiing in Austria. I told them about Bad Aussee and that I was looking forward to skiing in Switzerland. They said they were very happy I was seeing their country and said I should ski in the Tirol too. I said I wanted to see the Matterhorn and having done that, if Switzerland proved to be too expensive, I planned to return to Austria to ski.

An elderly woman came on board at Villach with a broom, dust pan and rags. She travelled with the train, cleaning up the compartments while the train was in motion. I thought this was an excellent idea as it did not disturb the passengers at all really and kept the train clear of rubbish. Probably she got off at the next stop and cleaned a train that took her back to her starting point. The train stopped in Velden a town on the shore of lake Worthersee, which the Austrians said was the largest lake in Carinthia, the region of Austria through which I was travelling. From then on nearly all the way to Klagenfurt the train line ran along the shores of the lake stopping at another town Portschach by the lake The train reached Klagenfurt at 4 p.m. after a journey of approximately 170 km. I said goodbye to my Austrian acquaintances who were a lovely couple to talk with.

KLAGENFURT

My first impressions of Klagenfurt were that many of the buildings had suffered bomb damage. There was not very much evidence of any restoration work being carried out, probably because it was winter time. However, the bahnhof had been rebuilt, which probably would have been a prime target. There was a partial thaw and some of the streets were like rivers, which was not a pretty sight. Klagenfurt had trolley buses and trams, which were fitted with wedge snow ploughs and ran on a narrower gauge than standard.

I found Klagenfurt to be a singularly uninteresting town, unkempt, with no attempt by the authorities to clear away ice and snow from the streets, which the trams, trolley buses and cars just ploughed through. After some trouble I found the YH. It appeared to have been built quite recently, but it was closed. A notice on the door said it was only open between the hours of 7 p.m. and 8 a.m. This was not at all helpful, so I lugged my rucksack and skis back to the bahnhof where it was warm, and watched the trains go by, all of them steam trains. I found it quite remarkable how well the Austrian trains kept to their timetables in winter. During heavy snowfalls, track workers had to be continually inspecting and cleaning the points to free them of snow build up, to make sure that the point blades were free to move fully from side to side, a mammoth task.

70

I had observed that on electrified lines point blades are kept free of ice and snow by electrical heating elements inserted in the area of the points. The trains on which I have travelled in Austria so far have crossed over many level crossings some unprotected and others with red stop lights and simple boom gates, which were mostly installed on electrified lines. Very few I saw were manually operated gates. I didn't know what the accident rates were for level crossings, but strangely, I saw an old photo of a level crossing accident between a truck and an Ischl Lokalbahn train.

I left the Klagenfurt bahnhof at 5 p.m. and found a beaut restaurant, the Landhauschiler. I didn't know whether the YH served meals, so I thought I would treat myself to a good meal. I ordered *rindfleisch mit gemuse*, (roast beef with vegetables) a delicious dinner. The atmosphere in the restaurant was very pleasant, with dark wood panelling and a violinist playing Vienna waltzes. After the meal I had a drink of Schnapps (the national drink), a colourless spirit which tasted like weak Scotch but was very warming. The manager came around and wished each person *'gute nacht'* (good night) in a very hospitable manner.

I left the restaurant in a very relaxed state after paying 45 Asch, which I thought was quite reasonable for the excellent dinner, wine and music. It was quite late as I made my way back to the YH. The warden welcomed me into the building, which really was new and clean inside, as distinct from the appearance of the warden, who was a bit scruffy. I signed in and after having a good wash I went straight to bed. As I lay in my sleeping bag I decided to move on the next day. I did not relish the idea of spending the day looking for any historic, architectural, or physical attractions that Klagenfurt might have to offer. Klagenfurt is the headquarters of the British Occupation Forces in Austria, but what a difference there was between it and Salzburg. Both cities were the headquarters of two of the armies of occupation. Salzburg was lousy with Yanks and a beautiful city, while Klagenfurt was a dirty, bomb damaged and an ill kept city, where hardly a British soldier was to be seen. I didn't even see a Union Jack anywhere.

Thursday 14th February: I woke up early the following morning and after breakfast I paid the overnight fee of 5 Asch and 3 Asch for breakfast and left, or I should I say that I was pushed out at 8 a.m. It was snowing heavily as I made my way to the bahnhof to catch the 8.35 a.m. train and bought a ticket to Vienna that cost 66 Asch. I think a snow plough had cleared the tracks because they were well free of snow quite unlike the streets of Klagenfurt. To visit Vienna, the British traveller must pass through the Russian Occupation Zone, one of the largest occupation zones in Austria, extending south from the Czechoslovakian border to the Hungarian border. Whether travelling by road or rail between Klagenfurt and Vienna, the only permissible route was via the Semmering Pass. I had already procured the required Grey Pass in London with Leon, because he said he wanted to visit Vienna.

iiiiiiiiiiiiiiiiiiiii

KLAGENFURT TO VIENNA

I boarded a steam train to take me on the 234 km journey to Vienna and once again the weather was foggy so there was very little to see from the train window of the surrounding mountains. Train travel in Austria in the wintertime was so vastly different to anything I had experienced travelling by train in Australia. All the normal rail sounds were muffled, the clickety-click as the train passed over the rail joints were hardly heard. In the 1950s welded rail was beginning to be installed on railways in Europe, and I think that some of the trains that I have been riding on were sometimes running on welded rail, but not this one. Leaving Klagenfurt the train, which I discovered had begun its journey in Villach, wheeled along from one sparsely populated valley to another, interspersed by a couple of towns Knittelfeld and Leoben were two that I noted. About two hours after leaving Klagenfurt I noticed that the land began to rise

72

perceptibly, which was also confirmed by the locomotive's exhaust beat becoming louder. The cloud base and fog had lifted a little and I was able to see a short distance up the sides of the valleys. It was quite frustrating that there was so little of the mountains to be seen, but at least the fog was never so thick as to prevent me from seeing some of the lakes and villages in the valleys as the train moved along. After all I thought, what is the purpose of travel such as I am doing if not to experience new sights and sounds. After stopping at a town called Murzzuschlag, the train, which was carrying many passengers, began to gain height quickly winding its way around the side of, rugged mountains and over bridges and coming to a stop at the Semmering bahnhof. This was the summit of the Semmering Pass, 897 m (2,943 ft), where our train crossed over into the Russian Occupation Zone.

A young Russian soldier, complete with rifle, fur cap and a long, dark green overcoat, came into my compartment to check passports and Grey Cards. My camera was on the seat beside me. He looked me up and down and seeing my camera pointed to it, neglecting to look at my passport and Grey Card, which I offered up to him. He asked me in *Deutsch: "Was ist das?"* (What is that?). "A camera," I replied. Then he looked at my passport and sneered: "British!" "Oh yes," I said, as he pointed to the Red Cross badge on my parka, a St John's ambulance course I had completed when skiing on Mt. Buller with YHA.

He then asked me: *"Sind sie Soldat?"* (Was I a soldier?) "No, it is a Red Cross badge," I replied, but I felt like saying: 'You should bloody well know what it is, any intelligent citizen all over the world does.' However, he seemed satisfied, and after checking the other occupants of the compartment he left. I was very glad he hadn't taken my camera, but I should have had the good sense to hide it beforehand. Lesson learned. At the far end of the bahnhof as the train moved off I saw the portal of a tunnel, which the train slowly entered.

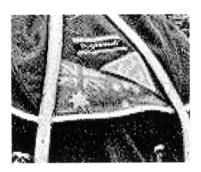

Looking back along the train near Bad Gastein

The Australian flag and YHA logo on the author's rucksack

A steam train passing by under an overhead gantry ready for future line electrification on the way to Klagenfurt

The countryside approaching the Semmering Pass

A large village by Worthersee as seen from the train approaching Klagenfurt

The author and the Red Cross badge

74

The Semmering Pass marks the boundary between two regions of Austria, Styria and Lower Austria, and also between the British and Russian zones of occupation. As the train made its noisy way through the tunnel, we closed all the windows of our compartment to prevent the smoke entering. The tunnel was 1.430 m long, its length indicated by a sign on the portal and in a matter of minutes the train emerged into the light of day, where it was pleasing to see that it was nearly clear of fog, and the surrounding snow clad mountains could be seen. Interesting to note are weather changes after crossing high mountain divides such as this and the Arlberg Pass, with distinct changes of weather conditions from one side to the other.

Now it was all downhill. The train crossed many high arched bridges and went through many tunnels of various lengths, short and long. The train coasted down the winding rails with hardly any noise from the locomotive, except for a high pitched whistle every now and again. This side of the pass is more heavily wooded and mountainous than the country on the Klagenfurt side and the snow thinned out a little as the train came to a stop at a town called Gloggnitz. This town seemed to mark the end of the high mountains, forests and heavy snow. Further on the train passed many acres of vineyards with a sprinkling of snow on the ground between the vines, and then after passing a large industrial town called Wiener Neustadt (Vienna Newtown) the train arrived in Wien (Vienna) in the late afternoon.

A

VIENNA

Emerging from the bomb damaged railway station I consulted my *YHA Guide Book* to find the way to the YH. It directed me to catch a D streetcar to Schotten Ring and change there to a No. 41 tram to its terminus at Potzleinsdorf, a 5 km journey. I rode in comfortable and fast trams arriving safely at the Potzleinsdorf terminus, where directly across from the terminus I saw a large white building standing in a park surrounded by a few trees and snow covered lawns. This was the YH, which looked to me more like a high-class hotel than a YH. The very friendly warden welcomed me and showed me around.

The warden told me that the YH was formerly a castle built on Potzleinsdorf Park, which was passed over to the city after the owner died. It then became a guesthouse for youth organisations and eventually a YH. There was absolutely every comfort imaginable, including clean sheets, beautiful toilets, lockers, nice warm rooms with hot water and hot showers, but the warden said that the showers were only available until 9 a.m. The YH also supplied meals, dinner, called supper and breakfast, each costing 8 Asch.

I had supper consisting of a plate of soup followed by spaghetti with meat. There were two other hostellers, Hank, a tall, jovial American and Jacques (Jack), a short vivacious Frenchman with red hair and a red moustache. He said he was a freelance journalist. After supper I was very tired, so I excused myself and climbed into a very comfortable bed, not really believing I was in Vienna one of the most famous cities in the world. I think I was more excited than when I arrived in London, probably because this time I was by myself.

Friday 15th February: First thing in the morning I had an exhilarating hot shower, which was absolutely out of this world. I was really clean all over for the first time I think, since leaving England. At breakfast the two other hostellers told me that the YH was supposed to close at 12 midnight, but was permanently open thanks to the warden. Austria at this time of the year was celebrating the Fasching (*Fasting)* Season, which really meant having a good time at parties and balls before the advent of Lent. Jack gave me a few hints on how to get around the city and also about the Art Club, which Hank had already visited. He said it was a good place to have a beer and talk to the locals.

It was a great relief to be able to leave the YH and to explore the city without having to take my skis and rucksack with me. With only my bum bag containing my valuables around my waist, I left the YH

76

and rode into the city on the No. 41 tram, for 1.30 Asch. The ticket allowed me to change from one tram to another, provided the one direction was maintained. There was some snow on the streets and footpaths, but no hindrance to walking around admiring all the new sights. One of the first was seeing gangs of men and *women,* some quite old, clearing snow from the streets. They shovelled the snow into trucks that carted it away. It appeared to be very cold, hard work and none of them looked very fit. I found Vienna to be a very large city and contrary to popular belief it does not really lie beside the blue Danube River, but alongside the Danube Canal. The canal was cut many years ago from the Danube River to facilitate trade closer to the city centre. Another important feature of Vienna is the *Ring Strasse* (Ring Street) in the form of a large 'D', with a straight section alongside the canal. Much of the main city area and streets lie within the Ring Strasse.

I decided to first have a look at the Art Club located in a small street off the *Karntner Strasse,* one of Vienna's main streets. I entered the club cautiously, because I didn't know what to expect, even though Hank said it was a good place. I sat down at a table in the long narrow club room and ordered a beer. Cheap meals and drinks were available in the club, which I reckoned was an Art Club in name only, because I was not asked for a membership card or other identification when I entered. I talked with a couple of Austrian blokes and a girl, all of whom spoke good English. I was able by this time to speak enough *Deutsch* to make myself understood, but I was not so good at understanding *Deutsch* when spoken to me. I had to ask the speaker to *"sprechen sie langsam bitte"* (speak slowly please). The club gave me the impression that it was a cheap Bohemian drinking saloon where people of all nationalities, and from all walks of life came to relax, drink, eat and talk. I didn't think by their dress that many had much money, but came to the conclusion that some were artists in one form or another. After I had finished my beer when I got up to go, the Austrians I had been talking to said that

I must come back again at night when there was dancing in the club. I thanked them and said I might.

For the rest of the afternoon I read in the US Information Centre. I learned how Vienna was administered by the occupation forces. Vienna was the headquarters of the Russian Occupation Force in Austria. The city was divided into four zones, French, American, British and Russian, all working together to administer the city and its environs. To this end, members from each of the zones met once a month at a round table conference in the centre of the city in the Inter-Allied Commission building, which flew the flags of the four powers. Every month, each of the occupation powers took it in turn to control the city and suburbs. It was said to be the only place in Europe where the four powers worked together, efficiently and amicably. I was told that one method of knowing which occupation force was in charge on any particular month, was to note which soldier of the four powers was driving an American jeep patrolling the city. After learning about the very interesting role of the occupation forces in Vienna, I returned to the YH.

Saturday 16th February: I left the YH after a shower and breakfast and took the tram into the city. I walked towards the Danube Canal along the Ring Strasse around which trams ran swiftly in both directions. There was much bomb damage evident in buildings and wharves, with some restoration work being carried out. The warden told me later that the restoration work was hampered by the lack of cash and it was taking a long time to see significant results. Although I was walking in the Russian zone of the city, there was no restriction to my movements. This was the same for all of the city zones. There were always a few Russian soldiers around, but I was never aware who controlled which area or city zone, or whose zone I was in. After having a good look around, I turned toward the city centre and looked at the shops along the Rotenturm and Karntner Strasse. Both of these streets converged on St. Stephen's Cathedral, its spire rising above the city skyline, and not in any way rivalled by

78

the highest building in Vienna, the Hoch Haus, (high house) only 12 stories high on the Karntner Strasse. In one of the shops I saw amazing photos of the Semmering Railway. I never realised what fantastic structures the viaducts were that I had travelled over on the way down from the Semmering Pass.

I vowed that on the way back I would make sure to see the double storey arches of the Semmering railway. I decided to leave visiting St. Stephen's for another day and carried on walking around the city. The central area of the inner city was virtually undamaged. The window displays in the shops were very inviting showing a vast range of beautiful clothes, shoes, jewellery and many other fine goods, all at seemingly reasonable prices.

Leaving the Karntner Strasse, I came to the Bristol Hotel, which the Americans were using as their HQ in Vienna. Except for the two US military policemen standing guard at the front doors, one would not have recognised the importance of the building. After walking around further I came to the much larger Imperial Hotel, which the Russians were using as their HQ.

By comparison with the Bristol Hotel, which only had a small frontage, the Imperial Hotel took up a whole block adjacent to the Karntner Ring. All the footpaths around the hotel were barricaded off and patrolled by Russian soldiers with Sten guns. Pedestrians were required to cross to the pavement on the other side of the street to pass by. There was no doubting the importance of that building and its occupants to the Russians.

Across from the hotel there was a square called Stalin Platz (Stalin Place), in the centre of which, a large olive green, Russian tank with a red star painted on the side stood on a concrete base. It was a Russian war memorial. I was not critical of using a tank as a memorial symbol, in fact I thought it rather appropriate. I was however, critical of the square being called Stalin Platz, later learning that the Russians had renamed various landmarks of the city. Stalin Platz was actually Schwarzenberg Platz, named after an Austrian Prince.

I was getting very hungry and I soon found a restaurant called the Althofkeller that looked very inviting. On entering and taking a seat I soon discovered it was where the cast and technicians dined when on location in Vienna, during the filming of the movie *The Third Man*. I had a tasty meal, a bowl of soup and spaghetti washed down with a beer, while a musician played the theme song from *The Third Man* on a zither. The cost of the meal was very reasonable, only 25 Asch. The *Third Man* was released in 1949 and was a huge success. The action in the movie took place on the streets of Vienna in its underground sewers, and in the Prater amusement park on the giant Ferris wheel. Leaving the restaurant I saw a street poster advertising the opera *The Magic Flute,* so I purchased a ticket for the following night's performance. What more appropriate place to see an opera and a Mozart opera than Vienna, I thought.

I went back to the Art Club, and had a wonderful time drinking and dancing with a gorgeous redhead called Ilsa, who seemed to take a liking to me. I had never danced with any girl before who moulded her body into mine like she did, it was as though we were one. For many years afterwards, I could remember that pleasant experience. Ilsa had to go home early, but we arranged to meet at the Art Club again the next morning. It was not to be, however, because shortly after she left, I had to retire to the toilet, where I was violently ill. I spent the night there, and did not recover until early the following morning. It was the inevitable consequence of mixing beer with a cheap, but nice red wine. It was a horrible experience and could have had disastrous consequences for me. I hoped I had learned another lesson.

Sunday 17th February: I left the Art Club at 7 a.m. after falling asleep, cold, sick and tired. I managed to find my way along the deserted, freezing streets to the 41 tram and back to the YH. I had a rejuvenating shower and fell into bed at 8 a.m., not waking up until

80

2.30 p.m. I suddenly realised that I was too late for my appointment with Ilsa the beautiful Austrian redhead, but I only had myself to blame. I hoped I might see her again at the Art Club. After supper I was nearly back to normal again, such were my powers of recovery at that young age.

I was very glad that I was fit enough after my misadventure of the previous night to go and see The Magic Flute *(Die Zauberflote)*, by Mozart. It was performed by the State Opera Company in the *Theater an den Wien,* located outside the ring road, a short way across from the Opera Ring. The opera was performed in this imposing venue, because the Vienna State Opera House was being repaired after being damaged by bombs during the war. It did not reopen until 1955. This was a pity because I would have liked to have seen inside this famous opera house, however the brilliant performance of *The Magic Flute* made up for this loss.

The opera is set in Egypt and has some connection to the Masons. The Egyptian décor, with large stage buildings, together with the costumes worn by the singers made for a truly wonderful spectacle. Although at that time I was not aware of the complete storyline as I only had a German program, it is now one of my favourite operas. My favourite aria was *'Ein Vogelfanger Bin Ich Ya'* (Yes I am a bird catcher), if my *Deutsch* translation is correct. I decided after that very enjoyable experience, that I must go to the opera again in Vienna. So cheap too, well within my daily budget.

Monday 18th February: After breakfast and a beaut shower, I decided to explore Vienna, this time by walking all the way around the Ring Strasse, a distance of about 4 km. I commenced at Schotten-Ring, where I got off the tram and walked in an anticlockwise direction. I was in no hurry, the weather was quite good with a low overcast sky. As I walked along I noted down the name of each section of the Ring. After Schotten-Ring, which I believe had something to do with Benedictine monks, came the Dr. Karl Lueger-Ring, named after an early *Burgermeister* (Mayor ofVienna).

Walking further on I came to Parliament-Ring, adjacent to the large parliament building of white, Grecian style architecture, with high columns in front supporting a Greek arch, flanked on both sides by low, off white–what I would call Renaissance type structures, which I imagined housed all the parliament's offices and employees.

The Burg-Ring with the adjacent Natural and Art Museum buildings was next on my walk. These museums are housed in two wings of a long, Gothic style building, with a central dome, which reminded me very much of the Exhibition buildings of my home town Melbourne. Across the other side of the strasse are two gardens the *Volksgarten* and the *Burggarten.*

Next I crossed the wide, vehicle and tram track Ring Strasse, being careful to avoid the fast moving trams, to get a closer look at the famous, world renowned, Vienna State Opera House building. Of course the Ring Strasse here is appropriately named Opera Ring. I began walking along the length of the huge building, which as far as I could tell from my little, but ever broadening knowledge of architectural styles, is of Gothic style, having large high, arched windows in front, and with a long cupola on top. It had not escaped some bomb damage during the war, and was bedecked with scaffolding erected all over it, which certainly did not completely detract from the immensity and grand appearance of the building.

After leaving the opera house, I kept on the same side of the Ring Strasse where the Karntner Strasse, Vienna's main shopping street, joins and crosses the Ring Strasse, hence the name Karntner Ring, named after a road that led south to Carinthia, a province of Austria bordering Yugoslavia. I was now about half way round the ring and approaching the Danube Canal. Next came Schubert Ring, which requires no explanation, then Park Ring adjacent to the *Stadt Park* (Town Park) and Stuben-Ring. The name Stuben Ring comes from *Stubenstifl,* fortifications that were part of the city walls in 1156. I could not see any sign of a wall, but there was a row of nondescript buildings along one side of the strasse.

82

The Ring Strasse then turned sharply to the left, and ran along beside the Danube Canal. It was named Franz Josef Kai, in honour of Emperor Franz Josef, Austria's last emperor, who ruled from 1848 to 1916. Another turn to the left brought me back to Schotten-Ring. It was a great walk along this famous, very wide, Ring Strasse, with rows of deciduous trees separating the vehicle road from the tram tracks

Afterwards I went to the US Information Library and looked up some of the Ring names I didn't recognise, after which, I felt I knew a little more about Vienna and Austrian history. During my walks around Vienna I saw very few soldiers of any of the occupation forces, which I found surprising. From time to time, I saw a Jeep with one soldier from each of the occupation forces, sitting in the Jeep patrolling the city. I was quite thrilled when some years later, I saw a movie, filmed in Vienna in 1951 called; *Four in A Jeep*. It was a story about a Viennese girl who was in trouble, and called on the patrol for help. It was a very dramatic story that brought back to me, memories of the happy days I spent in Vienna.

Tuesday 19th February: Back I the city I saw an advertisement displayed on a large advertising post for the opera *The Barber of Seville* for the following night. I bought a ticket and also a ticket for the elevated and underground railway that only cost 1.30 Asch. I joined the electric train at Hietzinger bahnhof. The line is really not all underground, but a mixture of underground, elevated and surface line. If nothing else, it provided me with very good views over the city as I rode around the full circle, but it bore no comparison to the London tube. I then wandered back over the canal to the city and went into a cafe on the Karntner Strasse for a coffee.

A new coffee innovation was sweeping through Vienna. It was being advertised everywhere: 'Espresso Coffee served here.' Around every corner in Vienna there seemed to be a coffee cafe. Espresso Coffee is made from special coffee beans, brewed quickly under pressure by boilers mounted on the bar. I went into one of the cafes and ordered an Espresso Coffee. A dinner suited waiter came to my table and presented me with an English newspaper on a frame complete with handle, a wonderful wooden device, because it made the newspaper easy to read without getting the pages all over the place. To me and I suspect many of the other patrons, the appeal of these charming Viennese cafes, was to be able to sit at a table and leisurely drink the very smooth tasting Espresso Coffee. A trolley with a selection of delicious looking cakes was wheeled around from time to time, and I couldn't resist purchasing one that tasted as good as it looked on the trolley. No one rushed me and I was able to sit and leisurely read any of the newspapers supplied, Austrian, English and American for as long as I liked.

After the evening meal at the YH, I returned to the city to see *The Barber of Seville (Der Barbier von Seville)*, a comic opera by Rossini, performed again in the *Theater an den Wien*. I saw that some of the singers were the same as in *The Magic Flute,* in fact it was the same State Opera Company. The music was excellent and once again the sets were stunning. There was even a rain squall. When one character with a large hat, with the sides rolled around (the barber, I thought), came on stage and bent over to talk to another player, two jets of water issued from his hat drenching the other player, it brought the house down. There were many other amusing incidents like this that really made the opera enormously enjoyable. This State Opera Company performs on many nights of each week in Vienna, and judging by these two operas I had the pleasure of seeing, I couldn't help but marvel at their vast repertoire and the excellent quality of their performances.

Wednesday 20th February: In the evening I went into town with Hank and dined at the Lindenkeller, a beautiful place with a man playing the piano. I had a dinner of soup, pork chops, fried potatoes, cake and beer, costing in all just over 100 Asch with taxes. I left Hank and returned to the Art Club where I hoped I would see Ilsa the red head, but no luck. I drank sensibly, no red wine, only beer

84

and a Coke now and again. I had learned my lesson. It was lovely and warm in the club and I fell asleep, but no one woke me, with the result that it was 4 a.m. when I left the Art Club. I thought I needed an Espresso coffee, so I went into a cafe nearby and had a much needed coffee. I saw some prostitutes looking for customers. They propositioned me, but of course I declined.

Thursday 21st February: I stayed in the YH and planned my next movements and wrote letters to my family, but I was not going to post them until I left Vienna, because I had been told that they might be opened by the Russians, and censored. The meals at the YH were excellent. Supper was usually a bowl of noodle or goulash soup (vegetables and meat). The main course was a plate with various forms of macaroni, potatoes or rice, which was certainly filling. Breakfast was mostly bread and cheese or an egg omelette. The Australian Vienna loaf bore little resemblance to the Viennese bread. Most of the bread baked in Austria was of the same shape as ours, but was mostly brown bread and when fresh was like eating firm cake.

After supper, Jack told me a little about the German occupation of France. He said there was a great difference between the strategy of the British and American bombing of German and French targets. The Americans bombed from a great height, with a strong force of planes, whereas the British came in low over the targets and were therefore much more accurate. For that and other reasons, the French did not particularly like the Americans. Jack told me of an Austrian newspaper reporter's view of the Russian occupation. He said that when an Austrian was killed in either the French, American, or British zones, there was always a proper legal, democratic trial or a court martial held into the case. When an Austrian was killed in the Russian zone nobody did anything. The Americans, he said, were good for the Austrian economy, because they were big spenders. The Russians in Vienna on the other hand, were a dead loss, because they were not big spenders. He concluded by saying that any Austrian woman living with an American in a life of luxury in Austria, was in for an unpleasant shock if she married and returned to America.

Friday 22nd February: There were intermittent light falls of snow during the last few days, but today was the first day of sunshine for many days. I went for a walk through the city to the *Roten Armee Brucke,* (Bridge of the Red Army), which crossed the Danube River on Lassalle Strasse. This bridge was actually the *Reichsbrucke,* (Empire Bridge), another of the Russian name swaps, which wouldn't have endeared them to the Viennese. My map showed both names, as it also did with Stalin Platz.

I decided to walk across the bridge to the other side, to see a little of the Russian zone, as I believed that the far side was not under the four-power city control, but in the Russian occupation zone. I was probably taking a risk, but I was curious. After crossing the bridge the banks of the Danube sloped gently upwards for a 400 m, before there were any signs of houses or life, so I returned back across the bridge, noting as I did that the Danube was not blue, but a dirty brown colour. Lucky for me, I was not on the bridge, when on Sunday August 1st 1971, without warning, the bridge suddenly fell into the water in the early hours of the morning. Four people died. The cause was attributed to undetected rust erosion.

Lassalle Strasse led me directly to the Prater and the Ferris wheel, which dominated the sky. Prater, Vienna's amusement park, was closed for the winter. The Ferris wheel was invented by an American, George Ferris. It was built in 1897 for the World Exhibition. The Ferris wheel in the Prater was almost totally destroyed in the war, but was one of the first structures to be rebuilt. The wheel stands 67 m high. Each of the passenger cabins is about the size of a present day, small shipping container. One revolution took 10 minutes. I was sure that there must be great views of Vienna from the top of the wheel. The Ferris wheel, although already famous as an engineering marvel, achieved greater fame when it was featured in the movie *The Third Man.*

86

The Prater was also the birthplace of the Strauss waltz, first danced there in 1820. On the way back into the town centre I stopped to visit an underground toilet. Descending the stairway to the toilet entrance, I beat a hasty retreat because there were women there. I thought I must have got my *Damen* and *Herren* mixed up, but no, I was in the correct toilet. Women tended these toilets, and the minute the cubicle was vacated they moved in and wiped down the seat. I had to get used to seeing women doing all manner of unexpected work in order to earn a living in Vienna and Austria. There was a 'French letter' or condom vending machine on the wall, a very good idea I thought, so I tested it out and purchased one, in a little white packet. I was a Boy Scout whose motto was 'Be Prepared' and so now I was with this 'pragmatic souvenir' tucked inside in my wallet.

I had a bite to eat, then went to the Art Club, where I spent a pleasant evening talking to a blonde with long hair. We talked about Australia and she told me a little about her life as a student in Vienna. I got back to bed in the YH around midnight with no dramas.

Saturday 23rd February: A beautiful sunny day. One of the best so far in Vienna. I went with Hank by tram and bus north of the city through the small village of Grinsing up into the Vienna Woods. Two low mountain summits Kahlenberg, 483 m, and Leopoldsberg 424 m are the highest points in the woods, which rise up from the Danube. We walked from Kahlenberg to Leopoldsberg, where there was a restaurant in which we had an expensive, but excellent steak dinner. The view from the Vienna Woods with Vienna in the distance and the Danube below that was really blue, under the blue sky, making quite a contrast with the snow covered vineyards in the foreground.

I was struck by the similarity between the Vienna Woods and the Dandenong Ranges, in my home state of Victoria. They are very nearly the same height and skyline profile as the Vienna Woods. Both are located much the same distance from their respective cities

Vienna and Melbourne. The forests of the Dandenong Ranges are mostly eucalypts and are denser than those in the Vienna Woods, which are mainly conifers and deciduous varieties. Both areas attract many local and overseas tourists. The Dandenong Ranges lack only the history and musical connections that Vienna is famous for, but it has the famous Puffing Billy narrow gauge tourist train. We returned to the YH for supper, then it was bed for me after an extremely enjoyable day, good weather, good company, new sights, good but expensive food, and a special treat because we saw that the Danube could be seen as the 'beautiful blue Danube.'

Sunday 24th February: A sunny day again. In the afternoon I went by a local train about 6 km from Vienna, to see a ski jumping competition at Hutteldorf, The atmosphere was like a suburban Aussie football match with plenty of wild cheering and fun. This was the first time I had seen real ski jumping, having only seen the big Olympic jumps on newsreels and in photographs. The Winter Olympics were being held in Oslo Norway during this month, and today was the second last day of the events in Oslo, so it was quite a coincidence that I was witnessing this event on this day. Each contestant had two jumps, which were judged on a combination of distance and style. There were only a few falls, even though the length of the longest jump was only 36 m. This was quite short by Olympic standards of the time, where the longest jumps were about 80 m. I thoroughly enjoyed the spectacle and was surprised by the loud thump the skis made on landing.

Monday 25th February: To save money I was rolling my own cigarettes. I bought a packet of Austrian tobacco, but it was awful stuff because after a short time it turned into powder. I also bought a couple of Austrian cakes, which were delicious. I had supper at the YH and met a couple who came from Hitchin. It's a small world, but they didn't know the Bakers. We talked together about ourselves and the places we had visited. They left the next day and I kicked myself for not asking them about employment prospects in Hitchin.

88

Tuesday 26th February: I decided it was about time I went and had a close look at St. Stephen's Catholic Cathedral. On my walks and visits to the city the cathedral was rarely out of my vision, whether it was its tall spire, or when closer its steeply pitched roof covered with tiles in a colourful, patterned mosaic. St. Stephen's was not on the top of my list of places to visit in Vienna. This may have been because I was brought up a Baptist, but was not baptised, so I consider myself a failed Baptist, or a Baptist without a ticket. Back home, churches were only open on Sundays, except for some large churches in the city. Catholic churches being the exception.

In Vienna I discovered that not only were churches places of worship, but they were a prime attraction for tourists to inspect, study and admire the various religious and architectural features both inside and outside the church. I was about to become one of these tourists, with my first visit to a foreign church. I walked through the large ornate doors of St. Stephen's with some unease, but this was quickly dispelled as I took a seat in a pew. It was the perfect environment for me to sit quietly and think or meditate, with the sound of an organ playing softly in the background. My thoughts went to my mother and father and for the first time I felt very homesick. This I believed was the way a church should be, with its doors always open to everyone no matter what their beliefs or station in life, enabling people to walk in off the street at any time in their normal street clothes to ponder, just like I was doing.

I sat there for quite some time listening to the organ music. I saw people lighting candles and crossing themselves and I heard bells ringing, but I wasn't sure why. I soon discovered where the noise of the bells came from when a member of the clergy came around with a long stick on the end of which was a money sack and a bell. The bell tinkled as he walked around. I put a coin in. When I left I purchased a small book from which I learned about the cathedral.

The cathedral was built in the 11th century. It had been the centre of many important events in Austrian and Viennese history. Mozart was married there in 1782 and his funeral took place there in 1791. The church was damaged by fire during the war, but much of this had now been repaired. I then became a more complete tourist by paying a small fee to climb St. Stephens's 37 m high, knobbly spire. I climbed the 50 revolutions of the spiral staircase inside the spire and when I finally reached the top I was completely exhausted and giddy. The view over the city and surrounding country was really extensive with the Vienna Woods in the distance and the summits of Leopoldsberg and Kahlenberg on the horizon. I was also able to get a close up look at St. Stephen's very large, steeply sloping roof adorned with a large mosaic in pink and green tiles, arranged in chevron and diamond patterns.

At this stage of my journey I knew virtually nothing about architectural styles. From the small book I read that St. Stephen's was an odd mixture of Gothic and Roman, whilst the interior was in the Baroque style that I found to be too heavily ornamental for my taste. I supposed as my touring continued I would learn a lot more about churches and cathedrals.

Leaving St. Stephen's I went walking around the city. Although I was no admirer of Austrian tobacco, I was completely in love with Austrian *kuchen* (cake) sold here in Vienna, and also with the Austrian *Deutsch*, which is spoken in waltz time. I purchased 3 Schillings, 10 Groschens worth of the delightful cakes, and presented a 10 ASch note. The change was given to me and counted out in waltz time as follows:*"Guten tag—drei schilling zehn—danke schon—drei schilling zehn—und zehn ist zwanzig—und zehn ist dreisig—vierzig—und funfzig, is vier schilling—vier schilling—und ein schilling—and funf, is zehn schilling—danke schon—auf wiedersehen—auf weidersehen—guten tag."*

Translated into English this is as follows:

'Good day—three shilling and ten—thank you very much—three shilling and ten—and ten is twenty—and ten is thirty—forty—and fifty, is four shilling—four shilling—and one shilling—and five is ten shilling—thank you very much—goodbye—goodbye—good day.'

Another endearing *Deutsch* turn of speech was to exclaim with a drawn out *"AH SO, ah so"* when a point or a word of a conversation was finally understood.

Back at the YH I settled down to work out the route I wanted to take after leaving Vienna. The route I chose after returning to Klagenfurt was to go to Venice, Milan and Zermatt. Having seen the Matterhorn I would then decide where to go and ski in Austria before meeting Netta in Grindelwald. This route would also allow me to visit Venice, a unique historic city, which I definitely wanted to see, while not deviating too much from a direct line to see the Matterhorn in Zermatt. I went into Vienna to find the cost of a ticket to Zermatt that would allow me to break my journey on the way.

I tried four travel agencies including Cooks. All of their quotes were about the same, around £7 Sterling. All except Cooks gave me the price after a few minutes work, but not so Cooks. They told me to come back in 90 minutes and they would have it all worked out for me. I went back in 2 hours, but they told me I was too quick, to come back in an hour's time. Needless to say I didn't go back. I decided in the end to purchase the rail tickets as I went along from place to place. Besides, because of the poor exchange rate in Austria, I thought that it was probably better to first just buy the ticket I needed to get me to Klagenfurt.

Wednesday 27th February: It was snowing again. For much of the time since I had left England I was plagued with a cold. I suppose it had something to do with the constantly changing temperature conditions, the lack of good basic meals each day, and mixing with many people at close quarters. I thought it was about time I washed a few clothes especially my underwear. The dirt that came out of all of my clothes was unbelievable. I hung them all up to dry in the attic of the YH. My socks needed darning but I couldn't be bothered, I decided to be extravagant and buy new ones.

Instead of washing my clothes myself, I could have taken them to one of the Bendix laundries that I had seen. There were usually about ten machines in each one of these places and they did a roaring trade. It was quite amusing, as there were usually dozens of Viennese people outside the laundry, just looking through the window at the machines washing the clothes. The purchase of a washing machine would not have been possible for the average Austrian on their very low wages.

Later Hank, who had friends in Vienna, came back from a party and told me that Jack was in trouble. Jack's girlfriend was going to have a baby! Poor Jack. The news from Paris that he was to become a father completely devastated him. His demeanor had gone from 'oo-la-la' to 'la-oo-oo'. Jack had to return to Paris. He had invited me to stay with him in in Paris, but that will not be happening now.

Before we wished each other goodbye he told me that I must not leave Vienna before I had seen the *Die Dreigroschen Oper*. So in the afternoon I went to the city and booked a seat for the *Die Dreigroschen Oper* and then had a beer in an Expresso Coffee café, where I read the *Daily Mail* from cover to cover. The *Daily Mail* is a broad sheet newspaper, not a tabloid, a type of newspaper I detest. I decided to leave Vienna in three days,' time.

Thursday 28th February: Even though my cold was still bad, I visited Schonbrunn Castle (Schloss Schonbrunn), a truly magnificent building painted in yellow ochre. The name Schonbrunn means 'beautiful spring.' I joined a guided tour as I believed this was the only way to obtain a true appreciation of everything about the castle. I learned that it has hundreds of rooms but only 45 were open for viewing. It is a very long building, built by the Empress Maria Theresa around 1700. It became the Summer Palace of the Hapsburgs and is situated just outside the city, set in the extensive grounds of the Schonbrunn Palace Park. We saw Emperor Franz Joseph's rooms and the iron bedstead in which he died. The chandeliers in the rooms were beautiful, everywhere there was gold leaf adornment (and probably pure gold as well). In a breakfast room, all the chairs were beautifully embroidered. We saw the Hall of Mirrors where Mozart, at the age of six, performed for Empress Maria Theresa and her court, then the Chinese room, which contained wonderful porcelain vases. The guest rooms where Napoleon stayed were in royal blue.

There was just so much to take in and wonder at. I am usually not impressed by opulence on this scale, whether it be in churches, buildings or castles, but I could not help but admire everything about this palace and its surrounds. Outside in the park there was a zoo, which I didn't visit because I did not want to have the possibility of seeing a kangaroo in a cage. A beautiful fountain adorned the park and to complete the grandeur, on a hill at the far end of the park is a huge beautifully styled colonnade. I have just about run out of superlatives describing this spectacular building, but every one of them was well deserved.

I left Schonbrunn and made my way to the Technical Museum, which had some very interesting displays, particularly cross section models of mines, but compared with the magnificence I had seen during my visit to Schonbrunn, it was something of an anti-climax.

Besides the ski jumping I saw at Hutteldorf, I saw another winter sport in Vienna, one that I considered must be the coldest in the world. As I was on my way back to the YH, I passed a narrow back alley in which highly vocal men were playing some sort of game. I stopped and found a game of curling in progress, a sport I had seen in a photo in one of my mountaineering books. All the players were rugged up to the neck.

I was fascinated as I watched one player slide a large circular stone along the flat icy surface of the alley, while another player brushed the ice ahead of the stone with a small broom as the stone approached the target. The object of the game, like lawn bowls, was to see who could slide their stone nearest the target. I said it must be the coldest sport in the world because the rink, if that is what it was called, had to be located in a place where the light of the sun never fell, such as that back alley. After a while the cold became too intense for me, so I left them to their game and returned to the YH. When I went up in the attic to get the clothes I had washed the day before, I found they were all frozen solid and sheathed in ice!

Friday 29th February: After supper I went to see *Die Dreigroschen Oper* (The Threepenny Opera). The Groschen is an Austrian coin, 100th of a Schilling. I thoroughly enjoyed the opera, staged at the Volkstheater just outside the Burg Ring. It was a different theatre than where I saw the other two operas, but just as elaborate in architectural style and interior decoration. It was a special performance that night, because the Premier of Austria, Leopold Figl was in attendance. I was dressed in my ski clothes, but did not feel out of place. People attending opera in Vienna, even on that occasion, did not dress up to the extent that was usual in Melbourne. In Austria opera going is a recreation, not so much an elite social occasion.

The sets, the actors and costumes were all very good. From time to time signs written in *Deutsch* popped out from the side of the stage carrying the titles of each song, which I likened to ballads more than operatic arias, but I could not understand many of the words written on them. I left the theatre with the very enchanting theme tune in my brain. I was certainly very grateful to Jack for telling me not to miss seeing *Die Dreigroschen Oper,* and also introducing me to the Art Club.

The story of the *Die Dreigroschen Oper* takes place near Newgate Prison in London. The main characters are the Peachums, receivers of stolen goods, obtained by getting them from a beggar's organisation they run. Polly their daughter is in love with a highwayman called MacHeath. She marries him despite her parents wanting a more suitable marriage for their daughter. They try to frame MacHeath to get him arrested and sent to the gallows, but after much complication, a happy end ensues for Polly and MacHeath. *The*

Dreigroschen Oper's music is by Kurt Weill and libretto by Bertholt Brecht, I have subsequently seen many versions of the opera and also *The Beggar's Opera* on film, TV, in various countries as well as on stage in Melbourne in 1966. I have always thoroughly enjoyed it, especially the Weill and Brecht version for its earthy plot, entertaining true to life characters, raucous ballads and satire. I was certainly very grateful to Jack for telling me not to miss seeing *Die Dreigroschen Oper.*

I was very sorry to be saying goodbye to Vienna as I had spent such a good time there getting to know the city and its people. However, I felt it was fitting that I left Vienna, a city in which music has played such a large part with two tunes ringing in my head, *The Third Man* theme and a tune from *Die Dreigroschen Oper*, which I didn't then know its name.

Tomorrow, after living in Vienna for two weeks I will leave the world-famous, war damaged city, which in the past decade or so since the *Anschluss,* when the Germans took over the country has had such a traumatic history, but not to the extent that its functions were marred. The people of Vienna on the whole were undeniably poor, but seemed happy. They said: "We are living for today and letting tomorrow take care of itself." The fact that it was winter time for my stay didn't really put a damper on the enjoyment of the sights of Vienna, nor did it hinder my ability to enjoy the opera, Art Club, restaurants and coffee cafes.

To add to the uniqueness of my stay, there was the four-power control of the city, with the Russians giving me some insight into their way of doing things. The military occupation of Austria by the four powers did not come to an end until 25th October 1955.

The time I spent at the grandiose, well run YH was wonderful, with its modern up-to-date facilities, especially being able to have a shower every day. It was also a relief to be able to leave my skis and belongings in the very secure and well run YH. My final thought on leaving Vienna was that I hoped it retains for ever its charming

The Vienna State Opera House

The Bridge of the Red Army

The View from Kahlenberg at the edge of the Vienna Woods The blue Danube can just be seen at the left hand edge of the photo

St Stephen's Cathedral
showing the roof and spire
Photo courtesy G W Smith

Schonbrunn Castle
Photo courtesy G W Smith

The Ferris wheel in Prater

96

character of beautiful buildings, unique street system, vibrant café and theatre going life, and above all its wonderful Viennese people.

Before I went to bed on my last night in Vienna I packed my rucksack ready to make a quick getaway in the morning. I thanked the excellent warden and paid the hostel fees to save time in the morning.

||||||||||||||||||||||

VIENNA TO KLAGENFURT

Saturday 1st March: I just managed to catch the 7.15 a.m. train, which was crowded with standing room only. The weather was fine, and I was anxious to see more of the magnificent mountain scenery between Vienna and the Semmering Pass, particularly the bridges and viaducts that I had seen pictures of in shops on the Kartner Strasse. As usual it was a corridor carriage. I had to stand with other passengers in the corridor and I didn't think I was going to see much of the scenery.

I hadn't had breakfast and as the train began to climb up the Semmering Pass, I asked a fellow passenger if he would please mind my rucksack and skis while I had breakfast in the dining car. He said it would be no trouble. I worked my way up to the dining car and took a seat at a beautifully laid table beside a large window. This was a great move because besides having breakfast, I was able to watch the spectacular countryside go past the window accompanied by the loud beat of the locomotives exhaust as it began the climb. I knew breakfast was going to cost me 'an arm and a leg' but I didn't care. I ordered bacon and eggs and coffee, which were elegantly served by a uniformed waiter. I was in no hurry to finish breakfast and was engrossed in enjoying the magnificent scenery of snow capped mountains and snow laden forests. The train passed through 14 tunnels, crossed over 16 magnificent viaducts, working hard climbing 460 m, to the Semmering Pass. Because the train was running along the top of the bridges, I only managed to get a few glimpses of one or two of the great double storey bridges when the train went around one of the many curves. The little I saw, together with many photographs I had seen, filled me with admiration for the bridge builders of old. I realised we were approaching the Semmering Pass so I paid the bill and was pleasantly surprised because it only cost 27 Asch. Money very well spent. I returned to the man who was minding my skis and thanked him in *Deutsch,* which I think surprised him.

The train passed through the Semmering tunnel and stopped at the Semmering bahnhof, where I discovered that there was an important event about to take place later in the day. My train was to be the last train from Vienna to pass through the old tunnel. I looked out of the window and saw the bahnhof decked out in Austrian flags, but of much more interest was the ribbon strung across the portal of the new tunnel. I had not seen any Russian border guards. None had entered the train to check passports, but I wasn't taking any chances. I hid my camera under my parka and went into the toilet at the end of the carriage and took some photos of the decorated bahnhof and the ribbon across the tunnel portal. The train finally moved off with not a sign of a Russian anywhere. Strange, I thought, but I supposed they didn't care who left their zone, only who came into it. As I write I have discovered that the Semmering bahnhof has been shifted to the Vienna side of the tunnel.

In 1998 UNESCO granted World Heritage listing to the Semmering Railway, defined as the 41 kilometres between Murzzuschlag *and* Gloggnitz. *It recognised that this section of alpine railway with its high standard of tunnels, viaducts and other works has ensured the continuous use of the line up to the present day. It runs through a spectacular mountain landscape and there are many fine buildings built when the area was opened up, due to the advent of the railway. Construction began in 1848 and completed in 1854.*

I still have the photos, which I thought they might be a collector's item. I wrote some years ago to the Austrian Railway

98

Historical Society, they said they had many photos of the opening, thank you.

Between Semmering and Klagenfurt the weather cleared as the train descended from Semmering. At last I was able to see much more of the snow covered countryside than on the way to Vienna. In the distance to the south I saw a range of high, snow covered mountains that gave me quite a thrill. I reckoned they were in Yugoslavia. Most of the railway carriages I have travelled in so far like this one were corridor type with vestibules at each end. The passengers have to be careful when descending the steep steps from the vestibule on to the platform, most of which are concrete strips at ground level or slightly raised about 20 cm. Nothing like our trains back home and the UK, where platforms are at the same height as the carriage floors, with just a step on from the platform. I did wonder how disabled persons were able to travel on these corridor type trains.

KLAGENFURT

The train arrived in Klagenfurt around 6 p.m., which was still the same rather unattractive city. I posted all the letters I had written in Vienna, and then realised I had to wait an hour or so for the YH to open, so I decided to stay on the station and watch the trains go by. When the YH opened I met a tall, blonde Austrian named Gerhart Pack. We talked for a while and seeing I had my skis, he persuaded me to ski with him the next day, as he said the weather would be 'prima.' We talked further during the evening and after a meal of macaroni and some sort of tasty meat I went off to bed.

KLAGENFURT TO VOLKERMARKT

Sunday 2nd March: The morning dawned cold, but sunny and so after breakfast Gerhart and I paid the charges and left the YH. We caught a bus that went along the shores of the upper reaches of Worthersee, the large lake that I had seen on the way to Klagenfurt.

99

The Volkstheater on the front page of the program

A page from *Die Dreigroschen Oper* program

A photo showing of one of the several two storey bridges on the Semmering Railway

The ribbon waiting to be broken for the opening of the new tunnel

Austrian flags celebrating the opening of the tunnel at the Semmering Bahnhof

Gerhart said it had the warmest water of the lakes in Carinthia. We skied alongside the lake for over an hour, just striding along with our skis sliding effortlessly over the new snow. It was an absolute pleasure. I had decided to bring my rucksack with me and not leave it at the YH, because I wasn't sure I would be returning there. Skiing along with a heavy rucksack on my back was not a new experience for me, nor did it diminish the enjoyment of our tour. In the distance I could see the high range of snow covered mountains that I had noticed yesterday. "Are they in Yugoslavia?" I asked Gerhart. "Yes, they are." he said. We then skied well away from the water to a road where we boarded another bus that Gerhart said would take us to his family's home in Volkermarkt for lunch. From Volkermarkt the road continued on to Graz, Austria's second largest city and the capital of Styria.

VOLKERMARKT

We alighted from the bus and walked a short distance through the small town to Gerhart's house, which was made of wood with plaster walls inside, decorated with many pictures and wallflowers. I was introduced to Gerhart's middle aged, mother and father and his sister Maria, an attractive girl about 18 years of age. They all gave me a very warm welcome and sat me down to big bowl of soup, followed by a plate of sausages and mashed potatoes. After lunch we talked together and I told them all about my travels, about Australia and the operas I had seen in Vienna. I showed them the programs, which impressed them immensely.

I mentioned *Die Dreigroschen Oper* and how much I enjoyed it, but couldn't get one of the tunes out of my head. There was a piano in the room that Gerhart's sister played, so I asked if she could play the tune I had in my head. Maria asked me to hum the tune while she played the notes on the piano, which she wrote down on a piece of paper for me. None of the family knew it. The tune I hummed that day became a hit tune for Sammy Davis Jnr some years later. It was

101

called *'Mac the Knife'*. It was late afternoon when I said goodbye to the Pack family and thanked them for their kind hospitality. They wished me good luck. It was a very happy and interesting diversion on my tour and allowed me to see a little more of the Austrian way of life.

VOLKERMARKT TO KLAGENFURT

I caught the bus to take me the 20 km back to Klagenfurt, arriving there at 6 p.m.

⌂

KLAGENFURT

The bus stopped at the railway station and I purchased a ticket, but not to Venice as that would have meant changing a £10 traveller's cheque, but to Tarvisio, just over the border in Italy. This ran my Austrian money down to 3.7 Asch just enough to get me to Tarvisio, where I would cash the cheque into Italian Lira.

I really didn't have enough money or inclination to stay the night at the YH, because the train to Tarvisio left at 7.30 a.m. in the morning. I decided that I had enough money to go to a café and have a bowl of goulash soup and a beer, both of which I had become very fond. After I finished my beer I returned to the station to spend the night, with only 3 Groschens in hand. I congratulated myself for drawing down my Austrian money to the lowest possible amount, and settled down to spend the night in the cold waiting room, happy as I reflected on the very interesting and enjoyable day. I wondered, when the Pack family heard *'Mac The Knife'* on the hit parade charts years later, if they remembered the Australian their son brought home to them with a tune in his head.

||||||||||||||||||||

KLAGENFURT TO TARVISIO

Monday 3rd March: I caught the 7.30 a.m. train to Villach going

102

over the same route that I had taken on the way to Vienna, but this time there was a big difference. The weather was clear and it was a thrilling revelation to look across Worthersee to the high, snow covered mountains in Yugoslavia. The steam train sped along quite close to the lake for much of the 45 km journey to Villach. On arrival at Villach there was no wheel tapping this time, but there were some important changes to my mode of travel. Three in fact, from an Austrian to an Italian train, from a steam train to electric, and a change of platforms to board the Italian train the carriages of which, were once again corridor. In Villach too, I saw a person in a wheelchair lifted on to the train by a form of fork lift where the wheel chair and its occupant would spend the journey in the vestibule. One of these three changes, from steam to electric was not required after 1956 when the Semmering Railway was electrified.

I changed into the Italian train that left Villach with a whistle that sounded like a cross between an Australian steam train chime and the more common peep sound. Picking up speed it ran along a flat valley where it crossed a bridge over the Drau River. From then on the train climbed gradually. I could see a range of high mountains in the distance that were gradually getting nearer. After crossing another river, our train came to Arnoldstein a station with a loop where it stopped to let another train pass by.

It was a lovely day as the comfortably filled train, ran around many curves and along valley walls as it climbed toward Tarvisio, eventually crossing over a relatively low pass into Italy, where it came to a halt at the border town of Tarvisio, a 30 km train journey along which I don't think there were any tunnels, or if there were I was asleep. In fact there were tunnels!

CHAPTER 8

ITALY

TARVISIO

There was no customs check on the Tarvisio station, but I was able to change a traveller's cheque for Italian lire, an urgent necessity as I had no Italian money. I received 16,000 lira for my £10 Sterling cheque. Now flush with Italian lira all in notes of numerous denominations, I purchased my rail ticket to Venice, costing 1.100 lira. I bought a packet of cigarettes for 200 lira and went and had a good look at the huge Italian, electric locomotive that was to haul my train. I bought a ham roll and a litre of milk for 300 lira. That was my breakfast, which made me feel more like a young man again, and ready to enjoy the next stage of my tour to the wonderful city of Venice that I had read so much about.

!!!!!!!!!!!!!!!!!!!!!!!!!

TARVISIO TO VENICE

Precisely at 12.27 p.m. my train left for the 154 km journey to Venice. The sun was shining brilliantly and straightway I left my seat and went into the corridor and poked my head out the window. What I saw was a high, snow capped mountain piercing the sky in the distance. The train began descending along the side of a snow filled gorge with a small river flowing down its centre, a tributary of the Tagliamento River. It was a truly a magnificent scene. The railway was mostly cut into the rock faces of the steep sides of the gorge and where this was not possible, short tunnels of various lengths were

104

bored. The gorge widened into a valley, the steep sides of which culminated in high snow covered peaks. On the right the eastern fringe of the Italian Dolomites (the Venetian Alps) and on the left, the Julian Alps in Slovenia (Yugoslavia). The train's descent continued along the side of the river passing through some snow sheds as the sun lit up the rugged landscape in brilliant, *'National Geographic Magazine'* like colours, particularly the river, which was a vivid green. The river with the railway making its way down the steep sides of the gorge was the most spectacular beginning to a railway journey that I think I have ever experienced.

The train gradually emerged from the high valley enclosed by snowy peaks, stopping at the town of Gemona where the mountains were not quite so high, but still carried a lot of snow. The high mountains gradually dropped behind the train as it descended through scattered trees, low hills and valleys. I saw women washing clothes in a river and a crop, which looked very much like cane, together with some type of vegetables growing alongside the railway line. Peculiar looking trees were being grown in extensive fields, which I was told later, would most likely have been olive trees. The train then passed through a small village called Resiutta, which had suffered massive war damage. The exact words I said to myself were: "It had hell belted out of it." What snow there was on the ground was nearly gone by the time the train reached the large city of Udine, which appeared to have escaped with virtually no war damage at all.

Looking forward from the train, I saw a great bank of cloud that the train soon passed under, causing all the colours and long views to regrettably, disappear. Further on I saw a bridge at the village of Casara, which had suffered major bomb damage. From then, on except for the country on the approaches to Venice, there was hardly a place that had not suffered war damage. All the way along the route

The electric locomotive at the head of the author's train at the Tarvisio railway station

The view from the train of the Italian alps left and the Jugoslavian alps on the skyline

My first view of a bridge over a canal in Venice after leaving the train

From the train looking down the Tagliamentor River flowing down the centre of the valley with a tunnel portal just visible on the left hand edge of the photo.

106

there were damaged and derelict railway rolling stock, buildings and equipment, even the rusted hulk of a big locomotive. The carriage I was travelling in was I thought, in better order than the Austrian one I had been in from Klagenfurt. The painted panels and seats looked nearly brand new. This was rather ironic considering the scenes of rolling stock devastation I was seeing after leaving the mountains.

Another bridge, this one undamaged that the train crossed, was over the Tagliamento River, then a little further on the train passed large vineyards. The area that the train was passing through was the scene of heavy fighting during World War II. It was not liberated until May 1945 by the British with great help from the Italian resistance movement. The train reached Venice (Venezia) at 5.30 p.m. approaching the city over a long 3.8 km causeway, bringing to an end a spectacular railway journey, which I have never forgotten. It was most fitting that its destination was the magnificent city of Venice.

▲
VENICE

After alighting from the train with my rucksack and skis I walked along the platform, and out the front of the station I looked at my map for directions to take me to the YH. Directly in front of me I saw a canal with a bridge crossing it a short distance away. I knew it wasn't the famous Rialto Bridge, which I had seen so many times in photos, but I imagined the canal was part of the Grand Canal. I kept on walking very interested in what I was observing in this famous city. Although it was dusk everything was so colourful.

When I walked further on I was again surprised how quickly I became immersed in the unique architecture and features of the city of Venice. The light was fading and the lights of the city were reflected in shimmering colours from the surface of the Grand Canal, along which many gondolas were slowly moving. A delightful and ideal hour for a tourist like me to get their first look at Venice and the Grand Canal. I realised that I was actually in Venice, the city I had read about and seen so many pictures of since my early childhood. 'THIS IS REALLY LIVING!'I exclaimed to myself. I followed the map to the YH that went by the long name of 'Ostello Casa San Georgios.'

The YH was actually on the island of Giudecca so I had to take a ferry ride of about 400 m across the Giudecca Canal to get there, which was a big thrill. The YH had quite good amenities and cost 250 lira per night, which was very reasonable, meals were also supplied for a small sum. I was very tired because it had been a long but interesting day. I had a meal of spaghetti with a glass of Chianti, a nice light red wine served from a large bottle wrapped in a straw cover. Because of the Italian custom of drinking wine with their meals, drinking Chianti is permitted in Italian youth hostels. After a cleansing wash, no showers though, I climbed into my sleeping bag.

Tuesday 4th March: The city of Venice is situated at the top of the Gulf of Venice, at the northern end of the Adriatic Sea. I suppose it could be said that it is in Italy's groin. I could not think of leaving Venice until I had seen the things I remembered learning about over the years. The Rialto Bridge, the Bridge of Sighs, the Grand Canal with its gondoliers and St Mark's Square. These famous features of Venice were my objectives as I set out in the morning after a breakfast of bread rolls and cheese.

I took the ferry across to the main island and walked through the city, losing my way many times until I found the Rialto Bridge over the Grand Canal. This world famous bridge was the first to be built to span the Grand Canal. The bridge had been rebuilt many times since it was first constructed, but it was not until 1557 that a permanent stone bridge was built. The span is 48 m long and 7.5 m above the water level. After crossing the bridge several times and admiring the view down the canal, I came to the conclusion that the famous Rialto Bridge was quite beautiful, its shape and architecture quite pleasing to my eyes. I then took a gondola from the Rialto

108

Bridge to St Mark's Square. An amusing incident occurred as I attempted to pay the gondolier for the journey. There was a gentle breeze blowing and I had not realised before that there were no coins in the Italian currency, it was all paper money. This involved all sorts of gymnastics on the part of the gondolier to accept and give change from piles of notes held down by various weights. I believe I could have made a fortune if I had brought along some Melbourne tram conductor's tickets and money bags and sold them to the gondoliers.

St Mark's Square (Piazza San Marco) is a large square populated both by people, tourists like me and flocks of pigeons. The square is bounded on three sides by imposing buildings and on the other by the Grand Canal. Along one side of the square is the Doge's Palace, the residence of the rulers of Venice. From the 9th century they were elected for life by the Venetian people and presided over a form of republic as Presidents. The palace is a beautiful three story structure of Gothic arches, the top level constructed with creamy yellow patterned masonry, with large Gothic style windows.

St Mark's Church stands at the head of the square, an impressive church with a highly decorated facade of large Gothic arches at ground level and more Gothic arches above these. The roof has five domes topped with minarets. I learned that the floor plan of St Mark's was also in the form of a crucifix, the long axis with the cross arms called the right and left transepts forming the conventional design. Up to this point, I was not aware that many churches were constructed in this form. The interior of St Mark's was extremely beautiful and ornate with lovely paintings and murals. I was most impressed by the floor, inlaid in a Venetian mosaic of various coloured stones, mostly rectangular, forming patterns of Biblical themes and icons. The walls and parts of the roof were lavishly adorned in the same themes.

Opposite the Doge's Palace on the left-hand side of the square, there was a variety of marvellous shops beneath a long colonnaded facade. The shops sold all manner of beautiful wares: clothes, shoes, silks, but in particular, Venetian glassware made into wonderful shapes. In the front of St Mark's Church in the centre of the square, a high brick tower with an open belfry topped by a triangular spire rose majestically. It was called the Campanile and is actually the bell tower of St Mark's. The Campanile stands 98 m high and was first built in the 9th century. It has fallen and been rebuilt several times. I found that I could get to the top of the bell tower by paying a small fee. I entered a lift that I operated myself. The lift took me up to the belfry from where there was a spectacular view of Venice and its surroundings, well worth the entry fee. I read that in suitable weather the Italian Alps can be seen, but today there was a low overcast.

I was about to enter the lift and descend, when all the clocks around me in Venice struck the hour, it was 10 a.m. Across from the Campanile rising above the shops I saw a clock tower, its clock face made of gilt and blue enamel. The clock recorded the time, the phases of the moon and the zodiac. High above the clock face there was a large bell, which was being struck by two mechanically operated bronze figures known as 'The Moors.' I was alone and a bit peeved because there was no sound from the bell directly above me, so. I decided to do something about it.

I discovered that I was just tall enough to reach the bell clanger and I swung it bit by bit until it eventually struck the bell. There was one very loud gong, which sounded all over Venice, about one minute after all the other bells in Venice had sounded ten times! Immediately I heard the lift start up and after a minute the attendant emerged from the lift door. He began abusing me in Italian. When he had finished his tirade, I said: "I am sorry I don't speak Italian." He replied in very good English: "I know you don't." With that, we both got back into the lift and returned to ground level without a further word being spoken.

Leaving the Campanili with a feeling of fulfilment, I walked along the Grand Canal until I reached the Bridge of Sighs perched over a small side canal. The Bridge of Sighs is so called because

110

prisoners were taken over this bridge on their way to execution. The bridge is adjacent to, and connects with, the Doge's Palace. I was surprised how small the Bridge of Sighs and the canal really were. Leaving there, I walked to the end of the main island and back, and the further I walked from St Mark's Square, the more unkempt and less attractive the buildings became.

I learned that the posts along the side of the Grand Canal that the gondoliers tie up their gondolas to, some looking like barber's poles are colour coded to identify the owner of the mooring. I spent a delightful half-hour or so sitting beside the Grand Canal having a cup of coffee and thinking how good it was to be here at this time without the crowds. I then returned to the YH after a tiring, but interest filled day. I found that I was getting a liking for spaghetti, which was much more tasteful than I had been having in Austria, irrespective of the sauce served with it.

The island of Giudecca where the YH is situated is about 2 km long and crossed by many canals. I did not explore it except for a short walk to visit a large church nearby the Chiesa del Redentore (Church of the Most Holy Redeemer). This church can be seen from many places on the main island, displaying a classic architectural style, its large dome and twin spires standing tall on the edge of the Giudecca Canal, I found it more to my liking. It is much less ornate than St Marks, which although famous for its architecture and embellishment, is diminished somewhat by being surrounded by other buildings of historical and architectural significance.

Wednesday 5th March: The morning was foggy, but the fog cleared away at noon. I took a ride in a water bus to the Lido, a journey of about 5 km. Motor driven open launches called water buses holding about 20 persons are used as ferries between the various islands of Venice. The Lido is an island 23 km long and over 7 km wide at its widest part. It fronts the Adriatic Sea on one side with good, long, sandy beaches. It was spring and surprisingly there was not much tourist activity, however in summer the island becomes a very fashionable beach resort, with big luxury hotels, a casino and cinema lining the foreshore. I walked around the island, which was nothing like Venice, because there were buses, cars and taxis running around, all ferried across from the mainland. There were many interesting shops, but business was slow at this time of the year. The Italian name Lido (meaning beach) has been adopted by many beach resorts around the world to indicate that it is something above the ordinary.

The island has a permanent population of around 18,000 people and in the summer hosts an International Film Festival. I walked out to the widest part of the island, called Alberoni and had a look at the 18 hole golf course, which was only open in summer. I don't know why because it was excellent golfing weather. I wandered along a couple of the fairways that were very much in need of cutting. Some of the fairways had concrete bunkers at their sides, a legacy of the war. I thought. The Lido is well worth visiting even in early spring, if for no other reason than to appreciate the contrast with Venice and its flamboyancy.

I returned to the YH and had another colossal meal of spaghetti and red wine. I had enjoyed my visit to Venice immensely. I had seen my five objectives and much, much more, too much, in fact, to take it all in. Venice was a complete change from any town or city I have seen or could imagine. It is a truly unique place, founded in 8011 AD. Venice encompasses 117 islands, 150 canals and 400 bridges. The buildings were originally built on pine wood piles, sunk 7.5 m into clay and sand, and then topped with masonry and bricks. Venice is slowly sinking, but thankfully there are engineering plans being devised to halt and stabilize the sink rate. I believe that I got to know Venice quite well in the three days I spent there. The weather for the three days I was there was mild and misty, quite pleasant for this time of the year. To stay any longer would have been time wasted. I decided to leave for Milan on the noon train tomorrow.

112

Thursday 6th March: Although the roads were clear of snow. I had given hitchhiking to Milan no thought being lumbered with skis. Besides I couldn't wait to get to Switzerland to put them to use.

!!!!!!!!!!!!!!!!!!!!!!!

VENICE TO MILAN

I boarded a train at 12 noon for the 5 hour journey of 276 Km to Milan. The carriage I was in was full of middle age Italian men, dressed in rather well worn black suits. It would have been a rather monotonous train ride, except for an argument that developed between the Italians There was no doubt that I was the catalyst for the argument, because they began asking me questions, pointing to me and saying: "Americano." "No, Australian, Melbourne, Sydney," I said, pointing to the small Australian flag I had on the flap of my rucksack. They were quite friendly, despite their arguing and at last seemed to understand my nationality. As the train ambled along stopping at all the stations along the way, their argument or discussion continued unabated with the word "Americano" still being uttered every now and again.

A peculiar aspect of their discussions about me was that when the train stopped at three large towns on the way, Padova, Verona and Brescia. At each of these towns one or two of my fellow passengers got off and their place was taken by others. I was introduced to the newcomers as an 'Austaliano', and after a short time the discussion appeared to continue in exactly the same vein as before. The pity of all of this was that, none of the Italians were able to speak English, or even attempted to do so. I wondered if such a circumstance would occur on a similar train journey in Victoria. We in Australia would have been more likely to talk about Aussie Rules football, albeit, maybe the politics of these games. The argument or discussion, I was not sure which that took place in my compartment was another instance of the behaviour I had observed when sitting down at a table with some Italians by the side of the Grand Canal in Venice the previous day. There was a lively political, or so it seemed to me discussion taking place between the coffee drinkers, with complete disregard for me.

We in Australia have a very stable political environment compared with Italy, which does not lend itself to political talk so readily. I reasoned that this was because we had not experienced the traumas of war, or the degrading spectacle of seeing our political leader, the dictator Benito Mussolini and his mistress Clara Petacci, shot by partisans, and strung up by the heels in Milan.

I saw very little war damage from the train as it sped across the Plains of Lombardy, nothing like I saw from the train on the way to Venice, and as the train approached Milan the weather cleared enabling me to see and be thrilled by a brilliant view of the distant snow covered Italian Alps. The train arrived in Milan *(Milano)* late in the afternoon.

▲

MILAN

I took a number 1 tram from the Central railway station to the North station and found the YH easily, a rather ugly building in a park right beside the North railway station. There were a few other hostellers at the YH. I talked with them before I retired to my sleeping bag with the thrilling prospect that in a couple of days I would be in the mountains of Switzerland.

Friday 7th March: In the morning I walked around the big modern city, its traffic lousy with Fiats, Lambrettas and Vespa motor scooters, which I thought were all being driven by maniacs. There were various places that my guidebook said I should visit in Milan. One of these was the zoo, but not for me because again I didn't want to see a kangaroo in a cage. However on the top of the list was the Duomo Cathedral, which my guidebook described as 'Milan's centrepiece' so this was where I went first. To my eyes the Duomo is ugly, because of the proliferation of 135 spires on its roof and many statues and gargoyles. The cathedral is built in the Gothic crucifix form, and has one strange peculiarity, not one of its spires contains a bell; in fact the Duomo Cathedral has no bell tower. I entered the cathedral through its huge doors that had suffered some damage during the war, the marks of which were still visible. The interior was huge, with large columns supporting the roof and beautiful stained glass windows. The Duomo is said to be the greatest Gothic cathedral ever built, and the third largest church in the world. When full it can hold 40,000 people. It is fronted by a large square, the Piazza del Duomo where there were many small stalls selling various wares. I bought a coffee and sat at a table watching the passing parade of people and traffic.

Leaving the Duomo Piazza, I wandered around the large city, an important industrial and commercial city situated on the plain of Lombardy in sight of the Alps. It was heavily bombed during World War II, but I saw very little evidence of this, except on the doors of the Duomo. Milan was liberated by the Partisans before the advance of the allied troops. It has quickly become a thriving city. This was quite evident as I explored the streets admiring all the beautiful shops, and the well dressed people I passed in the streets. Italian men all seemed to be wearing pointed shoes and long lapelled suit coats, while most of the women I saw were well dressed and attractive. I finished my walk in the park near the YH, where I sat on a seat close to a large traffic junction, watching the traffic.

Nearly every car was a Fiat, but best of all was the multitude of motor scooters, Most seemed to be driven by young Italian lads with their girl friends behind, sometimes riding side-saddle, their beautiful long hair streaming behind in the wind. Sitting there watching, I vowed I would get a motor scooter one day, and of course a beautiful girl to ride behind me. I never did get a motor scooter, but I did get a Morris Minor, a beautiful girl Dilys, who became my wife. Back at the YH I had a big plate of spaghetti and savaloys for tea.

Saturday 8th March: My second and last full day in Milan was

The Campanili bell tower in St. Marks Square

'The Moors' clock tower above St Mark's Square

The Bridge of Sighs

The open air cafe on the Grand Canal where the author enjoyed a refreshing coffee

Lake Maggiori as seen from the train

Traffic in front of the Duomo Cathedral in Milan

116

very cold with intermittent snow showers. As much as I thought the exterior of the Duomo Cathedral was ugly, I decided I would like to take a second look at the interior, particularly the stained glass windows, so that was where I went first. The stained glass windows are beautifully coloured, with pictures depicting a wide range of themes, some Biblical, which I recognised easily, but others, I had no idea what they were about. One even showed a python, in the act of swallowing a man. Maybe the snake was swallowing Adam. However, I thought it was well worth the second visit and afterwards, as the weather had cleared up, I sat in the Duomo Piazza again and had a coffee and cakes.

To satisfy my morbid curiosity, I attempted to find out where in Milan Mussolini and his mistress were hung. The warden said he didn't know, or maybe didn't want to know, so I didn't bother to enquire from anyone else as I thought it might embarrass them. Then I went to the North railway station and purchased a holiday rail ticket to Zermatt, Switzerland, costing 1.740 lira, which left me with about 2.000 lira. That purchase put me slightly over my budget, so from now on I would have to spend my money more wisely.

The last place of interest I visited in Milan was the Sforzesco Castle *(Castello Sforzesco)* at the end of the Via Dante. The castle was originally built as a fortress, but it is now a big museum holding sculpture, applied arts and a large picture gallery. I only had a cursory look around because I had seen a surfeit of various art forms. I hurried back to the YH where I had a good clean up ready for an early start in the morning. Over a large plate of spaghetti and sauce I talked with a couple of hostellers, all English, but no Australians. I retired early, excited that the next day would see me in Switzerland.

As I lay in my sleeping bag waiting for sleep to come, I reflected on my stay in Milan. Although I had only spent two full days there, I liked what I saw. Apart from the motor scooters, a new exciting form of transport I hadn't seen before, Milan was a lively, busy city, a city in which I felt at home with trams just like

Melbourne and something of the same atmosphere, and of course because Milan is in sight of the Alps.

Sunday 9th March: On the final morning of my stay, I had a breakfast of the same rice based porridge as was served each morning while I was there. It was certainly filling, but not as enjoyable as corn flakes or bacon and eggs. I wished the warden goodbye and paid him a total of 730 lira (200 lira/night plus meals) and made my way to the Central station to catch the 9.30 a.m. train to Brig. At last I was on my way to Switzerland.

IIIIIIIIIIIIIIIIIIIII

MILAN TO BRIG

Precisely at 9.30 a.m. my train hauled by a huge, Italian, electric locomotive moved slowly out of the Milan station. Once out of the suburbs the train sped up and ran for many kilometres across extensive plains with pastures and some vineyards. It tended to be a bit boring in comparison to the last rail trips I had taken lately.

From the time the train left Venice until it reached Brig, I realised that I was following the same route as the famous Venice-Simplon-Orient Express and was enjoying the same views from the train that its well-to-do passengers would have enjoyed. I had read about the Orient Express in my train books many times in my youth, so the train journey was especially thrilling and full of interest for me. The train became more famous after Agatha Christie's book *Murder On The Orient Express* was published in 1934.

The train was comfortably filled and only stopped at large towns. The first one of these was Gallarate where soon after, the scenery changed to a region of forests. The train crossed a bridge over the Tieino River and I could see from my map that the train line was nearing Lake Maggiore, and quite suddenly the lake appeared and the train stopped at Arona, a town on the side of the lake where some passengers got off and some joined the train. Sadly none of the passengers in my compartment took any interest in me and for about

118

the next 30 km the train line was cut into the slopes above the lake providing me with stunning vistas across the lake and the mountains beyond. The next stop was Stresa the principal tourist town for Lake Maggiore, where this time more people got off, but few joined the train. Most of Lake Maggiore is in Italy, but the northern end is just inside Switzerland. The part of the lake that I was seeing from the train is its north western extremity.

After leaving Stresa the lake was no more to be seen, replaced by a broad plain. The train then entered the Orsollo Valley running up its left hand side, where down below a river ran between pastures. Every now and again a small village or town appeared, but of more interest to me was the view across the valley, where I could see some very high, snow capped mountains. I began to get itchy feet because they wanted to be on skis. The Orsollo Valley is very long and I dozed off a couple of times as the train sped along.

However, there was no way that I would be asleep and miss the most exciting part of this trip, and what more historic and thrilling journey could there be I thought, than to cross the border and enter Switzerland through the famous Simplon Tunnel? At last after about an hour the valley narrowed and the train came to a stop at the large town of Domodossola overlooked by high mountain ranges. I was wide awake. I looked at my map and saw that the nearest station to the Simplon tunnel marked on it was Iselle, but wasn't sure exactly how far away it was from the tunnel entrance, so as soon as the train reached Iselle I decided I would go into the corridor and keep a lookout from there on.

There was still about 60 km to travel before reaching Iselle and the train was gradually climbing as it wended its way along the sides of very narrow valleys with rocky cliffs rising on both sides. On the way the train went through many tunnels of varying lengths, one quite long, before emerging from the last of these, a kilometer or so short of Celle, a small town where the train came to a halt. As soon as the train began moving again, I quickly got into the corridor and with my camera at the ready at an open window. There were two tunnel false alarms, which I knew weren't the Simplon tunnel portals from pictures in my railway books. The train next passed by a small settlement, but didn't stop. Then, after going through another short tunnel, at last the double portal of the Simplon tunnel appeared. I quickly took a photo and returned to my seat as the train entered the tunnel, roaring through at 90 km/h, by my timing.

The Simplon Tunnel is a two-track tunnel, 20 km. long, which took six years to bore and was completed in 1904. Steel bracing was used to reinforce the masonry due to very high rock pressures. Large amounts of cold air had to be pumped in to reduce the heat in the workings. At the time it was bored it was the longest rail tunnel in the world. It is a wonderful engineering feat, as there was not the modern hard rock drilling techniques and equipment available as there are today.

I have great empathy for those hard rock tunnellers of years ago. because I became acquainted with 'hard rock mining', after I returned to Australia, where I worked as a tunnel fitter, boring an underground power station on the Kiewa Hydro Electric Scheme in Victoria.

120

CHAPTER 9
SWITZERLAND

SWITZERLAND

A map of Switzerland showing the author's route from Milan to Zermatt and Grindelwald. Then back to Hitchin through Paris.

BRIG

After 13 minutes the train emerged into the daylight and I was in Switzerland! I managed to take a good photo of the Swiss portal before the train continued on for about another two kilometres before pulling into the large Brig station at 12.15 p.m. Brig is on a small

121

tributary of the Rhone River, which commences its journey from the Rhone Glacier in the Alps north east of Brig and flows into Lake Geneva. From there the river flows down the Rhone Valley of France below Brig, said to be the indigenous home of Shiraz wine. The Rhone finally enters the Mediterranean Sea near Marseille. I changed my lira in Brig and cashed a traveller's cheque for Swiss francs, 12 Swiss Francs (Sfr) to £1 Sterling.

The train for Zermatt was not due to leave until 2.15 p.m. so I curbed my excitement watching trains of all descriptions entering and leaving Brig for many destinations. Brig is an important rail junction where trains converge from many European cities, such as Paris, Brussels, Berne and Basle. Brig for a rail fan like me was a very exciting place to be, especially seeing many carriages carrying destination boards on their sides with the names of these and other famous continental cities.

!!!!!!!!!!!!!!!!!!!!!!!!

BRIG TO ZERMATT

On the dot of 2.15 p.m. the train left Brig for the climb of 945 m (3,100 ft) to Zermatt. The train was a narrow, metre gauge, rack assisted train, a train of a type that I had read about in my railway books. A rack railway is used where it is necessary for a railway to climb steep terrain, too steep for normal adhesion or grip between the steel wheel and rail. The rack or cog method, commonly referred to as a rack railway, is a positive traction method for both up and down movement. Steel rails in which teeth have been cut (a rack), are laid centrally between the running rails, and a revolving gear wheel on the train's power car meshes with the rack, driving the train up steep sections of the line as there are between Visp and Zermatt,

The 44 km line was first opened in 1891 for summer traffic, but by 1927 in the winter months it was possible to travel the full distance to Zermatt by rack train. Leaving Brig the train ran alongside the main line until it reached Visp, where the line made its way along the side of the Visptal valley, a lovely picturesque scene with many Swiss cottages or chalets tucked into the steep slopes on both sides of the wide valley. Climbing steadily towards Zermatt, the train turned to the left and entered a narrow valley. Soon the train encountered the first incline, where it slowed a little as the rack was engaged with a 'clunk.' Without any further slowing our train quickly climbed the incline. At various sections of the route where the train came to a flat section, the rack would be disengaged, then later the slowing and clunk was heard again as the rack was re-engaged.

At the village of Stalden the train came to a halt while some Swiss passengers alighted and boarded a cable car, the wires of which were slung across the narrow, deep valley to the village of Gass on the opposite side. It must I thought, be one of the most spectacular rides home in the world on the highest cable span I had ever seen.

The train was filled with many tourists and Swiss folk and as it progressed steadily upwards towards Zermatt a humorous episode took place concerning a middle aged English lady with a very upper class English accent. She announced to everyone in the carriage within hearing: "This is the time to come to Zermatt, not before. I have just spent a week in St Moritz and two weeks in Davos. The money for my baggage cost me more than my ticket. I have to economise." "I was to stay at St Moritz for three months, but I developed this terrible cough. I came out first class and will go back to England first class. The weather in England is terrible. I travel around third class. I don't feel as well as I hoped to feel. Everybody says I look well, but I sleep so badly. At home I get to bed about 10 p.m. and, if I am not disturbed, I go to sleep at once. I get an allowance. Not much mind you, I have to think before I drink, you know." As the train passed some chalets: she asked: "What do the people do who live in these chalets?" She pronounced the word *chalet* phonetically, which was quite strange I thought. "A number of families live in the chalets, they are small farmers," a fellow passenger replied: She responded incredulously: "What, two or three families in one chalet? Oh how awful!"

She then discovered that she had to go to the toilet, which the conductor told her was in the next carriage accessed by an open corridor connection. She exclaimed to the conductor! "I couldn't possibly do that. Oh no, I couldn't." She was too scared to go at first and had to be helped across by the conductor. When she came back by the look of jubilation on her face, you would have thought she had just climbed the Matterhorn.

There really are some characters in this world, I thought, and that night I noted the comical incident verbatim in my notebook, because I thought it was so hilarious. Telling us of her visits to Davos, St Moritz and now Zermatt, three of the most expensive ski resorts in Switzerland, raised a rather puzzling question for me. British travellers to Europe at the time were severely restricted by the total amount of money that could be taken out of the UK for tourism. I imagined that she must have known of someone high up who helped her get around those impediments. This restriction did not apply to me because I was using Australian Pounds, converted to Sterling.

From then on the train track clung to the right hand side of the valley through wooded hilly terrain. The next station was St Niklaus, but I saw no evidence of Father Christmas there, although with a sprinkling of snow on the ground and mountains all round, I could have imagined it was one his outposts. The deep valleys, with some more like gorges, continued to surround our train as it battled upward. The next station was Randa cut into the side of the mountain.

As the train progressed upward, so did a road that every now and again ran alongside the track, with cars travelling in both directions. A break in the skyline revealed a thrilling sight of a high snow covered mountain peak that a passenger seated alongside me

124

said it was the *Kleiner Matterhorn* (Little Matterhorn). At last the steep side valleys were left behind and our train came to the next station Tasch, situated on a large flat area where many cars were parked. Tasch was in effect a large car park, because this village was as far as motor vehicles are allowed to go as none are permitted in Zermatt. Quite a number of travellers some with skis, left their cars here and boarded our train to take them to Zermatt. Leaving Tasch the train travelled along snow covered ground all the way to Zermatt and I didn't see any more of the high snowy summits because cloud had closed down any view. The train arrived at the Zermatt bahnhof at 4 p.m. My first ride on a rack assisted train was spectacular for the novel sight and sounds I experienced as the train made its way up the steep narrow valleys to Zermatt and the on board entertainment. I have never forgotten her words: "I have to think before I drink."

⌂

ZERMATT

Leaving the train at the Zermatt Station, I walked up the unimpressive main street of the famous ski resort, but the Matterhorn was covered in cloud. My first priority was to find a cheap hotel, pension or boarding house in which to spend the night, with the hope that the next day would be clear and fine and I would be able to see the mighty Matterhorn. I would then have to beat a hasty retreat because I was under the impression that I could not stay in the YH here because I was too old. I didn't bother to look for the YH but I should have, because I found out later there was no age limit at all.

I found a travel bureau where I enquired about a cheap pension for the night. They directed me to the Tannenhof, where I booked a room for a reasonable 9.50 Sfr per day with two meals only. I had a quick look around at the shops, hotels and nightclubs, and then returned to the Tannenhof where I sat down to a massive meal at 7.30 p.m. The proprietor told me that it was not unusual for tourists to book in for a week without ever seeing the Matterhorn, and with that depressing comment ringing in my ears I retired, hoping that the

Matterhorn would look kindly on me, an Aussie who had travelled from afar to gaze in awe on its countenance. I tucked myself into a lovely warm bed with a big eiderdown over me. Soon, if I was lucky, I would satisfy one of my youthful ambitions of seeing the Matterhorn with my own eyes. The other mountain I had an ambition to see before I died was Mt Everest, which I thought was beyond my means, but one never knows what the future holds for them.

Monday 10th March: The Tannenhof pension, built of dark brown pine logs was not far from the centre of Zermatt. It was all I could have wished for, a massive evening meal and a lovely warm, comfortable bed. After an equally good breakfast I had a quick look to see if the Matterhorn was visible, but it wasn't. It was foggy and snowing lightly as I took a walk down the main and only street, lined with hotels, bars, restaurants, and many shops displaying ski equipment and beautiful ski clothes as well as many expensive souvenirs. There were no motor vehicles in Zermatt, although there were many battery driven carts and a few horse drawn sleds complete with bells, which gave Zermatt an enchanting atmosphere.

At the end of the main street I found the railway station of the Gornergrat Railway. I was amazed to find that a weekly ticket on this rack railway only cost 45 Sfr. The railway went up to the Gornergrat, 3.089 m (10,135 ft) in elevation. For a week of downhill skiing, I believed that 45 Sfr was very good value, so I purchased a weekly ticket. I returned quickly to the Tannenhof to ask the proprietor what was the lowest rate he could offer me for bed and breakfast, together with an evening meal for a week.

His offer was 72 Sfr, which I quickly reasoned was OK, and I gladly accepted his discounted offer and booked in. I was ecstatic. 'This is really living!' I thought. For a total of 117 Sfr for a full week, I could stay at this wonderful resort, skiing every day. Although 117 Sfr was above my daily budget allowance, there was no need for me to look for another place to stay and ski before

126

meeting Netta in Grindelwald the following week. All I wanted now was to see the mighty Matterhorn.

I went back to the Tannenhof to get my skis and bought some chocolate and an orange on the way back to the station, where I boarded the rack train that was filled with colourfully attired, happy skiers of all nationalities. This rack railway was built in 1898. It climbs from Zermatt, 1.604 m (5,262 ft) to the Gornergrat, a change in elevation of 1.485 m (4,872 ft).

‖‖‖‖‖‖‖‖‖‖‖‖‖‖‖‖‖

ZERMATT TO THE GORNERGRAT

Leaving the station the train first crossed a bridge over the Visp River then began climbing steeply, but there was no 'clunk' as the rack was engaged, because on this rack railway it is engaged permanently. Winding its way upwards through a pine forest by means of short bridges and tunnels, the train stopped at four stations on the way, Riffelalp, Riffelboden, Riffelberg and Rotenboden, where there were passing loops for the trains as it was only a single line rack railway. At some of these stations there were buildings, which provided meals, drinks and also accommodation. The tree line came to an end just above the Riffelalp and from then on there was nothing except huge expanses of glistening, white snow slopes. I think I was drooling at the immensity of the vista. At each of the intermediate stations, spaced at intervals of around 220 m (721 ft) in height, passengers got on and off the train to ski and sightsee.

When the train stopped at each station, it did so very suddenly because of the steepness of the line. I soon learned to hang on tightly when the train stopped, especially when I was standing up with my skis, because all the passengers including me were still moving forward with the momentum, following 'Newton's 1st Law of Motion. 'Everybody either remains at rest or moves with constant speed in a straight line unless it is acted upon by an external force.' It was very interesting to watch the wooden panelling of the carriage,

127

which also kept moving forward in a straight line, then being acted on by the force of the brake in the rack, settling back to the vertical at each stop. As the train approached the Gornergrat it traversed a large steep snow slope, prone to avalanches and drifting. The train was protected from these possibilities by passing under a long snow shed. This section was called 'The Gallery' by skiers, because the downhill side of the snow shed had been extended outwards to provide a relatively narrow concave ski run, with a steep drop on the outer edge.

GORNERGRAT

After about 45 minutes the train arrived at the Gornergrat, but sadly there was no view of any of the high peaks at all. It was misty and snowing lightly. I decided to ski up and down between the two top stations, Rotenboden and the Gornergrat, a height difference of 507 m (1,663 ft). After the first exciting run down, I caught the train back to the Gornergrat, then on down to the Riffelberg. I skied confidently, the Toko brand ski wax I had purchased working very well on the beautiful firm snow surface. A shuttle service was maintained for skiers between Riffelberg and the Gornergrat, and I did not have to wait more than 10 minutes at the most, for a train to arrive and take me back up again.

I skied up and down for a few hours, and then decided to test myself and take the plunge, (just about literally) and ski all the way down to Zermatt. It took me about an hour with only a few short pauses to catch my breath and look around to admire the spectacular mountain scenery. I skied on perfect snow conditions, powder on a firm base for most of the way down, until I reached the tree line, where the snow became very icy. I skied very carefully, without a fall, during my descent of 1.485 m (4,871 ft). My legs were very tired and I returned to the Tannenhof, where I lay down and had a short rest, but my day wasn't complete by a long shot.

I had seen a notice for the Zermatt Museum and off I went. The entry fee was 1 Sfr. It wasn't a large museum, but it was certainly

128

very interesting, containing many photographs of the Matterhorn, as well as many unique exhibits of the first ascent of the Matterhorn in the summer of 1865, by Whymper and his party, and the fall by some members of the party on the descent. I knew well the story of this first climb having read about it in my mountaineering books. The relics of this tragedy were on view in the museum. Most fascinating, was seeing sections of the actual climbing ropes. The 12 mm Italian hemp rope, the 12 mm Manila hemp rope, and the broken 6 mm sash line were all displayed in a glass case. There was also a diagram showing how each rope joined the members of the party, together with a diagram of the north face showing where the falls occurred. Displayed in a glass case was a boot belonging to Lord Douglass and a hat and rosary belonging to Cross found in 1897 at the foot of the Matterhorner Glacier. It was the best museum I have ever visited.

Total downhill descent today: 2.653 m (8,700 ft)

Tuesday 11th March: I woke up to a beautiful cloudless day and dressed quickly. Walking out of the Tannenhof I rounded a corner and there it was behind the church. **THE MATTERHORN.** What a revelation! The snow plastered east face of the mighty Matterhorn was a brilliant white, lit by the early morning sun. It was a scene I had seen hundreds of times before, in books, travel brochures and chocolate box lids, but none of those images could compare with what I was seeing up close with my own eyes.

I returned to the Tannenhof for breakfast, elated after seeing the Matterhorn. The meals at the Tannenhof, dinner and breakfast, were so large and good that I was not going to worry too much about lunch; instead I would smoke a few cigarettes and ski all day. Breakfast over, I hurried down to the station and caught the train to the Gornergrat. Nearly all the way up on the train the Matterhorn was visible, together with the surrounding peaks. The excitement among the passengers as the train climbed was infectious, as I imagined that many, like me, had seen the Matterhorn for the first time that morning. As soon as the train stopped at the Gornergrat, most of the

The Italian portal of the Simplon tunnel

Swiss portal of the Simplon tunnel at Brig

The not so elegant main street of Zermatt

My very first look at the Matterhorn behind the church

Joyfull passengers on the Gornergrat-Bahn

The Gallery with the Riffelberg Hotel on the left skyline

130

passengers moved out onto the balcony of the restaurant building, once described as the 'Royal Box of the Mountain Theatre'. The view across the glaciers and snowfields leading up to the Matterhorn was staggering. I looked directly at its unbelievably steep, snow-covered east face.

The magnificent skyline of the Pennine Alps that one sees from the Gornergrat is close to a 180 degree arc. Starting from the left, or eastern end of this awesome skyline that marked the border between Italy and Switzerland, there were seven mountain peaks whose summits were over 4.000 m (13,123 ft). They are called the '*Four Thousanders*'. I took many photos of this magnificent panorama, pinching myself to make sure it was truly me here in real life and not a dream. Assured of the reality of it all, I skied some more from the Gornergrat, before turning north for home, toward the Sunegga-Blauhard ski area that was served by ski lifts. The line I took was through 30 cm deep untracked, virgin powder snow. I managed it fairly well, although I had a few falls, and I learned a very valuable lesson: When a fall is unavoidable, keep your mouth closed, because once when I fell, I got a mouthful of powder snow and nearly choked. I finally skied back to Zermatt, after a truly wonderful day. As well as religiously entering in my diary the events of each day since the first day of 1952, I kept a daily record of my downhill skiing.

Total downhill descent today: 2.195 m (7,200 ft)

Wednesday 12th March: I rose early to another lovely sunny day and despite having only a monochrome camera, I had the intention of taking a photograph of the east face of the Matterhorn lit up in the colours of the rising sun, but I was too late. There were no colours, although the east face was a brilliant white in the sunshine. I walked over the Visp River on a bridge in the centre of which there was a religious chapel. It consisted of a large concrete box with a gable roof. Most of the front was enclosed by glass and behind the glass was a statuette of the Virgin Mary and Child.

To my amazement, as I moved forward, the view of the Matterhorn, which I had just been admiring was reflected perfectly on the glass. I quickly took a photograph, with my 1940 vintage Baby Brownie camera, not knowing what the result would be. The reflection of the Matterhorn in the glass cover of the chapel was a rare apparition, which if I were a Roman Catholic, I suppose would have had some profound spiritual significance for me.

An English couple I met on the day I arrived in Zermatt gave me some lift tickets that they didn't need as they were leaving Zermatt the next day. I used the tickets to go up in the chair lift and T-bar to Blauhard, skiing back to Zermatt down the same valley as yesterday. It was the first time I had used a T-bar and thought it was much better than a poma, and for that matter a rope tow. I then took the train up to the Gornergrat and skied between there and the Riffelberg all day with the Matterhorn cutting into the sky in front of me on the skyline, a magnificent sight.

For my last run of the day, I again skied down from the Gornergrat to Zermatt on the valley floor. This time I noticed that an enterprising Swiss farmer had set up an outdoor bar, which consisted of a few tables and chairs in front of his barn holding the cattle. So here, among the not unpleasant smell of cows and hay, I stopped and enjoyed a beer while sitting in the sun appreciating the magnificent mountain scenery above me.

I reflected on how lucky I was to be having such a wonderful time skiing in Zermatt, how perfect it was to finish a day's skiing enjoying a beer in this bucolic bar. "This is really living!" I exclaimed to myself. Finishing my beer I walked on my skis the short distance back to the Tannenhof where I lay down and fell fast asleep, having to be woken up for dinner by the proprietor's wife. *Total downhill descent today: 3.566 m (11,700 ft)*

Thursday 13th March: I did a little shopping in the main street, which would have looked much more elegant with a cover of white snow, instead of the patchy dirty surface that was out of keeping with

132

the classy shops and hotels along its sides. In stark contrast to the main street there were many elegant and beautiful ladies wandering everywhere in colourful ski and town wear. I thought that yellow and black skiwear, especially when worn by ladies with blonde hair and sun tanned faces, was 'absolutely bloody beautiful.' Hair styles were 50/50 long and short; I myself like long hair. I bought some handkerchiefs, ties, badges and other souvenirs.

I took a short walk to the cemetery, where many climbers who fell to their deaths on the Matterhorn are buried, including Hadow, Croz, and Hudson. I could have spent a lot of time there, reading the epitaphs on the tombstones, because there were many well-known mountaineering names, but on with the skiing, because that was what I was here to enjoy, not explore a cemetery, however historic it was.

I climbed aboard the 11.30 a.m. train to the Gornergrat. This time on the way up there was a group of German skiers all singing in *Deutsch* a familiar song that I had sung many times in English. 'She'll be coming round the mountain when she comes, she'll be riding two white horses when she comes', and other songs in *Deutsch*, which made it a very joyful journey.

It was truly wonderful skiing in the sunshine. I skied all the afternoon up and down between the Gornergrat and Riffelberg stations, returning to the Gornergrat by rack train after each run. On the way home at the end of the day the only section I found difficult was 'The Gallery', because I was not game to take it straight, except near the end. Instead I resorted to stemming and snow ploughing, but I was nevertheless very pleased with my overall standard of skiing.

The tourists were predominantly French and German spoken with quite a few Americans, but only one Aussie that I knew of, me. Apart from the sun tanned men and elegant women I saw in Zermatt, there were some crippled people hobbling around on crutches, skiers I supposed. There were many children in Zermatt too; most sporting badges from St Moritz, Davis, St Anton, and other Swiss and Austrian ski resorts

133

Sketch from the author's notebook showing where some of Whymper's party fell to their deaths after the successful first ascent

The author's first look at the sunlit east face of the Matterhorn

The author and behind him the superb panorama of the mountains and the Matterhorn as seen from the balcony of the Gornergrat

The reflected Matterhorn and Virgin

The climber's tombstones in the cemetery

The Matterhorn from the Riffelberg

I was always very tired at the end of each day, especially after the huge meal, but this evening I forced myself to go and have a look at the Zermatt night life. It was a beautiful night. A vivid white moon was lighting up the Matterhorn's east face. I decided to go to a night club and chose a club called *The Jug*. It was a serendipitous choice, which led to a fantastic outcome for me. *The Jug* was an enchanting Zermatt night club with a three piece band, piano, guitar and drums playing what I imagined were Swiss tunes with rather a jiggy, cow punching twang that complemented the candle lit tables. *The Jug* was a beaut nightclub. The chairs and tables were all polished hardwood and the bar was set off by lattice glassed cupboards behind it. The standard of dressing was not high and in keeping with the surroundings was rather informal.

There was a conjunction of nationalities. The bottle holding the candle on the table in front of me advertised Black and White cigarettes in English. The beer glass drip mats boasted of Bier Fine from Sion Swiss. The band's singer sang in *Deutsch*; while all around the babble of voices in many languages made for a very exciting atmosphere. After downing my first beer I ordered another and began talking with a German man of about 45 years and his wife, who were seated at the same table as me. His name was Walter Holz and he told me that he wanted to go on a ski tour to Monte Rosa, and had put a request over the PA system for a guide to take him there. Hearing this, a couple of mountain guides came over to our table. They told him that no guide would take him there at the moment, because the wind up on Monte Rosa was too strong and too cold. He said he was anxious to go on a ski tour, if not to Monte Rosa then to the Theodule Pass.

He asked me if I would like to join him. He seemed to be a competent skier with an understanding of the route to be taken, and from our conversation together, he must have considered that I possessed enough skiing ability to accompany him. We arranged to meet at the Zermatt station, weather permitting, to catch the 8.30

a.m. train to Rotenboden. From there Walter said we would ski up the glacier to the Theodule Pass on the Swiss-Italian border and do a traverse around the base of the Matterhorn and ski back down the valley to Zermatt. We wished each other good night and left *The Jug* together. It had been a most enjoyable and rewarding night. I climbed into bed looking eagerly forward to tomorrow's ski tour.

Total downhill descent today: 2.895 m (9,500 ft)

SKI TOUR TO THE THEODULE PASS

Friday 14th March: On a very beautiful morning, I walked to the Zermatt station stopping only to buy an orange and some chocolate. I met Walter and we shook hands and boarded the rack train to the Gornergrat. We left the train at Rotenboden station and put on our skis and skied down towards the Gorner Glacier. The snow did not cover the rocks of the lateral moraine so we had to take off our skis and walk across to the smooth icy surface of the Gorner Glacier from where we skied easily on to the adjoining Upper Theodule Glacier. The slope of this glacier was quite steep, so we stopped and put on our skins, which enable a skier to climb steep slopes and even ski downhill to a very limited extent. Skins are made of sealskins cut into strips and sewn on to a web backing about the length of a ski and half the width. Straps attach them to the bottom of the skis, with the sealskin hairs pointing to the rear of the ski. This produces a ratchet effect, allowing the skis to slide forward preventing any backward slip.

We began the long climb up the Unter Theodule Glacier noting with dismay that the wind was blowing clouds of snow from some of the high peaks ahead of us, although it was completely calm where we were. However, as we climbed higher the wind began to blow strongly around us. We were passed by a guided party of five men and a woman and paused to watch as their guide stopped and roped up his party. I wondered whether this was for effect or really a necessary move. A little further on, however, the glacier's surface hinted that there could be a crevasse or two beneath the coating of

136

snow. Climbing slowly, I stopped for a breather. Looking back, I saw the magnificent sight of Monte Rosa rising majestically at the head of the Gorner Glacier, its snowy slopes glistening in the sun. I marvelled at the beauty of the spectacular scene, and Lyskamm's large triangular north face in shadow, rising abruptly above the glacier. Monte Rosa looked very high, but looming up ahead of us the Matterhorn, although 150 m (492 ft), lower seemed to dwarf the height of Monte Rosa.

Walter and I followed the guided party climbing on our skins, passing the Breithorn on the left with a very beautiful icefall dropping from its side. The wind commenced blowing in horizontal sheets of snow behind us. It was icy cold and soon my fingers became quite numb.

We reached the top of the Theodule Pass at 12.15 p.m., where we quickly found refuge on the Italian side of the mountain under an overhanging slab of rock, at an altitude of 3.322 m. (10,896 ft), the highest I had ever been, although I felt no adverse effects of the altitude. The Theodule Pass is a natural funnel for the wind, which must have been blowing at about 100 km/h, raising willy-willies of snow on the lee or Italian side of the pass.

The guides who had talked to us at The *Jug* the previous night certainly knew what they were talking about. I thought I had better put on some more sun cream, but when I pulled it out of my bum bag it was so cold it had frozen solid! With both of my very cold feet in Italy once again, I looked down into the Italian valley of Aosta, where the villages of Tournanche and Breuil are located. A ski lift from Breuil climbed towards us, but it did not reach all the way to the pass. It was from Breuil that Whymper made his first attempts to climb the Matterhorn.

The Matterhorn's south face as seen from the Theodule Pass is a rugged conglomeration of steps, stairs and shoulders, not nearly as impressive as from Zermatt. Because the sun shone on this side of the Matterhorn nearly all day, this face tended to hold less snow than

137

View up the Gorner Glacier towards Lyskamm right and d
two of Monte Rosa's many summits

Sheltering from th wind behind a
rock at the Theodule Pass

The view down into the Aosta Valley
in Italy

The south Face of the Matterhorn as
seen from the Theodule Pass

The author trying to warm his hands
on the Theodule Pass with the French
Alps in the distance

138

the south face in profile, I could quite easily understand why early climbers would have thought that it was the easiest route to the summit. Away to the west the French Alps rose in an ocean of peaks. I was sure I could pick out Mount Blanc the highest mountain in France and Europe by its shape and height. 4.807 m (15,770 ft). Apart from its height, Mount Blanc is very recognisable by its long snowy summit ridge. Although it was some 70 km away, it was quite a thrill to see it for the first time, even from that distance.

There are huts on the eastern side of the Theodule Pass and we made an attempt to climb up to them, but the wind and blown snow drove us back to our shelter. I tried to thaw out my hands in my trouser pockets, but to no avail. However, I managed to eat some chocolate and take a few photos, but found to my dismay that I had to change a film.

My camera has only eight exposures to a roll of film Changing the film became an agonising exercise with numbed fingers, particularly as the new film tore as I was fitting it, so I had to start reloading it all over again. I used my teeth to help wind the film on, chipping a tooth in the process. Then to make matters worse the lens of the camera fell out in the snow. I managed to replace the lens and clean it of snow, so I just hoped that the next lot of photos would come out OK. We were sharing our rocky shelter with a number of parties, one of which skied down to Breuil in the Aosta Valley below. Walter and I remained on the pass for about half an hour, admiring the spectacular, but cold panorama across to the Italian and French Alps with the Swiss Alps behind us.

Leaving the pass, we skied down into the teeth of the gale taking a route toward the north, then turned gradually towards the east face of the Matterhorn. As we skied down a long slope on beautiful powder snow, I stopped to take a couple of photos with my frozen hands. At last we reached the floor of the Furgg Glacier, which ran from the base of the Matterhorn's east face. We were now protected from the wind and the feeling began returning to all of my fingers at the same time. It was excruciating, but a welcome agony that lasted for about five minutes We looked up at the massive 1.219 m (4,000 ft) high east face of the Matterhorn's 4.478 m (14,692 ft) high summit. It rose at an incredibly steep angle from the glacier, first a bergschrund, (a depression between the glacier and the rock face) then ice cliffs, then rock and snow until the angle increased to appear nearly perpendicular at the top. Most of the face was covered with a plaster of snow, frozen to the precipitous east face. Even the pain in my fingers did not dim my appreciation of the awesome sight. What a contrast it was, as we stood there in the burning sun and complete calm, listening to the sound of the wind blowing and buffeting against the mighty east face of the Matterhorn. We skied a little further down the glacier and climbed up onto the medial moraine. We sat there on a rock and smoked a cigarette, soaking up the lovely warm sun. I stood in the centre of the glacier, gazing up at the east face for many minutes, awe struck by this 1.219 m (4,000 ft) high wall of rock. It was a spectacular, mind boggling perspective that I have never forgotten.

I turned around and beheld a dazzling panorama of alpine summits on the eastern skyline. It was a breathtaking view. Monte Rosa, Lyskamm, the Breithorn, Castor and Pollux and the sharp rock peak of the Kleiner Matterhorn all brilliantly white, with their mantle of snow contrasting with the deep blue of the sky behind. Reluctantly we left behind the fantastic panorama of snow clad peaks and glaciers and skied down, turning west into the valley of the Matterhorner Glacier where we were brought to a halt by a border patrolman on skis.

He asked us: "Have you come from Italy?" "No we are doing a round tour from Zermatt and return." We replied. He then asked to see our passports, but neither of us had them with us. He seemed satisfied with our explanation and after thanking us, skied quickly down below us in very expertly executed, parallel christies. He really looked a picture. If only I had film in my camera.

Whether he was an Italian or Swiss border patrolman I wasn't quite sure. He was dressed in an olive green ski uniform with a slouch hat with a chin strap and an ostrich feather in the band of his hat. Slung neatly across each shoulder were his sealskins, crossed at the front and tucked into a belt. If he had a firearm as part of his equipment, it was certainly not noticeable. It was a very enjoyable encounter to end the best ski tour of my life.

We skied on down for a short way and pausing for breath we looked back at the Matterhorn. Our eyes were met by a particularly menacing aspect of the mountain, so different from the beauty of the scenes we had just been witnessing. This was the vertical north face of the Matterhorn, down which four of Whymper's party fell to their deaths, their bodies coming to rest on the glacier just above us.

After contemplating the horror of that event, we pointed our skis down towards Zermatt. As we descended the valley became very narrow and we found ourselves skiing down a path among pine trees with a beautiful icicle covered gorge on our left. After crossing a bridge, we took off our skis and walked the last kilometre into Zermatt, arriving there just as the church bells chimed five. I shook hands with Walter, who had been an excellent skiing companion. After exchanging addresses we went our separate ways. I did not see Walter again in Zermatt, but we wrote to each other a number of times.

The day had been truly, the most awe inspiring and exhilarating day I had ever spent ski touring, gazing on three of the Matterhorn's four faces, each completely different in their awesome form. Meeting with Walter in *The Jug* was a classic case of serendipity, one which made my visit to Zermatt a never to be forgotten experience. As soon as I returned to the Tannenhof, I wrote a long description of the day in my note book.

Total downhill descent today: 1.707 m (5,600 ft).

The east face of the Matterhorn with the Dente Blanche right

My companion Walter leading the way towards the base of the 4,000 ft high east face of the Matterhorn

Looking back on the near vertical north face of the Matterhorn

The author looking up in awe at the east face of the Matterhorn. Behind from L to R are Monte Rosa, Lyskamm and the Breithorn

142

Saturday 15th March: Another beautiful sunny day in Zermatt. I caught the 9.30 a.m. train and skied between the Gornergrat and the Riffelberg all morning, then transferred to the pomma ski lift at the Riffelberg for a few runs until 1 p.m. I returned by train to the Gornergrat and had a rest before I skied back down to Zermatt, stopping as usual to have a beer at the outdoor bar before going back to the Tannenhof.

I was keen to have a look at what lay beyond the little church in an easterly direction towards Staffelalp and the Zmutt Glacier, so I set out with my skis and a new roll of film in my camera. I walked up the valley on a snow covered path by the Visp River, with the sunlight streaming through the pine trees. I soon came to the native parts of Zermatt, away from the tourist hustle and bustle. I passed small farms with barns where the cows were housed, milked and hand fed during the winter months. I soon reached Staffelalp near the snout of the Zmutt Glacier. Except for the rather dirty, jumbled ice and snow of the forward extremities of the Zmutt glacier, it was a beautiful alpine scene with the vivid white, upper reaches of the glacier hidden by a forest of conifers. Up to my left, the brooding north face of the Matterhorn overlooked this scene. I was seeing the same view of the north face that I had looked upon in awe on the way back from the Theodule tour. I believe the word 'beautiful' can only be used truthfully to describe the Matterhorn when it is viewed from Zermatt.

What really amazed me was how the pyramid of the mighty Matterhorn was created by geological forces millions of years ago, particularly with regard to the much less spectacularly shaped peaks immediately surrounding it. I took some photos and made my way back to the Tannenhof after another very enjoyable day.

I picked up all the rolls of film I had taken in Zermatt, including those from the Theodule tour, and was very happy to find that all had come out very well, though the cost was an enormous 3.70 Sfr! I was particularly ecstatic that the photo of the reflection of the Matterhorn

143

in the glass front of the chapel had come out perfectly. I treasure this photo today.

Total downhill descent today: 3.200 m (10,500 ft

Sunday 16th March: My final day in Zermatt. Once again it was a beautiful sunny day. Going up in the train at 9.45 a.m., I noticed that some of the peaks had small cloud plumes rising from their summits. When I arrived at the Gornergrat a cloud plume was beginning to build above the Matterhorn, and as I skied up and down it grew larger and larger. This phenomenon was a result of an easterly wind coming up against the east face of the Matterhorn and being forced to rise, condensing as it did into a cloud. I suspected that this indicated a change of weather, with the air becoming more humid than it had been for the past week. Towards the end of the day the Matterhorn's cloud plume gradually grew in size to become the largest plume on any of the surrounding peaks. It was most impressive. Starting from near the top of the east face, the cloud obscured the summit, and I estimated that it rose a further 1.500 m (5,000 ft), above the summit. I took a photo of the cloud plume from the Riffelberg, before I returned to the Gornergrat to have my final run down to Zermatt.

When I returned to the Gornergrat, I stood gazing at the wonderful panorama of glaciers and mountains, which I had been able to witness for nearly a week of beautiful weather. The cloud plume made it look as though the Matterhorn was on fire, but more likely it was a curtain that was about to be drawn on the final scene of my wonderful week of viewing and skiing. My week staying in the comfort of the Tannenhof also contributed immensely to the enjoyment of my week in Zermatt.

With the spectacular cloud plume on the Matterhorn in the background, I prepared to take my last long and steep ski down to Zermatt. I had one last look at the skyline, in particular the Theodule Pass, finding it hard to believe that I had been there only two days ago. I skied down to Zermatt, stopping for my usual beer at the farm

144

bar. I timed how long it took me to ski from the Gornergrat to Zermatt. The result was 44 minutes. After drinking a final thirst quenching beer and taking in the glorious vista before me, I skied back to the Tannenhof. My total downhill skiing for the week was *64,900 ft (19.780 m)*. More than twice the height of Mt Everest, all for 45 Sf (£4), thanks to the Gornergrat rack railway.

Monday 17th March: I was up early to catch the 6.35 a.m. train to Brig to connect with a train to Grindelwald. It was another sunny morning, but with a high overcast covering the sky. I paid the bill and told the proprietor how much I had enjoyed the spectacular week skiing in Zermatt, and thanked him for his hospitality and tasty meals. Leaving the Tannenhof I looked along the path toward the church to see the now familiar sight of the sun on the Matterhorn's east face. It was not so brilliantly white as usual, because of the overcast. I walked down the street to the station and bought a ticket to Brig.

!!!!!!!!!!!!!!!!!!!!!!

ZERMATT TO BRIG

I climbed aboard the train and as it left Zermatt and I couldn't help but wonder if the English lady who caused all the amusement on the way up in the train a week ago, had enjoyed her stay in Zermatt as much as I had, and if she still had to 'think before she drinks'. I noted a few changes on the journey down to Brig, the rack didn't seem to engage as smoothly as on the way up and there were a couple of injured passengers, one with his arm in a sling and another on crutches. Thankfully I was not one of them.

BRIG

Arriving in Brig I bought a ticket all the way to Grindelwald. So far I have not had to book a seat on any train, or for that matter in a youth hostel. The only crowded trains I have been on were from Salzburg to Bad Ischl and from Vienna to Klagenfurt, most others have been around half their capacity. I had about half an hour to wait

The church and the
path to Staffelalp

The snout of the Zmutt Glacier

The author and the
Matterhorn with its cloud
plume

The fully developed
cloud plume viewed from
the Riffelberg

Enjoying my final beer at the farm bar
after my last downhill run at Zermatt

146

for the train and while I was waiting I took a photo of one of the locomotives that usually haul Swiss passenger trains such as the one that took me from Milan to Brig. Right on time a long train that had come through the Simplon tunnel pulled up at the platform. The train had route boards on the sides of some carriages that carried the names, Venice, Simplon, Milan and Basel. These cities were no longer just names in an atlas or a geography book, they had become part of my life. Many people alighted from the train some with skis and rucksacks, just as I had one week ago.

¦¦¦¦¦¦¦¦¦¦¦¦¦¦¦¦¦¦¦¦

BRIG TO SPIEZ

I climbed aboard the train for the 75 km journey to Spiez. I had read in my railway books about the double spiral tunnels of the St. Gotthard railway and the two double loop, spiral tunnels on this Lotschberg railway, I was quite excited to be able to travel on the railway under the Fisistocke mountains, and after finding a seat and parking my rucksack and skis, the train began climbing along the northern side of the Rhone valley. I went into the corridor looked out on to the Rhone Valley below as the train began running over small and large bridges cut into the side of the mountain, and through many short side tunnels where spurs protruded from the mountainside. The train passed a couple of stations perched on the side of the stations, but I was not sure where the people lived to use these stations because I hadn't seen any houses.

A little further on the train turned away from overlooking the Rhone Valley and into more small tunnels and then into wild, wooded valleys, where the line transferred from one valley side to the other and snow appeared on the ground as the train wound around many curves weaving its way forward.

Around about 30 minutes after leaving Brig the country opened up a little and the comfortably filled train came to a halt in Gopperstein, a town surrounded by snowy peaks. I returned to my seat. A short distance past the station the train entered a tunnel. It was the 13 km long, Lotschberg tunnel, which took about 10 minutes to pass through before emerging into daylight. The train then ran on a kilometre or so, before arriving at Kandersteg located on a high plateau with much snow on the ground. I had heard of the name Kandersteg many times before and I was sure it had something to do with Scouting. I was right. In fact it is the Kandersteg International Scout Centre, which is open for Scouts all year round.

When the Lotschberg tunnel was being bored an undetected glacial valley was opened up and flooded the workings, resulting in the loss of 25 tunneller's lives. Tunnel boring began again later on a different line and was completed without any further setbacks. All the tunnelling on the Lotschberg railway was completed in 1910.

Leaving Kandersteg the train ran along at a steady speed of around 80 km/h. There was a thermometer on the wall of the carriage which showed a comfortable 22° C temperature, but I would have preferred it to have been a speedometer. The train then came to a wide high valley called Kandergrund, with Swiss houses dotted along the way.

Soon the valley was left behind and the train entered a series of tunnels one of which was quite long. I felt that the train was losing altitude, but other than that I felt no sensation to tell me if the train was in a curved tunnel or straight, except that its speed slowed a little. Emerging from the tunnel the train went along a bench and over what I knew to be an arched stone bridge, where I got a brief glimpse across a valley to mountains on the far side, before the train entered another tunnel. Some minutes later this tunnel came to an end and the train emerged from the portal on to a bench, and over the same form of arched stone bridge as before

This time the train was at a much lower level above the snow covered fields with a few houses on floor of the valley. There is a photo of the bridges in my railway book *The Iron Horse. The Wonders of Railway Progress* by Cecil J Allen. (see photo on page

148

155). I wondered if the train had already passed around any one of the two loops, but I didn't feel that the train in any of the tunnels was travelling around a curve, except that we were constantly losing altitude. The train entered another tunnel and emerged into daylight at the Blausee-Minholz station where it came to a halt and some people got off. From there the land soon opened up to a flat valley with houses and green fields where the train went around a very long sweeping curve, which I don't think was banked to any degree. The train then dived into another long tunnel from which the train exited providing a lower view of the valley, before arriving at the large town of Frutigen where again the train stopped.

Further on the land opened up on to the main valley floor, the snow was gone and the scenery changed to green farming countryside. After going around big curve, the train crossed a large viaduct over the Kander River and sped along in open country amongst green fields with signs of civilization becoming more apparent. Next came a couple of short tunnels, then one about two kilometers long, before the train pulled up at the large station of Spiez along the side of a large lake, the Thunersee. Between Brig and Spiez, I counted 32 tunnels through which the train passed. but I was not aware of any sensation of banking that would have indicated that the train was on a curve in a tunnel.

In my research for this book regarding the enigma of the locality of these so called spiral tunnels. I discovered that that 'Lotschberg's famous spiral tunnels,' do not really exist! One is merely a 180° loop in a tunnel, termed a 'spiral loop' a Google description. The other is not a tunnel, but an open air, 180° long radius loop. According to my dictionary of technology and science, a 'loop' is not a 'spiral.'

However, leaving all that aside, all are railway engineering marvels and achievements, especially as many of these tunnels and associated earthworks were completed before the advent of modern tunnelling infrastructure tools and tunnel boring machines that are available as I write. If a reader would like more information about

149

the Lotschberg Railway, its tunnels, bridges stations and way points a Wikipedia strip map can obtained by Googling: 'Lotschberg Railway Wiki Rail Route Map,' and also for other main rail routes.

||||||||||||||||||||||

SPIEZ TO GRINDELWALD

I changed trains at Spiez for the journey to Interlaken and Grindelwald. While waiting for the train to start, a gentleman, I think he was Swiss, asked me: "Where are you going?" "Grindelwald." I replied: "Where?" He asked me again. "Grindelwald." I repeated. He still didn't understand, and I said it again, He was still none the wiser so I kept repeating: "Grindelwald, Grindelwald," each time with the accent on a different vowel, but that didn't help either. Finally, I got out my map and pointed to Grindelwald. He peered at the place where my finger pointed and then with great surprise he exclaimed loudly: *"Ah, so, ah so, Grindelwald!"* I noted for further use that he sounded the 'd' as a 't' and the 'w' as a 'v'. I'm gradually learning the language. So correction, I am going to *Grintelvolt,* with the accent on *Grindel.*

By now I was used to Swiss trains starting off right on the dot of their scheduled time and so did this train. It took a little while getting used to as there was no guard waving a flag and blowing a whistle. Just a single gong on a bell was the signal for the train to slowly move off. The train ride of 14 km to Interlaken Ost ran along beside the Thunersee with lovely views of this big blue lake. It stopped at a couple of stations and ran through a few tunnels where bluffs dropped down into the lake, and after about 25 minutes the train arrived at Interlaken Ost, where the Swiss gentleman wished me goodbye.

In Interlaken Ost I changed trains to the narrow gauge, rack assisted railway line to Grindelwald and sat back to enjoy the 20 km ride. The train consisted of four wood panelled carriages with double doors in the centre. Leaving the station the train entered a picturesque wide valley and I was thrilled to see snow on the high mountains on the skyline. The train passed farms dotted with Swiss style houses and some 10 minutes later the train came to a town called Zweilitschinen, a large rail junction. This was where our train turned to the left to go to Grindelwald. The line to the right went through the spectacular Lauterbrunnen Valley to Wengen.

Immediately the land changed as the train entered a narrow valley and began climbing through wooded highs cliffs with level crossings every now and again. The railway line was accompanied by both the road to Grindelwald and the Schwartze Lutschine River. Sometimes the line ran next to the road and other times the river, while other times neither were to be seen. Patches of snow began to collect on the ground just before Lutschental station where the train stopped for a couple of minutes. Leaving the relatively flat area of the station the rack was engaged with a familiar clunk, and the train began to climb steadily around curves cut into the hillside beside the river for around some ten kilometres, where again a flat area was reached and the rack disengaged.

It was here that I beheld a fantastic view of a high rocky snow covered mountain. Once again the train entered a wide, lush green flat valley, along which the train travelled for perhaps five kilometres before coming to a halt at Schwendi station. The rack was engaged again and as the journey continued and the snow became deeper on the ground. This was the steepest section on the line and for the next 10 minutes the train worked hard ascending this section.

I was overwhelmed by the wonderful views of the high rocky snow plastered summits I was seeing every now and again from the train. Two of these, the Wetterhorn and the Eiger were familiar forms to me from my mountaineering books. At last after one final steep pinch the train arrived at the large alpine town of Grindelwald.

GRINDELWALD

The time was 12.15 p.m., which I think was wonderful for such a long journey through the mountains, with all credit to the Swiss

Federal Railways. Following the directions that my YHA friend Netta had given me I climbed up a steep snow covered path to the Friends of Nature House (*Die Naturfreundehaus*). I booked in and soon found Netta and her companion Nellie Hobern. I had met Nellie and her daughter in London, but her daughter was not with her thankfully, as I don't think she approved of me. I would just be skiing with Netta, because Nellie didn't ski, but told Netta and me to go and enjoy ourselves. Nellie said she would be quite happy shopping and exploring Grindelwald and the surrounding area. We sat down to a cup of coffee and talked non-stop for the next hour, because we had so much to tell each other.

The Friends of Nature House (FNH) is a solidly built, large Swiss chalet, constructed of varnished pinewood. It looked down on to a huge snowfield with high mountains on each side. The rooms were large and everything was spick and span. Bunk beds were provided, with separate rooms for male and female guests. It was not necessary to belong to the organisation that ran these houses, they were open to all. The rates were quite reasonable, just a fraction dearer than a YH. Netta and Nellie had only just arrived and hadn't had time to visit the town before I showed up. After I had settled in, Netta and I took a walk down to the town with the massive bulk of the Eiger in full view across the valley below the town.

We enquired about skiing on the slopes and facilities for downhill skiing. We each purchased a 31 Sfr weekly ticket for the rack railway from Grindelwald to the Kleine Scheidegg, a high pass, then continued on down to Wengen. There was also a branch line from the Kleine Scheidegg to the portal of the tunnel through the Eiger. For 10 Sfr we also purchased 10 tickets each for the T-bar lift from the Kleine Scheidegg to the Lauberhorn. Happy with the tickets in hand, we returned to the FNH for an appetising dinner, talking our heads off again until it was time to retire.

Tuesday 18th March: After a breakfast of cereal and bacon and eggs, Netta and I walked down to the town with our skis, on a fine,

152

but cloudy day. I couldn't wait to get on my skis again and the same for Netta, who hadn't skied at all since she left Australia.

!!!!!!!!!!!!!!!!!!!!!!!!

GRINDELWALD TO THE KLEINER SCHEIDEGG

We boarded the narrow gauge rack train to take us to the Kleiner Scheidegg. The train was much the same wooden panelling style, three carriage rack train that took me to the Gornergrat. There were four intermediate stations between Grindelwald and the Kleiner Scheidegg, Grund, Brandegg, Alpiglen and Salzegg. The rack was engaged all the way to the Kleine Scheidegg. Our tickets didn't allow us to travel down to Wengen, but we could travel to the Eigergletscher (Eiger Glacier), the last station before the train entered the tunnel into the Eiger.

KLEINER SCHEIDEGG

The Kleiner Scheidegg is a high pass that separates the Grindelwald valley from the Lauterbrunnen valley, where the ski resorts of Wengen and Murren are situated. The railway line is called the Wengenalpbahn. We left the train at the Kleiner Scheidegg where there was about a metre of snow. The trip had taken us 30 minutes for the 10 km journey. We sat down and had a beer outside one of the three large hotels and admired the magnificent panorama around us. To the north behind us the Lauberhorn rose to 2.471 m (8,106 ft). The ten tickets we had bought were for the T-bar that went straight up to its summit.

Best of all, however, was the magnificent view to the south, where we gazed in awe at some of the famous peaks of the Bernese Oberland and two more of Switzerland's '*Four Thousanders*'. The Monch at 4.099 m (12,493 ft), so named because its snow covered summit is said to resemble a white cowl over a monk's head, and the Jungfrau (the Virgin) at 4.169 m (13,677 ft), to the right, a beautiful triangular faced mountain. Last, but by no means least was the Eiger, 3.975 m (13,041 ft), both famous and infamous in the annals of alpine history. The view we admired from the Kleiner Scheidegg was truly spectacular.

Having enjoyed this wonderful panorama, we put on our skis and skied down toward Grindelwald to Grund, a vertical descent of 1.026 m (3,365 ft). As we returned to the Kleiner Scheidegg in the rack train we gazed in awe at the Eiger, its enormously steep and menacing north wall (the Eigerwand) dominating the southern sky. We skied many times between the top two stations, finishing with a long run back to Grindelwald from the Kleiner Scheidegg before returning to FNH for our evening meal, which was nearly as good as I had at the Tannenhof. When skiing down the ski runs in Zermatt, I always had the mighty Matterhorn facing me in my line of sight. Here in Grindelwald, when we were skiing down from the Kleiner Scheidegg, less than a kilometre away the menacing north wall of the Eiger towered above us on our right. Grindelwald, at 1.036 m (3,502 ft) is a totally different ski resort to Zermatt. Grindelwald does not have the same variety of ski slopes, nor were they as steep. There is no restriction to car traffic in Grindelwald however, although there were not that many cars to be seen. The shopping centre was much wider and had a more traditional continental layout than Zermatt.

Wednesday 19th February: Netta and I skied up and down from the Kleiner Scheidegg in cloudy, but pleasant weather. We skied in a very similar manner, having both learned to ski by the Arlberg technique. Myself with the Rover Scout's Austrian skiing instructors on the Bogong High Plains, and Netta with a skiing instructor Maurice Selle on Mt Buller with YHA. We could ski together without either of us having to lag behind or slow down for the other, which was a perfect way to enjoy skiing with a friend.

I had read many mountaineering books about the Eiger, especially about climbing the north wall the Eigerwand, but I hadn't connected the town of Grindelwald with the mountain. The Eiger and the Matterhorn are two of the most famous mountains in the European Alps. The Eiger however, is a unique mountain, first

154

because of the rack railway bored through it, and the manner in which the train emerges from the tunnel at the Jungfraujoch, a high saddle at 3.456 m (11,340 ft), the most spectacular railway terminus in the world, Second because of the history of the attempts to scale the Eiger's north wall.

Mountaineers are always seeking greater challenges to test their skills, and by 1930 many of the well known alpine summits had been scaled including the Eiger, which was first climbed in 1858. The cost of a return ticket to go to the Jungfraujoch was 42 Sfr, which neither Netta or I felt we could afford. I was not sorry that I did not take the journey, however I could not speak for Netta.

Mountaineers are always seeking greater challenges to test their skills. By 1930 many of the well known alpine summits had been scaled including the Eiger. Interest then turned to climbing various mountains by their steeper walls and faces. The first attempts to climb the Eigerwand were in 1935. This face is 2.042 m (6,700 ft) high, very steep, slightly concave and raked by falling stones and avalanches. Many attempts were made to climb the Eigerwand, some with tragic results. It was not until 1938 that a successful climb was made by the Austrian Heinrich Harrer and his three companions.

By 1964 there had been 40 successful climbs, but many others had resulted in deaths every year. While we were in Grindelwald there were no winter attempts taking place, but between 6th and 12th March 1961 a party of four made the first successful winter climb. spending six nights on the wall in temperatures of –30°C (–23°F). The next challenge was to climb the wall solo. A Swiss achieved this remarkable climb in 1962

By 1964 there had been 40 successful climbs of the Eiger's north wall, but many others had resulted in deaths every year. In his book, *The White Spider*, Heinrich Harrer describes all the climbs on the Eigerwand between 1936 and 1964. The 'White Spider' is an ice field resembling a white spider with outstretched legs near the final stage of the climb, across which the climbers must pass to reach the

155

My Grindelwald Kleiner-Scheidegg ticket

This photo shows three levels of the Lotschberg railway where the train emerges on to stone arch bridges on its transit passes through the two loop tunnels.
Photo from the book The Iron Road

The Jungfrau as seen from the Kleiner Scheidegg

The Eiger with the town of Grindelwald below

Netta at the Kleiner Scheidegg with the large hotels and Eiger in the background

156

summit. It forms a natural path for falling stones and avalanches. It was thrilling for me to look up at the tremendous Eigerwand and see in detail all the various features of the wall that I had read so much about.

I had kept a close eye on my budget ever since I calculated my daily allowance in Bad Ischl. Since leaving Venice and entering Switzerland. However, the daily costs had begun to mount, although I still believed I was within my budget. When we returned to the FNH I thought I had better discover how much money I had in traveller's cheques to get back to England. I found I only had one £10 cheque left. Adding what it would cost to spend the full two weeks in Grindelwald with Netta, the rack train fare, accommodation, beer, cigarettes and all the other sundry expenses, plus I was not sure how much it would cost to across the English Channel and get back to Hitchin. But there was nothing I could do about it. I would just have to return to England after only a week skiing with Netta.

It came as a shock to discover that I would have leave, because I certainly wanted to stay longer, even though the snow conditions were beginning to deteriorate. I consoled myself with the thought that I had already enjoyed a magnificent fortnight of skiing in Switzerland, much, much more than I could have ever imagined.

When I told Netta about my finances she was very disappointed. She didn't want me to leave because she was enjoying skiing with me. She asked me whether I would stay on if she loaned me the money I needed for the extra week. I said I would think about it.

Thursday 20th March: It was raining and sleeting outside, the first time I had experienced bad weather in Switzerland; but after all it was now the third week of spring. It was relaxing however, just to have an enforced day to talk together about our experiences since we left Australia. I decided I would accept Netta's offer. She was delighted, saying we should celebrate with a visit to a nightclub in

157

Grindelwald. The warden of the FNH recommended *The Rendezvous* so off we went after dinner.

The nightclub had a small band that played excellent dance music, waltzes, fox trots and sambas. The nightclub had a small band that played excellent dance music, waltzes, fox trots and sambas. Netta was very easy to dance with and we danced all night, having a marvellous time together. I tend to believe that good skiers are also good dancers because a sense of rhythm is required for both. We talked to a Viennese man alone at the next table, who was very interested in my experiences in Vienna. He wanted to ski with Netta (with no mention of me). Netta accepted his invitation, which annoyed me, although I was careful not to make this evident. Maybe my ego was a little dented, but I didn't want to miss a minute skiing with Netta. The Viennese man asked Netta for a dance and I suppose that was when she arranged to meet him, but she never mentioned it to me. We were drinking a very nice brand of Swiss beer, but finished up on Bol's Banana Liqueur a great drink.

Thursday 21st March: The weather was snowing heavily and certainly not suitable for skiing in the morning, After lunch however, the weather cleared, so we caught the train to the Kleiner Scheidegg. It could not take us any further than Brandegg until the snow ploughs cleared the line, so we only had a few short runs, but we both skied well on the deep, dry powder snow and neither of us mentioned the Viennese gentleman, and thankfully he never showed up. I told Netta of my experience skiing in powder snow and warned her to keep her mouth closed if she fell. Skiing in deep powder snow is a great sensation: the skis make a whispering sound as they move through the powder, instead of the more grating sound on other types of snow.

Saturday 22nd March: It rained all day, so I just mooched around and talked all afternoon with Netta and Nellie. I felt sorry for Netta, because the rain was preventing her from getting the most from her two week skiing holiday. We feared the rain would produce very

158

poor skiing conditions, but hoped it was snowing further up the mountain. After another large evening meal of pasta, with a meaty topping, we decided to go to the *The Rendezvous* again, this time taking Nellie along with us. Once again we had a very enjoyable night drinking beer and finishing off with a Bol's Banana Liqueur. The Viennese gentleman was not in the nightclub, which pleased me greatly. The band played, a very rhythmical samba called *El Cumbanchero,* which I hoped to get a record of in England.

Sunday 23rd March: At last the sun came out again, although it was a little cloudy. The skiing conditions were perfect. It had snowed up on the Kleiner Scheidegg and on the lower slopes, leaving about 50 cm of new snow. Netta and I skied up and down between the two top stations in perfect snow conditions. We then used up some of our ten lift tickets to ride the T-bar on the Lauberhorn. This was really good skiing, as the slopes were much steeper than from the Kleiner Scheidegg. We had a beer and lunch again at an outdoor cafe of one the huge hotels on the Kleiner Scheidegg.

These hotels are perfectly situated to provide wonderful views across to the north wall of the Eiger. On the hotel terraces there were coin operated telescopes and binoculars. When climbers are on the Eigerwand, their progress or otherwise, can be viewed through these binoculars. Many climbing tragedies had been observed close up by this means. While we sat drinking our beers we were startled to hear a noise like thunder. Looking across at the Eigerwand, we saw an avalanche falling down over the rock ledges on the wall. It looked rather harmless, as if someone had spilt a big load of white sugar, but the noise it produced told us otherwise. We thought the noise must have been due to rocks and stones coming down with the snow.

Monday 24th March: We went skiing in the afternoon until suddenly the rain came down in torrents and we both got very wet. Netta and I had met first at the YHA in Melbourne, and went on many skiing trips together. Netta was quite attractive with lovely, thick brown hair, but her complexion showed the effects of too much sun. This was a common characteristic of Australian girls compared to the 'peaches and cream' complexion of English girls, as I became increasingly aware during my stay in the UK.

Netta was older than me, and that was why she had booked into the FNH and not a YH. Skiing together in Grindelwald we found we had many interests in common besides skiing. We were thrilled to be sharing so many new and exciting experiences, skiing, dancing, drinking, talking and enjoying the sights of the great ski resort of Grindelwald. Although I found Netta attractive, we were of different religious upbringing, so our relationship would have to remain purely Platonic. At that time a difference of religion was an obstacle to serious relationships between the two sexes.

Tuesday 25th March: The rain continued falling, but in the early afternoon it suddenly stopped. Our tickets allowed us to go to the Eigergletscher station where the rack railway enters the tunnel into the Eiger, so we decided to take the train there and have a look. We did. The Eigergletscher station is very close to the magnificent Jungfrau that was draped with a pure white mantle of new snow. There was no doubt why it was called the Jungfrau. After gazing in wonderment at this beautiful mountain, we were preparing to put on our skis to ski down to the Kleiner Scheidegg when we beheld another beautiful sight. The complete snowfield down to the Kleiner Scheidegg, up and across to the snow covered slopes of the Lauberhorn was a magical, translucent light blue colour. I imagined that the newly fallen powder snow was of such a crystal shape and size as to act as a perfect reflector of the sky, just like a still lake reflecting the blue above. It was a unique and beautiful phenomenon, which for all the time I have spent skiing, I have never seen before or since. We only had one run down to the Kleiner Scheidegg that was on surprisingly good snow after the rain, then we transferred to the T-bar lift on the Lauberhorn. As if the blue snow that we had just witnessed was not enough, another phenomenon was about to reveal itself. Many mountain climbing books that I had read told of the

160

ability of mountains, including the Eiger's north wall, to be able to generate their own local storms and weather conditions. Here at the top of Lauberhorn, this was occurring before our very eyes. As we gazed across at the Eigerwand and the summit of the Eiger, cloud suddenly formed and obscured it from our view. It was a remarkable scene, as we were virtually on the same level as the Eigerwand, enabling us to view the full face of this enormously high and steep wall front on, with its amazing cover of cloud.

Here, leading down to Wengen, we also saw the site of one of the World Cup downhill ski racing courses, which I have seen on TV. The course dropped away very steeply right from the start. It has been especially thrilling for me to ski here in full view of the Eiger, because it was one of the mountains about which I had read so many enthralling accounts.

Wednesday 26th March: It snowed heavily during the night but by morning the weather was clear and sunny. We again skied on beautiful deep powder and were both very pleased that we were skiing so well, literally getting on top of the beautiful powder, with few occasions when we needed to keep our mouths closed.

Thursday 27th March: Another fine day. As we were skiing down from the Kleiner Scheidegg during the afternoon we came to a young Swiss boy and his mother. The boy had fallen and twisted his ankle so badly that it prevented him putting his skis back on. While Netta and his mother took his skis back up to Alpiglen station, I put the boy on my back and skied carefully down to the next station, Brandegg. I waited with the boy until he rejoined his mother on the next train back to Grindelwald. Our good deed for the day. While I was skiing in Zermatt and Grindelwald, I don't think it ever crossed my mind what the dire consequences of hurting myself would have been. I carried no insurance, but this never bothered me. I had complete confidence in my skiing ability, such is the confidence of youth. Besides I am a British citizen with a passport to prove it!

Netta admiring the blue snow with the Lauberhorn behind and the three hotels on the Kleiner Scheidegg below

The storm cloud on the Eigerwand as seen from the Lauberhorn

Netta amidst the pine trees

The author in deep snow on the slopes in Grindelwald

Netta and the author at the Kleiner Scheidegg with the Eigerwand behind

162

I would I think, have been covered by National Health. Thankfully the question never had to be resolved.

Netta and I were using Kandahar cable bindings the standard type of binding of the time. They were not like the present day so called 'safety' bindings. We skied with these in the full down pull position, which meant that the ankle, boot, and ski were virtually a rigid fixture, which allowed the best control of the skis. By relaxing the down pull adjustment of the Kandahar bindings, our skis could be used equally well for both ski touring and downhill, such as when I went on the ski tour to the Theodule Pass.

Friday 28th March: Two completely unexpected but pleasurable events occurred on our last day of skiing in Grindelwald. While we were waiting on the station for the train to take us up to ski, a small boy approached me and offered me a large block of Swiss chocolate. I thanked him and asked him: "What is this?" As the boy walked away, Netta pointed to the boy's mother who was watching. I then realised that the boy was the one I had taken on my back the day before and the chocolate was a gift in gratitude. We were pleased to see his ankle seemed OK, and thanked him and his mother.

We later enjoyed eating the lovely chocolate for which Switzerland is famous. We skied all day with just a stop for a light lunch and a beer at Grund, then sadly the time came for us to take our last run down to Grindelwald.

We pointed our skis down towards Grindelwald and we had only just begun our descent when a skier skied over beside us and greeted me, saying: "Hullo, do you remember me?" The skier seemed vaguely familiar, but not waiting for me to reply said: "I'm Ernie Gertz, we were both in the Rover Scouts together." I was amazed and asked him: "How the hell did you recognise me?" "By the gloves you have hanging from your belt by a blanket pin." Earnie said. I knew Ernie quite well, but to be recognised on the other side of the world, as a rover scout from Victoria by the simple rover scout practice of attaching a spare pair of ski gloves to our trouser belts by a large blanket pin, was one in a million. I introduced Ernie to Netta and we talked for a while about our travels. We wished each other well before parting with a Rover Scout, left hand, hand shake.

It was to be our final downhill run for the fortnight. We decided, however, to have one more run. When I finally took off my skis after the last run, I was sure it would be the last time I would be putting them on for some considerable time, because my future plans did not include skiing. That day in Grindelwald was to be the culmination of three weeks of exciting skiing in Switzerland. In my wildest dreams, I never contemplated that I would ski in Switzerland for three weeks in two of Switzerland's top ski resorts. One never knows what fate and luck have in store for us.

Saturday 29th March: It wasn't a very good day, and fog shrouded the mountains, so we were not tempted to go skiing. I decided to catch the 6 p.m. train from Grindelwald, but hadn't bought my ticket, so Netta and I went down to the travel agency in the town. For some unexplained reason I could only buy a ticket as far as Bern. I would have to buy another ticket and change trains there for the remainder of the journey through France. While at the travel agency we discovered something that was a shock to us, as well as a great disappointment. The proprietor asked how we had enjoyed skiing from the Kleiner Scheidegg down to Grindelwald and Wengen. We said our ticket wasn't valid for Wengen. He said that although the ticket only showed 'Grindelwald-Kleiner Scheidegg and Kleiner Scheidegg-Eigergletscher,' in the winter we could have used it to go to Wengen, as many times as we wished.

For the whole two weeks we could have been skiing from the Kleiner Scheidegg up and down between Grindelwald and Wengen. Missing out on the marvellous opportunity to explore the famous ski resort town of Wengen and view the surrounding mountain panorama from the other side of the Kleiner Scheidegg was a bitter disappointment. However, we consoled ourselves when we reflected

164

on the wonderful two weeks we had spent skiing on the Grindelwald side of the Kleiner Scheidegg up close to the Eiger.

I packed my rucksack and thanked the staff of the Friends of Nature House for the marvellous accommodation and facilities, which I believed were a feature of the organisation's hostels. Netta and Nellie accompanied me to the station where I wished them goodbye and good luck on their travels. With a kiss and a hug for each, I boarded the train. I would not be seeing them for about a month, when they arrived back in London. They were leaving the next day to travel to Spain and Italy.

|||||||||||||||||||||||

GRINDELWALD TO BERN

I waved to Nellie and Netta as the train pulled silently away from the Grindelwald station exactly on the scheduled time of 6 p.m. It was nearly dark so there was nothing much to see except lights dotting the landscape here and there and at the stations I changed trains at Interlaken Ost and Spiez, where I had to wait for about half an hour for a train to Bern.

While I waited I reflected on my last three weeks skiing holiday. Skiing with Netta for two weeks in Grindelwald and a week in Zermatt under cloudless skies was the ultimate skiing holiday. What I ask, could have been better? The train arrived and on the way I wrote up my notebook and dozed off every now and again. The train was about half full and stopped at a few stations along the way, but I couldn't see much in the dark before arriving at Bern the capital of Switzerland around 8 p.m., where I tried to buy a ticket to London, but this was also not possible, only as far as Paris, which was a bloody nuisance. Before getting on a Swiss train to take me to Paris I had time to buy a bar of lovely Swiss chocolate, and a soft drink.

|||||||||||||||||||||||

BERN TO PARIS

Leaving Bern I settled down to the long journey to Paris and I

165

promptly dozed off to be awakened every now and again by the conductor checking tickets. I noticed once when I walked along the corridor to go to the toilet that many of the passengers were sleeping too. The train crossed the border into France at les Verrieres, where there was a ticket check, but no custom check.

Travelling by train in Switzerland had been a joy. Most were corridor carriages, which were always clean and warm, even in third class. It was thrilling to travel behind huge Swiss electric locomotives and experience the marvels of Swiss railway engineering, diving through tunnels, over bridges, and climbing up the sides of valleys and mountains.

I had read about the Swiss railways in my youth and now I had seen them first-hand. I had also gained the impression that Swiss trains went faster up hills than downhill. I should say that the Austrian Railways were not very far behind the Swiss in all aspects of their many wonderful railways.

CHAPTER 10
FRANCE

Sunday 30th March: Some time after midnight the train arrived at Dijon. From there on I dozed off again waking later when the sun rose, but I was wide awake during the last kilometres to Paris.

PARIS

At last after travelling through the suburbs of Paris and filling up with commuters along the way, the train pulled into the Gare de Lyon railway station at 6.30 a.m., exactly twelve and a half hours after I left Grindelwald. It was a long trip of about 470 km. involving five train changes, but thanks to the comfort of the Swiss railways carriages I slept and travelled well. I now had to get across Paris to the Gare de Nord station, but had no idea where it was. I decided to hire a taxi and was charged, *correction,* slugged 100 Ffr by a 'taxi getter,' and then 400 Ffr, for the taxi from the Gare de Lyon to the Gare de Nord.

The little I saw of Paris looked very attractive in the morning sun. While I was in Vienna, Jacques invited me to visit him in Paris. Had he not had to leave Vienna in a hurry because his girl friend was pregnant. I am sure I could have looked him up.

PARIS TO CALAIS

Netta had loaned me a total of £14 Sterling and 800 French francs. I was especially thankful that Netta had made sure I had some

167

French Francs with me, so in Paris I was able to buy a ticket right through to King's Cross Station in London.

Electric traction gave way to a steam hauled train that left the Gare de Nord at 8.15 a.m. The journey of over 200 km on the comfortably filled French train between Paris and Calais, in no way rivalled the high standards of the Swiss railways. I was travelling third class, and the carriage I was in was a bit rough and not well maintained especially the upholstery, which was well worn.

I opened up my map to see where the train would take me to get to Calais, the same cross channel port as I had begun this very long, but incredibly interesting journey. I saw from the map that the route to Calais was through the war torn area of the Somme, which brought back memories of the 1914-1918 Great War and the 'Battle of the Somme' that I had learned about as a youth in school.

From the train I saw much evidence of the war. The country was pock marked with various size craters and the unmistakable earth works of trenches. All of this devastation was somewhat softened by a covering of green grass. Small forests, tree lined dirt roads and scattered trees that survived the heavy fighting were also part of the landscape. About halfway through the journey as the train approached Amiens I saw damaged buildings, and much more in and around the city, the railway station and yards. The fighting, called the 'Battle of Amiens' was centred around the Somme River which flows through the city. Finally on 31st August 1944 Amiens was liberated from the Germans by the British.

I had enough French money too to buy a ham roll, chocolate and drinks in Paris, and after the train left Amiens I tucked into these as I watched the same sort of battle scarred, scenery pass by as I had seen before Amiens. After a not too tiring journey of over four hours the train reached Calais.

CALAIS

The ferry to take me across the Channel was close by. I bought a ticket and without any trouble passed through customs and boarded

168

the ferry for Folkstone.

CALAIS TO FOLKSTONE

The crossing was rough and cold and when the ferry arrived at Folkstone it was freezing, colder than any day I had experienced since I left England, except of course on the Theodule Pass. I was not surprised to learn that I had missed the coldest March since 1871.

CHAPTER 11

ENGLAND

FOLKSTONE

iiiiiiiiiiiiiiiiiiiiii

FOLKSTONE TO HITCHIN

As I went through customs and boarded the train for London, I noticed that there was a sprinkling of snow on the ground. It was great to see English faces and talk English again. Best of all however, was to be able to step off the platform directly into a compartment of the swing door carriage with the same floor height as the platform. The train ride to Victoria Station was quite fast as the English train took me through the now familiar English landscape. Unlike last time when I landed in England I could see out the window as it was not fogged up. What relief it was that it was not a corridor train, and when I heard the loud sound of carriage slam doors being closed before my train departed from the stations, I knew for sure I was back in dear old England.

At Victoria station I joined a Circle Line tube train to King's Cross this time making sure I went the correct way round. It was rush hour in the tube and I received many enquiring, and I liked to believe, admiring glances as I manhandled my skis in the carriage. I was still wearing my ski boots as they were extremely comfortable and easier than carrying them in my rucksack. I bought a ticket to Hitchin and climbed aboard my last train journey for the tour. The train pulled into Hitchin station in the dark at 5.45 p.m. I had travelled approximately 2,500 kilometers by train since leaving Hitchin two months ago, not counting the distance I had travelled in rack trains skiing in Zermatt and Grindelwald.

HITCHIN

I arrived back at the Bakers to a rather indifferent welcome, but was not surprised at my less than enthusiastic welcome, because I had not being able to give them an exact date and time of my return. Leon was there at the Bakers. He gave me a perfunctory welcome, then kept out of my way, ostensibly because he said: "I have caught some sort of bug." From the little he did tell me, I was sure his tour wasn't as exciting or enjoyable as mine. He never attempted to tell me any of the highlights of his tour, whereas I was bursting to tell him all about mine. He probably had a bit of a guilty conscience after the manner in which he abandoned me in Bad Ischl.

It was a great relief to put my rucksack and skis down, particularly my skis, which were always awkward to carry around. I unpacked and read all the letters that had accumulated from my parents, YHA friends and my mother's relations in Scotland. The letter from my parents said they were well, but missing me very much. Mrs. Baker made me tea and scones, which I was very grateful for as I was very hungry. It had been a long day and I didn't have much to eat on the way. After talking for a while I retired to bed with the thought that in the morning, I would have to look for a job and having found that, board and lodging.

Monday 31st March: When I woke up in morning after a well-earned sleep, my first thought was how was I going to go about looking for a job. While we were having breakfast Mr. Baker told me that he had talked to George King, a Conservative Party friend of his, who had a large engineering factory in Stevenage.

Mr. Baker said that if I was interested, I should go and see him straight away, because he was sure I would find a job there. I thanked him and said I would go to Kings straight after we had finished breakfast.

I decided that his advice was too good to be missed, so after thanking Mr. Baker I took a double decker bus to Stevenage, a town 4 miles from Hitchin on the way to London. I walked over a small, masonry railway bridge spanning railway lines, where I found there was a big modern factory with the words HITCHIN GEO. W. KING STEVENAGE written in big red letters on one side of the factory, and CRANES CONVEYERS on the other. I found the reception desk and was sent to have an interview with King's employment officer Mr. Furlough, a middle aged bloke with a pleasant manner. After I had shown him my tradesman's certificate, he signed me up for a job as a fitter, starting next Friday 6th April.

Better still, he told me that Kings ran a boarding hostel in Stevenage for its workers, ten minutes walking distance from the factory. Mr. Furlough said that if I wished I could board there. Full board he said was not expensive and would be deducted from my pay. I gladly accepted his offer of work and board. He gave me the address of the boarding house and told me to report to the manager there at 9 a.m. on Friday 4th April, sign in, then come to the factory ready to start work. I couldn't believe my good fortune. A job and full board, all secured in one interview on my first day back in England. I rushed back to the Bakers to thank Mr. Baker for his help. Leon had not begun working and he never told me about his plans for his stay in England. There was a letter for me from Maurice Spanger a YHA member. Maurice wanted to know if I would like to go to the south of England with him at Easter.

I soon discovered with a shock that Easter was only a little over a week away! It sounded an interesting trip with just the two of us for four days. Although Maurice was still a bit of a mystery man, I wrote back saying: I would be pleased to go with him, and asked for more information about his plans. I spent the rest of the day writing letters and looking around the shops in Hitchin.

172

Tuesday 1st April: There were three days to go before I started work, so I decided to go to London the next morning and learn more about the city and see a few shows. The journey to London by double decker bus was much more relaxing than before, because I was not worrying about my lost rucksack. Sitting in the top deck of the bus was different for another good reason. There was a weak English sun shining with hardly any fog or haze to prevent me from seeing the lovely green countryside. The bus took about an hour to travel the 51 km (by rail) to London, travelling along the not so wide, but excellently surfaced main London–Edinburgh A1 Highway, (The Great North Road). The countryside gradually changed from rural beauty to a crowded unbeautiful, residential and industrial landscape, as the bus went through the London suburbs of Finsbury Park and Golders Green.

In London I went first to my bank to draw out some money. Then I went to Netta's bank and put the money I owed her into her account. In London the sun was struggling to shine through the grey haze, or was it pollution. I wandered around getting to know more of London that seemed to be focused around Piccadilly Circus and Trafalgar Square. From there I walked down Whitehall towards the Houses of Parliament. Rising high above these buildings was the icon of London, Big Ben the nickname for the bell in its clock tower, a familiar sight to people all around the world. The sound of its bell is used by the BBC to chime the hours. As it was still early, I decided to go to the movies, or the cinema as it is called in England.

I saw *A Streetcar Named Desire*, a very enthralling movie about a neurotic woman, with Vivien Leigh and Marlon Brando. I now had money so I went back to Hitchin by train. I wasn't able to see much of the countryside going past the window because the fog had descended on the scenery, but I thoroughly enjoyed being behind a steam locomotive again.

Wednesday 2nd April: I went by bus to London. I rang Judy, but she wasn't at home. I walked miles around the streets of London. It was always a great thrill to come across street names that I was familiar with from playing Monopoly. I called in to Australia House on the Strand at Aldwych and studied the notice boards, which carried lots of useful information. I was especially interested in the job advertisements, many for nurses, stenographers and other office workers. A couple were for various tradesmen, carpenters, plumbers, but none for fitters and turners. The Orient Line had a notice requesting Australians to register with the company for passages to Australia, and although I had no intention of returning home until after the Coronation, I decided to register my name.

At 2 p.m. I went to the Stoll Theatre in Kingsway and saw a program of short excerpts from a number of ballets, *Les Sylphides, Don Quixote, The Dying Swan, Concerto Grosso en Ballet* and *Scheherazade.* It was all very enjoyable and colourful as the ballets were a great variety of form and subject matter.

Thursday 3rd April: Today was the last day I of my holiday before I embarked on the working part of my 'working holiday.' I decided to go and see Ralph Bateman, the Australian dentist I had met before I went on my tour. He greeted me with a cheery: "Gooday mate." Ralph had a look at my teeth and said that I needed a filling. I made an appointment with him for a day next week after work. Ralph was a great bloke with a ready smile. His said to me: "It won't cost you a thing mate."

I managed to sell my extra sleeping bag to a friend of the Bakers, but I still had two rucksacks. I wrote letters to my family, my relatives in Scotland, Roy and a couple of other YHA friends. I packed up all my gear and asked the Bakers if I could leave my skis and boots with them. Mr. Baker said he would put them in the shed, where they would be safe and dry. Although I was glad I would be leaving the Bakers in the morning, I would always be extremely grateful to them for their hospitality. It wasn't the happiest of households, quite apart from the feelings between Leon and me. The Bakers never seemed to stop arguing about politics and Mr Baker's

174

'pram.' I finally worked out what the pram was. Mr Baker had a large lounge chair in which he sat. The 'pram' was all those things he had on the floor around his chair that he liked to keep handy, newspapers, books, glasses cases, pencils and pens etc. I must admit that I also have a pram around my chair in my retirement, which is sometimes not very tidy either. The Bakers were also always criticising the socialist government, saying how much better it was under the conservatives. I was very surprised and somewhat disappointed when in 1945 just after the war, Winston Churchill and his Tory Party were voted out of office in favour of the Labour Party led by Clement Atlee. Churchill had virtually won the war for the English, and it seemed to me that they couldn't get rid of him quickly enough. In fact unbeknown to me, in October 1951 a month prior to me leaving Australia, Winston Churchill became Prime Minister again. I went to bed that night, looking forward eagerly to the morning, and the exciting experience of being an Aussie, working and earning some money in an English factory.

Friday 4th April: After breakfast. Leon as usual was nowhere to be seen when the time came to say goodbye. Mr. Baker gave me a warm handshake, and with a kiss and a hug from Mrs. Baker, I again thanked them for their hospitality. Mrs. Baker gave me back my ration book, which they would have used to enjoy extra rations while Leon and I were away. Mr. Baker assisted me with getting my luggage on to the bus to Stevenage, one large case, one small case, my rucksacks, and golf clubs. I thanked him again for getting me an introduction to Kings. His parting words to me were: "You know where we live." I managed to carry all my belongings the short distance from the bus stop to King's hostel by following a small map the employment officer had drawn for me.

⌂

STEVENAGE

Mr. and Mrs. Page, the manager and his wife welcomed me with big open smiles. The hostel, called *Fieldview,* was a double story

175

building with lots of windows and with some ivy growing up the front wall. It was really quite an attractive dwelling in a rural setting. Mr. and Mrs. Page, who I thought were not much older than me, showed me around Fieldview. First of all the communal dining room where I remembered to pass over my ration book, then the lounge, bathrooms and a large dormitory type bedroom. It was all clean and tidy, just like the outside. I was given a key to a locker, where I could hang up my clothes and lock away my valuables.

I changed into my work clothes and deposited my cases, rucksack and golf clubs in a locked storeroom, then set off to walk across the Great North Road and the bridge over the railway tracks to the modern factory, which. was only a short walk of about 10 minutes. Inside the large airy workshop, Mr. Furlough met me and introduced me to my foreman Harry Hammond, a dark, middle aged man with a ready smile. He in turn introduced me to Bob Chapman a fitter, who I was to work with assembling a large overhead travelling crane. Bob was a tall, middle aged Englishman with buck teeth. This seemed to me to be a common feature of the English, together with the more charming and beautiful peaches and cream complexions of many English girls.

Bob told me that King manufactured cranes, conveyor systems and many other items of mechanical handling equipment, both large and small. The first job that Bob had me do, was installing grease nipples and piping at various locations on the crane, interesting and easy work. I was pleased that the work was quite clean, as was the factory, but I would need to get some overalls and a few basic tools, although most of the tools I needed were supplied. In another welcome surprise, I was asked if I would like to work the next day Saturday at time and a half. Of course I accepted. There was a canteen at the factory where I could buy sandwiches or a hot meal, as lunch was not included in my full board, except at the weekends.

Back at Fieldview after my first work day, I was introduced to the other eight boarders who all worked at various trades at Kings.

176

They came from many different places in England and Scotland, but I was the only Australian. They were all very friendly, although some of their English and Scots accents would take some getting used to. They flung questions at me right, left and centre. I flung a few back, all in the process of getting to know one another. They were all very interested in the working conditions in Australia, and from the information I gave them they were quite impressed, saying: "How about we all emigrate to Australia and leave Gordon here." Much of the questioning took place while we were partaking of a very appetising meal of mashed potatoes, vegetables and slices of meat.

Fieldview was equipped with hot showers, a rarity in English houses, but a necessary feature in a boarding house for manual workers. Before I had a shower and went to bed, I wrote a thank you letter to Mr. and Mrs. Baker and letters to Scotland, my family, my Aussie rover scout best friend, Roy and a few others. I wrote about my new job and board, my new address and how thrilling and rewarding it was, to begin my English working life.

Sunday 6th April: Mr. Page invited me to come and have a drink with him at one of the local pubs, the Two of Diamonds. We talked a lot as we drank our room temperature English beers, which although not as cold as Australian beer seemed to have more taste. I realised that living in England, I would just have to get used to the ambient temperature of the beer or go without, and that was not worth thinking about. Mr. Page told me that there were many workers travelling around the UK looking for work and a place to stay, or 'digs' as the English called it. In some areas, the prospect of finding a suitable job with board close by was not easy, so he said I should consider myself very lucky, which of course I did.

Mr. Page said that George King was not only the owner of Kings, but was also a leading business, social and political identity around the district of Stevenage and Hitchin. George King realised that the availability of cheap, nearby accommodation, was an

177

important factor with which to attract the workers he needed. To facilitate this need, the company purchased and renovated *Fieldview* as a communal boarding house for use by their single employees. *Fieldview* had been operating for a couple of years before I came, and its aim of attracting and recruiting suitable tradesmen to the factory was a complete success. Over drinks we certainly learned a lot about each other.

My second week working at Kings was to be a short one, because the week finished on Thursday before Good Friday. I rang Maurice Spanger to tell him of my new address and find out about his plans for Easter. He wanted to travel by coach to Minehead in Somerset, and from there hitchhike around the west of England. Maurice had booked the coach for us and accommodation at the Minehead Youth Hostel. That sounded OK by me. He said to come and stay with him at his digs on Thursday night, and we would catch the coach the next morning.

Thursday April 10th: I received my first pay, £2 odd. Not much, but my board at Fieldview had been taken out of this and of course, I had only worked for part of the pay week. Back at *Fieldview* I had tea and a quick shower before I caught the bus to London.

STEVENAGE TO LONDON

This time I was travelling light with only the essentials in my rucksack and suitably dressed. I easily found Maurice's digs at Notting Hill Gate. When he opened the door to me, Maurice was no longer a mystery man. I remembered seeing him at Youth Hostel Association (YHA) functions many times.

A woman who was with him left as soon as I entered his digs. Maurice didn't introduce me, but said rather apologetically: "Women are like flies in London."

⌂

NOTTING HILL GATE

Maurice was a tall, well built, and handsome man of dark complexion and seemed a nice sort of bloke. Maurice had been in

London since the previous May, and was working as a waiter in a London restaurant. We had a cup of coffee and talked a lot before we went off to bed looking forward to the morning and our trip together. Although experience had demonstrated to me the benefits of travelling alone, this journey was only for three days, and I was quite happy with Maurice's plans to explore the south west of England.

CHAPTER 12

THE SECOND BACKPACKING TOUR

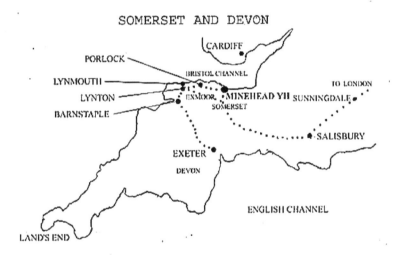

A map of Somerset and Devon showing the route and towns
Maurice and the author visited on their Easter tour

LONDON TO MINEHEAD

Good Friday 11th April: Although it was the start of the Easter holidays there did not appear to be many people travelling as we boarded the coach at Victoria Street station for the journey to Minehead. Our first stop was for lunch at Salisbury, about 140 km from London. We were aboard a tourist coach, which allowed us time during the lunch break to visit Salisbury Cathedral. My tourist

180

brochure said the cathedral was built in the remarkably short time of 46 years during the 13th century. It has the highest church spire in England, 403 ft (123 m), and the top of the spire leans 2 foot 6 inches (75 cm) from the vertical. We didn't venture inside because there was a Good Friday service in progress.

After lunch the coach travelled across the Salisbury Plain into Somerset. The countryside was a beautiful green, with some flowers in bloom heralding the beginning of spring. On the way to Minehead the coach passed through the counties of Surrey, Wiltshire and Dorset before reaching Minehead in county Somerset at 4.30 p.m.

$$\text{\AA}$$

MINEHEAD

We quickly located the YH and booked in for bed and breakfast for 4 shillings. The YH was a nice big place with good facilities. After a dinner of some form of meat and vegetables we explored the town, located on the southern shore of the Bristol Channel. Wales and the city of Cardiff were about 30 km away across the Channel. The tide was out at the time, which left Minehead detached from the waters of the Channel by a huge expanse of flat rather unattractive, dark sand. Maurice said that Somerset was renowned for its apple cider, so of course this is what we drank at a pub we visited, which surprisingly was open on Good Friday. Cider was a bit too sweet for my liking, but it did have a good effect on my outlook on life. Maurice was good company and we were getting along well together.

MINEHEAD TO LYNTON

Saturday 12th April: On an overcast morning we left the YH after a breakfast of cereal and bacon and eggs. We took a bus to Porlock and tried to hitch a ride from there to Lynton to the west of Minehead, but we had no luck, although very few cars passed us going in the direction we wanted to go. I am sure that if we had been two girls we might have been given. a lift. However, we gave up and didn't have long to wait before a bus came along to take us to Lynton. The bus wound its way through the rolling uplands of Exmoor and the countryside that drops down steep cliffs and gullies to the shores of the Bristol Channel. It afforded us great views back across the rural country of Exmoor and in the opposite direction down to the Bristol Channel and across to Wales. I saw too, the small, picturesque villages of Exmoor, which was the setting for the famous historic novel, *Lorna Doone,* written in 1869 by R D Blackmore, a book I began to read, but gave up after a few pages because I didn't like the writing style, far too many adjectives.

The journey from Minehead to Lynton across Exmoor reminded me very much of the landscape on the road between Cape Schanck and Flinders, overlooking Bass Strait on the Mornington Peninsula in my home state of Victoria.

LYNTON

The bus arrived at Lynton just on noon. Lynton is a small town located on the top of high cliffs beside the Lyn River, a small river wedged between the town and high cliffs. We admired the spectacular view of the rugged, hilly, Somerset coastline. Directly below Lynton, down the steep 100 m high cliffs we could see the small seaside village of Lynmouth where the Lyn River entered the Bristol Channel.

LYNMOUTH

The two towns were connected by a cable railway powered by the waters of the Lyn River. There was no YH in either Lynton or Lynmouth, so before deciding on our next move we walked down the steep path to Lynmouth, a popular beach resort and fishing village.

Lynmouth might be a popular beach resort by English tastes, but was not the sort of beach that we were used to in Australia. The sand was a very coarse, grey colour, not very suitable for building nice sandcastles. We had a rest and a bite to eat and admired, not its beach, but its picturesque location surrounded by bare hills rising steeply from the coast.

182

We decided to ignore the expense and book into a hotel in Lynton, not that we really had any other choice. We took a ride up the cliffs in the cable car, and booked into a hotel called *The Globe* for two nights. We had a sumptuous mixed grill for dinner helped down with a few beers; Maurice had cider.

In the evening we went to a dance in the Lynton town hall. We were surprised how the English really let their hair down in a rather unattractive and rowdy manner, nothing like the good mannered and well dressed dancers at our Saturday night town hall dances that I was used to back home. Neither of us enjoyed the dance very much because the dancers were not very friendly.

LYNTON TO BARNSTAPLE

Sunday 13th April: It was a beautiful Easter Sunday morning as we boarded the bus to take us south to Barnstaple. The bus travelled around the western edge and forests of Exmoor to Barnstaple a small town situated on the Taw River that flows into the Bristol Channel. The bus dropped us at the railway station, and soon a steam train came along going to Exeter.

!!!!!!!!!!!!!!!!!!!!!!

BARNSTAPLE TO EXETER

I got a brief glimpse of the locomotive that was to haul our train. It was a tank engine with the unique design characteristics of most GWR locomotives, the square Belpaire type firebox and the tapered brass steam dome. It was especially thrilling to see the locomotive in real life that I had seen in my railway books.

We scrambled into a swing door compartment of a carriage of a GWR (Great Western Railway) train to Exeter, a 34 mile journey. It was great to hear the steady beat of the locomotive's exhaust as it hauled three swing door carriages along quite briskly, on a delightful journey through a landscape of hills and dales. There were many bends in the line, and with the pleasant sound of clickity clack from the rail joints the train ran along. The countryside opened up and was

183

mainly pasture, but with very few sightings of any form of cattle. The line followed the Taw River, crossing over it a couple of times. There were a few stations I noted among others where the train stopped. Chulmleigh, Langford and Crediton. At one of these there was a passing loop where we crossed a train from Exeter. The Taw River disappeared to the west after leaving Langford.

Just before the train reached Exeter the main GWR railway line from London joined ours. When the train stopped at Exeter station and we stepped on to the platform. I was ready to take a photo of the locomotive, but was surprised to quickly discover that this was not the end of the train's journey, and almost immediately with a shrill whistle and a blast of steam from the release cocks, it carried on its way to the real terminus Exmouth, 11 miles further on.

EXETER

Leaving the station we walked around and explored the big city, which had suffered extensive bombing in 1942. The raids were called the 'Baedeker raids.' This was because it was discovered that the Germans were using the excellent *Baedeker Tourist Guide* books and maps to help them pinpoint their targets in Exeter.

We had a look at the large, Gothic Church of England Cathedral of St Peter, which despite the bombing had only sustained superficial damage. The construction of the cathedral began in 1275, but was not completed until nearly 100 years later. It was quite beautiful inside, where an Evensong service was about to start. Although neither of us are overly religious, but because this was Easter Sunday, we thought it appropriate to stay and be part of the service, which we both enjoyed. I got a little emotional thinking of home, much the same as I did in Vienna, when I sat in St Stephen's.

We had a good look around Exeter, a city that we thought was quite liveable, especially with the beach at Exmouth only a short distance away. By this time we were very hungry so we had a very tasty meal of fish and chips sitting in the park near the church until it was time to get back to Lynton. We maybe should have taken the

184

train or bus to Exmouth to see what the coast and beach was like, but we didn't think we really had the time as it was late afternoon.

EXETER TO LYNTON

We caught a bus back to Lynton because it was cheaper than the train. The bus took a much more interesting route than the train, calling into all the towns along the way, but it took two hours for the journey. After another big meal in the hotel we relaxed in the lounge.

There was a small bookcase in the lounge and I looked to see if there was anything interesting to read. Imagine Maurice's surprise, and mine, when we pulled out a large book about the Holocaust. It was full of the most horrifying graphic photos of piles of dead bodies, stores full of hair, false teeth and glasses, and much more of the same. I don't know about Maurice, but these were the first photos I had seen of the atrocities in the various concentration camps, except on newsreels and in newspapers. I don't think I slept too easily that night. I thought that maybe the proprietor was a Jew and wanted his guests to be aware of the Holocaust outrage.

LYNTON

LYNTON TO STEVENAGE

Monday 14th April: We woke on Easter Monday to pouring rain, so we wasted no time in catching a coach back to London. The coach travelled through the small village of Simonsbath, the highest village on Exmoor. Exmoor that day looked much like my preconceived idea of an English moor, dull, damp and mysterious.

The coach followed much the same route by which we had come, but there was nothing much to be seen because of the rain. When we reached the outskirts of London, somewhere near the famous Sunningdale Golf Course in Berkshire about 40 km from London, we got caught in a huge traffic jam. I didn't see any sign of the golf course, because the rain was still coming down in buckets.

Geo. W. King's factory where the author worked for three months

The author and *Fieldview*. The boarding house run by Geo. W King

The author waiting for a lift on the A39 to Lynton
Photo Maurice Spanger

The author in Lynmouth with Lynton above on the cliff
Photo Maurice Spanger

A GWR locomotive and train similar to the one that took us to Exeter.
Photo *The Iron Horse*

Exeter Cathedral

186

The coach finally reached London in the late afternoon, where I said goodbye to Muarice, thanking him for being such good company, and for inviting me to come with him on a very pleasant Easter tour. We parted with a firm handshake and a resolve to keep in touch..

Back at *Fieldview* that night, I reflected on the tour. Maurice and I got on famously, with no arguments when we discussed our plans for each day. I would probably not have visited that part England of my own choosing. Although we had no luck on our only attempt at hitchhiking, the prospect of two male hitchhikers carrying large rucksacks trying to get a lift together, was, I thought, rather slim.

STEVENAGE

Tuesday 15th April: It was pleasing to be back at Kings earning money after ungrudgingly spending quite a lot on our trip to the south of England. I had a letter from Tom Webb, with a work reference that I had asked him for, because I thought I might be asked for one when I applied for work in England. There was also a letter from my mother, with a note from my father asking me to fill in the enclosed tax form and post it back to his accountant. I didn't know why, because I was required to get a tax clearance before I could be issued with my passport and boarding pass. I was kept quite busy at night writing letters to everyone about my work and life in Stevenage, and in return it was always a thrill to get letters almost every day. I was keeping in touch by letter with my relatives in Scotland, who had offered to have me stay with them when I come up to Scotland in August.

Friday 18th April: It was going to be a very hot day according to my fellow boarders at *Fieldview,* 70°F (21°C). I didn't think that was very hot, but strangely the temperature of 70°F seemed much hotter than a similar temperature in Melbourne. The day turned out to be not only hot, but also full of surprises. It was pay day and I received my first full pay packet, £7/0/2, which apart from making me feel like a millionaire, led to a puzzling incident with my workmate Bob.

When I worked with the VR in Melbourne, the first thing we did on receiving our pay envelopes, was to open them and check the amount we had been paid against the pay slip. Then we compared them with our workmates, to make sure there were no mistakes. When I opened my King's pay packet and looked at the amount, I turned to Bob and asked him; "I got £7/0/2, what did you get?" Bob didn't answer me, but reacted as though I had asked him a most insulting, private question. He quickly put his pay packet in his pocket without answering me, and we both returned to our work on the cranes without further talk.

I wasn't sure what I had done wrong. He was not going to divulge how much he had been paid, but he certainly knew how much I was earning. The next surprise was when Bob Langley, Leon's older brother, came to Kings to invite me to Hitchin after work to see the Bakers. He seemed to be quite a nice bloke. I told him I had an appointment with the dentist and arranged with Bob to go to the Bakers after that.

From nearly the first day I began working at Kings, a cheery English worker called Mack had attached himself to me and took great pleasure in making fun of me as an expatriate Australian. It was beginning to annoy me, but he was not such a bad bloke, as I gradually got to know him. He soon became a very good friend and confidant. Mack was a Cockney from the East End of London and talked with the characteristic quaint Cockney accent.

He said he had served with the Merchant Navy and was married and lived with his wife in a council house in Stevenage Newtown. Mack told me about his experiences in the Merchant Navy during the war, which were quite enthralling. It was the first time I had been told a personal account of the war by someone who served.

I told Mack about the pay packet experience with Bob that had continued to puzzle me. He explained that the fitters at Kings kept

188

the amount they were paid strictly to themselves, because each could be paid slightly different hourly rates, although the difference might be only one or two pence. I told Mack that fitters and turners working for the VR were all on the same award wage, so there was no difference in the amount they were paid.

On the way after work to see Ralph at his surgery, I took my two suits to get cleaned and pressed, because I thought that as a novice ironer I might ruin them. Ralph filled my tooth and we talked about ourselves. I told him about my voyage to England and my first tour of the Continent. As yet he and his wife had not ventured across the Channel, but they had made a few sightseeing trips around England, before he set himself up in a dental surgery in Hitchin.

Afterwards I walked to the Bakers, where Mr. and Mrs. Baker and Bob Langley welcomed me warmly. The visit was quite pleasant, but there was no sign of, or talk about Leon. I told them about my trip at Easter and my job at Kings, thanking Mr Baker again for his help in getting the job.

Bob suggested that the two of us go for a drink on my way back to Stevenage. We went to a pub called The Cock, where I was very pleased to find that Bob Langley had a totally different personality than Leon. We agreed to have a drink together again sometime. When I returned to *Fieldview*, for some reason I took the brave decision to shave off the moustache that had been with me since 1948 that I first grew it on a two-week skiing holiday with the Rover Scouts on the Bogong High Plains.

Saturday 19th April: There was no overtime, so I went shopping and spent nearly all of my pay. I bought a pair of overalls for £2/0/11 and an expensive pair of sunglasses costing £3/5. Before going to bed that night, I wrote to Mrs Wiltshire, an English woman my mother had regularly sent food parcels to after the war. My mother had asked if I could visit her while I was in England, which I intended to do. I had another important task to perform before I climbed into bed, putting my watch forward one hour for the start of daylight saving. This was an English innovation to make use of the lengthening days, allowing more time for daylight pursuits and saving electricity. It was not until the 1990s that Australia adopted daylight saving, which I believe had greater benefits for us than in England, especially for our southern states.

Sunday 20th April: I went to Knebworth to have a game of golf, which cost 7/6. I started badly, but after a bit of practice I managed the first nine holes in 47 and ended up breaking 100, which pleased me greatly. Knebworth is a small town 3 km down the line from Stevenage towards London. The golf course was described in my golf guide as an easy walking, parkland course, 5,877 m off the back tees. I thought it was an interesting course, especially the first few holes alongside the railway line with steam trains speeding past every now and again in full view. What I ask could be a better sight to accompany me in my game of golf? It reminded me of watching football at the Hawthorn Football ground with trains going by on the embankment, some of which slowed down to watch the game.

Back at *Fieldview* I decided that I would have a go at ironing. I had no trouble ironing my handkerchiefs and then decided to iron my badly creased gabardine raincoat. I had not yet learned how to control the iron properly with the sad result that I scorched the lapel. It was an expensive raincoat I had purchased at Henry Bucks, the leading Melbourne men's wear store, before I left for overseas. I was devastated! I thanked my lucky stars that I had sent my suits out to get cleaned and ironed and not tried to iron them myself.

As the April days passed by I was quite contented with my job and life at *Fieldview,* but I did get terribly lonely at times and thought it was about time I found a nice, English girlfriend. Maurice Spanger might be correct that 'women are like flies in London', but I reckoned I would have to get out and see what the Stevenage and Hitchin girls were like.

I wrote to Netta at her London address and planned to go and see her as soon as she returned from her travels. I had plenty of lively

190

company and conversation with my fellow boarders at *Fieldview*. They were all really good blokes, although the Scotsmen tended to be a whingeing lot, their Scots accents making the whingeing sound even worse. I hoped to hell my Scots relations, were not like the complaining ones down here. I was still working overtime, which was allowing me to save about £2 each week.

If the weather was fine, during my lunchtime at Kings, I sometimes sat with other blokes from Kings and watched the trains go by. It was just pure chance that I came to Hitchin where Leon's relations lived, and then found a job in Stevenage, because I don't think I ever looked at a map to see where in England Hitchin was located. As a railway enthusiast, if I had searched the length and breadth of England for a place to live and work, I could not have found a better location than Stevenage.

Sitting on the grass of the low embankment outside Kings, I was able to view close by, some of the most famous passenger trains in the world, speeding along one of the most important railway routes in Great Britain. Each day on the way to and from Kings I walked over a bridge, just down the line towards London, spanning the same railway lines that I was watching the trains go by in my lunch time.

There are the four tracks of the London and North Eastern Railway that link London with many large cities in the north, Edinburgh, Doncaster, Newcastle and York. It reminded me, when I was skiing in Zermatt enjoying the fabulous view of the Swiss Alps from the Gornergrat–being described as the 'Royal Box of the Mountain Theatre.' Likewise being able to see a cavalcade of trains go by beside Kings–was certainly the 'Royal Box of the Railway Theatre.'

In 1946, Prime Minister Atlee's Labour government nationalised all the railways of Great Britain. Although the trains I was seeing in 1952 were now administered by British Railways (BR), they still retained the colours and other characteristics of their former private owners. In the months I lived in Stevenage and

191

worked at Kings, I was in fact witnessing a significant period of railway transition that of the LNER to BR, the demise of one of the most famous and well known railway companies in Great Britain and the world. The end of the steam locomotive too was not very far away.

Sunday 27th April: It was a lovely sunny day so I walked over to the railway bridge I crossed to go to work each day. I wanted to take a photo of the famous *Flying Scotsman* picking up water from the Stevenage troughs, which I had watched in amazement on many occasions. The *Flying Scotsman* left King's Cross daily at 10 a.m. on its non-stop journey to Edinburgh in Scotland. I got myself into a good position in the centre of the bridge with my camera at the ready. I had to wait about half an hour, but right on time the *Flying Scotsman* roared through as I clicked the camera and hoped I got a good photo, which I did, a very good one in fact.

Running beneath the bridge were four railway tracks of the LNER. The outer two were for the 'Up' (to London) and 'Down' (from London), slow speed local and goods lines. The two central tracks were the 'Up' and 'Down' express lines along which trains sped to and from the north of England.

These two tracks were equipped with water troughs, about 45 cm wide, 15 cm deep and approximately 400 m long, between the rails. The troughs were kept filled with water by means of a float valve connected to a small water treatment and pumping plant adjacent to the rail lines. The water troughs were a means of replenishing the water supply carried in the locomotive's tender, while the train was moving at speed, enabling it to run non-stop between London and Edinburgh, a distance of 633 km. The tender was designed to carry enough coal, but not enough water for this non-stop journey. Water troughs were located along the route every 50 km or so. The locomotive's tender had a narrow passage connecting the locomotive to the rest of the train, enabling a change of driver and fireman along the way.

192

The pick up of water was accomplished by the fireman lowering a mechanical scoop beneath the tender, which entered the trough, forcing the water up into the tender at a rate of 2000 gallons or 9100 litres in 10 seconds. Although water could be picked up at a speed of 90 km/h, 65 km/h had been found to be the most effective speed. The most spectacular part of the process was where the tender reached full capacity, and the excess water was vented by an overflow from the tender, spraying water everywhere until the fireman retracted the scoop. This usually occurred just before but sometimes directly under the bridge. It was a spectacular sight to see, with the excess water looking like a huge water spout.

Water troughs were also installed on many other long distance, non-stop rail routes in Great Britain and some even in the USA. Approaching the water troughs for a water pick up, the driver blew the locomotive's whistle using a code that was the signal for passengers to close any open windows to avoid being soaked with water. The same whistle code was also used before a steam train entered a tunnel. I was now familiar with this whistle code warning of the approaching tunnels at Welwyn, but the first time I used the train a fellow passenger had to tell me to: "Close the window please."

I was very fortunate too that Stevenage had two good golf courses close by, Knebworth where I had already played, and Letchworth a town a little north of Hitchin. In the afternoon after taking the photos, I went up to the Letchworth golf course and played a passable game of golf with an English bloke. The green fees were very expensive compared to those back home, as golf is considered to be a rich man's sport in the UK.

In the evening I rang Bob Langley and arranged to have a drink with him in a pub in Hitchin. He was glad I had rung because he was returning to Australia next month and wanted to see me again. We had a pleasant drink together and I was eager to ask him about Leon, but as usual there seemed to be an invisible wall of silence regarding Leon's wellbeing and movements, which I couldn't quite understand.

While working at Kings there seemed to be one pleasant surprise after another. The next was when Mr Furlough, King's employment officer said that as I was only going to be with Kings for a few months, instead of me being eligible for sick pay, Kings would pay me a little more per hour. I was very grateful to Kings for this arrangement. I told him I would be sorry when it came time for me to leave, because I was very happy working at Kings. I didn't tell Mr Furlough exactly when I would be leaving although I had a tentative date in mind of Friday 12th August.

Tuesday 29th April: I received a letter from my mother. There is no doubt about my mother, she kept up a steady flow of news with her letters that were always so beaut to receive. She enjoyed writing letters and had a beautiful clear style. She wrote that she was missing me a lot. I wrote a long letter back telling her all was well with her son. The spring mornings were quite cold, but the days were fine with plenty of sunshine. The sky, however, was never quite as blue as back home as there was always a slight haze.

I also got a letter from the Orient Line notifying me that I would be put on their waiting list when I sent back the enclosed application form. I filled it in that night to post in the morning. I probably should have enquired what the current waiting time was and the cost of the passage, but I didn't. The Coronation date had not been announced and I certainly wasn't going home until after that. Through letters back and forth to Scotland, it had been arranged that I would be staying with Uncle John and Auntie Greta in Glasgow. Uncle John was the brother of my mother's Aunt Ruby.

I planned to travel by coach or train to Glasgow, where I would stay with my relations for a couple of weeks. I then planned to fly from Scotland to Norway, but I had yet to decide on the route of my next tour.

194

Friday 2nd May: The month of May began badly when the filling Ralph put in my tooth fell out. Ralph apologised for the faulty filling and very soon he refilled it, saying that this time it was in there for good. He also said that he and his wife Gladys were going to a dance that night with a few English friends. He invited me to come along. I had a shower and tea, got dressed and went along to Hitchin to a dance organised by the Conservative Party. Conservative, Tory, Socialist or Labour, I didn't care, because I was about to enter the social life of the county.

When I arrived at the dance hall I was introduced to Ralph's English friends, Brian and Sheila Day, Jim and Jean Spicer, both young, attractive married couples about the same age as me, 24. Ralph pointed out George King, the manager of Kings. Emboldened by a few beers, I approached Mr King and managed to have a short talk with him. I wasn't trying to ingratiate myself, but I bought him a sherry and told him how I was enjoying working at his factory and living at *Fieldview*

I danced with Ralph's lovely wife Gladys and with Sheila and Jean. I also danced with an attractive girl called Marie Lore, who Ralph had introduced me to, as one of his friends. She had brown wavy hair, and very slight buck teeth. I had quite a few drinks, which gave me the courage at the end of the evening to ask Marie if I could see her next weekend. She said she would like to and gave me her phone number. It was a thoroughly enjoyable dance and my entry into the social life of Hertfordshire.

Saturday 3rd May: I went up to London, where I was surprised to see so many people in the streets. It was the soccer, sorry football Cup Final, and many were dressed in the colours of their teams, black and white for Newcastle United, red and white for Arsenal. Most of the shops had their windows decorated with the colours of the clubs. (Newcastle United won the Cup 1 nil). My first objective was to find an overnight place to stay. I intended to spend the night in London and also have a place to stay on other occasions,

195

especially when Netta returned. Strangely, I never thought of looking up the address of a London Youth Hostel.

I went to Australia House where I had seen advertisements for various lodgings when I was there last time. I selected what looked like a suitable one in Clapham Common and travelled out on the tube to have a look. I was elated when I was able to use my limited *Deutsch* to explain to two Iranian men who only spoke *Deutsch* on the platform, how to get to where they wanted to go.

The room in Clapham Common was quite suitable and cheap for my needs, so I booked in for the night. I went back into the West End and walked around London for a while, finishing up at Trafalgar Square where a union demonstration was in progress, a belated part of the May Day celebrations. I was quite interested and stayed to watch for a while. I had been involved in unions soon after I joined the Victorian Railways as an apprentice in 1944. Although apprentices were not required to join a union, my period of apprenticeship coincided with a union campaign for a 40 hour week, to replace the existing 44 hour week in Australia. The campaign was led by the Communist president, J J Brown of the Australian Railways Union. Many mass meetings were held during lunch hours at the workshops, which I attended, first out of curiosity, but later because I was interested in the workings of the union.

Very early in my working life, I learned about the false reporting and distorted truth that newspapers print, when I read the reports on the proceedings of the mass meetings in a newspaper on the way home in the train that night. The reports bore little resemblance to the conduct and agenda of the meetings I had attended.

I believe that newspapers, with very few exceptions are greater distorters of the truth today, than they were 50 years ago. The tabloid newspapers in London that week had been running an exposé of the Masons and one can't help but wonder, how much of this was fact. Very little, I suspect. After a series of rail strikes over six months in

196

1946, the 40 hour week was won and all workers, union members or not, benefited by the shorter working hours and other benefits. During the strike I could not get to work, and had to serve an extra six months to complete my apprenticeship.

I went to a travel agency and enquired about the cost of tickets to Glasgow by coach and rail. The coach ticket was much cheaper. Although I would have preferred to travel by rail, I chose to go by coach and booked a seat for Sunday 3rd August. By booking well ahead I was able to get a discount. The ticket cost me about £5. The coach was scheduled to leave from Victoria Station at 8.30 p.m. for the overnight journey to Glasgow, arriving there at 7 a.m. the next morning. Then I bought tickets for the 5.30 p.m. performance of *The Merry Widow* at the Stoll Theatre and for *Call Me Madam* at the Colosseum at 8.30 p.m. I bought a cheap pair of opera glasses £3 odd, ready for an intensive afternoon and evening of theatre going.

I decided after a quick lunch that I had time to visit Madame Tussaud's Waxworks in Marylebone Road. I found that the wax figures and facial features of many famous people, royals, sportsmen, prime ministers and others were extremely life like and a trifle eerie. The Chamber of Horrors lived up to its name. I was really horrified, so much so, that I advise anyone with a weak stomach to avoid this section. In the Chamber of Horrors there were wax figures of many criminals and murderers, some depicting their gory acts of murder. The most terrifying of all were the models of instruments of torture, showing lots of blood and flesh being ripped from bodies on spiked carousels, the rack and other gruesome exhibits. These more than any of the other wax replicas, have remained in my mind for a long time and I can recall them even to this day.

Leaving the blood and gore behind I entered a new world at the Stoll Theatre again in Kingsway. I was so glad to have the opportunity of seeing *The Merry Widow,* one of Franz Lehar's musicals so soon after being at his summer retreat in Bad Ischl, where he gained so much inspiration for his music. The show was

197

spectacular with lovely music, songs and dance routines, including a lively can-can. I knew none of the cast, but they were all first rate. There are at least two film versions of *The Merry Widow*, one in 1925 and another in 1934. Clark Gable appeared as an extra in the 1925 film and his wife Carole Lombard had a role in the 1934 film.

The next show on this very busy Saturday in London was *Call Me Madam*. To quote the sixpenny program's sparse notes, 'The musical is about a mythical country called Lichtenburg and the United States of America. The action starts when the American government appoints Mrs Sally Adams, a leading, party giving, society lady, to the post of Ambassador to the Grand Duchy of Lichtenburg. She has no diplomatic experience whatsoever, but she has plenty of money and knows how to throw fabulous parties. Her appointment leads to many exciting and amusing events in Lichtenburg, including complications with the American government. She is however, able to transcend all of these with a combination of charm and money.

Call Me Madam surpassed *South Pacific* that I had seen before I left on my first tour in every way. The only member of this cast I had previously heard of was Shani Wallis, a lovely redhead I had heard on the hit parades. She played the part of Princess Marie. Billie Worth played Mrs Sally Adams and Anton Wallbrook took the part of a Litchtenburg Conservative Party leader. Mrs Sally Adams, the ambassador and 'hostess with the mostest,' was modelled on an American hostess, Perle Mesta, who was famous for her party giving and money raising in Washington DC, and was appointed Ambassador to Luxembourg.

I was quite familiar with her exploits, which were reported from time to time in *Time* magazine. It was an absolutely wonderful musical. To my mind, the only other musical in its class that I have seen to this day is Lil Abner. On later visits to London I bought many 78 rpm records of the songs from *Call Me Madam*, and I still have these today in my record collection.

198

Sunday 4th May: After paying 10/6 for board I made my way to Petticoat Lane. I had heard the name Petticoat Lane many years before I came to London, so it was a place I wanted to see. Back at Stevenage I had looked for Petticoat Lane in the index of my map, but couldn't find any such name. My fellow boarders at *Fieldview* told me a little about Petticoat Lane and I found a further explanation in an English guide book. There is no such lane as Petticoat Lane, the name originated in 1602 for the area around Middlesex Street E.1, where traders of that time erected stalls selling cloth and clothing. Due to this activity it became known as 'Petticoat Lane'.

I went by tube train to Aldgate, which was near the centre of the streets set aside on Sundays for street stalls. The stalls now sold much more than cloth and clothing, electrical goods and many other small items. The spruikers on the stalls were quite entertaining, but I found their Cockney accents very hard to understand. I spent an hour or so looking around the stalls, but didn't purchase a thing, except fish and chips for lunch. Then it began to rain, so I caught the bus back to Stevenage, having spent a very busy but rewarding weekend in London.

When I got back to *Fieldview,* I was delighted to receive a letter from Netta in France saying she was having a great time and would tell me all about it when she returned to London at the end of the month. A letter from Roy, my best mate back in Australia, brought me up to date with all the latest YHA news. There was a letter too from Mrs. Wiltshire, saying she would be coming to London and would contact me.

Sunday 11th May; I decided to go down to the railway bridge to try to get some more photos of locomotives picking up water. I managed to get a graphic photo of an express passenger train just as the tender overflowed, but I wasn't able to discern the name of the A4 locomotive or the express train as it all happened so quickly. It was always an exciting experience watching the water pick up either from the side or top of the bridge, especially when the water began to spill just as the tender went under the bridge. I had the strange feeling that in one of my railway books, there was a coloured photo of the *Flying Scotsman* emerging from under a bridge as it picked up water.

I decided that I must put my thoughts into action straight away and write to my parents to see if they could find the book with the picture. I wrote asking my parents if they would look for one of my railway books that had a hard, red cover, with black lettering. I wrote saying that I couldn't remember the name of the book, but if they found it, to see if it had a coloured picture of a locomotive coming under a bridge picking up water from water troughs. If they found it with the picture, would they write and let me know if there was any wording under the picture and any other details in the book. I explained to them why I wanted to know, and if it was what I suspected, it might turn out to be a wonderful coincidence. However, the information was going to take at least ten weeks to get back to me, as both letters went by mail ships to and from Australia

I saw that a local theatre group from Stevenage called The Lytton Players were performing *The Mikado* on 14th May. I was most interested to see my nickname *Nanki Poo* in the comic opera. I rang Marie Lore, the English girl I met at the Conservative dance and asked her if she would like to come with me to see it. She said she was sorry, but was going out that night, I booked a seat.

Wednesday 14th May: I went to see *The Mikado*. It was a very good production. The plot involves Nanki Poo, a wandering minstrel who has come to the city of Titipu to search for and claim Yum Yum, who he fell in love with when he played in a band in Titipu. Nanki Poo is really the son of the Japanese Emperor (the Mikado), in disguise. Eventually, after many amusing events and trials, he gets to claim Yum Yum as his bride and it all ends happily. I don't think I ever looked like Nanki Poo, not the one in this opera anyway. I enjoyed all the wonderful tunes and songs, although not to the extent that I would want to buy any records. I was very amused at the

200

English accents of some of the players, which made some of the dialogue quite hilarious for me. Sometimes I was the only one laughing (quite out of context) at such phrases as "and never coom bark" and words like "joostice" and "pooblic".

I spent a great deal of time after work studying maps and youth hostel handbooks of various countries, trying to decide where I would go after I left Scotland. I had already decided to fly from Scotland to Norway and from Norway I planned a route through Sweden and Denmark, then down through Germany and back to England by way of Holland. I very much wanted to see both Paris and the French Alps, but that would have to wait until my next tour, whenever that was going to be. I wasn't sure at the time because the date of the Coronation had still not been announced, but I imagined it would be in June or July. I expected that immediately after the Coronation many Australians would be looking for a passage home, so I thought I had better decide on a date and book my passage as soon as possible, probably October 1953.

I took a bold step and rang Marie, and asked her if she could meet me in London around noon and I would take her to see a show. She said she would love to. Then I heard that there was a Test cricket match between India and England taking place at Lords. Although I am not a cricket fan and the match didn't involve Australia, I decided I would go along to the morning session to see the famous cricket ground.

Saturday 17th May: I went to London by bus, first to the bank to take out some money, where I received a most welcome surprise, £90 had been added to my bank balance. The bank said it was to do with exchange rates. With a happy heart I went to the Orient Line offices, where one of the brochures that I was given showed the ports that Orient Line ships called into, one of which was Naples. I had a brilliant idea, I would join the ship in Naples, after I had toured down through France and Italy. With a sense of relief, I booked a passage back to Australia from Naples in October 1953 and paid a deposit of

£10. The Orient Line said that they would let me know the exact date of sailing and the ship I would be sailing on. The die was cast.

I took the tube to St John's Wood, the nearest station to Lords. Unlike the Melbourne Cricket Ground, Lords is located unobtrusively in the midst of a residential district to the north of London. The cricket ground was just as I had imagined it to be. The stands are quite small and the playing surface certainly had a bit of a slope to it, much more than I had observed from photos and newsreels I had seen. Two Australian prime ministers have extolled its virtues: Sir Robert Menzies saying it was "the Cathedral of Cricket," and John Curtin, at the end of the Second World War, when he made a visit to Lords, said that "Australians will always fight for the twenty-two yards. Lords and its traditions belong to Australia, just as much as to England." Fine words, but I was certainly not impressed by Lords.

The game I saw was the second day of the Test between India and England, which England won by eight wickets, winning the four match series 3-0. The Simpson I saw, who eventually made 101, was the English R.T. Simpson, not the famous Australian R B. (Bobby) Simpson who captained Australia in later years. I left Lords in plenty of time to meet Marie as we had arranged at King's Cross Station. Marie looked lovely dressed in a neat brown dress that went well with her beautiful, wavy, brown hair.

Our first stop was a cinema nearby where we saw *Bet Your Life,* a comedy starring Groucho Marx. We didn't think it was very funny. We then we walked hand in hand down to Soho where we went into a nightclub called Balsams. Balsams was quite a pleasant place to have a meal with its typical English pub type atmosphere that I was becoming familiar with, but this time a little different, as it had a dance floor. After partaking of a nice meal there, we danced together on the small floor before it was time for us to head back to Hitchin.

I told Marie that before I met her, I had been to Lords Cricket Ground. I told her too that I had been to the Orient Line and had

202

booked my passage home on a ship in October 1953 after the Coronation. It was then about 7 p.m. but with daylight saving it was still quite light. We took the double decker bus back to Hitchin, and we parted with a couple of kisses. Marie said she enjoyed the day with me, and lent me her bike to ride back to Stevenage. It was a wonderful Saturday in many ways, especially now that it seemed I had won myself an English girlfriend.

That night I wrote to tell my parents they could expect me home sometime in October 1953 and all about my first date with an English girl. For my father's benefit, because he was a cricket fan, I told him about my visit to Lords. It was a great relief to have tentatively booked my passage home and into the bargain settle on the route of my last tour through France and Italy.

Sunday 18th May: I rode Marie's bike back along the not very busy Great North Road. Marie and I then went for a walk in a park in Hitchin. I went back to Stevenage by bus and then played golf in the afternoon at Knebworth on a very humid and hot day, 85°F (30°C). It was a surprise to me that it got so hot in England. My golf was not the best, maybe because of the heat, but back home I had never been bothered by this sort of temperature. I suppose it was the humidity that made me so uncomfortable.

I had hiked and camped with the scouts on Phillip Island, a popular holiday location in Victoria with its lovely, long sandy, surf beaches. The island had the added attraction of being able to view, on one of the beaches, the nightly intriguing spectacle of penguins emerging from the sea. I was aware that some place names on Phillip Island such as Cowes and Ventnor, had been so called by the early settlers, because of their perceived likeness to those places on the Isle of Wight in the south of England. I decided I must visit the Isle of Wight. After some thought I decided it would be a nice gesture to invite Bob and Leon Langley to join me. I wrote to each, telling them of my plans. I received Bob's reply the next day. He was very sorry he couldn't come to the Isle of Wight with me.

203

Lord's Cricket Ground

The Flying Scotsman picking up water at the Langley Stevenage troughs

The locomotive tender of an express passenger train spilling excess water

A Merchant Navy photo of my friend Mack

The author at the May Day demonstration in Trafalgar Square sans moustache

Marie my English girl friend

204

He didn't mention Leon, but I was sure he wouldn't be coming. There was no YH on the island and because it was a holiday weekend, I looked up a couple of hotels on the island to stay. I decided to try and book a room at the Channel View Hotel in Ventnor for Saturday 31st May and Sunday 1st June.

Monday 19th May: **It is my birthday** and I was 25 years old on a hot and very muggy day. I really felt the heat in England much more than I ever did back home. No one knew it was my birthday, but over the next week I received many letters from Australia with birthday wishes, as well as one from Auntie Ruby, who I would be seeing in Scotland. I hadn't yet invested in a radio and all there was at *Fieldview* was a communal radio in the lounge room. My fellow boarder's tastes didn't really conform to mine, especially when I wanted to listen to a bit of opera or classical music on the Third Program, a BBC station that broadcasted classical music. The Third Program would be termed 'highbrow', because its programs consisted of talks, plays and the like, similar to our ABC Radio National station in Australia. It goes without saying that the Third Program didn't get much of an airing at *Fieldview.*

Tuesday 20th May: I went by myself to Hitchin to see the movie *The Tales of Hoffman* with Moirer Shearer and Robert Helpmann. The plot is based on Jacques Offenbach's fantasy opera *The Tales of Hoffman.* It is about a student who has bizarre dreams about various stages of his life. Hoffman was actually a real person, an opera composer and novelist. Robert Helpman (now Sir Robert) was an Aussie expatriate in the UK, who was on a working holiday like me, except that mine was not to further my career in the theatre. It was a fantastic movie. Robert Helpmann played the part of four characters brilliantly. This movie with its colourful costumes, make up, décor, dancing, music and singing had everything. Moirer Shearer had a leading role as a ballet dancer, and she also sang. One film guide writer wrote that: 'It was an overwhelming combination of opera, ballet and rich production design, an indigestible hodgepodge with flashes of superior talent.' Another critic, Richard Mallet of *Punch* magazine, wrote: 'An arts director's picnic, I marvelled without being enthralled.' I on the other hand marvelled and was completely enthralled.

This film marked a turning point in Sir Robert Helpmann's life, for it was at this time that he gave up ballet dancing as his forte. His swan song was a three act ballet version of *The Merry Widow,* which he produced and staged at the Sydney Opera House in November 1975. I was glad I saw *The Tales of Hoffman,* because of its unique nature, a combination of ballet and opera.

Friday 23th May: Kings were entering an exhibit in the mechanical handling show in London in June and there was a great rush to complete a segmented wheel I was working on. It was one of the items to be exhibited as part of a conveyor system.

I received a reply from the hotel saying that I was booked into the Channel View Hotel in Ventnor as requested. Ralph told me Jim Spicer invited me to join them that night at a pub where they went each Friday night to wind down after the week, and of course I accepted the invitation. They were the English friends of Brian and Sheila Day who were already there and so too was Marie. It was a pleasant surprise to see Marie and I gathered she had been with them to Henlow on previous occasions.

When we left the Brewhouse Inn, we drove to Brian and Sheila's farmhouse, where. Brian took me down in the dark to show me his hothouses and the big boiler. All of a sudden he opened the firebox door to reveal a huge inferno. In my intoxicated state I thought I was in Hell, but no, this was the boiler and fire that provided the steam to heat the hothouses where tomatoes, cucumbers and other vegetables were grown by Brian.

We played records at Brian and Sheila's farmhouse, dancing together and having a great time. To end the night Brian took Marie and me home. I found that *Fieldview* was locked, so I had to climb through an open window at 2 a.m., much to the amusement of my fellow boarders, who I think were a bit jealous of me for having a good reason to be out so late. This brought the exciting Friday night to a conclusion, a wonderful night with a very friendly group of young English people and my initiation into the social life of Hertfordshire.

Saturday 24th May: I was suffering from a rather big hangover, but I went to work, because I needed the overtime now, to support my newly acquired social life. After work I showered, had dinner and changed. I met Marie and with all of my new English friends went to a dance in Welwyn Garden City, about 20 minutes down the road from Stevenage on the way to London. Brian drove a Hillman station wagon and Jim his Morris Oxford. It was so beaut to have the company of this group, 'the mob' as they called themselves.

The dance was at the 'Cherry Tree' a large dance hall where the band played all the popular tunes I was used to, foxtrots, waltzes and all the other usual dances. I got quite a surprise to see that there was a bar at each end of the dance floor where alcohol could be purchased. Nobody there seemed to have had too much to drink, which to me was understandable, because English beer is never really cold and I found that I was full in the stomach before I was 'full' (drunk), as we say in Australia, although this was not so the previous night. I was both full and drunk.

There were a lot of dancers and almost everyone at the dance was drinking beer including us. I danced with all our girls and Marie, who was lovely to dance with. It was a great night, but afterwards on the way home I was very tired, so I asked Jim to drop me at Stevenage. They were all going back to the Days, but I don't think I would have been very good company if I had gone along with them. One can have too much of a good thing, but the weekend was not over yet. I fell into bed a happy and contented Aussie!

Sunday 25th May 1952: In the afternoon as planned, Jim picked me up and I went with 'the mob' swimming and punting at a place north of Hitchin called Hurdleford where we went punting. It is quite a pleasant experience propelling a boat, or punt, by means of a long pole along a beautiful, small, placid English stream. 'Punting' has no connection to a method of kicking a football in Aussie football. I had seen punting scenes in romantic movies, paintings and photographs. They always seemed to portray a typical English Sunday country escape, the man, complete with a boater hat with ribbon, with his sweetheart, punting in idyllic leafy surroundings. The only difference was that I didn't have a boater hat and ribbon, but I did have my English sweetheart, Marie in the punt beside me.

After we had punted, it was decided we would all go for a swim so I put on a brave face and endured the cold water. If only the English beer was that cold. Then we returned to the Days and played records including some I had purchased of *Call Me Madam.* I asked Marie if she would come with me to London on Saturday week. I wanted to go to the mechanical handling exhibition at Earls Court, and afterwards, I said I would take her to a show in the West End. She said she would, so I wrote to the Colosseum for tickets to see *Call Me Madam,* as I was sure she would love the show and it was so good, and I certainly didn't mind seeing it again.

Monday 26th May: While working on a new project the segmented wheel, Harry Hammond, my foreman, a great bloke, drew me aside to have a talk. He told me that before he worked at Kings, he was a chauffeur-gardener for Mr King. He said that he was very interested in my future plans, especially as Kings were making a large conveyor for Austin of Birmingham, the big English car company. He wanted to know if I would be interested in going to Birmingham to help install a conveyor. The segmented wheel was an integral part of the conveyer. It would be going to Birmingham as soon as the mechanical handling exhibition had closed and the conveyer was complete. I thanked him for the offer, but told him I had booked to go to Scotland in the first week in August. He said that was a pity, but he realised I was on a working holiday. I probably would have accepted his offer, if I had not already booked my ticket on the coach to Scotland. In hindsight I was glad I had, because I was very happy in my current working situation and life in general.

The next day after my talk with Harry I was a very enlightening talk. It was like a match being lit in the darkness. I had been puzzled by the lack of trade knowledge of some of the fitters employed by Kings. However, I was reluctant to ask too many questions about their lack of expertise, after the pay envelope incident. The puzzle was about to be solved, when Bob asked me to make up a sheet metal cover for a paper lifter. These paper lifters were not in continuous production at Kings, they were only manufactured when an order was placed for one. They were used for lifting heavy rolls of paper, the design allowing the rolls to be stacked vertically close together with a saving of storage space. To make the sheet metal cover, which was in the form of a frustum of a cone, I obtained a sheet of 16G steel, and with dividers and rule set about developing the cover. Developing is a method of solid geometry that enables the shape of the surface of a curved object, to be converted into a shape in a flat plane. Having marked the shape out, I took the sheet to the guillotine and cut out the shape, finishing it off with a file before placing it in a roller to bend it to the desired curvature. The whole process took about two hours.

I took it back to Bob and asked him to give me a hand to fasten it to the enclosure. Bob looked very surprised saying: "You did that quickly, how did you do it so fast?" When I told him I had developed it, he obviously didn't understand what I meant, so I asked him. "Didn't you do geometry and development in your apprenticeship?" He replied: "I never had an apprenticeship, I am what is called in the trade. 'A dilutee.'

Bob explained that after the war there was great shortage of skilled workers in most trades. Men and women were recruited and given basic training, enough to allow them to obtain work in the various trades up to their level of competence. I was now very curious to learn Bob's method of making a cover when one was required for a paper lifter, so I asked him. He told me that he would get a large piece of thin cardboard, lay it over and around the enclosure, cut it to the required shape with a pair of scissors to make it fit. He would then use this as a template to trace out the shape on the metal sheet, prior to cutting to the required shape.

Now I realised why I have been offered advancement at Kings, and why I had been puzzled by the lack of expertise demonstrated by some of the 'tradesmen' employed there. One further point of interest in this enlightening experience was that Bob took me aside, and asked me to show him how I developed the frustum shaped cover, but to please not show any of the other dilutee fitters.

Those two enlightening experiences at Kings, especially the last one, prompted me to have a good think about my future. Kings was a very good company to work for. They were offering me more responsibility and wanted to upgrade me. That would have been great, especially the extra money together with more interesting work. I thoroughly enjoyed living in Stevenage, even the climate that I had experienced so far was quite pleasant. I had ready access to London as well as a couple of golf courses nearby. My social life with my new English friends and my girlfriend Marie could not have been better. She seemed to enjoy my company and I hers, but I certainly didn't want to let it get serious.

Wednesday 28th May: Mack, my cockney friend at Kings, invited me to tea with him and his wife Mary. I was glad to accept. After work I walked with Mack to his house in Stevenage Newtown, about a kilometre behind *Fieldview*. I met his charming wife, and we had a very nice hot meal of stew together. Afterwards we talked about ourselves. They asked me to tell them all about life in Australia and my family, which of course I did.

They told me they were very happy living in Stevenage Newtown, as everything was really new. It was quite a large development with most of the houses, including theirs, in row upon row of cottages, with very little front or back garden, bordering the newly made streets. Mack told me they were paying 35 shillings a week for their two bedroom, double storey unit. I thoroughly enjoyed the evening and meal with them. It was most interesting to see Stevenage Newtown a large new development, and a very valuable asset to Stevenage and to the working man.

Just before the Whitsun holiday weekend we completed the indented wheel, much to our foreman Harry's relief. It was now ready in good time for showing at the mechanical handing exhibition.

CHAPTER 13

THE THIRD BACKPACKING TOUR

A map of the Isle of Wight showing the location of towns and villages the author visited and the rail and coach routes along which he travelled.

STEVENAGE TO LONDON

Saturday 31st May: It was raining a little when I caught an early train from Stevenage to King's Cross. When I alighted from the train who should I see, but Bob Langley. It's a small world. We both had time to spare, so we went and had a drink together. I hadn't expected to see him again before he left for Australia, and this meeting was a pleasant bonus. Bob was always very guarded about offering any information about Leon's movements. This occasion was no different, but I should have 'thrown caution to the winds' and asked Bob straight out: "What was it with Leon?" I didn't, and regret it to this day. Whether Bob would have told me anything I don't know. Bob however, was always good company. We parted with a warm handshake and good wishes, for his safe voyage back to Australia.

LONDON TO PORTSMOUTH

I took an electric, third rail train to Portsmouth. The 63 mile journey was quite fast and by 11.30 a.m. I was in Portsmouth.

PORTSMOUTH

PORTSMOUTH TO RYDE

I left the train at the famous town of Portsmouth, the home of the British Navy. It was heavily bombed during the war and there was still some bomb damage visible. I straightway boarded the ferry to Ryde and on the way I saw various grey warships, including *HMS Eagle,* a huge aircraft carrier tied up at the extensive wharves. I left the ferry at Ryde, the port on the north eastern shore of the Isle of Wight, where there was a steam train waiting to take me to Ventnor.

RYDE ISLE OF WIGHT

RYDE TO VENTNOR

From Ryde I caught a train to Ventnor. Along the 14 mile trip the train passed through the small town of Brading, then along the east coast above the villages of Shanklin and Sandown, through undulating land broken up into pastures and fields by hedges and Cyprus trees. At 3 p.m. the train arrived at my destination of Ventnor the terminus of the line. The train was hauled by a small tank locomotive. The carriages were certainly not modern, but comfortable. There was no doubt that during my visit I would not be able to refrain from comparing the island with Phillip Island in my home state of Victoria, which of course was the reason for my visit.

VENTNOR

I expected to see lots of tourists, but there were not many to be seen on this Whitsun holiday weekend, with the following Monday being a bank holiday. Whit Sunday is the seventh Sunday after Easter, commemorating Pentecost, the Jewish harvest festival.

I found my way to the Channel View Hotel quite easily. It was high above the sea, which accounted for its appropriate name. After booking in, I strolled down to the township and had a meal. Ventnor was the first town on the island I visited with the same name as one on Phillip Island. Ventnor on the Isle of Wight rises from the English Channel in a series of terraces to a height of 600 m. Ventnor on Phillip Island is also on the ocean. It has no cliffs, and is on flat ground behind Ti tree covered bluffs that separate the beach from the town.

I purchased an *Isle of Wight Guide Book* and had a good look around the town. I booked a coach tour of the island for the morning. In the evening I went to a dance which was very enjoyable. The long day ended when I climbed into a very comfortable bed and fell fast asleep.

SOUTH OF ISLAND COACH TOUR

Sunday 1st June: In fine weather, I boarded a large coach that left Ventnor and climbed steeply above the town. After a short drive

214

we came to Wroxhall, a village surrounded by high downs. The dictionary defines a 'down' as 'open high land.' There were about a dozen tourists on the bus, and by their accents I thought most were English and Scots. After Wroxhall the coach made its way up to the downs, where we passed through the small villages of Branstone, Horringford and Downend.

The bus driver was a bit of a comedian and kept us entertained with plenty of information about the countryside, interspersed with a few inane jokes like the following example: Just before we entered Downend, he brought the coach to a halt, and pointed to an old church at the bottom of the hill, saying in his quaint English accent: "If the brakes don't work, we'll all finish up in Sunday school, Ha Ha!" The brakes did work so we continued on our tour, descending gradually from the downs and turning to the east until we came to Brading, a village that I had passed through yesterday in the train.

St Helens was the next town on our tour, an unusual place as the town was built around a large green. Nelson used St Helens as an anchorage for his ships because of its small protected inlet. The coach drove around to the south side of the inlet, and crossed over the branch railway line to Bembridge that left the main line at Brading. The gates were manually operated by the signalman.

Bembridge our next town on the tour was endowed with beautiful, wide, sandy beaches bordered by high cliffs. My guide book said that there was a nine hole golf course in the town, but I didn't catch a glimpse of it when the coach took a short tour around the town.

Leaving Bembridge we travelled down to the picturesque beachside town of Sandown, which has a jetty and a long esplanade, with hotels and guest houses along one side of the esplanade, and the beach on the other. I was pleased to see not only that the beach was nice and wide, but that the sand was a clean, sandy colour, much the same as Bembridge. Sandown I thought was an ideal beach resort for children because of its gently sloping beaches. The coach driver told us there was a golf course here also, with a green shaped like the Isle of Wight, surrounded by water, a classic island green, which I would very much have liked to have seen.

Melbourne has a suburb called Sandown, but it is a long way inland from a beach, nothing like Sandown on the Isle of Wight. I couldn't help but wonder how the early English settlers could see some comparison between the two. Perhaps they didn't. They just wanted to use the name, maybe because they came from Sandown on the Isle of Wight.

We stopped for a short while to allow us to walk down to the beach where it was pleasing to see people sunbathing, although I noticed that not many were in the water. The last stop on the coach tour before returning to Ventnor was the seaside town of Shanklin, about 5 km further along the long, curving coastline from Sandown. Shanklin the guide book informed me, 'has held the British annual sunshine record for more years than any other resort.' The Shanklin jetty just short of a kilometre long, was used as the starting point for Pluto, a pipeline that extended under the Channel to Cherbourg in France through which petrol was pumped during the war to supply the Allied Forces.

The coach took us back to Ventnor, where we thanked the driver for his commentary. I went back to the hotel and talked to two Australian girls who had just booked in. They were qualified nurses and were both nursing in a hospital in London. They said they had no trouble finding nursing work as there was a shortage of qualified nurses.

VENTNOR TO RYDE COACH TOUR

Monday 2nd June: During yesterday's coach tour, I saw a large part of the eastern side of the Isle of Wight. Today the last day of my holiday, I joined a coach tour to the western side of the island. The tour ends in Ryde where I will catch the ferry to begin the journey back to Stevenage. After paying the Channel View Hotel's bill of £2/3/6, which I thought was quite reasonable, I climbed aboard the

216

coach that took us to the west over the downs. We passed a number of small villages with names all ending in stone. Brightstone, Limerstone, Matterstone and Milverstone. My guidebook explained that this was because of the proximity to the famous 'Long Stone,' a huge, rough, quadrangular pillar, of iron sandstone, but sadly the tour never took us to see it, a highlight of a coach tour I would have thought. Next was the village of Freshwater, a short distance inland from Freshwater Bay. Freshwater is the terminus of another branch of the extensive Isle of Wight railway, which the coach crossed. The gates here were also operated manually.

Further on the coach entered Totland, a small seaside village on the shores of the Solent, the stretch of sea that separates this island from the mainland of the county of Hampshire. The Solent provides access for large liners going to Southampton. I wondered if our ship the *Moreton Bay,* had taken this passage along the western side of the island, or whether it was the eastern passage between Ryde and Portsmouth.

The next point of interest was Alum Bay, but the coach could not take us all the way there. We had to leave the coach and walk down a steep path to the beach, where at the extreme end of Alum Bay I could see the famous Needles, with a lighthouse standing at the far end. The Needles are three massive chalk rocks rising 90 feet from the sea. Originally there were four, but the fourth, a sharper needle collapsed into the sea in 1764.

The Nobbies and Seal Rocks on Phillip Island in Victoria bear a vague similarity to The Needles, as both rise above the sea and are located on the south western end of the island. The Alum Bay sandstone cliffs are stratified with different colours, red, green, yellow and grey. Stalls had been set up on the small beach to sell samples of these coloured sands in little bottles, but I wasn't tempted to buy any.

On most of the island downs, I saw farms here and there, with small scrubby trees scattered around, together with the ubiquitous, cypress bordered fields. Here and there large vineyards could be seen. The wine from these is said to be some of the best in Great Britain.

The next stop was Yarmouth, another seaside town and a favourite anchorage for yachts. We had lunch there before moving on to Cowes 10 miles away. On the way we passed a large forest, about the only concentration of trees I saw on the island. I was aware of Cows since my early childhood. Mrs Clarke whose husband was killed in WWII lived in our street in Rosanna. She managed a large guest house called the *Isle of Wight Hotel* in Cowes on Phillip Island. Not only are both townships of Cowes the largest seaside towns on their respective islands, but both are identically located in the centre of the north coast. Cowes on the Isle of Wight lies on the west side of the River Medina, which forms an estuary where it enters the Solent. Across the water I spied a large building like an aircraft hanger. The driver said it was Saunders Roe, a company that built many types of aircraft including flying boats.

The coach stopped, and we had a short walk along the Cowes foreshore looking out across the Solent to the mainland. I felt that Cowes and its foreshore promenade, was not as pretty as the foreshore and beach at Cowes on Phillip Island. Queen Victoria and her husband Prince Albert spent their holidays in Cowes at Osborne House, a large mansion in East Cowes, where Queen Victoria died in 1901. Our Government House in Melbourne, built in 1872 is a replica of Osborne House in Cowes, another link with my home state of Victoria. Cowes main claim to fame is centred on yachts, in fact it is regarded in yachting circles as the 'Home of Yachting.' Each year in early August a regatta is held in Cowes, which plays host to many members of the Royal Family, distinguished people and famous yachtsmen who come from around the world to sail and race.

The coach then drove us to Newport on the River Medina, just before the river opens out to become an estuary. It is quite a large town with many historic buildings and churches. Newport is a name

218

that is very dear to my heart, for I served my time as an apprentice fitter and turner at the Newport railway workshops in Victoria. Both Newports are alike as both are railway junctions. Newport, as well as being the railway hub of the island is also its commercial centre. It is the central place to stay to make excursions to the Isle of Wight's towns, villages and beaches by either coach or rail. Railway lines radiate from Newport to Ryde, Freshwater, Cowes and Ventnor, the town I travelled to on Saturday and stayed in the hotel there.

The Isle of Wight's railway system had a total of 55 miles of lines across the island. The railway was gradually built between the years 1862 to 1920. I was very fortunate to travel on the section from Ryde to Ventnor because beginning in 1952 the year of my visit, the railway was being dismantled, although I saw no evidence of this. Leaving Newport, I had my last look at the island's countryside as the coach travelled across a gently, rolling green landscape to my final island destination of Ryde,

RYDE TO PORTSMOUTH

I caught the ferry back to Portsmouth and then boarded the train back to London.

|||||||||||||||||||||||||

PORTSMOUTH TO STEVENAGE

The train from Portsmouth was a corridor train and I went for a walk along the train. Imagine my surprise, when I discovered that a local pub had been spirited aboard the train! Was I dreaming? No, it was a complete replica of a small local pub with polished wooden bar, stools and tables. It was in fact a 'club car,' which was sometimes attached to holiday trains. Of course I had a pint of brown ale, which was a great finish to an enjoyable and instructive three days on the beautiful Isle of Wight. I arrived back at Fieldview at 9.30 p.m., tired after a marvellous Whitsunday weekend. I had spent about £6 odd, which I thought was money well spent. and a valuable birthday present for myself.

219

The street where Mack lives in Stevenage Newtown

Mack and his wife Mary on the front porch of their house

The high speed electric train to Portsmouth

A tank locomotive hauling an Isle of Wight train

A view of the Ventnor foreshore from the Channel View Hotel

The long lovely Sandown beach

Saunders Roe hangers in Cowes

Osborne House Cowes

STEVENAGE

Now that I had explored the Isle of Wight, I found that the similarities between Phillip and Wight were very real. Both islands, Phillip and Wight are similar in size and shape. The Isle of Wight is 36 km long and 20 km wide, whereas Phillip Island is 33 km long and 16 km wide. Both are also roughly the same shape, with a peninsula in the south west that extends out to the ocean. Phillip Island does not have inland down country, but a gently rolling, low landscape, with many isolated clusters of eucalypt trees. It is the home of many koalas, and penguins can be seen emerging from the sea each night on the southern side of the island.

Two large differences are immediately apparent. Phillip Island is connected to the mainland by a bridge, but has no trains. The similarity of names is of course striking, with towns that have identical names, such as Cowes, Ventnor, Sandown and Newport, and it was very pleasing to see that the Isle of Wight has many sandy beaches just like Phillip Island.

Back at Stevenage all was going well. I now had an English girl friend Marie, but I made doubly sure there was to be no hint of any it becoming serious because I would be leaving on my next tour in August !952. My social life with the English married couples and Aussie mate Ralph was very pleasurable. My fellow boarders at *Fieldview* were a great lot of blokes too. I got to know a few different things about my workmate Bob and how an Englishman in the work force differs from an Aussie. I discovered that Bob was not a tradesman but a 'dilutee' so called because men like him were trained to do a particular job in a factory. Tradesmen were scarce after the war and these dilutees played an important role in getting the UK back to industrial strength after the war.

Friday, 6th June: I worked only until 5 p.m. then after tea I went to Henlow with the mob. I had a great time, especially with Marie at my side. I asked Marie if she would like to come to London with me tomorrow to see an exhibition and then go and see a show. She said she would. My parents sent me a roll of newspapers, both local and daily, that brought me up to date with some of the events back home. It was a nice thought of my parents to send them and I wrote back straight away to tell them how much I had enjoyed reading them.

Saturday 7th June: This was the day of the Mechanical Handling Exhibition in London. I worked until noon, then met Marie and we went by bus to London. We took the tube out to Hammersmith, the nearest tube station to the Olympia Exhibition Centre. This centre is one of the main sites for exhibitions held in London. I was thrilled to see my paper lifter and the segmented wheel I had worked on at Kings, as well as many other wonderful exhibits. Mechanical handling equipment was really a new technology for me, but I found all the exhibits very interesting and informative. Marie was also interested in the show, especially as I was able to explain to her some of the uses of the machines on display, and at the same time educate myself. After the Exhibition we returned to the West End, where I bought a 78-rpm record of a song from *Die Drei Groschen Opera,* and some records from *Call Me Madam.* I explained to Marie what the *Die Drei Groschen Opera* was all about, and where I first saw it performed, but I don't think she was too interested.

Neither of us realised that today was the Queen's official birthday and the Trooping of the Colour ceremony. The only part of this traditional, colourful parade we managed to see, was at the conclusion of the parade. The Coldstream Guards Band at Whitehall, with their pussy willow hats, heralds and beautifully trained horses were absolutely magnificent. I decided that I must remember the date for next year. I told Marie that in Victoria my home state, the weekend was also recognised as the Queen's Birthday. To mark the occasion Monday was a public holiday. The weekend however, was more important to us skiers, as the official opening of the ski season.

We had a quick meal and then it was off to see *Call Me Madam,* which I thought was even more enjoyable than the first time I saw it. I suppose part of the enjoyment of this performance, was because I had Marie to share it with. When Jean and Jim Spicer heard that we were going to see the show, they decided to book and come along too. Although they weren't sitting next to us, we had arranged to meet them after the show, to get a ride home in their car. Jean and Jim agreed that it was one of the best musicals they had ever seen. The song 'You Are in Love' had five encores. To end an especially enjoyable day in London with my English girlfriend, was exciting to be driven home along the Great North Road at an extremely fast speed by Jim Spicer in the Morris Oxford.

Sunday 8th June: After lunch I played golf at Knebworth, but it started to rain so I gave up after three holes. In the evening I went up to Marie's, where I met her brother, who seemed to be a good bloke, but I didn't meet Marie's mother and father as they were out.

Tuesday 10th June 1952: Before I left for work this morning, a uniformed man came to the door at *Fieldview* and asked for me. It was quite a shock, but I had a clear conscience. He handed me a packet and asked for 8 shillings and 1 penny customs duty. I was rather taken aback, but he explained that he was a customs officer, and that the packet contained a satchel of tobacco. I paid him the money and off he went. I suddenly remembered that in a letter to my mother a couple of months ago, I had asked her to send me a packet of Havelock ready rubbed tobacco. I had been rolling my own cigarettes, because cigarettes and tobacco were expensive in England and not the best quality. I had been reduced to buying cheap Wild Woodbines in packets of five, but they weren't very good either. That night I wrote a letter to thank my mother for the tobacco and asked her not to send any more, as it didn't work out any cheaper.

It was much more relaxing working at Kings after the exhibition at Olympia and it was back to work with Bob on the overhead cranes. That afternoon, the next event of significance in my working life at Kings, was a row I had with my workmate Bob. The argument was about unions, or lack of unions, at Kings. I told Bob that the union slogan: 'In unity there is strength' applied equally to a tug of war as it does to many other team endeavours in life.

I told him that I believed in compulsory unionism and the 'closed shop,' a practice that many professional alliances also adopt, and defend vigorously. I said to Bob: "Any gains won by union activity should not pass on to parasitic workers, who are perfectly willing to let others do all the hard work." I hoped that I had made my point, and had given Bob something to think about. We returned to our work without any hard feelings. I didn't say so to Bob, but I reckoned that dilutees like him, lived a charmed life in industry. They have a good job, but do not want to join a union, and do not really appreciate what having a trade is all about.

My next tour itinerary was only in the initial stages, except for the fortnight I intended to spend in Scotland with Uncle John and Auntie Greta. I had not booked into any youth hostels in the countries I intended to visit, but purchased YH guide books for Norway, Sweden and Denmark. I already had a German guidebook. With all of these I was checking out which towns and cities had youth hostels, and if there were any conditions that applied, such as an age limit, but there wasn't. Belatedly, I realised I was only 24 years old when I was in Zermatt, so I could have stayed in a YH there, but it could not have been better than staying in the Tannenhof pension. Chances are too that I would not have serendipitously met Walter, and gone on the tour around the Matterhorn.

Friday 13th June: I received my pay packet, the best so far, £9/10. There was some sort of a tax rebate included. Being Friday night, it was up to the Brewhouse again. Poor Marie, silly girl, mixed her drinks and suffered the consequences. Normally she just drank beer with me, but this night she decided to have a few gin squashes as well. She was sick all the way back to Sheila's house. Brian took Marie home, where she discovered she had lost her handbag. Ralph rang the Brewhouse and found she had left it there, so he went and got it for her.

224

I had given Sheila a record from *Call Me Madam,* which we played as well as other records. I was so fortunate to be part of the Friday night mob, because it was always great fun, that is, except for this time for Marie. I eventually climbed into bed back at *Fieldview* in a rather poor condition.

Saturday14th June: On a lovely evening after work I went to Hitchin to see Marie. I was glad to see that she had made a full recovery. We went for a walk in a park amidst lovely flowerbeds and trees in blossom. It was nearly 10 p.m., but the sun had still not set. I had been surprised by the absolute abundance of beautiful flower displays everywhere in this country in springtime. In Australia, I had never been as conscious of the advent of spring as I was in England, witnessing the rapid blooming of flowers of all shapes and vivid colours that seemed to be everywhere I looked. The song, *'Spring is Busting Out All Over,'* from the musical *Carousel,* was certainly true of this time in England.

Although the display of flowers was beautiful, I am more excited by the sight of a beautiful woman, or a snow covered mountain. Back home in an exercise book, I had a pressed many lovely species of alpine flowers I collected while hiking on the Bogong High Plains. It could not be said that I was completely lacking in my appreciation of the beauty of flowers, certainly not the alpine variety anyhow.

I rode Marie's bike from Hitchin back to Stevenage, which was quite an experience as it was then nearly dark. Although Marie's bike had good lights, I had to be very careful cycling at night along the Great North Road, because there was quite a lot of traffic.

Sunday 15th June: When I rode back to Hitchin the next afternoon, Marie invited me to stay for tea. I met her parents, a charming, middle age couple. They put on a nice tea of sausages and vegetables, thankfully not a Baker style high tea. Afterwards we all retired to the lounge, where I was asked a lot of questions about myself and Australia. I enjoyed meeting Marie's parents, but I thought I would have to be careful about my friendship with Marie because that was all it was. Although I was very fond of her, I felt she was getting a little too involved with me for her own good, even though I had told her the day we were in London together that I had made a tentative booking to return to Australia next year.

Friday 20th June: Instead of the usual trip to the Brewhouse, it was the Conservative ball, a black tie affair. Once again my dinner suit came in handy. I was so glad I had brought it with me along with my golf clubs. I sent the suit out to get pressed before the ball because it had contracted a bad case of the creases. The ball was a gala affair and most enjoyable. Marie and I danced most of the dances, but I felt very sorry for Ralph without a partner. Of course all the girls danced with him. I had a short talk with Mr King, but I didn't offer to buy him a sherry this time. Besides, it was his turn to shout me and perhaps tell me what a wonderful job I was doing at his factory, but he didn't do that either.

I had written to my former girl friend Judy about coming to London on this coming Saturday. I asked her if I could take her to a show and stay the night at her place. The next day we could visit two YH girls, who we both knew. The last time I had seen Judy, she said if I ever came to London I could sleep on the couch. Judy and I had been lovers, and we dated regularly. Back home, the first time I took Judy back home after a show in the city, I found she lived in a large, double storey house in Kew and her father was a very successful estate agent.

This revelation gave me an acute inferiority complex, because I didn't think I was Judy's social equal, although I was proud of my trade as a fitter and turner, and was making a lot of money in my new job with Tom Webb. Judy said she didn't care what work I did, because she loved me. I was certainly in love with Judy, an elegant, square jawed blonde. It was a happy and exciting time for both of us, dating and going on trips together with YHA. Then all of a sudden Judy kept making excuses for not being able to see me. When we did

226

at last get together again, she told me she was going overseas. I was devastated. Judy left Australia for the UK in an Italian ship, the *Ugolino Vilvaldi* of the Lloyd Triestino Line. I didn't go to see her off, because she made a point of not telling me her sailing date and time. However, Judy was the catalyst for me leaving Australia and going abroad. So I have Judy, Tom Webb and of course Leon, to thank for the wonderful life I have had.

The last time I phoned Judy, we agreed that we would keep in contact with each other. This we did, a few letters passing between us over the year before I left Australia. A day or so later, amongst the mail from my mother and Uncle John in Glasgow, was a reply from Judy saying it was OK for the next weekend. However, there was a postscript written in *Deutsch; 'Aber es ist kein moglich zu schlafen zusammen.'* ('But it is not possible to sleep together'). Why did Judy write this in *Deutsch*? I believe she was too much of a lady to write such delicate words in English. In just over a month I would be leaving on my next tour, and if Judy and I were to get together again, it would have to wait until I returned to London. Besides, I was very happy in Stevenage. I was still managing to save about £2 from my pay each week, even with the rather hectic social life I was leading.

Saturday 21st June: I went to London as usual by double decker bus. As the bus passed through Hatfield from the top deck I could look over the brick wall to where the de Havilland Aircraft Company had its factory. De Havilland was the manufacturer of the beautiful new, four engine jet, passenger aircraft, the *Comet*. I could see some of these aircraft on the tarmac with their silver fuselages gleaming in the sun. In the previous month the *Comet* had made its first scheduled flight between London and Johannesburg, a great advance in aviation.

As soon as I arrived in London, I made a booking with SAS (Scandinavian Airline System) for Thursday 25th August, to fly from Prestwick in Scotland to Stavanger on the west coast of Norway. I paid a deposit of £5. I just loved being in London. I took the tube out to Judy's digs in Earls Court. It was exciting to meet and be with Judy once again. I took her in my arms and kissed her. I told her I loved her and how much I missed her, but got little response.

Neither of us mentioned the *Deutsch* phrase she had used in her letter. We talked about what we had been doing and our plans for the future. Judy said: "That considering our previous relationship, we were both now literally in a different world and it would be best to just carry on seeing each other as we are now." She went on to say; "I am working for the Brazilian Embassy and have a Brazilian boyfriend."

In the evening we saw the musical *Blue For a Boy*, a sentimental, enjoyable musical, no more, no less. It was quite an unusual feeling to come out of the show to find that it was still daylight, but at this time of the year, it didn't get dark until after 10 p.m. Judy said it was the longest day of the year. Back at Judy's place we had a cup of coffee and a nice cuddle, but that was all. Then it was off to bed, Judy to hers and me on the couch. Back in Melbourne years later, I could not find any mention of *Blue For a Boy* in any musical reference book. I don't have the program, Judy must have kept it.

Sunday 22nd June 1952: We lazed around and talked in the morning, then in the afternoon we went to Rosemary and Joan's flat in Notting Hill. It was great to get together again. There were hugs and kisses all round The last time we had seen each other was back home at YHA in Melbourne. I was very surprised to see Bruce Norman there, another YHA friend of ours from Melbourne. He had just set foot in London. We were introduced to another man, Joc Cordner, who was to be married the next day. He was not a member of YHA, but a friend of the girls.

There was a constant babble of voices from the animated gathering of expatriates, as we all recounted our experiences of living in the UK. Rosemary and Joan were nursing in London through an agency. Soon it was time for Judy and me to leave, so we

228

wished Joc Cordner good luck for his marriage the next day. Joan and Rosemary asked us to keep in touch, and with hugs we left. I took Judy back home where we kissed goodbye, with both of us expressing the desire to see each other again.

Monday 23rd June: There were many letters waiting for me on Monday evening, one from my mother and one from Roy. Another letter from Lois Sandwell telling me not to write to her again, as she had fallen madly in love with Teddy Mohn a very good YHA friend of mine, and was going to marry him.

I had been dating Lois before I left for the UK. The last time I saw her she asked me to write to her every now and again about my experiences. I wrote to Lois about once a month describing the highlights of my journey, but I had actually stopped writing to Lois a month or so ago, because in all that time she had never written to me once. I discovered later that Lois was using the contents of my letters in some sort of travel segment, broadcast from a Perth radio station. I sat down to digest it all. There were more letters to read. An invitation to John Loughnan and Lois Nutting's wedding. They were both two, 'beautiful, YHA people' and a perfect couple. I looked out a special card to send to them, but sadly I wouldn't be able to be at their wedding.

Wednesday 25th June: I wrote to everyone asking them to address their letters to me care of Australia House. All of the mail sent from Australia to the UK, except that sent by airmail, took four to five weeks by steam ship. From this time on, any mail from Australia, would arrive after I had left Stevenage. Later that evening at *Fieldview* we were startled by a very loud whining noise and we all rushed outside. Above us, virtually blotting out the sky, we saw a large, dark, triangular, winged jet aircraft, which was very low and appeared to be moving very slowly, heading north. The boys at *Fieldview* thought it was a delta wing *Vulcan* bomber, and was probably heading for an airfield near Bedford. It really was a menacing sight, the first jet aircraft I had ever seen and heard actually flying. The only other jets I had seen were the *Comets* on the tarmac at de Havilland at Hatfield from the top deck of the bus.

Friday 27th June: It was Friday night again and off we went to the Brewhouse. It was a hot night and this time it was me that had too much to drink. Afterwards as usual we went to Sheila and Brian's house to play cards, play records and dance, but I was too full to enjoy it. The next morning I was really in a bad way, but despite all logic, I went to work. At 10 a.m. after putting my fingers down my throat, I felt better. I left Kings and went back to *Fieldview* where I slept for 2 hours in the sun in the garden. After that I felt fit and healthy again. I returned to work in the afternoon. I wasn't going to miss out on overtime if I could possibly help it.

Sunday 29th June: It was a very hot day, 86°F (30°C) and I was still suffering from a hangover, but decided that a game of golf at Knebworth (10 shillings a round) might have a revitalising effect. I had a good game and drove the ball well. I felt much better after my game of golf. Many years later, I read that Nick Faldo the champion English golfer, was born in Welwyn Garden City in 1957. He learnt to play golf on the Welwyn Garden City course and was a member there in his amateur days. He also played on the Knebworth course.

I met Marie and we went to a cinema. Afterwards we went a walk in the park where we had a kiss and cuddle session. As we walked home, by the way Marie was acting and talking, I knew she was getting a bit too serious about me. I thought it was about time I told Marie my plans for the future. I told her that in August when I left Stevenage, I would probably not be able to see her again.

She paused for a moment and then said: "If that's so, I had better not see you any more then!" We talked a little more, both deciding that we would not see each other again until the next Friday night at the Brewhouse. I walked Marie home and held her in my arms for a moment and then we parted.

On the way back to Stevenage in the bus, I wondered if I had taken a gentlemanly course by telling her my plans. She was my first

English girlfriend and was a lovely, sweet companion. We had of course indulged in harmless 'love making,' but in no way had I led her on to believe that there was anything permanent in our relationship. From the time when we began going out together, Marie knew my plans for the future. I was very fond of her and would be truly sorry when I left her and Stevenage the following month. But I knew the difference between being fond of a girl and being in love, and I was not in love with Marie.

Monday 30th June: On the last day of June I received a long awaited letter from Netta saying that she and Nellie were safely back in London. Netta invited me to spend a weekend with her and stay overnight at her flat. She wanted to book a show for us in the West End. I wrote back straight away saying I would be looking forward to seeing her at the weekend, and going to a show together would be great. It seemed to be a very long time since I had left her and Nellie in Grindelwald. Netta's return was welcome in many ways, as I was looking forward so much to seeing her again and hearing all about her travels. Netta's return also served to take my mind off Marie.

After tea I went down by myself to Our Mutual Friend, a pub in Stevenage. It was a beautiful evening as I sat and drank in the beer garden, watching the sun go down. Netta's return had somehow brought me back to reality, So ended a busy month of letters going back and forth, and the not altogether successful relationships with the fairer sex.

Thursday 3rd July: The first week in July I received a swag of letters from various friends, among them one from Marg Edney. She invited me to a party in London, but I had to decline because the party was on a week day evening. I first met Marg, a very attractive blonde and university graduate, at a YHA party. I dated her a few times and was flattered that she found my company agreeable.

Friday 4th July: I went up to the Brewhouse with Ralph and the mob, but Marie wasn't there. I missed her not being by my side, but a pleasant night was had by all. Jean Spicer was very anxious to learn all about my relations with Marie, so I told her the story. She said I did the right thing by Marie–at the right time. We finished the evening with an egg and bacon supper at Sheila's.

Saturday 5th July: I worked until 4 p.m. and caught the bus to London. It was a nice trip admiring all to be seen from the top deck of the double decker. I met Netta at the Palladium in Argyll Street. We saw *The Jack Benny Show*. It was wonderful to see Netta again and we had a real big hug. She had bought tickets beforehand, because she knew I particularly liked Jack Benny's subtle, self deprecating, style of comedy. The best film I saw him in was *To Be or Not Be* with Carole Lombard. Jack Benny was accompanied by Billie Russell, an English comedian, who brought back many happy memories for me. I grew up listening to his act; 'On Behalf of the Working Classes' on one of my father's 78 rpm records. I was not impressed by the other supporting act, an American singer and comedian, but overall Netta and I enjoyed the show immensely.

Afterwards, back at the flat in Clapham, which Netta shared with other young people from Canada, New Zealand, and Ireland, she told me about her travels in France, Spain and Italy. Rome. I imagined would have had a great attraction and significance for Netta as a Catholic. Netta wanted to see a bullfight in Spain, but missed out because it was the wrong season.

Netta and Nellie hitchhiked quite successfully around all of those countries without any trouble or harassment. Riding in buses in Rome however, Netta said that she was repeatedly pinched on the bum by Italian men.

I told Netta and Nelly about my life in Stevenage and my job at Kings. They were impressed. Netta was back at her job as a stenographer with a London company. I slept the night on a very comfortable couch.

Sunday 6th July: After a late breakfast and lunch Netta and I strolled through Hyde Park. We watched and listened to the Sunday soap box orators, a new experience for both of us. They talked about

232

every conceivable subject. Religion of all persuasions, of course politics, including Communism and many other items of interests. There was a policeman on hand to subdue anyone who got too carried away in the repartee between the orator and the onlooker. Surely I thought, this was a true manifestation of a working democracy. Netta and I parted in the afternoon at Marble Arch. Netta went to an hour show, and I went to a tourist agency and paid a deposit on a flight from Scotland to Norway on my next tour, I went back to Stevenage by train. The two days I had with Netta were very pleasant. We enjoy each other's company and have so much in common. I was I think beginning to wish she wasn't a Catholic, no not really.

Monday 7th July: When I worked at the Victorian Railways I gave blood periodically to the Red Cross Blood Bank in the city. After our blood was taken, we were given a nice hot cup of tea and biscuit, and were required to rest for half an hour before returning to work. Not so at Kings. This morning the Red Cross came to King's factory in a special mobile unit. I volunteered because I thought it would be good for some of my Aussie colonial blood, to be infused into an English recipient. The procedure was nothing like it was back home. In I went, blood was taken, out I came. No cup of tea or biscuit, no rest period, straight back to work. I wondered if this had become such a common procedure under wartime conditions, that the niceties were not considered necessary.

Friday 11th July: It was off to the Brewhouse again. Marie was there too, but I was sorry to see that she had cut her hair. We talked casually during the night, but nothing more.

Saturday 12th July: I worked until 4 p.m. then went to a dance at Hitchin I danced with a girl called Vivienne from Letchworth, an intelligent girl who had the most beautiful skin I had ever felt, as we danced. I thought she liked me, so I took her home and made a date to meet her next Tuesday. I had to get a taxi back to Fieldview, which cost 12 shillings. Oh for Marie's bike. I wasn't looking for any permanency in this new date, I was just out to have a good time for my last month in Stevenage.

iiiiiiiiiiiiiiiiiiiii

STEVENAGE TO CAMBRIDGE AND RETURN

Sunday 13th July: It was a lovely day and I found on my map that the famous university city of Cambridge was only about 30 miles from Stevenage by rail, so I decided I should go and have a look at the town and its famous university. A return ticket from Stevenage was only a few shillings as it was deemed a 'Sunday excursion fare.'

The steam train first passed through Hitchin and then turned right on the branch line to Cambridge. The next station of interest was Letchworth where I played a couple of games of golf. It is a beautiful town and really earns the name 'Letchworth Garden City.' It was a stopping train and it was great to hear again the puff puff from the engine as it made its way along the line. Some distance into the journey through the ever so green fields of Hertfordshire, the train crossed into the neighbouring county of Cambridgeshire. Imagine my surprise, when the train stopped at a station with the double name of Meldrith & Melbourn! I wondered if there was any connection between Melbourn without an 'e' and my Melbourne? Maybe not. It wasn't much furher on through the county when the train final came to my destination of Cambridge.

CAMBRIDGE

I left the train in Cambridge, so called because it is on the Cam River. I wandered through the streets. The main street was called King's Parade and this led me to the imposing King's College Chapel, a large rectangular church building with many spires and one side formed by high Gothic arches. I took a photo and turned around to walk away, when there in front of me were two familiar faces, two YHA members from Melbourne, Lionel Kane, and Ian Meadows. Unbelievable! We shook hands and stood there talking for a while. I

234

said that half of our YHA members must be in England. They were like flies, which by the way, I didn't think they had in England because none had annoyed me so far. Together we saw through the beautiful King's College Chapel and other buildings in the grounds. King's College is one of 31 colleges that make up the complex of Cambridge University. Others include Queen's, St John's, Corpus Christi and Clare's. We also saw the impressive Cambridge University Press building, a name familiar to me from books I had read.

Lionel told me he was thinking of going to Canada where there were plenty of jobs available with good wages. He suggested that I should think about it too. Lionel said a passage only cost £50 (in fact, I had heard that the voyage was free if a contract was signed before leaving). We parted after an exchange of addresses, and looking forward meeting again. We wished each other good luck.

Having seen some of the most important institutions and buildings in this famous city it was time to head back to Stevenage. On the way back to the railway station, in the university grounds, I saw and photographed one of the King's College Chapel's choir boys dressed in a black cape, gartered black stockings and big black hat. I read later that to become a member of the choir, 'the applicant must be between 8 and 13 years of age, love singing and have a willingness to learn.' The choir has 24 full members and usually takes in 6 new boys each year. A boy who proves his worth can become a full member at age 9, retiring when his voice breaks.

It was such an interesting day at Cambridge seeing around the extensive grounds, especially with the absolute surprise and delight of meting Lionel and Ian. On the way home in the train I thought about what Lionel had said about him going to Canada and working there, but I quickly put any thought of that out of my mind.

An orator talking religion in Hyde Park. Marble Arch is behind left

The Meldrith & Melbourn railway station on the way to Cambridge

King's College Chapel Cambridge

Ian Meadows facing the camera and Lionel Kane, two of our YHA members I met in Cambridge

The Cambridge University Press building

A King's College Chapel choir boy

236

Monday 14th July: I knocked off at 7 p.m. Back at Fieldview there was an amazing surprise in a letter from my parents that I had been waiting ten weeks for. It confirmed by a hundred, thousand, or maybe million to one chance that the bridge I had been walking over from work each day was the same one that was pictured in the railway book of my youth!

I knew there was something familiar about the bridge and water troughs, but what a coincidence it was. Of all the places in the UK that I could have settled in, Stevenage turned out to be one that had a significant connection with my boyhood days. The book; *The Iron Road: The Wonders of Railway Progress*, by Cecil J. Allen, my favourite railway book, which I still possess as I write, although it is showing signs of old age like me.

Inside the front cover, a colour photo shows a locomotive, number 4472, picking up water as it speeds under a bridge, my bridge that I crossed twice each day while working for three months at Kings. The caption reads: *'Flying Scotsman* of the LNER, taking water at full speed from the Langley Troughs, near Stevenage.' The locomotive in the photo is the famous Gresley A3 Pacific, 4-6-0 named *Flying Scotsman,* the name also carried by the London to Edinburgh express.

This marvellous coincidence began during lunch times when I watched the trains going past Kings and something seemed familiar to me when I took a photo of a locomotive picking up water under the bridge. Most significant types of locomotives in England, like boats and ships of all sizes, are given names. Many express trains are also named. Besides seeing the famous *Flying Scotsman,* I saw many streamlined A4s with names such as *Silver Fox, Union of South Africa* and *Dwight D Eisenhower.* This locomotive was shipped to the USA, in the year 2000 to be exhibited in their National Railroad Museum.

I regularly saw two express trains speeding by Kings in my lunch hour. The *Dundee Pullman* and the *Tees-Tyne Limited.* The

Dundee Pullman began its long journey to London from Dundee on the Firth of Tay on the east coast of Scotland, a journey of nearly 600 km 'as the crow flies.' The route took it across the Firth of Tay on the famous Tay bridge, which during a violent gale in 1879, collapsed while a train was crossing with the loss of over 70 lives. Further into its long journey the train crossed the huge and also famous, Forth railway bridge over the Firth of Forth, just north of Edinburgh and thence on to London.

The other express I saw, the *Tees-Tyne Limited*, commenced its long journey to London from the northern city of Newcastle on the Tyne River, about 400 km 'as the crow flies from London.' The *Tees-Tyne Limited* was always hauled by a streamlined A4 Gresley, whereas the *Dundee Pullman* was hauled by an A3 class without streamlining.

A solid Pullman train included a restaurant car that served first class meals along the route. Some passenger trains may only have a few Pullman cars, the remainder being standard first, second or third class, depending on the demand on a particular route and time. The cavalcade of trains I saw and marvelled at while living and working in Stevenage, also included many smaller trains and locomotives of various classes hauling local passenger trains, as well as many types of goods locomotives, especially the *Austerity* 2-8-0 designs built during the war. These were nearly at the end of their working lives judging by the loud clanking noises coming from their motion gear (coupling and connecting rods) as they passed by.

I did not have the good fortune of seeing *Mallard*. This Gresley A4 locomotive that still holds the world's speed record for a steam locomotive hauling a multi-coach train. The record of 126 mph (202 km/h) was established in 1938, and maintained it for a distance of 8 km down Stoke Bank, about 100 km north of Stevenage. This speed may not seem remarkable compared to present day passenger trains on this line, which travel at 200 km/h for most of the journey between London and Edinburgh, covering the distance of 395 km in around five hours.

I told the blokes at work about the amazing coincidence of the bridge just down the line from the factory that they like me, crossed each day on the way to and from Kings. I decided to name the bridge: '*The Bridge of Serendipity*' and wished I could attach a plaque inscribed with that name on the bridge.

Saturday 19th July: I travelled up to London to pay the balance of my airfare to Norway. The total cost was £17/19. Then I went to the YH shop and bought a sheet sleeping bag for 2 shillings as my other one was worn out. A sheet sleeping bag is mandatory when sleeping in youth hostels with eiderdowns on the beds, but I also used it inside my sleeping bag as it could be easily washed and dried.

When I returned from London I met Vivienne and we went to a local dance in Letchworth. There was a good band and I was pleased at the standard of behaviour and dressing, much better than I had experienced at Lynton. Vivienne was a lousy dancer and not very good company either. She was very self-opinionated and accused me of being too short, which didn't do a great deal for my ego. I took her home but as far as I was concerned that was the end. I took the bus back to Stevenage, not a taxi this time. In Marie I realised I had seen the nicest of English girls and in Vivienne the worst example.

Sunday 20th July: I worked until 1 p.m. The overtime rate was double time for working on Sundays, time and a half for Saturdays and time and a third on week nights. Working at Kings could not have been more rewarding. I spent most of Sunday planning my next tour as best I could. I planned to be away for about two months, returning to England during the first few days of October.

My mother was a prolific writer, but I never got tired of receiving her letters. My father appeared to let my mother do all the writing; maybe she had more time than dad, but I think she just enjoyed writing so much, and keeping in contact with her eldest son. I wrote back to her quite frequently but not as regularly.

Monday 21st July: We welcomed a new boarder to Fieldview, a bloke named George Daly. He seemed a cut above the rest of us, well dressed and well spoken. He had a job in the office at Kings. What's more he owned a Morris station wagon, or 'shooting brake' as they call them in England. One day at work I broke a threading tap, a hand tool used to cut a thread for a screw, which caused me a big problem to rectify. I was very ashamed of myself. My mind must have been elsewhere. I was getting along quite well with George Daly who seemed to have taken a liking to me. The blokes at Fieldview nicknamed him Lord Woolton: They said he looked very like Lord Woolton the wartime Minister for Food who urged everyone to be creative with their cooking with rationed food, and to use more vegetables, especially potatoes. Surprise, surprise: I got a letter from Vivienne wanting to see me again; I didn't reply, but my ego went back up a notch.

Wednesday 23rd July: Today was a very significant day for me because I wrote my resignation to Kings, to finish on 1st August 1952. In the letter I wrote how much I regretted having to leave, as I had thoroughly enjoyed working for Kings, my first job in England. Working conditions at Kings were excellent, as was the friendship of my workmates. My resignation was received without much comment because they all knew roughly when I would be leaving. I also wrote to Uncle John and Auntie Greta and told them my travel arrangements.

Friday 25th July: It was my last night out with my English friends. It was a great night and a grand old time was had by all. My English girlfriend Marie was sad to see me go, but from the beginning of our relationship she knew it would not be lasting. Everyone told me that when I settled in London, I would have to come up and visit them as usual on a Friday night. They had all been so wonderful to me with their very open hospitality, for which I was very thankful. I would always remember and treasure the time I spent in Stevenage, which I have to this day.

240

Sunday 27th July: I wanted to try to get the *Flying Scotsman,* The Bridge of Serendipity and Kings all in one photo. Soon after breakfast I went down to the tracks opposite Kings and found a position where all three would be in the picture. On the appointed time the *Flying Scotsman* roared by with a little water still trailing from the tender. When I eventually had the film developed I was very happy to see that the 'Bridge of Serendipity' was in the picture, but looked very small in the distance.

In the evening I went with some of the blokes from *Fieldview* to the Yorkshire Grey pub for a few farewell drinks. I drank sweet martinis and chatted with a very lovely girl named Norma. She was very interested in all that I had been doing since I left Australia, and in my next tour. She said she would come up to London to see me, so I gave her my Australia House address and left the rest up to her. It gave my ego quite a boost. Maybe this is what Maurice Spanger meant when he said: "Women are like flies in London."

Monday 28th July: George Daly offered to drive me to the Bakers with some of the luggage, my golf clubs and skis that I wouldn't need on my next tour. They had kindly offered to keep them for me until I found a place to live in London, on my return. I thanked George for taking me to the Bakers. Over a cup of tea I told the Bakers all about my time at Stevenage and my English friends. I thanked them all for their help and returned to *Fieldview* on the bus after a pleasant afternoon, but still Leon was nowhere to be seen.

Thursday 31st July: I got a letter from Netta saying she was looking forward to seeing me on Saturday, but that she had some bad news for me. I couldn't imagine what this could be. I phoned to book a room in the boarding house in Clapham Common that I had previously stayed in. Looking back, it is really strange that I never gave a thought to staying in a YH in London.

I finished packing ready for the next day and in the evening I again took a few blokes from *Fieldview* to the Yorkshire Grey for a drink and brought some back for the others. I had a great final night.

241

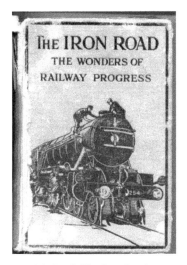

My book *The Iron Road*

A black and white copy of the coloured photo inside he cover of *The Iron Road* with the 'Bridge of Serendipity' and the *Flying Scotsman* picking up water

The *Dundee Pullman hauled by an A3 locomotive*

A fast passenger train hauled by an A4 locomotive *Silver Fox*

Flying Scotsman and Kings. The Bridge Of Serendipity, can just be seen in the distance.

The Tees-Tyne Limited

242

Friday 1st August: Before I knocked off at 4 p.m. I collected all the money due to me, about £20. I said goodbye to my workmates and my foreman Harry said to me: "Any time you want a job at Kings in the future, you will be most welcome." That was most encouraging. I thanked them all, and said a special goodbye to my Cockney friend Mack, who asked me to keep in touch. Bob was especially sorry to see me go. I thought this was because in the time I worked with him I had taught him quite a few things about the trade, quite apart from how to develop a shape.

I left the factory, and walked over the *Bridge of Serendipity* and gazed up and down the tracks for the last time. Sadly, there was no train to whistle me goodbye. Back at *Fieldview* I said goodbye to Mr and Mrs Page and the blokes. George Daly had kindly offered to take me up to London with him, as he was going to spend the weekend there. While I was waiting, I reflected on how fortunate I was to be able to stay at King's boarding house. If nothing else it kept me out of trouble, because I couldn't invite any girls back to my room.

STEVENAGE TO LONDON

It was a lovely balmy evening as George drove to London by way of Hereford, which was new country for me. George dropped me off at the boarding house around 7.30 p.m. I thanked him for his help, and he wished me good luck.

LONDON

I booked into my room for the night. Netta's flat wasn't far away, so off I went to see her. After a bit of a yarn, I asked her what the bad news was she had to tell me? With some hesitation, she said that I had an inferiority complex, and I should do something about it. I was astonished. Me with an inferiority complex, impossible! I asked her why she was of that opinion. She said that it was just the way I acted and approached life. I was always aware of the fact that I was a tradesman. I told her I was very proud that I had a trade and how helpful it had been to me in securing a job quickly in England. I told her that Kings had wanted to upgrade me, but unfortunately, I had naively told them I was only going to be there for a couple of months. We talked for a while around the subject and then we talked about Netta's tour and my next tour.

Before I left, Netta asked me if I would like to wander around London with her in the morning. I said I would love to. She went on to say that she had booked tickets for us to go to Covent Garden in the evening. I said that would be really great and gave her a big hug as we said goodnight.

I returned to my room and climbed into bed. As I lay there, I thought about what Netta had said about my personality. That I, Gordon James Robert Smith, was perceived to have an inferiority complex. I went through all the possibilities in my mind. Yes, I certainly did have an inferiority complex with Judy, but she said being a tradesman didn't matter to her, as she loved me. Netta however, was not aware of my intimate relationship with Judy. Yes, I did have an inferiority complex when I was dating Marg Edney. Yes, I did have a slight inferiority complex with the Friday night mob, because I couldn't compete on an equal footing with their marvellous hospitality and friendship. Not once, however, was I made to feel I was inferior, quite the contrary.

With regard to my social interactions here in England and back in Australia with the wide range of people from many levels of social standing I had come in contact with, I had not in any way experienced feelings of inferiority and had always been at ease.

In other areas of my lifestyle, I could say I was an above average skier, and classed myself as a good tradesman fitter and turner, coupled with a good education and interest in the arts. I had no trouble in attracting the attentions of the opposite sex. I was relatively good looking, having been told on occasions that I looked like Clarke Gable, which did no end of good for my ego. After that self-analysis, I thought that it was far more preferable to have an inferior complex than a superior one.

244

Saturday 2nd August: I met Netta and then we went to my bank in Berkeley Square, which was open on Saturday mornings. I drew out cheques, £60 pounds in travellers' cheques and £50 cash. This was much the same as I had taken away on my first tour, but I had already paid for my coach trip to Glasgow and the flight to Norway. I intended to hitchhike as much as I could, so would not be spending much on fares I hoped. Netta and I went into the West End, where we wandered around looking at the theatres and shop windows. I enjoyed Netta's company very much. Then it was back to her place for lunch and a lazy afternoon talking over cups of tea with Nellie and Jan, who seemed to have softened her dislike of me somewhat. We all went out for tea at a café and then Netta and I went off to Covent Garden to see the New York City Ballet.

We saw a varied selection of short ballets: *The Prodigal Son*, *Serenade*, *The Cage* and *Cake Walk*. We thoroughly enjoyed them, each different in theme and style, both classical and modern. Covent Garden is a grand theatre. I particularly admired the huge burgundy stage curtains and drapes with embroided gold borders of the royal coat of arms and crests.

My use of the name Covent Garden to describe the theatre is in fact incorrect. The name of the theatre is The Royal Opera House, and is located in the London district of Covent Garden WC2. This is the location of London's chief market for fruit, vegetables and flowers. The Royal Opera House was built in 1732, but was later destroyed by fire. The present theatre was built in 1858. Covent Garden has its own tube station directly under the opera house.

After the ballet we wanted to find a dance hall, but the nearest we got to one was a nightclub, the 'Club de Fourburg' in Compton Street. We couldn't get in but obtained membership forms. I took Netta back to her digs in Ramsden Road, where we parted after a very enjoyable day together, with a hug and kiss. I was still puzzled about Netta's reasons for telling me of the fault she thought I had in my personality, instead of just observing it and keeping it to herself.

245

Sunday 3rd August: This was the day of my departure to Glasgow. I woke up late and after breakfast went around to Netta's with my rucksack, case and bum bag. I would be leaving the case with Auntie Ruby in Scotland and asking her to send it to London when I returned there after the tour, as it only contained those things I would need in Scotland. It was certainly a pleasure not to have to carry the awkward skis everywhere on this tour.

Netta, Nellie and I spent a relaxing day talking about various subjects, our plans for the future, our impressions of the UK and its people, which on the whole were quite good, especially considering my experiences in Stevenage. Netta and I both loved London and were surprised by the number of YHA members that were over here, in particular YHA members from Melbourne that I had come across by correspondence, and in a couple of instances met by accident. There was no doubt that in the early 1950s YHA members were at the forefront of an exodus of young Australians who travelled to the UK on working holidays, and who would later be classified as 'backpackers.'

I had an evening meal with Netta, Nellie, Jan and some of the other boarders. It was then time to go and I gave my three friends a big hug and a kiss. We wished each other good luck until we meet again in about two months' time. Then I left in time to take the tube to Victoria Street Station for the beginning of my fourth tour.

CHAPTER 14

THE FOURTH BACKPACKING TOUR

LONDON

LONDON TO GLASGOW

My luggage was loaded onto one of the two large white coaches that would be travelling together on my journey to Glasgow. The coaches left promptly at 8 p.m. for the 654 km (409 mile) journey to Glasgow. I was lucky to get a front seat right across from the driver in the front coach. I asked the driver if he would keep me informed of the highways we travelled along, and the main towns we passed through on the way. The coach travelled through the suburbs north of London and then joined the A1 Great North Road, passing through all the towns now so familiar to me: Hatfield, Welwyn Garden City and my town of Stevenage, which evoked in me many pleasant thoughts as the coach sped through. Next came Baldock, a town in Hertfordshire that I had not visited. Both coaches stopped in Baldock to enable the passengers to have a snack and visit the toilet. The driver told us the coaches would be stopping about every hour and a half for us to 'stretch our legs.'

Leaving Baldock, the light began to fade, and by the time we had reached Stamford in Leicestershire and Doncaster in Yorkshire it was dark. My seat was very comfortable, giving me a driver's view of the road. Up to this point, the coach had been travelling in a northerly direction along the A1, generally following the route of the

LNER railway line to Edinburgh. Near Darlington in Durham we turned off the A1 on to the A66, travelling west to the town of Penrith in Cumberland and from there along the A6 to Carlisle, a large city where the coach drivers were changed. It was quite cold when I got off the coach to have a bite to eat and stretch my legs. During the journey I had been sleeping on and off, only waking up when the driver told me about a town we were passing or a route change, so I could enter it in my diary and notebook.

CHAPTER 15
SCOTLAND

This map shows the routes the author took visiting towns, cities and places of interest in the south west area of Scotland

The coaches crossed into Scotland shortly after leaving Carlisle on the A74. The border between England and Scotland begins at the east coast town of Berwick upon Tweed in Northumberland, then follows a line roughly south-west to Gretna Green in Dumfries and Galloway on the west coast of Scotland. Here it joins the sea at the Solway Firth (a firth is an arm of the sea or estuary). The coaches continued along the A74 until we reached Crawford in South Lancashire. I was asleep for most of this section of the journey, and was unaware that we passed the small village of Lockerbie.

Lockerbie was to hit the headlines many years later in 1988 when, four days before Christmas, Pan American Airways 747 Flight 103 crashed, killing all 259 passengers and crew on board, as well as another 11 residents of Lockerbie. The flight had left London bound for New York when a time bomb exploded in the plane, bringing it down in Scotland. It took 10 years to find the terrorists responsible for placing the bomb on the plane. Two Lebanese operatives were found to be the culprits and were brought to justice. I fell fast asleep after leaving Carlisle, waking up in Crawford as dawn was breaking.

Monday 4th August: It was raining like hell and now there was only our coach, the other must have left us for some other destination, probably Edinburgh I thought. Next was Hamilton, an industrial town about 16 km from Glasgow where a feeble sun was shining through the coach windows. From there on I was wide awake as our coaches made their way along the A74. They crossed over to a large road called the London Road, in the centre of which were double tram lines. It was along this road that I got the fright of my life and thought my end had come.

In Australia as in the UK, we drive on the left hand side of the road. We have trams in the city with lines going to the outlying suburbs the same as Glasgow. In Melbourne, a car driver who wishes to pass a tram can only pass on the tram's left or kerb side. Our coach was travelling quite quickly downhill on London Road and approaching a tram going in the same direction. Another tram in the distance was coming toward us on the other double line. I was expecting our driver to pass the tram on its left side as in Melbourne, but no! He drove our large coach *around* the tram, passing on its right side, quickly moving back after he had passed to avoid the approaching tram heading straight for us on the other line. That really was a scare. I wondered how many cars or buses didn't make it and became sandwiched between the two passing trams. I just had enough time to regain my composure before the coaches pulled up at the Glasgow coach terminal, where thankfully the rain had stopped.

GLASGOW

I stepped down from the coach and was greeted warmly by Auntie Ruby and her brother John. I had heard so much over the years about Auntie Ruby, my mother's cousin (as was Uncle John). Auntie Ruby was like my mother in so many ways: the same age, same height, same dark hair, and with the beautiful warm smile I had seen in many photographs my mother had shown me. Uncle John, on the other hand, was not a familiar figure: I don't think I had ever seen a photograph of him. He was short, with greying hair, and about the same age as Auntie Ruby or a little older, I thought.

We caught a taxi to Uncle John's house in Muirend, a suburb of Glasgow. It was a solid brick house with a small front garden. There waiting for us were the rest of the family Auntie Ruby's husband Bob, and Uncle John's very English wife Greta. Last of all John and Greta's 15 year old daughter Heather, who appeared to be rather frail. Her sister May was at college and I would meet her later. They were all very pleasant and made me feel very much at home.

I soon discovered that Uncle John was the manager of the Clydesdale bank. He looked the part. Uncle Bob was a tall man, always smiling and with a great sense of humour. He was a sales representative for a ladies underwear firm, so I imagined that was why he had such a whimsical countenance.

They were keen to know all about my family and especially about my mother. Realising that I hadn't had any breakfast, a meal was hastily prepared and eaten without any pause in the conversation. There was so much they wanted to know and after a while Uncle John and Uncle Bob went off to work, which provided us all with a more relaxed exchange of news and even a chance to look at a little television, which was all new to me.

During my stay in Scotland, I referred to Greta and John as aunties and uncles as a courtesy, although strictly speaking they were not direct relatives. Knowing that I must be tired after my coach journey through the night, Auntie Greta showed me the room and bed I was to sleep in. After a wash I got into my pyjamas, climbed into bed and went straight off to sleep.

Eventually I woke and had lunch, all the while talk never stopping. Lunch over I took the tram into Glasgow on a tramline that terminated just a short distance away from their house. I found Glasgow to be very like Melbourne in many respects. The streets were laid out in a rectangular grid pattern, which made me feel very much at home. One difference I noted was that some of the Glasgow streets were paved with cobblestones. Trams ran along some of these streets, once again very similar to Melbourne, but most of Glasgow's trams were queer looking, slab sided, double deckers. The similarities with Melbourne continued. The River Clyde flowed alongside Glasgow in much the same position as does our Yarra River to Melbourne.

Both rivers are dirty, so much so that it is said that Melbourne's Yarra River 'runs upside down.' The buildings of Glasgow were much older than those in Melbourne, and Glasgow presented itself as a rather dirtier city than Melbourne. I imagined this was due to the number of houses that have coal fires. However, I felt very much at home in Glasgow, the home city of some of my ancestors.

When I returned from the city in the evening we all went to Auntie Ruby's and Uncle Bob's flat in Newlands, south of the Clyde.

252

I had posted many letters for my mother to this address, so it was very familiar to me, but never did I think that one day I would be visiting there. Auntie Ruby and Uncle Bob live in a cosy, three room, upstairs flat. May was there too, a very attractive, brunette, of 18 years. The family suggested that one lovely place I should visit was the Isle of Arran not far away from Glasgow, so I decided to make that my first tour the next day.

|||||||||||||||||||||||||

GLASGOW TO ARDROSSAN

Wednesday 6th August: I was up bright and early and took the tram into Glasgow where I boarded a steam train for Ardrossan 27 miles away on the west coast of Scotland. Leaving Glasgow station the train crossed the Clyde River, but I didn't really see it from where I was sitting because of the high bridge parapets. After leaving the less than attractive industrial districts of the Clyde, the swing door train settled down to the journey accompanied by the sound from the locomotive exhaust and the click clack of the rail joints. It was a stopping train and the first big town the train came to was Paisley, situated amongst beautiful green wooded valleys together with a couple of lakes, or lochs. These were the main scenic attractions of the trip until the train reached train reached Saltcoats, where the line ran along the shores of the Firth of Clyde.

Then the line moved inland at Ardrossan South a short distance from the sea and where many types of boats were being built and repaired in yards along the way, and finally to the terminus at Ardrossan in Ayrshire.

ARDROSSAN
ARDROSSAN TO BRODICK

I boarded a ferry in Ardrossan to take me 15 miles across the Firth of Clyde to Brodick, on the east coast of the Isle of Arran. As the ferry approached the island I could see a range of rugged mountains to the north. The highest, Goat Fell was 2,687 ft (874 m)

253

and cone shaped. The tourist brochure said that the island was 19 miles long by 9 miles wide, and described it as a paradise for day trippers who go to the mountains in the north and the beaches in the south, its population trebling in the summer months. From what I had already seen I was sure the brochure was not exaggerating.

BRODICK

ISLE OF ARRAN TOUR

I had a bite to eat in Brodick and then boarded a coach for a tour around the island, which followed the coastline for most of the way. The coach was equipped with a public address (PA) system, which the driver used to keep us informed about the interesting features of the island. Not far north of Brodick the driver brought the coach to a stop above a river across which there was a large building. He said it was Brodick Castle, used by the Duchess of Montrose as a shooting lodge. The castle looked in very good condition, but didn't appear to be very ancient.

Soon the country became quite mountainous and we came into full view of Goat Fell, easily recognisable by its conical shape. As the coach travelled around the northern end of the island the inland mountains were always visible, very rocky and rugged but never higher than Goat Fell.

In lovely sunny weather we passed small seaside villages every now and again, as well as many stone ruins, some dating from the time of the Viking settlers. As the coach approached the southern end of the island the landscape changed, becoming a series of low hills and dales, totally different from the mountains of the northern end. The reason for the difference was the 'Highland Boundary Fault,' which cuts the island virtually in half from east to west. It is a favourite excursion venue for university geology students.

About 15 miles from the southern end of the island the large conical island of Ailsa Craig could be seen. As the coach followed the southern coastline, I saw a couple of golf courses and from the little I saw they looked very inviting. The coach driver said there

254

were seven golf courses on the island. The well paved road then turned north and followed the eastern coastline back to Brodick, passing through the seaside towns of Whiting Bay and Lamlash. It was evident that this area of Arran's south east coastline was where most of the hotels and guest houses were located and together with Brodick, were the most visited and popular part of the island. Back at Brodick after a lovely day, I caught the ferry back to Ardrossan.

||||||||||||||||||||

ARDROSSAN TO GLASGOW

I caught the train back to Glasgow. The London Midland and Scotland (LMS) carriages were swing door, but there was no loud slamming like I heard in England. The Scots must be more gentle. The coach tour of Isle of Arran had brought my first views of the Scottish countryside, which certainly looked like some of the photographs in the yearly calendars that Auntie Ruby sent my mother.

Thursday 7th August: Shortly after I arrived in Glasgow, I told Uncle John I would like to see over the factory where the R class locomotives were being built by the North British Locomotive Company (NBLC). Uncle John said the manager was a friend of his and he would try to arrange a visit for me. He did. On my return from Arran, Uncle John had arranged a visit for me to the factory the next day,

Thursday 7th August: It was a very wet day and I spent the morning talking to Auntie Greta and writing to my mother about my arrival in Glasgow. In the afternoon I went into the city and out to the NBLC located in the northern suburb of Springburn. At the time of my visit, the company had a contract to build and ship 70 R class4-6-4 Hudson, express passenger locomotives for the Victorian Railways (VR).

When I wentI went to the Newport workshops to see my former

255

The coaches at Baldock

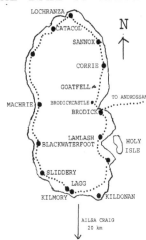

The author's route around the Isle of Arran

Auntie Ruby and uncle Bob Rintoul

The Johnston family L to R, Greta, May, Heather and John

Goat Fell across Brodick beach

An R Class locomotive

Brodick Castle

256

workmates there and tell them I was going overseas and wish them goodbye, they told me about the troubles they were having with the R class, which were being shipped from the NBLC to Port Melbourne as each was completed. They were finding a number of faults, including faulty bearings, misalignment of motion gear and improperly quartered (fitted) driving wheels. Sadly, this prevented these much needed locomotives from being put into service immediately, and resulted in a decision that no more locomotives were to be shipped until all the faults had been rectified.

Against that unfortunate background, I was very pleased to have the opportunity of seeing around the works. I presented myself to NBLC reception where. I was ushered into the office of the manager and asked to wait while they contacted him. While I was sitting there my gaze was attracted to a large calendar on the wall with an oil painting of the front of a speeding R class locomotive. I noticed that the tail disc (its function being to indicate to a signalman that a train was complete) was incorrectly displayed–unless of course the R class was speeding in reverse!

The manager came into the office and we introduced ourselves. I told him about my railway interests and how I had served my time as a fitter and turner in the VR, but of course I did not reveal that I knew about the troubles his company was having with the R class locomotives. I did however, point out the error on his calendar. The manager said: "Oh, we can't have that, can we?" He promptly got up on a chair and blanked out the tail disc with a pencil. He then introduced me to a foreman who took me into the factory, where I had an interesting tour around the works, much smaller than I expected.

I saw various sections of the locomotives being built. With regard to the R class faults, I didn't see anything amiss, and was sure that the main cause of the bad workmanship on the R Class locomotives was the lack of qualified tradesmen. However, when all the problems had been rectified the R class locomotives proved to be

257

very good machines, and as I write they are used extensively hauling tourist trains.

In 1951 an R Class locomotive, R 704, was exhibited in the engineering section of the Festival of Britain in Glasgow. I was very grateful to Uncle John for arranging the visit for me and, although I didn't have any input into correcting the R class faults, at least I had the fault in the calendar painting corrected.

In the evening I went to *The Joy Nicholls Show* at the Empire Theatre with May. It was a great show starring two expatriate Australians, Joy Nicholls and Dick Bentley, together with the irrepressible English comedian Jimmy Edwards. I remembered hearing Joy Nicholls on the radio back home. She and Dick Bentley were first class comedians, working together in radio comedies and revues. Both enjoyed successful careers in the UK in the 50s. They were both Aussies who like me, had journeyed abroad to the UK, but in their case it was to further their careers. They starred in many shows on the BBC, probably the best known and funniest being *Take It From Here*, about the Glum family, in which Joy Nicholls played a role with Dick Bentley, who had come over to the UK sometime after her. *The Joy Nicholls Show* was very funny, especially seeing Jimmy Edwards and Dick Bentley in person, having heard them so many times on the radio back in Australia. It was also beaut having May with me a lovely girl with the cutest of Scots accents.

THE THREE LOCHS TOUR

Friday 8th August: This seemed to be an ideal day to go on a tour called 'The Three Lochs Tour' even though the weather was not especially good. I joined the tour in the coach terminal in Glasgow. The tour coach passed through the towns of Dumbarton and Alexandria, about 30 km from Glasgow, and soon we arrived at famous Loch Lomond, which was very placid and beautiful although looking a little grey because the clouds covered the sun. The driver told us that Loch Lomond is 36 km (23 miles) long by 8 km (5 miles) wide. It is the third longest and third deepest loch in Scotland, and

258

the largest fresh water lake in Britain. It is fed by numerous rivers and is the source of fresh water for many parts of central Scotland. Loch Lomond empties into the Clyde by the Leven River.

There were a few Americans on the tour. They certainly were not backward in asking all manner of questions, 'to get their money's worth' as they said. The result was that all of us on the tour were getting more information than would be usual. My impression on tours both on the Continent and in the UK was that American tourists were not generally liked because of their demanding manner. They were tolerated because of the dollars they brought in to the countries they visited. I had been mistaken for an American many times, but I was always quick to let it be known that I was Australian and this usually evoked great enthusiasm as to my well-being.

The driver said we would only be seeing part of the western shoreline of Loch Lomond, before he drove across to Garelochhead. He said that if we wanted to see Loch Lomond at its best we should take the boat trip. That's good, I thought, because I had arranged to take that trip with May the next day. The coach drove west for about 10 km to the village of Garelochhead at the head of Garloch, where we stopped for a short while.

Some distance to the north there was a range of mountains, their summits covered in cloud. The driver said it was a pity the cloud was low because further back there was a mountain called Ben Arthur, which was also called The Cobbler because it was shaped like a boot. I was very interested because in the Victorian Alps we also have a mountain called The Cobbler, no doubt named after this one that sadly I couldn't see. Before I left Australia I had climbed Mt Cobbler, which at 5,341 ft (1.628 m) is twice the height of the Scots Cobbler at 2,890 ft (881 m). In Garelochhead I purchased a postcard of The Cobbler so I would at least know what it looked like compared to ours. There was a definite similarity.

The coach then took us along the western shore of Gare Loch, where there was a submarine base during WWII, then a short way to the west to Loch Long. Both Gare Loch and Loch Long open into the Firth of Clyde at their southern ends. Although it was not mentioned at the time, I wondered if they were true lochs. I always imagined that a loch was the Scottish term for a land locked expanse of water. My dictionary confirmed this, describing a loch as a 'Scottish lake, or land locked arm of the sea'. There is one essential difference however, between a true loch such as Loch Lomond and those such as Loch Long and Gare Loch. The latter two are salt water and subject to tidal influence, whereas Loch Lomond is not. My dictionary also defined 'firth' as an 'arm of the sea or estuary.'

After the coach left Loch Long the driver took us back to Glasgow by a short cut along the Firth of Clyde through Helensburgh. The tour of the lochs was a chance to see a few more of the brilliant scenes depicted in Auntie Ruby's calendars, but the vivid greens, browns and blues were absent because of the gloomy conditions.

A LOCH LOMOND CRUISE

Saturday 9th August: It was a very wet morning when May and I travelled on a coach toward Loch Lomond along the same road I had taken the day before. It soon cleared a little, although there was still very low cloud. We joined a single funnelled, rather large tourist steamer at Arden on the western shore of the loch and steamed north up Loch Lomond at its widest part. The steamer passed a number of islands. We were told over the PA system that there were over 30 islands of all sizes in Loch Lomond. The loch narrowed considerably, and the land on either side became much steeper as we went north.

It was great to have May along to share this journey. I never tired of her lovely Scots accent; in fact I was beginning to think she was the sweetest girl I had ever met. The steamer passed a place called Tarbet, which May said was the name of her parent's house. Next we saw a hydro-electric station on the side of the loch, fed by a pipeline coming down the mountainside directly above it. This was Sly Power

260

Station of the Sly-Shirr Scheme, one of the many hydro-electric schemes in the Scottish highlands. Little did I realise that after I returned to Australia I would be helping to construct a hydro-electric scheme in the Victorian Alps. We were told on the PA that on the other side of the loch, Ben Lomond, 3,185 ft (971 m) was the highest peak in the county of Argyll and Bute, but sadly, like The Cobbler it too was covered by cloud. As we steamed further north from Tarbet, Loch Lomond narrowed to its end at a village called Ardlui.

May and I left the steamer and walked along the pier to the shore, where we had lunch. The northern end of Loch Lomond is surrounded by 2,000 ft (600 m) high peaks, but they were all obscured by cloud. With the help of many photos around the walls of the lunchroom, I was able to gain some idea of the mountainous country that surrounded the loch. After a light lunch we relaxed and talked about ourselves while we waited for the steamer to take us back to Arden. It was a thoroughly enjoyable cruise of nearly six hours and 60 km with May, who I thought I was a beautiful young lady.

The steamer took us back to Arden, but the mountains were still covered by a blanket of cloud, so we didn't see any more of those that surround Loch Lomond. We took the coach back to Glasgow. May wanted to show me her city and its museum, so we decided to do that the next day. We arrived back at Muirend to find that Heather was ill. I watched TV before retiring to a very comfortably bed.

Sunday 10th August: May and I set off to go to the museum, which I probably would not have visited if May hadn't suggested it. We walked through the museum halls and saw all the usual exhibits, but it was not until we entered the art gallery that I saw an exhibit that really impressed me. On display were many of the works of the Spanish surrealist painter Salvador Dali. I had seen many of his works in books and magazines and was rather taken with his weird paintings. We came to a large painting that Dali completed in 1951, *Christ of St John of the Cross*. The cross was seen looking down on

A view of Gare Loch from the bus

A windswept May on the cruise ferry

Loch Long with The Cobbler obscured by clouds

The Sly hyro-electric power station and pen stock line above

The postcard photo of the Cobbler

The Ardlui pier at the northern end of Loch Lomond

it from above, floating horizontally in the sky with a lake below. I had seen many paintings and statues of the crucifixion in churches and elsewhere, most of which I thought were gruesome and uninspiring. This painting, on the contrary, was quite beautiful, painted in sombre brown hues. I didn't consider it surreal, unless it was the view from above. I am not sure what May thought of it and Dali's paintings. However, we enjoyed each other's company very much, and I am a real Dali admirer now because I enjoy his curious artistic style.

Monday 11th August: I slept in as usual, later going into the city to do some shopping and have a look around. After tea, I went dancing with May at the Plaza, a beaut dance hall with a great band. May is a very good dancer. It was a great night..

Tuesday 12th August: Late morning I went into town to have dinner with Uncle John at his bank. We were getting on well together and I enjoyed his company. We talked about all manner of things over the dinner table, but mostly about me and my family's life in Australia. Afterwards I went to a travel agency to book a tour to Fingal's Cave, but the tour didn't operate on the day I wanted to go. In the afternoon Auntie Ruby took me for a grand tour of the sights of Glasgow, culminating in a visit to the large, majestic Cathedral of St Mungo with its high spire in the centre of a long gable roof. The interior, whilst not as ornate as many churches I had visited, was very beautiful and impressive. It was one of the most massive cathedrals I had seen so far.

I tend to liken cathedrals and churches to mountains. In my opinion there are many beautiful mountains, and some not so beautiful mountains, such as the Dolomites in Italy. The most grotesque cathedral I had seen so far was the Duomo Cathedral in Milan. It was as though the architects of the Duomo were influenced by the nearby ugly mountain peaks of the Dolomites. In some way, Glasgow Cathedral with its huge central spire reminded me of the magnificent Matterhorn.

263

Wednesday 13th August: Auntie Ruby took me through the City Chambers and The Old House, a historic house, but these were not of much interest to me. When we returned to Muirend, Uncle John told me that the next afternoon he, Auntie Greta and Heather were going to England to visit relatives, arranged sometime before I came up to Scotland. He said Auntie Ruby and Uncle Bob were going to stay at Muirend to look after, or 'baby sit,' May and me while they are away.

I thanked Uncle John and Auntie Greta for their kind hospitality before they left with Heather for England, but it was a sad farewell. They would not be returning before I left for Norway. It was great to get to know them in the short time they were there. After tea with May, Uncle Bob and Auntie Ruby we all had a sing song around the piano before going to bed.

||||||||||||||||||||||

GLASGOW TO FORT WILLIAM

Thursday 14th August: I had to be up early to catch the 7.30 a.m. train from Glasgow to Fort William. On this journey I had my rucksack on my back again. It felt good and gave me a feeling of touring completeness. The train hauled by 4-6-0 locomotive resplendent in green livery, took me along the West Highland Railway (WHR) for a journey of 118 miles of about five hours duration to Fort William. The line was completed in 1894 and connects the fishing ports of Fort William and Malaig to Glasgow. It is a triumph of Scottish railway engineering.

For the first 31 miles of the journey the train climbed away from the Clyde up to Garelochhead and then followed Loch Long before descending into a lovely valley and on to Tarbet. Leaving Tarbet the railway line was cut into the hillside above Loch Lomond. It provided me with great views of the loch and the surrounding hills, but sadly the high peaks were still covered by cloud. The line then went past Ardlui, which May and I had visited by steamer. On that occasion I was quite unaware that there was a railway line up on the hill above the loch or even a railway station at Ardlui. In all the time we were on the cruise I didn't see any sign of steam or hear a train whistle.

I was becoming a little frustrated with the misty weather and low lying cloud as I very much wanted to see the summits of all the Bens. After the train left Ardlui it began to climb, passing through many valleys and around hills, even going around a horseshoe curve near a conical hill called Ben Dorian, 3,523 ft (1.074 m) high with its summit also covered in cloud. Thankfully the weather cleared a little and I was able to catch a glimpse of the summits of some of the lower Bens, but not Ben Dorian. The train crossed over many bridges and viaducts and went through one short tunnel, as well as passing a couple of isolated small stations called Tyndrum and Bridge of Orchy, but few people got on or off the train at these stations.

Leaving Bridge of Orchy, the countryside changed dramatically as the train was about to cross Rannoch Moor, which caused the builders of this line a great deal of trouble. The moor consists of peat bogs, small streams and heather covered marshy land.

To lay the railway track over parts of the moor required floating it, by building up layers of timber and branches placed crosswise until a stable base was established on which to lay the ballast. In Australia we call this method 'corduroying'. Looking out of the train window as the train crossed the 13 mile long desolate moor, it reminded me very much of our own Bogong High Plains (BHP), an elevated plateau of snow grass and moss beds surrounded by high summits. The BHP are 5,000 ft (1.500 m) above sea level; Rannoch Moor is only 980 ft (300 m), but the moor covers a much larger area. The similarity was so great that I could have easily imagined that I was travelling across my beloved BHP, where I had hiked and skied extensively. Although there is a great height difference between the two, I imagined that the weather conditions both in summer and winter would be very much the same, with snow in the winter.

Leaving the moor at Rannoch station the train climbed to the highest point on the line, 1,345 ft (410 m). It then began to descend as it passed Loch Treig, a true landlocked small loch, before joining the River Spean at Tulloch. Leaving Tulloch the line turned west, running along the side of a fast flowing river with mountains on both sides, then continued on through gorges, over bridges and viaducts, through the villages of Roy Bridge and Spean Bridge. The countryside opened out a little and the train gathered speed, finally reaching Fort William around 12.30 p.m.

FORT WILLIAM

Fort William is located at the junction of two Lochs, Eil and Linnhe. It is a large railway depot surrounded by mountains including the highest mountain in the UK, Ben Nevis 4,405 ft (1.343 m) the summit of which I was sorry to say, was obscured by cloud.

So ended one of the most interesting railway journeys of my life, a journey rated as one of the classic railway journeys in the world. The railway line doesn't end in Fort William, but continues on west for another 64 km to Mallaig, a large fishing port on the Atlantic Ocean. The railway's chief source of revenue is the fishing industry in Fort William and Mallaig, because between Ardlui and Tulloch there seemed to be no other revenue, except for tourists like me. I would very much have liked to travel on the WHR in mid-winter when there was snow on the ground.

The town of Fort William is a popular destination for climbers of Ben Nevis and hikers exploring the glens and surrounding high peaks. I had some lunch and left my rucksack at the bus depot, from where I would be leaving for Oban by bus at 2.30 p.m., as I had no intention of hitchhiking to my next destination Oban, 44 miles distant mainly because I did not know enough about the roads to Oban and the possibility of getting a lift.

I had a short look around the township and purchased a postcard that enabled me to see what Ben Nevis looked like behind the cloud. Oh to have seen Ben Nevis with my own eyes, but like all the other

266

Bens of Scotland on this tour, it was sulking behind bed sheets of clouds.

I decided to walk up the valley of Glen Nevis, between Ben Nevis and another large mountain. I thought I might get a little closer to the Ben and see what its lower ridges looked like, but the cloud was too low. Ben Nevis is a relatively low mountain by world standards, but provides great climbing difficulties because of its very steep and rocky sides and in winter it is a very formidable rock and ice climbing challenge. It was exhilarating walking along the road bounded by green fields with a picturesque tree lined, fast flowing stream keeping me company, but it didn't take me much closer to Ben Nevis. Having to leave Fort William without seeing the highest mountain in the UK was a great pity for a mountain loving man like me, but I consoled myself with the thought that I had seen the Matterhorn in ideal conditions. It could have easily been the other way round.

FORT WILLIAM TO OBAN

I caught the bus to Oban, further south down the coast. The bus was quite full as it made its way along a good road by the side of Loch Linnhe then across a bridge over the mouth of Loch Leven at Ballachulish. Further inland world famous Glencoe was situated, but our bus continued on. At last the cloud cleared a little to reveal a few glimpses of inland mountain peaks. The bus crossed a bridge over Loch Etive at Connel and the name Etive had me looking closely at my map. because it was one I had read about in climbing books. On the map I found the mountain, the Bauchville Etive Moor, 3,343 ft (1.019 m), but I could not see it from the bus as it was well inland and surrounded by other high peaks. My map also showed that most all of the lochs on the southern coast of Scotland are connected to the sea, so do not conform to my dictionary's definition of a loch. After a very interesting journey the bus arrived at Oban.

I was glad I didn't decide to try to hitchhike because I saw very few cars or other vehicles on the road,

Glasgow Cathedral and cemetery

My train crossing a bridge on Rannoch Moor

A view of Rannoch Moor from the train

The locomotive that hauled the author's train to Fort William

A postcard of Ben Nevis the UK's highest mountain and Fort William. The mountain was obscured by cloud the dayn I was there.

268

⌂

OBAN

Oban lies on the shore of the Firth of Lorne. Lorne is a familiar name to me, because Lorne is one of Victoria's top class beach resorts, which I have visited and stayed there many times. There was no YH in Oban. I booked into the ordinary looking, George Hotel. I then had a walk around the town. Oban is an interesting large resort town and tourist port, with a rather peculiar colosseum type structure called McCaig's Tower overlooking the town from a hill above. The tower was built over 100 years ago as an art centre, but was never completed and has become the most recognisable feature of Oban.

After taking a photo of McCraig's Tower I enquired about a boat trip to Staffa where Fingal's Cave is located. I was told there was no need to book. The boat also visited the Isles of Mull and Iona, neither of which I had heard of. I went back to the hotel and although I was feeling tired I decided to go to the cinema where I saw *Thunder Across the Pacific*, a good war movie about American B29 bombers.

A CRUISE TO THE ISLANDS OF IONA AND STAFFA

Friday 15th August: After breakfast I bought a ticket for the cruise to the Isles of Mull and Staffa, and boarded a sleek twin funnelled cruise ship the TSS *King George V* of 830 tonnes. I was very happy because it was a lovely morning with some cloud cover and the seas were calm. The ship cast off at 9.30 a.m. first crossing the Firth of Lorne and then entering the Sound of Mull, a sea passage between the large Isle of Mull and the mainland.

The ship then turned south along the west coast of Mull where the sea got a little choppy, but nothing more as we steamed along. It was great to be on board a steam ship again. After steaming along for about an hour, the ship dropped anchor at a small island just off the tip of the Isle of Mull.

IONA

We had arrived at Isle of Iona. We were told we had two hours

269

to explore the island, which is only 3.5 miles long and one mile wide. The island is mostly flat and has a population of around 130 who farmed, ran a few sheep and fished. As I walked from the pier I passed the ruins of St Margaret's Nunnery, then on to the cathedral (or abbey), which was built in the 13th century. The cathedral is quite small and without a spire. We weren't allowed inside because it was undergoing restoration. The guide told us that Macbeth was buried on the island along with many other Kings of Scotland, and that the cathedral, operated by the small community, is now the centre of a pilgrimage.

Back on board we had a sandwich lunch, which was included in the cost of the tour. After a coffee the *King George V* pulled up anchor and steamed off toward the Isle of Staffa and Fingal's Cave. The German composer Mendelssohn's *Hebrides Overture* was running through my mind. Mendelssohn visited Scotland in 1829. After making a visit to Staffa and other islands in the Hebrides, he composed the *Hebrides Overture*, sometimes known as the 'Fingal's Cave Overture' because it was reckoned that the music portrayed the sound of the sea and wind around the cave. Mendelssohn also composed the *Scotch Symphony*.

Very soon an island appeared in the distance and as we steamed closer I was able to discern a peculiar rock formation along the sides of the island. Our ship approached the island and dropped anchor a short distance away.

STAFFA AND FINGALS CAVE

This was the famous Isle of Staffa and Fingals Cave, an amazing sight, although it only covered an area of 71 acres (28 ha). I bought a small booklet about Staffa and had been reading it on the way. It said that 'Staffa was formed by volcanic action and the feature of the island was the hexagonal columns, which were caused by the slow cooling of the basalt that occurred over 60 million years ago.'

We were taken to Fingal's Cave by the ship's lifeboats, landing

270

on a small shingle beach and platform of rocks. From there we were ushered along a series of roped and railed walkways, up and down over rocky steps beside the water in the cave, until we finally reached as far as we could go to the back of the cave. Looking toward the cave entrance, it was rather dark and not really beautiful, but it was certainly a grand, dramatic and tremendous sight, with a little light glinting off the ripples on the sea inside. Fingal's Cave is 70 yards m long, 20 yards high and 15 yards wide. Only a certain number of people could view the cave at any one time, so we had to keep moving along a series of gangways. It was quite a scramble up and down over the rocks inside the cave.

Back on board, the *King George V's* the anchor was lifted and we steamed west to re-enter the Sound of Mull, then into an inlet at the head of which lay the port of Tobermory.

TOBERMORY

The *King George V* tied up at the quay and we were given time ashore to have a look at the small, but lovely fishing port and village. After having a good look around Tobermory, the *King George V* took us back to Oban. I was really lucky, the weather conditions could not have been more ideal for my visit to Fingal's Cave. If the sea is too rough it is not possible to leave the ship and visit the cave. The time was about 6 .p.m. and I should have caught a train back to Glasgow but I didn't. Instead after a large meal I went to the movies and saw *An American in Paris*, starring super colossal Gene Kelly and Leslie Caron.

Saturday 16th August: I left the George Hotel in the morning after paying a no ordinary, enormous fee, and then saw over a tweed factory, which I found it very interesting seeing the machinery used in the manufacture of heavy tweed clothing. Tweed however, is not my style, so I was not tempted to buy.

!!!!!!!!!!!!!!!!!!!!!!

OBAN TO GLASGOW

I caught the 11.45 a.m. train back to Glasgow 61 miles away to

McCraig's Tower above Oban

A view of King George V at anchor in Iona

The ruins of St Margaret's Nunnery

Approaching Fingal's Cave
(a postcard)

Fingal's Cave

The walkways in Fingal's Cave

the east. It was not a very fast journey, but an enjoyable one as the train stopped at every station along the way through rather rugged bushy country. A couple of stations I noted were Connel, and Loch Itive. Then the train joined WHR at Craigendoran, once again returning to Glasgow by Loch Lomond. I had hoped that the cloud would have lifted from the tops of the summits, but no, around Loch it was misty with low cloud covering the high summits

GLASGOW

When I arrived back in Glasgow I booked a coach trip to go to Edinburgh on Monday, from where I would have my last rail trip in Scotland going over the famous Firth of Forth Bridge. I finally arrived back at Muirend at 5 p.m. noon, and had tea with May, Auntie Ruby and Uncle Bob and then we all went off to a quadrille, a kilt and sword square dance show. It was quite skilful, with the dancers jumping back and forth over the swords. I enjoyed the display very much.

Sunday 17th August: In the evening, I went to Auntie Ruby's church. The minister welcomed me, which was very nice and later in the service Auntie Ruby sang a solo in a clear, contralto voice. I remembered my mother telling me that Auntie Ruby used to sing on the BBC. After the church service we went for a cup of tea at Auntie Ruby's and then to a friend's place for supper.

GLASGOW TO EDINBURGH

Monday 18th August: Instead of taking the shortest route to Edinburgh by rail or bus, I opted for a longer journey through some interesting Scots towns and countryside. The weather was passable as I boarded the coach, which drove north of Glasgow passing through Aberfoyle, then travelled on to Calendar, a popular tourist centre. Some parts of this town were renamed Tannochbrae for the TV series *Dr Finley's Casebook,* which I would see many times in later years. Leaving Calendar the coach turned west toward Stirling, with Stirling Castle a prominent landmark on its skyline.

From there the coach wound its way through various sized towns and villages and crossed and ran alongside railway lines, where I was lucky to see a few steam trains speeding by. After a very enjoyable three-hour journey of nearly 150 miles our coach reached the huge sprawling city of Edinburgh, the capital city of Scotland. situated on the Forth River at the head of the Firth of Forth.

EDINBURGH

I noticed flags flying on all the trams and found I had arrived at the time of the Edinburgh Festival. Edinburgh seemed to be a very cosmopolitan city, because it was teeming with visitors from all over the world. I thought that many of these visitors may have first been to the Olympic Games, which had just finished in Helsinki.

I found the YH and booked in, leaving my rucksack there to take a bus tour around the city. The tour took me up to the 11th century Edinburgh Castle situated on top of an extinct volcano core. The bus had to stop for a moment while the Duke of Edinburgh drove past in his open limousine. The tour then went around the city before going out to Holyrood House Palace, the official residence of the British monarchs in Scotland.

After the bus tour I walked around the city, but found it to be a mishmash of long and short streets. Princess Street and the parallel Queen Street seemed to me to be the limit of the city's street planning. The city of Edinburgh had no appeal for me quite unlike Glasgow, which gave me a warm and friendly feeling. However, very interesting to me was the Waverley Railway Station, the destination of so many of the express trains I had watched speeding through Stevenage. Waverley Station is situated at one end of a large depression called Princess Street Gardens, while at the other end the railway lines disappear under the Greek style National Gallery. Another feature of Edinburgh was a high hill called Arthur's Seat, 805 ft (251 m), which by no means dominated the city, but is seen a short way off from many points of view. We have its namesake in

274

Victoria, a very prominent landmark, which rises to 879 ft (274 m) on the shore of Port Phillip Bay.

Back at the YH, it was a joyous surprise to meet Rosemary Roberts, Joan Cooper and Ruth Pretty. It is such an exciting experience meeting members of YHA in cities so far from Australia. We talked happily together for a while before I went back into the city to the Church of Scotland Assembly Hall, to see *The Highland Fair,* produced by The Old Vic Trust Limited. It was a very entertaining operetta about the goings on between Clan Bracken and Clan Grelloch, which gave me an opportunity to see all the sporrans, kilts and tartans on display.

After dark, I walked up to Edinburgh Castle, a fabulous sight floodlit at night. I peeped through the closed gates where a military tattoo was in progress, being filmed by the BBC.

iiiiiiiiiiiiiiiiiiiii

THE FIRTH OF FORTH BRIDGE

Tuesday 19th August: I was up early the next morning, because I was off to see the fabulous Firth of Forth Bridge. I caught a train at Waverley railway station to take me to the bridge. It was a sunny day and in no time at all the train was on the approach viaducts. Then suddenly the train was enclosed by the massive steel construction of the bridge. I was able to look out of the carriage window and see the water a long way below, and managed to take a few photographs as the train moved across the bridge at around 30 mph. The bridge is truly immence and the train finally reached the other side of the Firth clear of the massive steel structure of the bridge and continued on to Dunfermline, the first station on the other side of the Firth. I had a ham sandwich in Dunfermline

DUNFERMLINE
DUNFIRMLINE TO NORTH QUEENSFERRY

I then took a bus back to North Queensferry to catch the ferry. I paid a very small fare and climbed aboard.

NORTH QUENSFERRY ACROSS THE FIRTH

Not long after the ferry left the wharf and began its journey across the Firth, I heard a noise. I looked up and saw what appeared to be small toy train coming across the bridge. I was lucky too, because another train crossed the bridge as I was crossing in the ferry. It was only when the ferry was in the centre of the Firth looking up that I realised how massive the bridge is. The ferry trip across the Firth below the bridge is a journey not to be missed if the grandeur and extent of this colossal engineering marvel is to be fully appreciated. My diary and notes do not record where the ferry journey ended on the south side of the Firth, I suspect it was called South Queensferry.

I bought a coloured postcard of the bridge in Dunfermline, which took up the top half of the card. The lower half listed the following statistics for the bridge, which I have converted into their S.I. equivalents shown below.

The labour of 5000 men, day and night for just over 7 years. Cost £3,500,000

Engineers: Sir John Fowler and Sir Benjamin Baker

Contractor: Sir William Arrol

Commenced December 1882, completed March 1889

Length including approach viaducts, 2.4 km, two spans 521m and two 210 m

Highest point above water level: 110 m

Height of viaduct: 48 m

Depth of foundations: 18 m

Diameter of largest tubes: 3.66 m

Dead weight on each main pier: 16,256 tonnes

Materials:

Steel 54,864 tonnes

Rivets 6,500,000, equivalent to 4267 tonnes

Granite 21,237 cubic metres

Concrete 101,600 tonnes

276

Certainly my train journey across the Firth of Forth railway bridge and being able to see the bridge with my own eyes that I had seen so many pictures of in books in my youth, was one of the many highlights of my visit to Scotland. Back in Edinburgh I had my last look around and climbed the 287 steps to the top of the Gothic Sir Walter Scott Memorial Tower where I had a great view of the city of Edinburgh, which has one feature in common with Oban. From the top of the Scott Tower in the west I could see a building with a number of columns. It was an unfinished memorial to the dead of the Napoleonic wars.

EDINBURGH TO GLASGOW

I caught a bus back to Glasgow along the M8, a more direct route than the way I had come. The bus passed through rolling countryside and the towns of Bathgate and Coatbridge. Scotland may be called 'the home of golf', but the courses were certainly well hidden, although I did see one on the way back to Glasgow.

GLASGOW

Wednesday 20th August: My last full day in Scotland. I began packing my rucksack and sorting out the things that would go in my case to be sent to me when I arrived back in London. I spent my last night in Scotland with Auntie Ruby, Uncle Bob and May, talking about my tours around their country and about my plans for the future, before retiring to bed for my last sleep in 'Bonnie Scotland.' As I lay in bed waiting for sleep to come, I reflected on my two weeks in Scotland with these wonderful people, my distant relations. It was truly exciting for me to be with them in person after hearing so much about them from my mother. If only the weather had been better, but I supposed the sort of weather I experienced was an intrinsic part of Scotland.

GLASGOW TO PRESTWICK AIRPORT

Thursday 21st August: I had breakfast with Uncle Bob, Auntie Ruby and May. I thanked them for their hospitality and for looking after

277

Entering the Forth Bridge

Halfway across with the
Firth of Forth below

Waiting to board the ferry at North
Queensferry

A centre span of the bridge as seen
from the ferry

A view of the bridge from he ferry

278

me wonderfully during my stay. Together with Auntie Ruby and May, we travelled to Prestwick Airport by tram and bus, 30 miles from Glasgow on the coast of the Firth of Clyde.

PRESTWICK AIRPORT

This was to be my first flight and I was looking forward to it without any fear. The time soon came to board the SAS DC 3 plane. With hugs and kisses with Auntie Ruby and May and grateful thanks for looking after me so well, I sadly I gave May a final kiss and hug. I climbed the stairs and paused for May to take a photo. It was a nice sunny day, and good flying weather. I took my seat at the back of the plane's narrow fuselage.

PRESTWICK AIRPORT TO NORWAY

A lovely SAS hostess in a very trim uniform gave instructions on how to put on the life jackets and leave the plane if the aircraft had to ditch in the North Sea. The possibility of that occurring didn't worry me at all. I had complete confidence in the pilot's ability, together with the knowledge that he loves life as much as I do, and would not place his life in jeopardy if he could hep it.

At 2.30 p.m. the air hostess asked us all to put on our seat belts and with a roar of the engines the plane began to move. After a surprisingly short time the plane was airborne. As it banked and turned to the east I caught a brief glimpse of the island of Ailsa Craig from the window, and then I was off to Norway. The DC 3 engines made a pleasant droning sound as the plane winged its way in steady flight over the North Sea.

Looking out the window I could see white caps mottling the surface of the dark blue North Sea below, and I guessed that the plane was flying at about 8,000 to 10,000 ft (2.500 to 3.000 m), because there was a stretch of puffy alto cumulus cloud just below the plane. I thought that flying was really good. I wondered if the fly on the window had a passport. Passport or not, it was going to have a terrible shock when the plane landed in Norway and its friends were back in Scotland. The 750 km flight to Stavanger took about two hours. Soon the cloud disappeared and all I could see from the window was the deep blue sea a fascinating sight. About halfway through the flight I was served a salad by the hostess both of which were very nice.

Soon after, but quite suddenly the plane crossed the Norwegian coast, and my first flight was nearly over. I thoroughly enjoyed the flight. The plane made a smooth landing in Stavanger, where the hostess said to reset our watches–1 hour forward, which I did as soon as I left the plane. I left the small Stavanger airport and took a taxi to YH that was not very far from the centre of the city.

CHAPTER 16

NORWAY

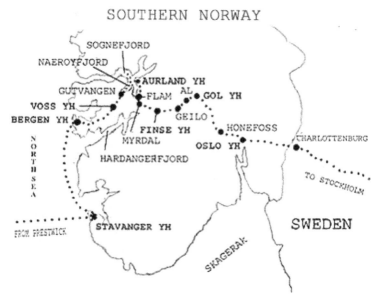

A map showing the route of the author's journey through Norway
youth hostels are indicated in bold type

⚐ STAVANGER

I booked in to the YH and settled in, and after a short rest I walked back into Stavanger, a fishing port with many canneries for the processing of sardines and herrings. The town's symbol is in fact, the key of a sardine can. Around the wharves in the town there were many stalls selling fish and other goods. At the time of my visit in 1952, Stavanger's principal and virtually only industry was catching and processing fish.

Since 1960, however, there has been a great change brought on by the discovery of oil in the North Sea. At the time of writing Stavanger is a very important town, where every type of business concerned with the oil drilling industry is conducted. Happily, in some sense, the discovery of oil coincided with a severe depletion of fish stocks in the North Sea, so all is still well for Stavanger.

The Norwegian language spoken here was very different to any foreign language I had encountered so far, and so was the money. I changed a traveller's cheque into Norwegian krone (Nkr): 1Nkr=100 ore; 20 Nkr=£1 Sterling. It was time to eat, so I decided to try the local product, a hearty meal of succulent sardines and chips.

Because I had moved further north it was still quite light at 10 p.m. Apart from the money and the language there was another difference, the traffic in Norway drove on the right hand side of the road, and not on the left, so I had to take great care when stepping off the kerb to cross a road. I walked back to the YH, which was only about 1 km from the town centre.

I thought it was a good time to work out my budget for the 40 days remaining, before I returned to London on 1st October. I still had a total of £50 left, so there would be no trouble keeping to a one pound Sterling daily budget, the same as on my first tour. This time, however, there would be no Netta to loan me money. If I was running short of cash. I could simply cut my tour short and cross the Channel back to England. Having worked out my buget, I climbed into my sleeping bag after a very exciting day.

Friday 22nd August: I went back into the town to a café and with my map and guide book, I had a beer and planned my next move, eventually deciding to go north to Bergen by boat. I walked down to the wharf and attempted to get a lift from a few boats, but to no avail,

282

so I booked a passage on a small ship to Bergen, sailing at 9.30 p.m. that night.

In the afternoon I stayed in the YH talking to other hostellers, getting a few ideas that were a great help in planning my journey after leaving Bergen. When staying in youth hostels, it is important to interact with all the other hostellers to glean as much information as possible about the vicinity, where to eat cheaply, places to see or not to see, where to get the best exchange rate. All manner of useful information can be obtained, and given. They should have told me to take a coach to Bergen as it was only 150 km away north.

I devoured another delicious meal of local fish and chips at a café near the hostel and drank a small bottle of vermouth and returned to the YH, where I suddenly realised it was time to catch the boat. Thankfully I had already paid the YH overnight fees, and I ran with my heavy rucksack to the boat, which was very hard work.

STAVANGER TO BERGEN

I just managed to climb aboard and show my ticket before the small gangplank was pulled up. I sat down on a hatch cover on the deck as the boat pulled slowly away from the jetty, to begin its voyage up the west coast of Norway to my destination of Bergen, 150 km north of Stavanger. I was not feeling at all well and soon began to dry retch, which caused me to spend the first part of the night time voyage close by the deck railing, just in case I was sick. I was lucky that the sea was dead calm and soon the feeling of nausea left me, but I remained by the railing for some time watching the white capped wake of the boat spread out in the dead black North Sea.

Saturday 23rd August: About half way into the voyage dawn broke and I could see the rugged rocky coastline close by. I saw one large inlet. I was told it was the entrance to the Hardangarfjord. In daylight the boat tied up in the Bergen at 7 a.m.

283

The Douglas DC3 aeroplane at the Prstwick Airport

To Norway the author and the SAS plane

Alto cumulus cloud above the North Sea

First sight of the coast of Norway

Stavanger

The Stavanger fish market

284

⚠
BERGEN

I found the YH at Floyen on the top of a steep hill above Bergen, which thankfully in my condition was accessed by cable car. I booked into the YH at 8 a.m. and a few minutes later I was fast asleep in my sleeping bag, where I remained until early afternoon. When I woke feeling much better, I decided to have a look at the city.

On the way I had a great view of Bergen from a high hill near the YH. Bergen's harbour has a tongue of land jutting into its centre, populated by many buildings and wharves. Low hills surrounded the harbour, but further inland they became a range of mountains. Bergen's harbour and city, with its many various coloured dwellings clustered around the water's edge, and back into the hills, looked very picturesque in the morning sun with a few clouds overhead.

I walked down the hill to a café where I had a large ham sandwich and a glass of Norge Export Beer and sat outside the cafe with another Aussie I met at the YH, Alan Hamano. We watched with eyes agog as gorgeous young, blonde Norwegian women passed by. Oh boy, but not like the ubiquitous bottle blondes that were around at the time in Australia. I noticed too that a lot of the people, both men and women, were wearing light grey, see-through plastic raincoats, as there had been a shower of rain a little while before. These were so light and thin that when not in use they could be rolled up and put in a trouser or coat pocket.

Sunday 24th August: With Alan Hamano I had a look at a couple of churches in Bergen, one the Domekirke (Cathedral), which was quite unusual in its style, dating from 1300. We then went into St Mary's church, which was from the same period but was of Orthodox Church architecture, Romanesque I believed, with Gothic spires and a very ornate pulpit. The main religion in Norway is the Evangelical-Lutheran State Church. Next we saw the Bryggen's

Museum, which had items from the 14th century found during excavations around the harbour.

After we had a ham sandwich it was time to go back to the hostel where I wrote to the family and May. I didn't plan to travel much further north, and decided it was time to move on into the fjord and mountain country for which Norway is famous. From Bergen I planned to travel west across the broad part of Norway and then south to Oslo. Further north beyond Trondheim Norway becomes a strip of country wedged between Sweden, Finland and the Atlantic Ocean. The main features of this rugged country that I wanted to see were the mountains and fjords and these were on the route I planned.

The first stop on this journey was Voss, about 160 km from Bergen, where there was a YH, but I decided not to try to hitch hike because the country looked very rugged on the map. The first train for Voss the next day left at 7.30 a.m. I decided to save some money and sleep overnight on the station.

After a fine cool day it began to rain and when darkness fell. I paid the very reasonable YH fees and around 11.30 p.m. I walked down the hill to the railway station in the rain. As I walked I admired the lights of Bergen below. They were very pretty, particularly the lights of boats moving across the dark expanse of water in the harbour. I didn't have too much admiration for the rain, but realised it was part of life in Bergen. At the station I took off my gabardine raincoat and got settled. I wrote up my diary and note book and then lay back and went to sleep and was not bothered during the night.

iiiiiiiiiiiiiiiiiiii

BERGEN TO VOSS

Monday 25th August: I woke up in the railway station waiting room after a good night's sleep. I had the bread and ham sandwich I had brought along for breakfast. I was the only person on the platform when the train backed in, but people began to arrive as the time approached for the train's departure. The train was hauled by a 2-8-0 steam locomotive and I noticed that the locomotive's cab was enclosed, which I thought was a necessity for the winter months. There were about six carriages and one I saw was an American style day coach, so I made a beeline for it and grabbed a window seat. A day coach is a railway carriage with seats that can be swivelled to allow a passenger to face in the direction the train is moving. The coach also had large windows and a centre isle with vestibules at each end with short stairs to access the low level European style platforms

With a loud whistle like a truck horn, and the sound of steam issuing from the locomotive's release cocks the train gradually drew away from the platform for the 73 km journey to Voss. For the first few kilometres it wound its way through the low hills that surround Bergen. Loud blasts from the locomotive's exhaust indicated that the train was climbing steadily and very soon the first tunnel was pierced. There were many more tunnels to come as the train ran along benches cut into the mountainside above the Sorfjord, a narrow fjord my first sight of one of Norway's many spectacular fjords. All the way along, the line clung to the side of the mountain from which spurs protruded and descended into the fjord below. It was these that were the reason for this line having so many tunnels, the length depending on the size of each spur through which builders of the line bored a tunnel. A massive, engineering achievement.

About halfway into the journey to Voss the fjord came to an end and the valley opened out as the train came to Dale, where we passed a train going to Bergen. Soon after leaving Dale the train entered a narrow gorge and burrowed through a very long tunnel. After traversing along more gorges and through tunnels the land changed to a series of luxuriant green valleys. Finally Voss was reached in a broad valley with mountain ranges on two sides, bringing to a close a very exciting journey through many tunnels above the fjord. I didn't count how many there were, but there must have been close to 50,

287

and we were not bothered by any smoke and steam inside the carriages at any time as the train went through all the tunnels.

▲

VOSS

The industrial city of Voss was bombed heavily during WWII and some bomb damage could still be seen. Voss is also a centre for skiing in the surrounding mountains. I had a bite to eat in in a café in the big city and then set out on the 3 km walk to the YH, a large wooden ski chalet type building in lovely grassy surroundings in a suburb of Voss. After an evening meal I slept the night there.

🖐

VOSS TO GUDVANGEN

Tuesday 26th August: After breakfast I paid my fees before setting out on the road for my second attempt at hitchhiking. My destination was Gudvangen at the end of the Naeroyfjord, a branch of the Sognefjord. The two bright and breezy Lancashire girls I met at the YH decided to come with me. Out on the road we went, but I was not sure what my luck would be with the two girls tagging along. However, I need not have worried because we got a lift quickly from a man in a car who took us along a thinly populated broad valley.

I am not sure if it was because I was with the two girls, but this hitchhiking attempt was off to an auspicious start. The driver took us a short distance down a switchback road past Stalheim, as he was not going any further. There was a large hotel at Stalheim perched on the side of the steep drop overlooking the valley of Naeroydalen, along which we had to go to catch a ferry to Gudvangen.

The view looking down into this valley was truly spectacular. The valley floor was only about 400 m wide with a river running down one side and the road on the other. It could hardly be termed a valley, it was more like a gorge with the sides soaring steeply up 500 m (1,500 ft) or so above the valley floor. The valley was in fact the

288

Noeroyfjord Gorge. As we walked together down the switchback road to the bottom of the gorge, the Lancashire girls and I chatted together commenting on the magnificent vistas that surrounded us.

Although their north of England Lancashire style of English was enchanting, it was not as melodious to my ears as May's lovely Scots brogue. We walked along the Naeroyfjord Gorge looking up at the steep sides of the gorge where we could see many large and small waterfalls cascading down the precipitous walls. It was a truly magnificent sight. Halfway along one side of the gorge there was a mountain shaped like a blunt pyramid, and in the distance we could see patches of snow clinging to the mountainsides. On the floor of the gorge we saw large wire racks, which were drying grass that had been harvested on what little flat land there was.

After walking about 5 km along the gorge as it twisted first one way then the other the weather began to get gloomier. We eventually came to the small village of Gudvangen at the end of the Naeroyfjord, just as it began to rain heavily. We sheltered there and had a sandwich from a stall while we waited for the ferry to arrive, which it did at 5.30 p.m. Thankfully the rain had stopped as we boarded the ferry to take us along Norway's narrowest fjord the Naeroyfjord, to Aurland.

GUDVANGEN TO AURLAND

After a while the ferry entered the Sognefjord, Norway's longest and deepest fjord, 200 km long and 1.300 m deep. We entered this fjord some 25 km from its end, where it is surrounded by steep cliffs that rose to snow covered mountains, 1,000 m (3,208 ft) above us and the water level in the fjord. Surrounded by magnificent scenery the ferry took us into the centre of the Sognefjord and along its length for about 2 km, where we were met by two other ferries. Midfjord we transferred from our ferry, which was returning to Gudvangen, and on to the ferry to take us to Aurland. Other passengers changed to a third ferry, which was going to a village further up the Sognefjord. The ferries were tied with the deck gates opposite each other so it was easy to step from one deck to the other. Never did I ever expect to see an interchange station in the centre of a fjord, all without any signposts. Once we got going again we returned a little way back along the Naeroyfjord toward Gudvangen, then branched off into the Aurlandsfjord that I had not noticed along the way.

A

AURLAND

This ferry took us to Aurland, where the YH was located on the side of the fjord. The time was 9 p.m. and it was quite dark. After a good meal in a well appointed YH with hot and cold water, I got into my sleeping bag and reflected on the wonderful country I had seen that day.

AURLAND TO FLAM

Wednesday 27th August: I set off with the girls intending to hitchhike to Flam, 8 km distant, but this time we had no offers. About halfway to Flam a bus came along, so we climbed aboard to take us the rest of the way to Flam. The bus drove along the side of the fjord, which ended abruptly at the town of Flam, beyond which a mountain range rose to a great height. Flam is the terminus for the Flam-Myrdal Mountain Railway. The girls said they would come with me to Myrdal, where they will take the train back to Bergen. I will catch the train there for Finse in the opposite direction to Oslo. From Bergen the girls were going to journey up the coast of Norway to Trondheim. We purchased a ticket to take us up the switchback railway to Myrdal to re-join the Oslo-Bergen railway line

¡¡¡¡¡¡¡¡¡¡¡¡¡¡¡¡¡¡¡¡¡¡

FLAM TO MYRDAL

The train to Myrdal began its upward journey and very soon it had climbed high enough to see magnificent views back down the length of the Aurland valley. The train consisted of six carriages with two electric locomotives, one pulling and the other at the rear pushing. Each carriage is equipped with five separate braking systems, any one of which could hold the train safely on its own on the incline. The skyline at the end of the valley was punctuated by a spectacular high mountain with a sharp peak and a high waterfall falling from its lower steep flanks. The train wound around sharp bends through some small tunnels, then switched back on itself as it quickly gained height.

A couple of times the train was stopped to allow the passengers to see some more magnificent views, then a little further on stopped beside a large waterfall, the Kjosfoss a huge cascade dropping down from ledge to ledge only metres away from the train. The train ran along a cutting or bench in the side of the mountain and then entered a long tunnel in which it performed a loop, reversed direction, and emerged high up on the side of the mountain at Myrdal. The magnificent train ride took about an hour to climb from Flam to Myrdal.

The spectacular Flam-Myrdal line is 19 km long, and climbs 886 m (2,841 ft) with a gradient of 1 in 18. It is claimed to be the longest, continuous adhesion, (without rack or cable) mountain railway in the world. After bidding goodbye to the Lancashire girls who were really good company, I purchased a ticket to Finse where there was a YH. I did not have to wait long before a train arrived going to Oslo and Finse. Most of the carriages were day coaches giving me great views.

iiiiiiiiiiiiiiiiiii

MYRDAL TO FINSE

Very soon after the train left Myrdal station it dived into the kilometre long Reinunga tunnel, emerging above the tree line where there were many large snow drifts on the ground. The train was equipped with a public address system, my first experience of this feature which kept we passengers well informed of items of interest and our whereabouts as the train travelled along, puffing its way through many snow sheds, protecting the railway line in areas prone

291

Bergen harbour from the YH

A view of Bergen and the mountain range behind the city

Photo of the switch back road from Stalheim descending into the Naeroydalen Valley

The author about to board the ferry on the Naeroyfjord for Aurland

The Flam Myrdal train in the station

Noeroyfjord Gorge waterfalls

Finse railway station in which is also the Youth Hostel all surrounded by fog

to the large build up of snowdrifts. Halfway to my destination of Finse 25 km away the train stopped at Haugastol railway station located inside a snow shed with a loop where an Oslo bound train passed ours. From then on the train passed by many small lakes and large snowdrifts, but as the train climbed higher the country became fog bound and finally it pulled into Finse.

A

FINSE

Finse is the highest railway station in Norway, 1.240 m (4,068 ft) above sea level. It is a popular ski touring destination surrounded by mountains, but they were invisible to me because of a thick fog. The YH is located in the Finse railway station building looked after by three pretty Norwegian girls.

I booked in and went for a walk in the fog. There were a few cottages near the station for workers who maintained the railway line. Their work would be especially important in the wintertime in keeping the track clear of snow. As I ambled along I heard the noise of an engine, so I went and investigated. The noise was made by the idling engine of a small seaplane on Lake Finsevatn, about a kilometre below the railway station. The pilot told me he worked for a company called *New Realm Pictures*. He was in Finse making a film called *Into the Unknown*.

The pilot said he was going to Oslo as soon as the fog cleared. I asked if he could take me with him. He asked me how much luggage I had? I told him only my rucksack. He said to be at the plane when the fog lifted and he would give me a lift. There was nothing to see at Finse in the fog and I thought it would be a thrilling experience to fly in a seaplane to Oslo, so I went back to the YH to get my rucksack.

I was about to return to the plane when I heard it take off. The fog appeared to me to be as thick as before, but it must have cleared enough down by the lake for him to get away. I was not really

293

disappointed as I was looking forward to seeing the countryside between Finse and Oslo.

Finse has an important place in the history of polar exploration. It was here that Robert Falcon Scott, the English explorer, trained for his ill-fated journey to the South Pole, which he reached on 17th January 1912. Finse was also one of the locations for the filming of *Scott of the Antarctic*, released in 1948, starring John Mills and Kenneth More. I would have liked to spend a couple of days in Finse and explore the area, but because the weather report for the next few days was for more fog and snow, I decided to move on to Oslo.

More history was made in this area in later years. Over this barren part of Norway, about 60 km inland from Stavanger, the English pilot Peter Twiss was granted permission to test fly his Fairy Delta 2 aeroplane, in preparation for breaking the world speed record of 1,000 mph (1.600 km/h). He had been banned from flying over France or any part of the British Isles because of the sonic boom that the test flights would produce. In 1956 he applied to the Norwegian authorities, and they welcomed him with open arms to test fly the plane in the area around Finse. Peter Twiss eventually succeeded in breaking the record in Sussex, England in 1956, after the bans were removed.

||||||||||||||||||||||||

FINSE TO GEILO

Thursday 28th August: I woke to a blizzard and with 25 mm of snow already on the ground and with Finse still enveloped in thick fog. I thought that I might be able to hitchhike all the 190 km to Oslo but it was not possible to begin this from Finse in these conditions, so I waited for a train to come along and at 12 noon a steam train emerged from the fog.

I thanked the girls, payed my fees and climbed aboard for the very comfortable, warm, 49 km ride to Geilo. It was a local steam train from Voss. The train with its car like whistle first went through a tunnel and a couple of snow sheds and then wound its way through a scrubby, rocky landscape that was all I could see through the fog, which cleared before reaching Geilo on the edge of the timberline. There were many ski runs cut into the small stunted pine trees, but there was no snow, because we were now below the snowline.

GEILO TO GOL

The next town on the way to Oslo with a YH was Gol, 50 km from Geilo. I left the train and decided to hitchhike to Gol. I went out on the road to try to thumb a lift south to Oslo, but had to wait a long time. I finally managed to get a lift in a car that took me to the village of Al. The next lift was in the back of an open truck to Gol, well within the tree line, which consisted of dense forests of pine trees. It was very cold as the truck drove down a winding road.

GOL

I was frozen stiff when I got off the truck at Gol. It was such a great relief to get inside the YH and warm myself by the fire, even though the YH was full of giggling, screaming girl guides. They quietened down at night and I slept well after a hearty YH meal.

GOL TO NESBYEN

Friday 29th August: Not having any reason to stay in the Gol YH especially with the screaming Girl Guides, I continued with my hitchhiking and got a 50 km lift as far as Nesbyen. I wanted to reach Oslo that day, so I decided to catch the train the rest of the way even though my hitchhiking had been very successful. I had to wait about an hour for the train.

!!!!!!!!!!!!!!!!!!!!
NESBYEN TO OSLO

The train was hauled by a large steam locomotive and I was very glad to sit down in the comfort of a lovely warm day coach for the long journey of 116 km to Oslo.

The train passed by small villages along the shores of Lake Kroderen, and bored through many short tunnels before coming to the large town of Honefoss, a big saw milling centre for pulp and paper production. The train was losing altitude all the time as it crossed a long bridge over the Begna River. Not surprisingly, I was developing a bad cold and dozed off for much of the journey. After passing along a beautiful valley and through heavily timbered hills, the train pulled into the large Oslo Station at 6 p.m. I was happy that I had not tried to thumb a lift for the remainder of the journey, because I am sure I would not have reached Oslo that day.

⛺

OSLO

I found the YH quite easily and booked in. After a good meal I had a long talk with some hostellers, during which I talked a couple of them into doing the trip to Bergen. Very tired, I hopped into my sleeping bag and read the large brochure I got in Bergen about the Oslo-Bergen Railway. The Oslo-Bergen Railway is rated as one of the classic railway journeys in the world. The line was completed in 1909. The highest point on the line is 1.320 m (4,235 ft), 96 km of the line is above the tree line and 73 km of its 490 km goes through over 200 tunnels, or snow sheds.

The train journey is advertised as seeing 'Norway in a nutshell.' I had now been on four classic heritage listed rail journeys in Europe, Bergen to Oslo, Glasgow to Fort William and the famous Semmering Railway to and from Vienna over the Semmering Pass, an imposing collection of wonderful historic railway journeys.

Saturday 30th August: I was up early to a beautiful day, ideal for sightseeing in and around Oslo. The city gave me the impression of being a small city, but I found this was not so. Oslo is situated on the

Oslofjord and has a large harbour with many wharves. The modern trams cost 30 ore to travel anywhere on the tramway system.

The city centre is dominated by the Oslo City Hall, an ordinary unadorned, brick, block style of architecture. It had an interrupted construction history. The German occupation brought the building to a halt and it was not until 1950 that the City Hall was completed. I had a look through the modern interior, with the inside walls decorated with beautiful murals.

I joined a coach tour going to the Mek-Verksted shipyards where a 9,000 tonne ship *Buffalo* was being built for the Fred Olsen Line. We were told that the shipbuilding yard was on the site where ammunition ships were blown up during WWII. I was extremely interested to see a 900 cm diameter propeller shaft being turned on a huge lathe and many other shipbuilding machines in operation. The ship's 7 cylinder diesel engine was rated at 7,830 kW (10,500 horsepower). The crank shaft alone weighed a huge 150 tonnes and the pistons were 1 m diameter by 1.2 m long. Probably unlike the average tourist, I found this very interesting. Even though this ship was not a really large one, it gave me an interesting comparison to the 75-foot ocean-going tugboats I had helped to build in my apprenticeship with the Victorian Railways (VR) during the war years of WWII

My next visit was of a more artistic nature. I went by tram to Frogner Park, better known as Vigeland Park, where there is a magnificent collection of sculptures by the Norwegian sculptor Gustav Vigeland. The most striking of these is the granite obelisk 17 m high made up of 121 nude figures struggling to reach the light, surrounded by a series of 12 radial steps. At the sides of each of these are pedestals with figures representing all the situations that occur in daily life.

The obelisk gives the park its image. As well there are many other exhibits, including one set of sculptured figures depicting life from birth to death. Frogner Park is a wonderful and unique park full of interest, which no visitor to Oslo should miss seeing. Next on my list was the Holmenkollen ski jump, which of course held great interest to me.

The jump is situated in the hills to the north west of Oslo. A light railway took me all the way up to the ski jump, which was first built in 1892 and then rebuilt for the 1952 winter Olympics. Although Holmenkollen was the centre piece for these games, other events were held in other venues around Oslo. The base of the jump tower was occupied by a ski museum, which housed all sorts of skis tracing the development of skiing from before the times of the Vikings, around 800 AD. Some special exhibits were the beautifully carved skis from Finland, elaborately carved ski stocks and a pair of Austrian bamboo skis. On view in the centre of the museum was equipment from the Nansen and Amundsen polar voyages.

I bought a bottle of beer and took a lift to the top of the jump tower, then climbed the final steps to the take off point. It was a frightening sight as I stood as near as possible to the take off position and looked down the jump run. I tried to imagine the thoughts of a jumper getting ready to take the downward plunge. The landing and run out area at the time I was there in summer is a large lake, which freezes over and is covered with snow in the winter. I walked across to one side of the jump ramp and sat down on one of the wooden seats that line both sides of the ramp. This provided me with an unimpeded view of Oslo and the Oslofjord, which I admired as I drank my tasty Norwegian beer. I hadn't had any lunch, so after I left the ski jump in the late afternoon, I decided to lash out and have dinner at a hotel as I was still well within my budget.

I selected the Grand Hotel, Oslo's premium hotel. It was superb dining in the heart of luxury and the cost was reasonable for a succulent meal of beef steak and vegetables washed down with a cold beer. I also had a desert of fruit salad and ice cream. Unlike the first tour, where I spent most of my time in ski clothes and ski boots, I came away on this tour with some smart casual clothes, plus my

298

good gabardine raincoat and my parka to wear in bad weather. One might have even described me as a 'gentleman backpacker.'

Sunday 31st August: I woke up with a bloody cold. I supposed this was not surprising considering how cold I was in the truck that gave me the lift. However, the joy of being a tourist in a foreign country must continue. I visited the Viking Museum, where I saw three Viking ships found in the mud beside the Oslofjord. Next was the Fram Museum, where I saw the *Fram,* a three masted schooner used by the Norwegian explorer Amundsen for his North Pole expeditions during 1893 to 1896, then by another Norwegian explorer, Sverdrups, for his polar expedition during 1898 to 1902

The building also contained the *Kon-Tiki,* the balsa raft that Thor Heyerdahl and five others, four Norwegians and one Swede constructed and sailed from Peru in 1947, to prove that the people of Polynesia originally came from Peru on similar rafts, driven west by the prevailing wind and ocean currents. His voyage was successful in proving this theory.

I decided to leave Oslo for Sweden the next day. I was not going to attempt to hitchhike with my cold. I walked around for a while, but my cold got the better of me, so I went back to the warm YH and wrote letters. As I climbed into my sleeping bag that night, I reflected on my journey through Norway. It was great to be amongst the mountains, the snow and the fjords. They were something new to my eyes. My only regret was that Finse was enshrouded in fog.

Monday 1st September: I bought a train ticket to Stockholm that cost 76 Nkr, about £3/10 Sterling, 3½ days budget money.

!!!!!!!!!!!!!!!!!!!!!!!

OSLO TO STOCKHOLM

The train left Oslo at 9.10 a.m. My cold had improved a little bit and I was hoping that the six hour train journey of 450 km would have some curative effect on my cold. The train was hauled by a big

299

The Oslo City Hall

A bronze pair by Vigeland

The Vigeland obelisk

Inside the Holmenkollen ski museum

Looking down the ski jump with the lake below

A view looking up the ski jump

electric locomotive and the carriages were day coach types, very comfortable, always great for viewing the passing countryside. After leaving the hills around Oslo the train followed Norway's largest river, the Glomma, which was chock-a-block with logs. They were floating downstream, but many appeared to be caught up in log jams on the side in eddies. The train passed by many lakes, crossing over into Sweden at Charlottenburg where our passports were checked, but there was no need to change money as Norwegian Kroner were accepted in Sweden.

CHAPTER 17

SWEDEN

SOUTHERN SWEDEN AND DENMARK

This map shows the route the author took and the
towns and cities he visited. Youth Hostels are shown in black type

The train continued on, again passing by many beautiful lakes of
various sizes, through cornfields and pine forests, stopping at the
towns of Karlstad and Kristinehamn on the edge of Lake Vanern, the
largest lake in Sweden, which has over 100,000 lakes, covering

about 9% of the country. So it was not surprising that lakes were forever in my view from the train.

I noticed that not only the train, but all the cars I saw from the train were travelling on the left hand side, not the right hand side as in Norway! More curious still was that all the cars seemed to have their steering wheels on the left hand side. I noted too that all the towns the train passed through were very clean and tidy. There was also a camouflaged pillbox guarding a railway junction the train passed by. I wondered why, because Sweden remained neutral during WWII.

The last hour or so of the journey was through seemingly never ending pine forests, which I supposed like lakes, was not surprising because these forests cover half of Sweden's land. From the train it appeared that Sweden was a land of pine forests and lakes. One town further on that the train stopped at had the very nice name of Katrineholm.

I met a bloke from Singapore called Basel on the train. He was on a university exchange program and was meeting his girlfriend in Stockholm. When we reached Stockholm about 4 p.m. after a very fast, comfortable and interesting train trip, Basel's attractive, girlfriend Kathleen was there to meet him

STOCKHOLM

They suggested I come and stay with them as there was a spare bed at a flat they were renting. They said it would only cost me 4 Skr per night. They seemed a genuine couple and they must have thought that I was a good bloke, so I agreed. We took a local electric train a short way to their flat. The train ticket was valid for anywhere for 1 hour at a cost of only 35 Ore (100 Ore=1 Skr). After depositing my rucksack in their room we went and had a meal in a nearby cafe. Very quickly I discovered that the road rules in Sweden were the same as in England and as I stepped off the kerb I had to get used to looking in the opposite direction than in Norway if I wished to stay alive. Most of the cars I saw in Stockholm were imported American cars, Pontiacs, Oldsmobiles, Fords and Chevrolets. All had their steering wheel on the left hand side, which further complicated the road rules.

When the driver of a parked car intended to enter the traffic stream, the driver using his rear view mirrors, and with trafficators illuminated and extended had to very carefully edge out to get into the traffic. In 1952 the Swedish car industry did not exist as it does at the time of writing. I saw no Volvos or Saabs, nor were there many English cars, which was surprising considering that English cars had their steering wheels on the correct side for the road rules in force in Sweden.

Tuesday 2nd September: I went into the city with Basel, but he dithered around so much about tips that I left him and walked around by myself. I thought Stockholm was a lovely city clean, wide, and handsome. I had never seen so many beautifully dressed blondes in all my life, even more than I had seen in Norway. It was a sight for sore eyes. The shops displayed beautiful goods, clothing, jewellery and many other enticing wares. I bought a quick-dry, nylon white shirt for 50 Skr and a nice tie to go with it for 14 Skr. I liked Stockholm very much.

Wednesday 3rd September: I saw signs advertising Puccini's opera *La Boheme*, so I decided to go that night. I was able to attend the performance in a nice white shirt and new tie. The dress standard of the opera going Swedes was of a high standard, more so than in Vienna, where it was not a social outing, as I suspect it was in Stockholm. I enjoyed the opera immensely, even though I could not understand any of the words that were spoken or sung, but I knew the opera was about a girl dying of consumption and recognised the beautiful aria, *'Your Tiny Hand is Frozen'*, and a few others. The opera was performed in Stockholm's opera house, the Kungl Teatern (Royal Opera House), 'Royal' because Sweden is a monarchy. The

304

Opera House is an attractive building, although not imposing. After the opera I washed the nylon shirt and hung it up to dry.

Thursday 4th September: It was another fine day and my nylon shirt was dry. The shirt will be a great asset on my tour: I would be able to wear it each day with my tie and look good as I did at the opera. I went on a boat tour called 'Under the Bridges' that travelled along canals that jut into the city centre. We passed beneath many stylish, reinforced concrete bridges. The Swedes certainly know how to build excellent structures. The boat tour allowed me to see many places that bordered the water, hospitals, wharfs, blocks of modern looking flats, factories and many other sights. It was a far different perspective than being viewed from a road.

Lastly the tour boat ventured out into the harbour on stretches of water called Lake Malaren and Lake Salsjohn, then along the waterfront of the Ridderfjord, all of which did not seem to earn the description of being either lakes or fjord. The tour was very good value, lasting two hours at a cost of 6.50 Skr that included a meal of very succulent cantaloupe and beef.

In the afternoon I visited Skansen Park, which cost 1.50 Skr admission. The park was mainly a zoo with a glass blowing exhibition and other demonstrations. A museum about Swedish life and culture cost 50 Ore. Every time I looked sideways it cost me another 50 Ore for something or other. Best was seeing the glass blowing, which I thought was a very skilful and rewarding trade.

Next on the list of sights to see was Slussen, a clover leaf style road interchange or crossroad. There were no traffic lights, but by means of signs a motorist coming to the crossroad was directed into taking the correct path, which allowed cars to merge into the traffic of their selected road. I was fascinated by the orderly flow of converging cars. At first Slussen appeared to be a complicated layout, but its efficacy was beyond doubt. It was the first example I had seen, of present day clover leaf highway interchanges, or roundabouts as we call them in Australia.

In the evening I went to the Tivoli Gardens, in Skansen Park, a big Luna Park type amusement centre. Every large city I have visited has an amusement park of some description and this park was one of the best. The admission cost was 50 Skr. I saw acrobats and then went to a dance for 50 Ore. It was the best 50 Ore or equivalent I had ever spent, because I met and danced with Oolah one of those beautiful Swedish blondes that I had been admiring, but never expected to have the good luck of being with. Oolah spoke perfect English and after the dance we had a coffee together. We talked about ourselves and our lives in our respective countries. Oolah said she lived in Eskilstuna, 30 km from Stockholm. She gave me her photograph and phone number and asked me to ring her in the morning, saying she would come into Stockholm and show me around.

Oolah told me that the Swedish government looked after the social welfare of all of its people, albeit with high taxes. There was no Swedish beer, except a poor excuse for one called, would you believe it, Vermouth Grog', which was quite harmless and tasted something like a soft drink I used to enjoy in my youth back home. But I did miss not being able to have a real, cold beer. Swedes could only purchase alcoholic drinks in strictly rationed quantities, which I imagined helped to maintain the clinical clean look, and well being of the city and environs.

I found where Eskilstuna was located and with the help of a tourist office employee I phoned Oolah. She said she couldn't get into Stockholm today, but I was welcome to come out to Eskilstuna any time to see her. Disappointed, I explored Stockholm further. I thought that it would be a great city to live in with its wide open streets, trams and buses. I particularly liked Kungsgaten, a city street with a slight curve, topped with an arched walkway from one side of the street to the other. Behind this on either side of the street were two brown brick office towers, and behind them in the distance was another small walkway. I next wandered down to the side of the

306

Riddarfjord, a section of Stockholm's waterfront, which was spick and span like the city, but with no resemblance to a fjord such as I had seen in Norway.

After tea, which we cooked in the flat, I went to the movies with Mr. Johansen, our landlord and Basel. We saw *Eldfagdn* (*Firebird*), an adaptation of Stravinsky's *Firebird.* Mr. Johansen explained to us much of what was occurring in the movie. I knew nothing of the Swedish language, but the movie was very colourful and interesting. I decided to leave Stockholm in the morning, having seen many interesting elements of Swedish life. I bought and mailed postcards to my family, May and Netta.

Friday 5th September: After breakfast I paid my rent and said goodbye to Kathleen and Basel. The Stockholm YH I learned later, was on a yacht moored at a Stockholm wharf. Many hostellers I met later raved about it. Boarding with Basel and Kathleen had been quite OK, but I imagined that the YH on the yacht would probably have been a little cheaper and more exciting, but I had enjoyed my stay in Stockholm, a very liveable city except for the traffic chaos.

♣

STOCKHOLM TO COPENHAGEN

I caught a bus to take me away from the city traffic on a main road to begin hitchhiking to Copenhagen, in Denmark, 500 km distant 'as the crow flies.' I studied my map and found that when I reached the town of Sodertajle, I would have to decide which way to go, to Oolah at Eskilstuna or Copenhagen.

As it transpired, the decision was made for me when along came a single spinner Ford. The driver indicated that he was on his way to Helsingborg, where I intended to catch a ferry to Denmark. He could not speak English or me Swedish. Thankfully I climbed aboard.

The waterfront on the Riddarfjord

A reinforced concrete bridge seen on the boat trip

Kungsgaten Street my favourite street in Stockholm

Slussen the Stockholm clover leaf road interchange

The Kungl Theatre Royal Opera House where I went to the opera

Oolah

We got on famously, as both of us had enough knowledge of *Deutsch* for a halting conversation. He said his name was Johan and was probably pleased to pick me up because I was a great help to him. Driving in a car with the steering wheel on the wrong side required a special driving strategy to avoid a possible head on collision with vehicles coming in the opposite direction. In order to pass a slower vehicle, whether a car, bus, or truck, Johan had to peer around the left side of the vehicle he intended to pass. If it was clear ahead as well as he could determine, he would then edge out to the right with trafficators and lights wagging and flashing and quickly pass, a very nerve racking manoeuvre.

Because I was on the correct side of the car, I could see the road ahead and when we caught up to a slower vehicle, Johan would edge out a little, and if I saw it was clear to pass, I would yell out: "OK." If not, I would yell out: *"Nein, nein"* (no in *Deutsch)*, until it was safe to pass, and around the slow vehicle we would pass with safety.

Further on we picked up a Swedish student called Paul, who wore a cap like a ship's captain. The hat, he told me, was worn by university students in Sweden. Paul spoke English, so from then on we were able to get a conversation going, while I still gave the passing commands.

Most of the journey was along a very good highway, through the ubiquitous pine forests, but not so many lakes. Every now and again we would stop at a garage, sometimes a short distance away from the highway where Johan would ply his trade in car accessories. Towards evening we arrived at the large town of Jonkoping, where Johan booked us all into a hotel, then took us to a restaurant for a tasty meal. Jonkoping is said to be 'the home of the safety match.' There was a large paper industry here, and also the 'Husqvarna' sewing machine factory and museum nearby. Coming back from the restaurant we walked into a fistfight between two Swedes, one a civilian and the other in the uniform of Sweden's militia. Johan was a big strong bloke and he separated them without too much trouble and sent them on their way. He told me that Swedish soldiers were not very popular with many members of the public, who didn't want anything to do with any aspect of war

⌂

JOHNKOPING

Saturday 6th September: After a big breakfast we left the hotel and Jonkoping in the rain at 10 a.m. There was a YH in Jonkoping and I would have liked to have stayed there. because there was a lot to see that would have been of interest to me such as visiting the match and paper factories, the Husqvarna factory and its museum. Exploring the shores here of Lake Vattern would have been of interest too, but it was raining heavily. I thought of the saying: 'when you are on to a good thing stick to it,' and the Ford Custom was a very good thing, so I remained with Johan and Paul.

We drove through the rain at 130 km/h, which was quite thrilling and probably a little dangerous considering the wet conditions. Paul took the front seat as this was much safer for us all, because Paul could tell Johan in his own language if it was OK to pass a slower vehicle. On the way to Helsinborg we called in at a town called Halmstad, where Johan did some business.

HALMSTAD

We had lunch there. Halmstad is on the southern end of the long arm of the North Sea called the Kattegat, which separates Norway and Sweden from Denmark. Its western end, called the Skagerrak, joins the North Sea, separating Norway from Denmark. I remembered learning about these in geography class at the Preston Technical School.

HELSINBORG

We drove on to Helsinborg, reaching there some time in the afternoon, and put the car on the ferry for the journey to Denmark.

HELSINORG TO HELSINGOR

In just over an hour the ferry took us across the 6 km stretch of Sea to Helsingor in Denmark

310

CHAPTER 18

DENMARK

COPENHAGEN

We left the ferry at Helsingor also known as Elsinore. The Elsinore castle featured in Shakesspeaqre's play *Hamlet*, but I didn't see the castle as Johan sped us on all the way to the city of Copenhagen 40 km further on where we parted company. Johan had to do some business in the city before returning to Stockholm, and Paul was going to a college here for a week of study. I thanked Johan for the great lift and he wished me good luck. I said goodbye to Paul and wished him well with his studies. I found the YH easily and booked in, then took the warden's advice and went down to the Tivoli Gardens not very far from the YH, where he said I could get a good cheap meal.

The Tivoli Gardens were beautifully lit at night by many Chinese lanterns of all colours. The gardens covered a very large area and contained all manner of amusements. There were Ferris wheels, shooting galleries, restaurants, cafes, dance halls, pantomimes and many beautiful flower shows. I found a cafe where I had a good cheap meal, then wandered around the gardens. They were much larger than the gardens in Stockholm, but not as clean and tidy, or as friendly.

With my hunger satisfied I walked back to the YH. Before retiring, I reflected on my good luck in getting such a wonderful lift with Johan. It was to be another 10 years before Sweden's road rules were changed to conform to the road rules in Europe and Scandinavia.

The manner in which this conversion was accomplished was quite interesting. All road traffic, with the exception of emergency vehicles were prohibited for two days from using the roads of Sweden. During this period all the traffic signs were altered to comply with the keep to the right side rule of the road. After those two days, all traffic was allowed back on the roads, but at a greatly reduced speed. The speed limits were finally lifted four days later when it was considered that the change had been successfully completed. The population knew well beforehand the date of the change over and many cars and vehicles had their cars converted to right hand drive, and those driving American cars had no need to change anything about their cars.

Sunday 7th September: I rose late for my first full day in Copenhagen and washed my nylon shirt, then went into the city at noon. I found the layout of the streets in the city rather confusing at first, but other than that Copenhagen was a thriving, well kept city with many attractive shops and buildings. It lacked a little of the elegance of Stockholm and there weren't as many big American cars to be seen, but there were plenty of bicycles. There were also many lovely blonde Danish women, but they were not as elegantly dressed as their counterparts in Sweden. Denmark was occupied by the Germans during the war, although so far I had not seen any evidence of this.

Denmark is a country composed of many islands, among which there are three large islands, Jutland, Funen and Zealand, separated from each other by small stretches of sea. These three islands account for most of Denmark's territory and population. Copenhagen, the capital, is located on Zealand, the eastern most of the three. I returned to the YH from my first short walk around Copenhagen. The first item on my list of Copenhagen's attractions and its trademark and icon, was the bronze statue of a mermaid. I wandered along the side of the city's harbour until I came to the beautiful dark bronze statue sitting on a rock beside the harbour. The statue is life size. She is sitting on a rock side on with her tail draped down the side of the rock, a beautiful sight with the harbour and the ships in the background. The statue was sculpted by a Dane, Edward Ericson, and unveiled in 1913. It was inspired by Denmark's famous writer, Hans Christian Anderson and his fairy tale, '*The Little Mermaid.*'

Back at the YH I was advised to go on a tour of the Carlsberg Brewery, and to make sure I went in the afternoon and not the morning. I booked a tour for the following afternoon. Once again I had to be careful when stepping off a kerb, because the traffic was now driving on the right hand side of the road.

Monday 8th September: I went into the city to the La Scala Restaurant, where I had a delicious meal of steak, eggs and vegetables, for quite a reasonable price, then took a local train to Valby, the suburb where the Carlsberg Brewery is located. The tour consisted of about 10 people of different nationalities, some from the YH. The fantastic tour through the brewery was very noisy and took, took 90 minutes. Then we saw the brewing and fermentation vats. It was much quieter there and I could hear what our guide was saying. Our guide then took us outside and showed us the beautiful, high, decorated chimney and other interesting architectural features of the brewery. The entrance is flanked by large stone elephants, above which was the brewery's motto: 'LABOREMUS PRO PATRIA.' ('Let us work for our country').

At the end of the tour we were taken into a large banqueting hall lined with beautiful works of art, where we all sat down at a long table loaded with bottles of Carlsberg's products, both alcoholic and soft drinks. Also on the table were a number of small flags in stands, one for each of the countries of the people at the table. Placing the national flag of a guest at a dinner table is a Scandinavian custom, which I thought was an excellent idea. Our guide told us that we could stay at the table as long as we liked, drinking the company's product. He said he was not allowed to join us with a drink, but would be with us to answer any questions we might like to ask him about Carlsberg. He told us the brewery produced 1.5 million bottles of various drinks each day and the workers were given three bottles of their choice *each* day. It was only when he began to tell us about Carlsberg that I realised how much of an asset the Carlsberg Breweries are to the people of Denmark.

I was very glad that I had a big meal before I came to the brewery and taken the advice of joining the afternoon tour, because many of us were quite inebriated when we left the brewery, as can be imagined after two hours of solid drinking. Before we left we were presented with an illustrated book, which told the history of the brewery, and an envelope containing a collection of bottle labels of all Carlsberg's products. After a short walk in the Tivoli Gardens, I retired to the YH to sleep it off.

Tuesday 9th September: For my last day in Copenhagen I decided I would like to see a few real tourist sights. First I saw the Grundtvig Church, designed by the Danish architect Jensen Klint, completed in 1926. It is a massive church built of yellow bricks and looks like a huge church organ, 35 m high and 76 m wide. This style of church is called a Grundtvig Church to honour Grundtvig, a very important man of the Lutheran Church in Denmark.

Then I visited the Aquarium. I didn't think I had been to an aquarium since I was a small boy, so although the fish and mammals were of the types that I expected to see, including sharks and stingrays, it was great fun. The aquarium was quite modern and the displays were very innovative.

I had a ham roll for lunch and then visited the large modern building of Radio House, which contained broadcasting studios and a large concert hall. The entrance hall and foyer were lined with beautiful marble panelling, with marble columns supporting the roof. I joined a tour of the broadcasting studios and the record library, and

314

then we were escorted into the concert hall where Eugene Ormandy was conducting a rehearsal. We were told we could stay there and watch and listen until the rehearsal was over, which of course I did. I had seen everything I wanted to see in the city, and for that matter in Denmark with its lack of mountains, fjords or other interesting features.

I decided to leave Copenhagen for Germany the next morning and hitch a ride to Konsor on the west coast of Zealand, and take a short cut by ferry across Kiel Busch (bay) on a western arm of the Baltic Sea. I was heading for Kiel where there was a YH, and taking the long way round across the islands of Funen and Jutland had no appeal for me.

I had another great meal at the La Scala Restaurant and returned to the YH. One of the hostellers, who had just been to Algeria, showed us a short movie of his experiences there, which was very interesting because the Algerians were striving for independence at the time. Then I talked with a few other hostellers and new arrivals and after passing on some tips to them, especially about visiting the Carlsberg Brewery.

|||||||||||||||||||||||

COPENHAGEN TO GLOSTRAP

Wednesday 10th September: I left the YH about 9 a.m. on a nice fine day and caught a local train to Glostrap, a suburb of Copenhagen to begin hitchhiking to Konsor.

GLOSTRAP TO KONSOR

I managed to get three short lifts one after the other to Konsor through very pretty farming country on the excellently paved highway and I spotted a couple more Grundvig style churches along the way. Arriving in Konsor, I was dismayed to find that there was no ferry service across the Kiel Busch to Kiel in Germany.

315

Copenhagen's mermaid

Carlsberg's spectacular
chimney

The road and rail bridge joining
Funen to Jutland

Radio House Copenhagen

The imposing entrance to the
Carlsberg factory supported by
two elephants

316

I discovered however, that there was a ferry going to Nyborg, on the island of Funen.

KONSOR TO NYBORG

There was no alternative but to take 'the long way round, so I boarded the ferry that took me across a stretch of water about 20 km wide between Zealand and Funen to Nyborg.

!!!!!!!!!!!!!!!!!!!!!!

NYBORG TO ODENSE

It was now late afternoon in Nyborg, so I took a train instead of trying to hitchhike, because I wanted to make sure I reached the YH at Odense, 50 km from Nyborg, before nightfall. The short train was hauled by a small steam locomotive and carried its passengers at a languid pace along flat farmland country, stopping at stations along the way where there was an interchange of passengers. There was hardly any talking between the passengers and I didn't raise any interest.

The bogie centre isle carriage was clean and reasonably comfortable. The rail joints clicked loudly beneath the carriage as the train made its way to Odense arriving as the sun set after a journey of 28 km and 90 minutes duration. Sad to say, if I had made enquiries about a ferry to Germany prior in Copenhagen, it would have saved me lot of time and money.

A

ODENSE

I booked in to the YH at Odense and was delighted to discover hot showers among many other good features of the YH. After enjoying a rejuvenating shower, I talked with a few hostellers as I sat down to a pasta meal at the YH. In both the Odense and Copenhagen YHs the meals were adequate and cost 2.35 Danish Krone (Dkr). I had a good look at my map to see where I had to go next. I was still about 250 km from Kiel, but I hoped to reach it the following day by

317

crossing over from Odense to Denmark's western and largest island, Jutland. From there I would have to work my way down to Flensburg, then across the border into Germany, and thence to Kiel. To accomplish this journey in one day I had to make an early start so with that thought was in my mind, I called it a day and retired to my sleeping bag.

ODENSE TO ABENRA

Thursday 11th September: The following morning I left the YH very early and walked through the town, having a quick look at Odense as I made my way out onto the main highway. Without waiting too long I got a lift a short way in a truck, then a lift in another truck that took me just short of the road and rail bridge, a little over 1 km in length, connecting Funen to Jutland. I was then picked up by a car that took me across to Fredericia, the town on the other side of the bridge in Jutland.

The driver, who spoke English said he was going to Abenra, which luckily was on my route to Germany. He stopped for a short while in Fredericia to do some business, and then we were off down south to Abenra. As we drove along I saw some thatched cottages in a farmland and one small Grundvig style church. I thanked the driver when he let me off in the small town of Abenra. He wished me luck.

ABENRA TO FLENSBURG

The small town of Abenra is the nearest town in Denmark that was on my route to the German border. I got a ham sandwich and waited on the road for a couple of hours, but couldn't get a lift. I supposed this was not surprising as the road to the south from Abenra crossed the German border. It was about 4 p.m. and I was still 50 km away from Flensburg and getting desperate, but fortunately a bus came along and it took me all the way across the border into Germany in Flensburg.

318

The impressions I took away with me from the Scandinavian countries I visited were of the diversity of natural features between the mountains and fjords of Norway, the pine forests and lakes of Sweden and the flat country of the islands of Denmark. The cities and towns were clean, tidy and modern. All the people I met were very friendly, and most spoke English.

CHAPTER 19

GERMANY

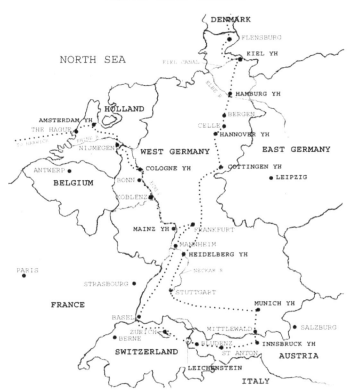

A map showing the author's route from Denmark through West Germany, Austria, Switzerland, Holland and return to Harwich in the UK. Towns and cities where the author stayed in Youth Hostels are shown in bold type

320

FLENSBURG TO KIEL

My passport was checked and the border guards helped me to get a lift on a big truck that was going all the way to Kiel. Thankfully I climbed aboard. Crossing the border into Germany from Denmark before it became dark, I noticed that the houses were untidy, far from being spick and span as they were in Denmark. As well, nearly all the men I saw were wearing dirty black peaked caps and the women were buxom and unattractive. The truck crossed a bridge over the Kiel Canal at dusk and I managed to get a brief look at the canal with its grassed banks, so different from the Suez Canal.

The canal was opened in 1887 to link the North Sea to the Baltic Sea, shortening the distance between the North Sea and the Baltic ports by some 600 km. The canal is 98 km long and runs from Kiel to the mouth of the Elbe River. In 1941 it was deepened to 11 m deep and 102 m wide. The Kiel Canal played a large part during both world wars with regard to the movement of German submarines some of which were stored in the canal.

KIEL

The truck driver, who spoke a little English, took me nearly all the way to the YH in Haus Bellevue, a substantial chateau like building, a long way from the centre of Kiel. I found my way in the dark arriving there at 8 p.m. The warden was very good and although it was late he made me up a meal. There were quite a few other hostellers in the YH some of them going north into Denmark. I talked with them briefly and gave them a few tips before I went off to bed.

Friday 12th September: After a good sleep and a filling breakfast of porridge, I left the YH and walked to the road where I intended to hitch a ride to Hamburg, but to my disappointment the road was lousy with hitchhikers from the YH. I thought I was never going to get a lift from there, so after two hours I gave up and walked into the city of Kiel and see if I could get a train from there to Hamburg.

I found the city of Kiel to be very badly damaged. It had certainly received a pounding in the war. There were a few modern buildings going up, but the Kiel Railway Station (Bahnhof) was just a shell and the ticket collector matched the condition of the station. He had artificial hands and his face was badly disfigured.

!!!!!!!!!!!!!!!!!!!!!!!!!

KIEL TO HAMBURG

The train I travelled on from Kiel to Hamburg was made up of vintage railway rolling stock, just like those I had seen in Germany during the war in newsreels and newspapers. The carriages were hard riding six wheelers with wooden bench seats. Furthermore the carriages were loose coupled. The locomotive was not much better, an 0-6-0 tender engine. As can be imagined, the journey of 85 km to Hamburg was very uncomfortable. What form of braking the train had I was not sure, although I think I heard the sound of an air compressor once when the train stopped at a station.

The one major town the train stopped at on the way was Neumunster The country I saw from the train was sparsely populated, flat farmland and scrub until the train approached Hamburg then it quickly became industrial. From the train I witnessed the first signs of war damaged Hamburg, the second largest city in Germany.

Thankfully at last, the two and a half hour journey was over. The most uncomfortable railway journey I had ever taken. The locomotive driver I think did his best to provide a smooth ride by braking and starting slowly as he took up the slack.

HAMBURG

Coming straight from the Scandinavian countries, it was a huge contrast seeing firsthand the destruction caused by World War II. I found Hamburg to be a large city and after booking into the YH, at 6.30 p.m., I went for a walk. I was attracted to a part of the city that was very brightly lit. It turned out to be the Reeperbahn, Hamburg's red light district, full of strip joints, topless cafes, and of course brothels.

Saturday 13th September: I was up early the next morning and I saw an advertisement for the opera *Don Giovanni*. I booked a seat, then decided to get out of the city and have a look along the Elbe. I took a tram to the Elbe River docklands, and began walking along the bank of the river downstream. I was struck by the amount of bomb damage still to be seen. The further I walked the more severe it became. The docks must have taken a terrific pounding in the air raids as there was hardly anything left standing.

There were some ships tied up to what was left of the port facilities. One was a four masted sailing ship with furled sails. For its age it looked in better condition than the surrounding docks. Although the city was badly bombed it did not look as devastated as this area along the Elbe. I climbed a hill and took a photo of St Michael's Church, then walked under the river by means of the Elbe Tunnel and after having a quick look at this side of the Elbe I returned to the city. Walking around I thought that Hamburg was a little like Venice in some respects because there were numerous canals running through the city.

Back at the YH, I had a meal and put on my white shirt and new tie and went off to the opera. The Hamburg State Opera House had been badly damaged and only part of the stalls area was in use. The balconies and the rear of the stalls were covered by large drapes of a black tarry material, some form of building sheeting I imagined

Don Giovanni (*Don Juan)* is a two act opera written by Mozart. Briefly, the plot is set in Spain and concerns a promiscuous libertine, Don Giovanni, who breaks into the bedroom of Donna Anna, the daughter of a commandant and tries to seduce her. Her father hears her cries for help and goes to her aid, and is murdered by Don Juan,

323

War damaged Kiel

Kiel Bahnhof minus its roof glazing

Flattened docks along the Elbe

A Venice-like Hamburg

The ruins of St Michael's church.

324

and that is the basis for the remainder of the opera, with Don Juan carrying on with his libertine ways and Don Attavio, who was betrothed to Donna Anna, swearing revenge for her father's death.

I came away noting many arias and the overture that I would buy records of when I returned to London. My favourite, sung by Don Juan, was '*Rietsch mir die hand Mein Lieben*' (give me your hand my love). Even though the opera house was in the process of being rebuilt, it was a great production with excellent costumes and stage sets. I came to the conclusion that I am a happy 'opera goer', especially if the opera is one of Mozarts. I felt very pleased to have supported the Hamburg State Opera company in staging the opera in their damaged opera house, a unique opera experience.

👍

HAMBURG TO CELLE

Sunday 14th September: I left Hamburg early the next day and went out on the road to Hannover. I tried for two hours to get a lift, with no luck. Eventually two girls called out in English for me to come back to where they were. I discovered they were Aussies from Sydney. They said the road was an autobahn, and the only place I would be picked up from was the entry ramp. Furthermore, it is prohibited to hitchhike on an autobahn. This was my first experience of these grand concrete highways that Hitler had built.

Very soon all three of us were given a lift to Celle 95 km from Hamburg through flat wooded country, the first 30 km of which was on the autobahn. The girls left me at Celle because they were not going to Hannover. I couldn't get a lift and as it was getting late, I gave up and caught a train from Celle to Hannover.

||||||||||||||||||||||

CELLE TO HANNOVER

Thankfully this steam hauled train that took me the final 35 km to Hannover was much more modern and comfortable than the bone-crunching train ride from Kiel to Hamburg. One station the train

325

stopped at was Bergen, the same name as Bergen in Norway, but the country here was flat, quite unlike the ranges that surround Bergen in Norway.

HANNOVER

Late afternoon I arrived at the Hannover YH, a large modern, double story building. I had a big plate of spaghetti and then I went to a large room downstairs where the warden had arranged for a small three-piece band to play dance music for the hostellers to dance to. It was an innovation for a YH to run and was great fun. I danced and talked with many of the hostellers, telling them of my travels. One English chap asked me if I knew that Celle was near the infamous Bergen-Belsen concentration camp? I said: "I didn't know that." I told him the train stopped at a station called Bergen with the same name as Bergen in Norway and after the war, Bergen-Belsen was the first concentration camp I ever knew about.

He told me that the town of Celle was a staging point on the route of the forced death marches to Bergen-Belsen concentration camp. Celle was also where an isotope separation laboratory was discovered in a disused parachute factory, a relic of Germany's attempt to make a nuclear bomb.

Monday 15th September: I went out to explore Hannover and discovered that a large industrial exhibition had just opened, the Hannover Messe. I went along and saw much of interest to me, wonderful new manufacturing processes, tools and appliances. I found Hannover to be a beautiful clean city. There were many new modern buildings, with very little bomb damage to be seen. In a shop I saw some photos of life in Hannover during the war. I bought three of them. They showed the terrible damage done to the city during the raids. The shopkeeper wrote on the back of each photo where each of the photos was taken. I looked at my map and found a couple of the streets shown in the photos, especially Kropsche Bahnhof Strasse, along which I had walked from the railway station. There was nothing to be seen of the bombed buildings. Each area had been rebuilt with modern shops and flats.

I had a ham sandwich for lunch, and then I decided that I would move on to Gottingen, 120 km distant, the closest city with a YH that I could find to the Russian Zone, which I thought might be interesting.

HANNOVER TO GOTTINGEN

Tuesday 16th September: It was just after 12 noon when I got out on the road leading to Gottingen. Very soon a two door Volkswagen driven by a middle-aged lady with another as a passenger stopped and offered me a lift. The car was full of their luggage in the back seat, but they insisted they could take me, so I squeezed in with my rucksack. They spoke good English and asked me all about Australia. They took me to the small village of Elsa, which was as far as they were going. I thanked them in *Deutsch* as I waved them goodbye, which I think surprised them as we had only been speaking in English.

I had another 80 km to go to get to Gottingen, but couldn't get a lift any further for quite a while. I cursed many large American Army cars that passed me with only a driver on board. I was wondering what to do when along came a motorbike: "Gottingen?" the rider asked. *"Ya, danke."* I replied rather tentatively, because I had never ridden on a motor bike before and certainly not as a pillion passenger, but I climbed up behind him and off we went.

To balance my rucksack I was leaning the wrong way as we went around curves. Soon one of my feet went to sleep and I had to take it off the foot rest and hang it out in the breeze, until I got the feeling back, then the same with the other one. I didn't get too much of a chance to view the countryside, because I was scared stiff trying to keep a hold on the motorbike. The little I did see was becoming more wooded and undulating. Thankfully the weather was fine and eventually I was very relieved to arrive safely at the very English looking city of Gottingen.

🔥

GOTTINGEN

After thanking my bike rider, I climbed off the bike and promptly fell in a heap on the pavement because I didn't have any feeling in my legs. I found a seat where I gathered my thoughts and body together. I needed a haircut and finding a barber nearby, I continued my rejuvenation relaxing in the barber's chair.

I found the YH and booked in. It too was an English style building. The YH didn't provide meals, but the warden said the best place to eat was in the British Army Canteen. It was only when I entered the canteen and saw some British soldiers that I realised I had been in the British Zone ever since I crossed the border from Denmark. Except for the canteen, I had seen no evidence of the British Occupation Force anywhere on the way. I had a succulent dinner of steak, eggs and mashed potato and then returned to the YH.

Gottingen is a University City and was founded by George II, King of England, in 1734. I was sure that accounted for the distinctly English Tudor nature of this city, with its buildings, houses and shops reminiscent of those I had seen in the UK, with black slats spaced across contrasting white walls of the buildings. While I was in Gottingen I didn't see any evidence that the Russian East German zone, only 40 km away however, I am glad I visited Gottingen, because of its English connection.

Looking at my map I found I was nearing Heidelberg where I spent much of my youth in my home state of Victoria. Tomorrow I will try to hitch hike to Heidelberg, where there is a YH.

👍

GOTTINGEN TO HEIDELBERG

Tuesday 16th September: It was a very foggy morning when I

328

left the YH and walked a couple of kilometres to the autobahn's slip road to get a lift to Heidelberg 300 km to the south. I didn't have to wait long before a big black Mercedes Benz came along and picked me up. The fog cleared after a short time and I was able to enjoy the beautiful scenery along the autobahn. The driver spoke English and said he was bypassing Frankfurt because of a polio scare. I sat back and enjoyed the ride, travelling at 120 km/h in the comfort and safety of the Mercedes Benz. At 2 p.m. we reached Heidelberg. I thanked my driver for the great lift and walked a short distance to the city.

Δ

HEIDELBERG

My first impression of Heidelberg was that it was a tucked in amongst low mountains with a big river the Neckar flowing alongside the main city. I caught a tram over the river to the YH at Handschuhsheim, a couple of kilometres from the city centre. Although I lived with my family in the small town of Rosanna in Victoria, I spent a lot of time in Heidelberg a large city a mile to the south. I walked there and back each day to school in Heidelberg and was a member of the 1st Heidelberg Scouts. I was very excited to be here and see how the two cities compared.

After booking in at the modern YH, I went into the city for a meal and a drink. I had a choice of two 'student' hotels. I chose the Roten Ochsen (Red Ox) gasthof on Heidelberg's main street the Hauptstrasse. Inside there were long, solid, oak tables and chairs, most of which were occupied by uniformed American soldiers. Some Americans invited me to have a drink with them. In fact they shouted me all my drinks for the rest of the night. They told me that Heidelberg was in the American Zone of Occupation of Germany. This explained why on my arrival I had seen so many American cars and soldiers in the city.

I told them how I had spent a few days at the marvellous US Recreation Area in Berchtesgaden in the winter. Many of them had not visited the area. They said they must certainly go to

Berchtesgaden. They were particularly interested too in Heidelberg Victoria and Australia in general. It was a great night with the Americans, but I drank too much and had to take a taxi back to the YH. The YH was shut, so I curled up under a window and fell fast asleep.

Wednesday 17th September: Although I was still suffering from a hangover, I set off for a tour of the Heidelberg Castle, which I found very interesting. I could have reached the castle on the hill above the city by means of a short mountain railway, but I opted to walk up the winding road and admire the view as I climbed. Our guide for the tour was a very cheerful young girl called Alleta, who showed us over the very old Heidelberg Castle (*Schloss*).

The castle was built in the 15th century and much of it was in ruins, but it still had an excellent courtyard. The highlight of the castle tour was going down into the wine cellar, where there was a huge oak wine barrel made from 130 oak trees. It was built in 1751 and could hold 49,000 gallons (222,700 litres), of wine, colossal. Beside the barrel there was a statue of the barrel's guardian, a dwarf named Perkeo who it was said, drank copious quantities of the wine and died when he drank a glass of water by mistake. From the terrace there was a great view of Heidelberg and the Neckar River with its surrounding hills.

Then I was off to the Heidelberg University, Germany's oldest, built in 1386. It was supposed to rival Oxford as a seat of learning. There are two universities in Heidelberg, the old and the new. The Old University was completed in the 18th century. The New University was constructed in 1930-32. I only saw over the Old University, a three story Baroque building that really wasn't of much interest to me. That is, except for going to a room that I was told was the student jail (Studentenkarzer). The walls and ceilings were covered with a strange type of graffiti, made by the students who were locked up there for their misdemeanours.

After the tour, I invited Alleta to have a cup of coffee with me. I

330

told her about my home town of Heidelberg in Victoria. She was very interested. I said I would write home for some photos and send them to her. We exchanged addresses and wished each other good luck. That night I wrote a letter to my father with a Heidelberg post mark on it. In the letter I told him all about Heidelberg and asked him if he would send me some postcards of Heidelberg to Australia House.

Thursday 18th September: I woke to find that it was raining heavily. I decided it was not worth going up the mountain railway above the Heidelberg Castle to the summit of a high hill called Konig Stuhl (King's Chair), 594 m, because it was covered in cloud. The rain stopped, so I went instead to the market place where the large Gothic style, *Heilig Geist Kirche* (Church of The Holy Ghost) stood at one end of the square. The Gothic style church has high arched windows, a domed roof and high steeple, but no transepts, a departure from the normal Gothic style churches.

I bought a cushion cover from the shopping stalls around the side of the church for my mother. It had an embroided view of Heidelberg Castle on both sides. I posted the cushion cover and postcards of Heidelberg with Heidelberg postmarks to my father. For myself I bought a nice ashtray inscribed with the name Heidelberg.

I returned to the YH to plan my next move, and decided to go to Munich, a German city that I had heard so much about during the war. I then went back into the city, and as my budget was still in good shape I purchased a coach ticket to Munich for 22 DM, which sadly was cheaper than the train.

This would give me a rest from hitch hiking, besides the weather looked a bit rainy. I had a ham roll, my usual lunch, very tasty and cheap. Then to wash it down I did a bit of a pub crawl of the lesser known hotels, where I drank and talked with the locals, who were very interested when I told them I came from Heidelberg Australia, although none offered me a drink.

The author looking down on Heidelberg from the castle

The Weender Strasse in Gottingen

The ruins of the Heidelberg Castle

The Church of the Holy Ghost

Perkeo the wine barrel guardian

The Neckar River looking upstream with the city on the right

332

Having spent three very enjoyable days in the Heidelberg, both cities–Heidelberg Germany (HG) and Heidelberg Victoria (HV) have many features in common–although quite different in many respects. With regard to significant buildings and architecture, HG has its universities, whereas HV has the Austin Hospital, a very large important teaching hospital complex. Both the university and hospital are situated on high land above their respective cities. The main streets, Burgundy Street in HV is a long street rising up and over the summit of a high ridge overlooking the city, from which a spectacular 180° view of part of the Australian Great Diving Range can be seen. The Haupstrasse in HG is mainly within the city centre.

Both cities are serviced by railway lines and have railway stations within the city, but only HG has trams. One of HG's churches dates back to 1300 and all are large, but no church in HV is more than 200 years old. The Neckar River runs through the centre of HG with land rising from the river on both sides, whereas the Yarra in HV is located a kilometre below the city on the river flats. The Neckar River is crossed by a number of bridges of various forms. One is called the 'Old Bridge.' The Yarra River has only one, an un-named iron culvert bridge. With regards to the arts, HV is the location for world famous 'Heidelberg School' of famous artists such as Tom Roberts and Frederick McCubbin. HG's main connection to the arts seems to be that Heidelberg was the location for Sigmund Romburg's excellent operetta *The Student Prince*.

The naming of HV Victoria comes from Richard Browne, an estate agent, when he first set his eyes on Heidelberg in Victoria in 1838. There were few dwellings with plenty of trees, and the alps of Australia reminded him of the Neckar River and the mountains around Heidelberg in Germany, so he named it Heidelberg.

HEIDELBERG TO MUNICH

Friday 19th September 1952: On a bright sunny morning, I said goodbye to the warden of the very good hostel and paid the low charges. At 9 a.m. I boarded a coach that joined the autobahn and drove toward Munich 344 km distant. There were a couple of noticeable things about the ride. First, there were no fences bordering the autobahn, and cattle could be seen in the farmland on both sides. Second, I was sitting at the rear of the coach, nearly on top of the dual rear wheels. Every 100 metres or so, the wheels would cross the joints in the concrete surface with a low thump. I wondered at the time of writing whether this annoying discomfort had been rectified by sealing between the joints with asphalt or with some other fix, as it detracted from an otherwise great coach journey. Riding in the Mercedes on my way to Heidelberg, crossing over these joints was only slightly noticeable.

About half way on the journey to Munich, the coach pulled in to Stuttgart, a large city where some of the passengers got off and others got on. There was just time to visit the adjacent comfort station and then we were on our way again. Leaving Stuttgart a large city of which I only saw parts from the coach window. For the remainder of the journey there was some beautiful countryside and sights to be seen. Potatoes or something like them were growing in large fields and also fruit trees in large orchards. I noted that women were working in the fields, alongside men with scythes. The journey in the coach was a really great trip, especially the brief look at the centre of the city of Stuttgart.

MUNICH

The coach arrived in Munich at 5 p.m. I took a tram to the YH on the *Wendl-Dietrich Strasse*, a kilometre or so outside the city. The YH was a modern building with good facilities and cheap meals.

Saturday 20th September: I was up early, breakfasted and out by 9 a.m. into Munich *(Munchen)*, named after a group of monks who settled nearby 1200 years ago. Looking at a Munich guide I noted two items of interest. The opera *Carmen* was on at the Munich Opera

334

House, so I straightaway booked for the following night's performance. Secondly, I discovered that once again, I had entered a city on the opening day of a big event, this time the Octoberfest. I seemed to have the knack of arriving in cities when there was a major event taking place. The Edinburgh Festival, the Hannover *Messe* and now the Octoberfest.

I went and had a quick look at the Octoberfest, held at the *Theresienwiese,* a very large exhibition ground not far away from the city centre. The site was crammed full of all manner of entertainments, but of course the major attraction was beer drinking and having a good time. There were many large halls put up by the major brewing companies of Germany, *Hofbrau* (farm brew) and *Lowenbrau* (Lion's brew) as well as many other lesser known beer companies. There were also many stalls exhibiting various products, not necessarily related to the brewing business. I decided however, that drinking and taking part in the festivities of the Octoberfest was not for me that morning.

Instead I had a ham sandwich and made my way to the Deutsch Museum, which I was told back at the YH was an excellent museum. It was in fact an absolutely wonderful technology and science museum. It had just about everything on display, the first Benz car from 1886, the first diesel engine from 1897, as well as many other firsts. It was colossal and very informative. The Deutsch Museum should not be missed by any visitor to Munich.

I returned to the YH, where I met an American named Greg who appeared to be a decent bloke, so after we had eaten we went together to the *Hofbrauhaus.* It has three floors; one of the top floors is a dance hall and the other a restaurant. It was built in 1897. The ground floor where we were drinking, can accommodate 4,500 drinkers. A large brass band blared out 'oom-pa-pa' type German music as everyone consumed vast quantities of the company's beer in litre steins. Each *stein* (stone beer jug) has a large blue HB on the side. We sat at wooden tables and talked to those sitting around our

335

table while eating *wurst*, a very tasteful, German style sausage, all at a reasonable price.

We had a great time there and entered into the spirit of the place, called *gemutlichkeit*, meaning conviviality. We also learned the Hofbrau song, which in part went: *'In Munchen Stadt, ein Hofbrauhaus* (In Munich town, a Hofbrau house), *Ein, zwei Zoompa* (One, Two, Zoompa). Those were the only words I could remember, but with the whole house singing the complete song, together with the band all swaying to the beat of the band, it was great.

We drank four litres of the rather sweet, Hofbrau beer, and when I left, I souvenired (stole) a litre beer mug (stein) under my raincoat. Once again I had no guilty conscience, but considered it to be a small part of the reparations that Germany had to make for starting and losing the war. Later that night rather inebriated, we made our way back to the YH.

Sunday 21st September: I slept soundly until 11 a.m. then just before noon I went off to the Octoberfest. I looked inside the huge and noisy Lowenbrau Hall, There was a large brass band in the centre of the gaily decorated hall filled with tables and chairs. I had tasted the Hofbrau beer at the Hofbrauhaus and here I tasted the other large brewing company's beer, which I thought was not as sweet as Hofbrau. People, some in traditional dress, were sitting at the tables consuming beer from large steins and eating wurst served by German waitresses in colourful dirndls.

I could not have picked a better day to go to the Octoberfest. It was the day when many of the German people came attired in their traditional dress, representing the different cantons and regions of Germany. I was amazed at the ability of the waitresses I saw serving the beer, because they had to have very strong arms and be fit to quickly carry as many as ten beer filled steins. I purchased some postcards, which I later sent to family and friends.

Back at the YH I had a quick meal and made my way by tram to the Prinzregenten Theater where Biset's opera *Carmen* was being performed by the Bavarian State Opera Company. The journey by tram to the opera house was a little complicated as I had to change trams, but I made it on time, just!

I had told the warden that I was going to the opera and might get back late. He told me to knock on the door and he would let me in. Biset's opera *Carmen* is a popular opera about bullfighters and their romantic problems. At the end of Act 2 the audience stamped their feet. A case for rubber props, because the scenery made a hell of a noise as it was shifted around. The role of Carmen was sung by Lilian Benningsen, who had about as much sex appeal as a rattlesnake, but she did have a good voice. Apart from those remarks, I noticed that the audience in general was more formally dressed than at the operas I attended in Vienna.

Thinking about *Carmen* on the way back to the YH in the tram, I decided that although the music and the plot were quite straightforward and enjoyable, there was no doubt that Mozart's music and operas are my favourites. I enjoyed *Carmen* in my off white shirt and a new tie I bought (my drip-dry shirt had lost a little of its pristine whiteness). As I had told the warden I was going to the opera and might get back late. He told me to knock on the door and he would let me in, but it took a lot of knocking before he opened the door for me.

My time in Munich was very exciting, but it was now time to move on. I decided to try to hitchhike to Innsbruck in the morning, and was looking forward very much to being in Austria again.

♣

MUNICH TO STARNBERG

Monday 22nd September: I left the YH in Munich at 9 a.m. I would have to cross the border between Bavaria and Austria somewhere along the way. Out on the road, I managed to get a 20 km lift as far as Starnberg, where it started to rain like hell, so I gave up hitchhiking and caught a train.

337

The Hofbrauhaus Munich

The Hofbrauhaus stein
stein I appropriated

Inside the Lowenbrau beer hall
a postcard

The Octoberfest fair ground
a postcard

The Lowenbrau beer hall
a postcard

An image from the program of
the Prinzregenten Theater where
the author saw the opera Carmen

STARNBERG TO INNSBRUCK

I couldn't see the mountains from the train, but I saw beautiful green luxuriant meadows. The rain changed to a thick mist as the train began to climb into the mountains and stopped at Garmisch-Partenkirchen, 97 km from Munich, I had heard of Garmisch-Partenkirchen, the town with the long name where the winter Olympics were held in 1936. The two villages of Garmisch and Partenkirchen joined forces to help stage the events.

If the weather had been fine and sunny I would have been tempted to get off to see the town and the surrounding mountains, including Germany's highest mountain, the Zugspitze. I had seen much of the Bavarian mountain country when I visited Berchtesgaden on my first tour.

However, I remained on the train as it ascended into the clouds. The steam hauled train journey was very exciting as the train climbed up the mountainside and through a couple of long tunnels. Hopefully this time in Austria I will get to see all the high mountains that on my first tour were covered in cloud.

MITTENWALD

The locomotive's exhaust sounded loudly as it laboured to gain height and soon it came to rest as it arrived at the German border town of Mittenwald, noted for its colourful painted houses, which I didn't see, and its famous violin making history.

339

CHAPTER 20

AUSTRIA

Passports were checked by customs officials, but this didn't take very long and very soon my journey to Innsbruck continued as the train departed Mittenwald in a cloud of steam and crossed into Austria. The descent of 56 Km to Innsbruck began by a stop at the ski resort village of Seefeld and then we were on our way again.

Miraculously, on the Austrian side of the pass the train emerged from the clouds high above the Inn valley in which Innsbruck is located, another case of a change of weather after crossing a high pass. My hope of seeing the mountains of Austria was realised. The railway line was so high up on the mountainside that I was looking down on planes coming in to land at an airfield in the valley. The views of the valley of the Inn River were very widespread and breathtaking. In the distance I could see right across to the mountains where the Brenner Pass crossed the border into Italy. As the train descended further the valley with its roads, scattered villages and the Inn River surounded by lush green fields came into focus.

🏔

INNSBRUCK

Early evening the train entered the large city of Innsbruck. I changed all the *Deutsch* marks I had left into Austrian Schillings, receiving a very good exchange rate with no need to cash another traveller's cheque. I found the large YH located in the buildings of a high school and booked in. After I had cleaned up I went into the city to a rather swanky restaurant, the Goldener Adler (Golden Eagle),

340

which I am told is still in business as I write. I had a scrumptious Wiener schnitzel for 23 A.sch, much cheaper than I had expected. I was sitting at a table with an attractive young English widow called Annabella, a Swede and a Yank. The three of us enjoyed each other's company so much that afterwards we decided to go to a nightclub together, where we had a great time talking about ourselves and our journeys as we drank a bottle of dunkel vermouth.

Annabella and I got on very well together, so that when the time came to leave at 12.30 a.m. she allowed me to escort her back to her lodging. She said she would like to see me in London, and wrote her full name and address on my menu, together with the dates when she would be there. Maybe I thought, she was just looking for another husband. After saying goodnight I returned to the YH only to find it was locked.

I decided to go to the railway station and spend the night there. It was very cold and I had a horrible night, trying to sleep on a seat between two doors that kept opening and closing, one to the street and the other to the platform.

Tuesday 23rd September: The YH opened at 6 a.m. so I made sure I was there as soon as the door opened. Thankfully it did, to the minute. I got straight into my sleeping bag and slept until 2 p.m.

I left the YH to explore Innsbruck, the capital of the Tyrol. On my first tour with Lyon on the way to Salzburg the train stopped at Innsbruck for a few minutes. It was dark and I only saw its lights. Innsbruck was the headquarters of the French Occupation Forces, but I didn't see any evidence of this.

The main street, the Maria Theresien Strasse is named after the Austrian Empress. It is really the showpiece of Innsbruck. Walking north along this famous street from where it first takes up its beautiful name, I passed under the Triumphforte (Triumphal Arch). A little further on I came to St Anna's Column in the centre of the Strasse. The beautiful imposing, column is quite high with a statue of the Virgin Mary on top and four saints around the base. Looking further north along the street, I saw a small, bright, yellow roof that stood out from the side of a building. When I got closer I saw it was the roof of a small balcony that jutted out from the third floor of a large building.

It was the *Goldenes Dachl* (Golden Roof) and as I walked towards it the roof became even more brilliant. It wasn't yellow, in fact the roof of the balcony is covered by 2,657 dazzling, gold plated tiles. The roof was constructed in the 16th century as a Royal Box for Emperor Maximillian. As I walked further along the Marie Theresien Strasse, a wonderful view greeted my eyes. Rising behind the buildings Hafelekar, a broad mountain range over 2.000 m high (6,500 ft) overlooks the city.

Wednesday 24th September: Because I enjoyed my meal at the Goldener Adler so much the previous day and liked the ambience of the restaurant, I entered its doors again. This time I had a succulent pasta dish, which was only 8 Asch, then I was off to Hafelekar.

iiiiiiiiiiiiiiiiiiiiii

INNSBRUCK TO HAFELEKAR

The ascent commenced from the valley floor in the *Bergbahn* (mountain railway) to the Hungerburg Plateau, at 870 m (2,854 ft). I then transferred into the Nordkette, a cable car. I had ridden in one before, but not as high and airy as this one. It was a thrilling and spectacular ride hanging in the small cabin by a slender cable above the precipitous mountainside. The feeling of being suspended in space was quite awesome. There was a pause at the intermediate station of Seegrube, 1.905 m (6,250 ft), then finally on to the Hafelekar summit station, at 2.334 m (7,657 ft),

Leaving the station I took a 10 minute walk on a path along the ridge to the actual summit of Hafelekar, only a metre or so higher than the summit station. As I walked along the path there were superb panoramic views of the Inn valley, with Innsbruck on the valley floor.

There was a slight haze, which is quite normal for clear days in Austrian alpine valleys, but this did not in any way detract from the spectacular view, in fact I thought the haze added to the beauty of the panorama.

Away to the north there were the high Wetterstein Mountains, while in the distance to the west a pointer directed my gaze to the Zugspitze, Germany's highest peak at 2.963 m. (9,721 ft). Another pointer indicated the Grossglockner, Austria's highest mountain, 3.798 m (12,460 ft) high, barely discernible about 100 km to the south-east. Although there was only a little snow on Hafelekar, some of the high mountains that I could see from this viewpoint were still covered by large areas of snow.

After a very expensive meal of sandwiches and a beer at the summit restaurant, I decided to save a little money and walk down the mountainside to the halfway station Seegrube. It was very steep and soon I came to a large scree slope (an area of small loose stones) down which I had to descend. To my surprise, I caused the scree to form small avalanches as I descended, making it difficult for me to keep my footing.

I thought the sooner I got away from this the better, before I caused a major scree avalanche, so I gradually made my way across the slope to more solid ground. It was very scary, but eventually I was able to move away from the scree area. Pausing to catch my breath I looked up. Directly above me. Silhouetted against the blue sky, I saw the cable car miraculously hanging in mid air, moving slowly upwards, seemingly without any support, because I couldn't see the cable. I joined the cable car at Seegrube and enjoyed the rest of the descent to Innsbruck. It was a tiring, but very enjoyable day.

I had a final walk around Innsbruck, where I came across the beautiful white Burghaus (town hall), then it was back to the YH to plan my next move. Although nearly devoid of snow at this time of

The Otztaler Alps and the Brenner Pass mountains above the Inn valley

Innsbruck on the floor of the Valley

The Goldener Dachl

A view along the Marie Theresien Strasse

The Goldener Adler Restaurant sign in Innsbruck

344

the year, Hafelekar provides a magnificent backdrop for Innsbruck. In the winter covered in snow. It must be a breath-taking scene.

On my first tour the only high Austrian mountains summits I saw from the train were at St. Anton where the cloud cleared. Tomorrow I will try to hitch hike through these regions and see the magnificent mountains and scenery that was denied to me on my first tour.

◆

INNSBRUCK TO ZURICH

Thursday 25th September: I left the Innsbruck YH on a beautiful sunny day and found the main road that went through the Tyrol and Vorarlberg to the Austrian border. I planned to get to Mainz next for a cruise down the Rhine to Cologne, then cross into Holland and leave from there for England, hoping to be there on 1st October as planned.

I didn't have long to wait before a large van with advertising for Ferrado and Lucas on the outside stopped and picked me up. The van was driven by two English blokes about my age, Paul and Ted, who were following the motor bike and racing car circuits, servicing brakes and clutches (Ferrado) and electrical systems (Lucas). As we drove along we talked about our lives, jobs and travels. They were on their way to Zurich and then to Spain. I told them I was a fitter and turner. They said I would be interested in seeing the lathes, drilling machines and other equipment that they had in the back of the van. I had a wonderful seat up front of the van, to view as we drove along the road the magnificent mountains of the Tyrol.

The mountains of the Tyrol varied in form, high grey rocky monoliths, jagged peaks and lower forested alps with scattered rocky outcrops, but all members of the Tyrolian alpine family. The road passed through many of the towns I remembered on the way to Salzburg by train, but kept mostly to the valley floor except at times winding around to cross low passes.

In some of these towns, multi storey chalets rivalled the vista of

345

A view along the Hafelekar path

The Nordkette cable car above
the scree slope

The author on Hafelekar

A balcony floral display of
an Austrian house

The Innsbruck Burghaus

Some mountains of the Vorarlberg

346

the spectacular mountain scenery in splendour. The small balconies on each level were adorned with a lovely profusion of beautiful flowers, with hardly a telephone or power line to be seen.

We stopped in St Anton for lunch, but this time not the beautiful mountain ski resort I remembered seeing from the train window in the winter on my way to Salzburg. Once an area becomes a designated ski resort its natural beauty, especially in summer is degraded. The cleared areas for the ski runs and lifts are transformed to long, ugly scars amidst the surrounding pine tree forests, but that is the price we skiers pay for progress. During lunch I had a look at the equipment in the van. It was quite a large array of machines, all of which I knew how to operate.

Leaving St Anton we drove up and over the Arlberg Pass, 1.802 m (5,900 ft), then down a winding road into Austria's western canton, the Vorarlberg, bordered by the mountains of Switzerland to the south and Germany to the north. The Vorarlberg is an excellent place for winter sports and contains two top ranking skiing resorts, Lech and Zurs. When we stopped for afternoon tea at Bludenz, Paul and Ted invited me to travel with them as far as I liked. They said I could probably give them a hand with their work, but they couldn't pay me.

However, back to this wonderful ride in their service van and a pause in busy, Bludenz an alpine town surrounded by high mountains. On the move again, we descended a twisting road to Feldkirch, where there was only a cursory check of our passports before leaving Austria to enter the Principality of Liechtenstein, sandwiched between Austria and Switzerland.

LIECHTENSTEIN

Liechtenstein is very small, with an area of only 160 square kilometres. We drove across a lovely valley containing many farms and vineyards. The houses were all typical alpine style chalets. High mountains surrounded us, except to the north and west, where there was a range of high hills covered by dense forests. As we drove across Liechtenstein, I gave some thought to travelling with the van but quickly came to the conclusion that it was really not an option. Liechtenstein in some respects is part of Switzerland, in that it uses Swiss currency and many other Swiss documents. Like Switzerland it remained neutral during the war. Its capital is Vaduz, a good question for Trivial Pursuit I thought.

As we drove across Liechtenstein, I gave the idea of travelling with the two servicemen a lot of thought. They said they were going to stop in Zurich in Switzerland for the night. I hadn't planned to enter Switzerland, certainly not to stop overnight, but there was no way I was going to leave the service van before we reached Zurich. When we arrived there I would have to make up my mind whether to stay or leave Paul and Ted. If I left them there, I would have to put up at a cheap Swiss pension for the night, if there was such a thing in a big city like Zurich, or sleep on the railway station.

I had not looked to see if there was a YH in Zurich so that might be another option. I thought if I accepted their offer to take me with them, I would need more money than I had with me, and Netta was not with me this time to give me a loan. To carry on with them for some weeks would have been a great experience, but I quickly came to the conclusion that it was really not possible.

I was told that Liechtenstein has no railway station, but our van was held up at railway boom gates to allow a train to speed by. After driving about 20 km from where we entered Liechtenstein we began to climb up through the mountains where it started to rain heavily. At the top of the climb we crossed into Switzerland, but there was no customs to pass through, and that was the end of the Principality of Liechtenstein.

348

CHAPTER 21

SWITZERLAND

As we made our way towards Zurich as night fell, I told Paul and Ted that thanks for the invitation, but I would have to leave them in Zurich. It would have been a wonderful experience, to have travelled with them, but I had to keep to my plan. It was now dark so I didn't see much of the countryside and soon we came to Lake Zurich on which the large city of Zurich is located. I thanked Paul and Ted for the wonderful lift in their truck when they let me off in the centre of Zurich. We shook hands and they wished me luck as they drove off into the rainy night. It was 8.30 p.m.

ZURICH

I looked around the city, which was glaring and expensive, then went to the railway station to have a look around and get something to eat. On the way to the railway station I admired the beautiful city lights reflected in the ripples on the surface of Lake Zurich. When I arrived at the station I found there was a train just about ready to leave for Basel. It couldn't have been better. I bought a ticket, grabbed a ham roll and soft drink and hastily boarded the train.

||||||||||||||||||||

ZURICH TO BASEL

As the train pulled out of the station I thought to myself. 'If that's Zurich I've been there, done that.' It was a pleasant train journey of about 60 km to Basel. As I relaxed in the warm carriage I thought back over the events of the long day. I had travelled some

349

170 km as the crow flies, from Innsbruck to Zurich, with my front seat in the service van giving me an uninterrupted view of the wonderful high mountains of the Tyrol and Vorarlberg as we drove along.

It was a pleasant train journey of about 60 km to Basel. When I wasn't asleep or dozing, all I saw from the carriage windows were lights of all colours flashing by. During the journey I couldn't help thinking again, how fortunate I was to get that great lift from Innsbruck in the service van with an upfront view of the wonderful mountains of the Tyrol and Vorarlberg.

BASEL

The train arrived in Basel at 1 a.m. I had been to Basel on my first tour with Leon and knew that it was a focal point where the three countries of Switzerland, Germany and France converged. This made Basel an important city for commerce and a hub for people moving between the three countries. Much of this activity was centred on the Basel railway station, where trains entered and left to all parts of Europe. I bought a rail ticket for Frankfurt, and more food and a drink. I changed a traveller's cheque for *Deutsch* Marks at an excellent exchange rate.

The timetable showed that a train was due to leave for Frankfurt at 6.35 a.m. Basel is in Switzerland, but I wanted to cross into Germany and sleep on the railway station before catching that morning train to Frankfurt. I thought that this would not be a problem as my passport and visa were valid for Germany. I passed through Swiss customs without any fuss, which evidently put me into French territory. I explained to the French customs official what I wanted to do, but he would not let me through into Germany and on to the platform from where I expected my train to leave.

I was beginning to get a little annoyed, so I decided that I would become an American and adopt their methods to get where I wanted to go. I had seen enough of American tourists on my tours to realise that the Americans believe they are doing a favour to the countries

350

they visit by helping their economy. They also believe it is a privilege that they should wish to visit their country. In return they expect to be treated with respect and have their every need satisfied, or they will raise hell. I didn't change my nationality or change my accent, but I ranted and raved American style and told them to let me onto the platform in Germany. It worked!

⌂

I slept soundly after all the trouble, but I think I actually slept on the Swiss railway platform and not the German one, because that was where the 6.35 a.m. train going to Frankfurt left from. On thinking back, in fairness that was what the French customs officials were really trying to explain to me as I ranted and raved.

When I woke I bought a couple of ham rolls and a soft drink for the journey. The train, composed of corridor coaches and hauled by a large red, German electric locomotive, with the letters DB (*Deutsche Bundesbahn*) on its front pulled in to the platform. As other passengers began to arrive on the platform we were informed that we could board the train. I found myself a window seat and relaxed in the warm carriage and well upholstered seat for the long journey of 295 km through the Upper Rhine valley to Frankfurt.

!!!!!!!!!!!!!!!!!!!!!!!!

BASEL TO FRANKFURT

At 6.35 a.m. right on time the train slowly moved away from the station and almost immediately crossed a large bridge over the Rhine River, which defines the border between Switzerland and Germany, and crossing the Rhine meant I was back in Germany again.

351

CHAPTER 22

GERMANY

It was not surprising to see that a DB (*Deutsch Bundesbahn*) locomotive was hauling the train now that I was back in Germany. For a short while the line ran along the bank of the Rhine a wide, grey water river, then the river was left behind as the train settled down to the task of taking me to Frankfurt along The Upper Rhine Valley as it is called, between Basel and Frankfurt (actually by definition, 'Biden'.

The railway line ran some distance to the east of the river stopping at various stations along the way. The first was Freiberg in a rural setting with a forest seen further east. Then a couple more small towns, Archern and Offenburg before arriving at Karlsruhe, a large city 172 km from Basel after which the scenery changed to scruffy bushes and trees.

There were many sounds from the locomotive's truck like horn that I had been hearing all the way from Basel as the train approached level crossings, most with automatic boom gates. The next city of importance was Mannheim on the Rhine River, where the train crossed a bridge over a river and a railway line.

I looked at my map and saw that Heidelberg was only 20 km away to the east and the river was the Neckar. It was really a pleasant surprise to be acquainted with my home town's name again so quickly. The Neckar River joins the Rhine in Mannheim, but I was unable to see the junction from the train.

352

Leaving Mannheim the Rhine was soon out of sight as the train resumed its journey 71 km north to Frankfurt. At one point the Rhine came in view for a short distance before the train approached the outskirts of Frankfurt where signs of German industry replaced farm houses and the rural landscape. The train reached Frankfurt 10 30 a.m.

FRANKFURT

I had had a look around the large city on the Main River and wondered what to do next considering the polio scare in this city. Back at the bahnhof I found I had to wait for 2 hours for the next train to Mainz. I decided to go a one hour movie news theatre on the railway station. I thought this would be a good place to wait considering the polio scare. In fact, I thought afterwards, it was probably the worst place. I would have been better out in the open air exploring the city

!!!!!!!!!!!!!!!!!!!!!!

FRANKFURT TO MAINZ

The journey of 32 km to Mainz was by electric train and by the time it got started it was quite full. Leaving Frankfurt a large bridge was first ``crossed over the Main River. It wasn't an express train and stopped at three stations along the way each with the name ending in 'heim,' Hatters, Russel and Hoch. At each of these there was a change of passengers. There was also station for an airport, then just before the train entered the Mainz bahnhof at 3.30 p.m., it crossed over a very big bridge over the Rhine, but 'this time I was still in Germany not into another country.

MAINZ

I found the YH, booked in and had a sorely needed meal in the YH. Mainz was heavily bombed during the war, including the cathedral, but it was pleasing to see that there was a lot of reconstruction work in progress. I booked for the ferry journey down the Rhine to Cologne the following day, which cost 20 Deutsch marks.

MAINZ TO COLOGNE

Saturday 27th September: On an overcast morning, just as I was about to board the large open cruise ferry to take me down the Rhine it began to rain heavily. Just my luck, I thought. I bought a map of the journey from the on-board shop. It was an excellent map about 20 cm wide, which unfolded vertically to a length of 1.5 metres. It was beautifully illustrated, showing everything of interest on the river from Mainz to Cologne.

The Rhine River begins its journey in Switzerland, and flows for 1360 km before entering the North Sea in the Netherlands. My voyage would take me 188 km from Mainz to Cologne. Through the pouring rain the first item of note was the large number of barges being towed by tugs. The Rhine is quite a busy river, but there was plenty of room for all this traffic as the Rhine is quite wide. I estimated it averaged 250 m wide, interrupted in many places by midstream islands, some of which had old castles on them.

The Rhine is a very famous river for many reasons, not the least for the part it played in WWII as the great barrier that the allied armies had to cross to overcome the German forces. More than a dozen bridges over the Rhine were destroyed, but many new and temporary bridges replaced them. Both banks of the river were quite steep and rugged. In many places I noticed railway trains and cars on roads running along both sides of the river.

Judging by the number of castles and fortresses I saw, there must have been a lot of fighting in ancient times along the river and on the mid-stream islands. The Rhine Valley too is famous for producing fine wines, and many vineyards could be seen where the banks of the river were not too steep and rugged.

There was a restaurant-cafe on board and about halfway along my voyage, I satisfied my hunger with a very costly ham sandwich and bowl of soup. The ferry passed Bignonia where the Nahe River

354

flows into the Rhine from the left, and shortly afterwards we came to the Laurel Rock (Fairy's Rock), a large cliff above the river on the east bank. Legend has it that on this cliff a beautiful girl would sit combing her long blonde hair, enticing the Rhine boatmen to their death on the rocks below the cliff where the water was 23 m deep.

The Rhine then made an S bend, and a little further on we arrived at Coblenz, (in Latin 'confluence') a large city on the left bank of the river, where the Mosel River joins the Rhine. Evidence of the destruction caused during the war could be seen as the ferry passed under two rebuilt bridges, beside the ruins of the original bridges. Further on the ferry passed the remains of another bridge and then a brand new bridge. Despite the incessant rain, the visibility was not too bad. I could easily see most of the castles and fortresses, many in ruins, some high on the hills just below the cloud cover. The ferry had a PA address system, with a commentary in German and English, which kept us informed of the sights as the ferry cruised along.

At last we came to the bridge that I had so much wanted to see, the Ludendorf Railway Bridge that crossed the Rhine at the town of Remagen, but all I saw were two of its stone piers rising above the level of the water in the river. In WWII the Germans attempted to blow up the bridge, but the Americans overpowered them and got across, breaking through this last German strongpoint.

Late afternoon the riverside suburbs of Bonn were passed on the left bank. Bonn is another large city on the Rhine and the seat of the federal government of Germany. After passing under a couple of new bridges my cruise was nearing the end.

The Rhine wound around a couple of bends and suddenly I could see the lights of Cologne in the distance. By now the rain was not nearly so heavy, and after passing under some more new bridges the ferry tied up at the wharf in the darkness at 7.30 p.m., which brought to an end a wonderful and interesting ferry cruise, not altogether spoilt by the continuous rain. Now to find the YH.

COLOGNE

Finding that YH was full, I was directed to take a 'D' tram to the substitute YH, the Hotel Zupp, a three storey, concrete air raid shelter with no windows and concrete walls, a metre thick on the Berliner Strasse. I booked in for 1.50 DM per night then went out and had a bite to eat.

When I returned to the YH I talked and flirted with the attractive *fraulein* in the office, and got quite a surprise when *she* invited me to come up to her room at 1.30 a.m. On the assigned time I knocked quietly and was invited to enter. When I did however, she looked at me and said: "I am not a plaything. Any man that wants me has to take the whole lot." I was dumb struck! I didn't want the whole lot, so after a little conversation between us, we parted with a *Gute Nacht* and I returned to my sleeping bag completely frustrated, and feeling a great fool. It was an interesting, bewildering experience. 'The ultimate tease'.

Sunday 28th September: I woke up very late, probably because there were no windows to let in the light. I quickly packed and paid the fees, thankfully to a different warden than last night. I caught the tram into the city. The perfume 'eau de cologne' derived its name from a chemist who settled in Cologne in 1709 and produced the scented water. There was nothing special I wanted to see in Cologne (*Koln)* except the cathedral. The city was still a scene of devastation except for the area around the cathedral, which was virtually free of damage. How the bombers had managed to destroy everything around, but miss the cathedral I could not imagine, but miss it they did. I supposed because of the great skill of the bomb aimers.

Cologne Cathedral took 600 years to construct, finally being completed in 1842. It is said to be one of the best examples of Gothic architecture with its twin spires. It certainly is a beautiful church. I paid a small admission fee to enter and climbed the spiral stairs

356

inside one of the spires. I was just enjoying the rather chaotic view of the city and its environs, when BONG, BONG, BONG the church bells rang out right alongside me. It was truly deafening and gave me a hell of a fright, because I was not expecting anything like that.

After having a further good look around Cologne from the spire, I descended the stairs and had a quick look inside the cathedral. It was magnificent with high fluted columns supporting the roof, and a statue of a religious figure attached to each column. Apart from those and the beautiful leadlight windows, there was little embellishment. I enjoy the simplicity of the interior of most of the Gothic churches I have seen besides this one, which was one of the best. It was time to move on.

!!!!!!!!!!!!!!!!!!!!!!!

COLOGNE TO AMSTERDAM

Just before noon I boarded a train to Amsterdam. I was delighted to see a steam locomotive at the head of the train and hear the noise of the exhaust and whistle as the train pulled out of Cologne station. The train first went through industrial cities of the Ruhr. From the train I saw a good deal of war damage, as well as many factories working full blast, judging by the smoke that was belching from their chimneys. It was a beautiful day and I could see for miles as the train puffed its way a little west of the Rhine River. The train soon came to the city of Neuss, which is located on the Rhine and I got a brief glimpse of the river as the train pulled into the station. The large city of Dusseldorf was not far away of the other side of the Rhine.

Leaving Neuss the train again ran along to the west of the river through a rural scene, stopping at stations along the way until after an enjoyable ride of 127 km at 12.45 p.m. the train crossed the border into Holland.

357

CHAPTER 23
HOLLAND

I crossed the border into Holland (or the Netherlands) and arrived at the border town of Nijmegen where my passport was checked and I changed my German money into Guilders, 1 guilder was equal to 2 shillings Sterling. Although the name Holland should only be applied to the north west of the country, I will use the name Holland, which I learnt in school and have always associated the name with clogs, tulips and windmills as well as the boy who put his finger in the hole in the dyke and saved Holland from being flooded!

I changed from the German steam train to a modern Dutch electric train. The carriages had large windows and a centre aisle with vestibules at each end. Leaving Nijmegen the train travelled north crossing first the Meuse River and then the Rhine over large bridges before reaching the city of Arnhem, where there were huge battles during WWII. From there the train travelled west across the flat country of the Rhine delta to the large city of Utrecht. It was from there on the way to Amsterdam that I saw my first Dutch windmills, but not tulips, and after a pleasant trip of 89 km from Nijmegen the train pulled into Amsterdam at around 2 p.m.

A

AMSTERDAM

I booked in at the YH, and went for a walk around the city to get something to eat. Once again it was spaghetti, which I had developed a liking for because it was cheap and filling. Afterwards I crossed a canal into the area where the nightclubs were. In fact they seemed to

358

be everywhere, as well as brothels where scantily dressed prostitutes sat behind large glass windows of flats, displaying their charms, which to my mind were not very enticing or seductive.

Monday 29th: September: I was woken at 9 a.m. by the hostel warden as the YH shut at 9.30 a.m. I bought a ham roll for breakfast and then looked for a travel office. I purchased a train and ferry ticket to London for Wednesday 1st October; for £5. The ticket was for the train to The Hague, then ferry across the North Sea to Harwich, and train to London. This meant I would be returning to London exactly to the day when I planned to be back. I also bought a ticket for a canal trip through Amsterdam in an open launch.

The canal trip took me along a centre canal with streets above on both sides. The canal dived under many small bridges connecting the streets lined with apartments and shops on both sides of the canal. After a kilometre or so the launch left the canal and ventured out into the North Sea Canal and Harbour, with wharves and large seagoing vessels. It was very interesting to see a different perspective of the cities, from that seen walking around the streets. It was a very enjoyable cruise.

Leaving the launch I couldn't believe my eyes when I passed a movie theatre showing *Die Drei Groschen Opera.* Of course I bought a ticket and went straight into the theatre. The movie was quite a contrast to the stage version I had seen in Vienna. I was given a very good illustrated program booklet containing all the words of the ballads, which gave me a better understanding of the opera even though it was in *Deutsch.*

I met an Australian, Russell Davis at the YH, which not only closed in the morning, but also at 10 p.m. at night. Hours not very conducive or convenient to allow its hostellers to enjoy the night life of Amsterdam, or maybe this was the idea. Russell persuaded me to find alternate board with him for the night, so that we could have a night out on the town. I said OK and off we went and quickly found a flat close by at 5 Guilders a night for bed and breakfast.

Once we had settled in we walked around to the nightclub district, ignoring the 'red light' area with its prostitutes eliciting trade behind the large windows of their brothels. We chose one and once inside, talked to a couple of attractive girls and bought them drinks. All of a sudden Russell said he was leaving and would see me back at the flat. I decided to stay on because I was having a good time with a beautiful, well groomed, Dutch girl who kept asking me to buy her drinks, which I foolishly did until all my loose cash was exhausted. When I was out of cash, and not prepared to cash a traveller's cheque, she said goodnight and left me.

The night was still young, so I went to another nightclub, where I bargained with a hooker, 10 Gilders for the room and 20 Guilders for her. I was safe this time, because I had no ready cash, the other hooker had taken it all. When she discovered I didn't have any money, not surprisingly, she left me too.

With that I decided that I had experienced enough of the goings on in that district of Amsterdam. Although it had cost me quite a bit of money it had been fun. It was time to return to the flat, where I found that Russel had booked out. I wrote up my diary and then got into my sleeping bag and fell fast asleep.

Tuesday 30th: September: I woke just before noon and left the flat and got a ham roll and a glass of milk for breakfast. I returned to the YH, but Russel was not there and I never set eyes on him again. I should never have accepted his suggestion, but looking back it gave me an insight into bar life in Amsterdam. I decided to see more of greater Amsterdam and visit an art gallery, but first I had to cash a traveller's cheque. In the end I couldn't be bothered going to the art gallery just to see Rembrandt paintings, because I was not a great lover of oil paintings, they are too slapdash for my liking. It started to rain so I had an ice cream and a glass of lemonade in a café. In retrospect I suppose I really should have gone to the gallery,

360

In the evening I went to the Casablanca Cafe with two Canadian girls and another bloke. We had a great time together swapping experiences and learning about each other's countries, and we were all back in the YH before the doors closed for the night.

¡¡¡¡¡¡¡¡¡¡¡¡¡¡¡¡¡¡¡¡

AMSTERDAM TO THE HOOK OF HOLLAND

Wednesday 1st: October: On this day, the last day of my second tour I caught a train at 9 a.m. through to The Hague, the centre of government of the Netherlands, as well as the location for most of the embassies. At the time of writing the International World Court is also in The Hague. There was quite a lot of interest to be seen on this short trip of 63 km.

Leaving Amsterdam the train soon crossed a couple of bridges over canals, which also ran along beside the railway line. The train stopped at about half a dozen stations along the way, one adjacent to an airport. Further on into the journey the train passed many farmlands with various crops some yellow, probably canola. All of these crops were surrounded by small water channels, but I didn't see any dams on farms like we have in Australia. I wondered if some of the crops I saw were in fact tulips. As the train neared The Hague, but still in rural flat country, I began to see a few traditional style windmills with their sails rapidly revolving, which was quite a thrill.

The Hague is large city, but I saw little of it as I was transferred to the wharf at the Hook of Holland, where the ferry the *Arhmer* a small ship with one funnel was waiting.

The journey of 80 km from Amsterdam took an hour and a half, and I was not really sorry to be leaving a country in which I could find little to interest me. The land is flat, and for me there were no features that I felt I must see while I was there. I certainly did not include the Amsterdam nightlife as one of those attractions.

361

The Ludendorf Bridge ove the Rhine River at Remagen

A postcard

The front cover of the Rhine strip map

The canal in Amsterdam

Cologne Cathedral

The cover of the Drei Groschen Opera booklet

362

The highlight for me was seeing the movie of the *Drei Groschen Opera*. I am quite sure however that when the tulips are in full bloom, this country becomes a place of beauty and a tourist Mecca. I decided to retain the impressions of Holland I had learnt in school, a fascinating country with windmills, clogs and tulips in abundance.

THE HOOK OF HOLLAND TO HARWICH

It was noon when I boarded the ferry for the long voyage of around 200 km to Harwich. On board I had a succulent meal of fish and chips and a beer, which filled a big hole in my stomach. I talked with a couple of Canadians about our countries as the voyage progressed across a calm North Sea under a clear blue sky. After nearly seven hours my voyage came to an end the ferry pulled into the harbour at Harwich.

CHAPTER 24
ENGLAND

iiiiiiiiiiiiiiiiiiiii

HARWICH TO LONDON

LONDON
LIVING AND WORKING IN LONDON

Back on English soil at Harwich, my passport was checked. I already had a ticket that took me all the way to London and a steam train was there on the wharf waiting to take me. It was pleasure to enter the carriage from a floor level platform. With a pip squeak whistle the train left the station for the 90 mile journey through Colchester and Chelmsford to London, arriving there in the dark at 9 p.m.

The supreme event of the following eleven months was the crowning of Queen Elizabeth II in Westminster Abbey on June 2nd 1953, after which I watched the magnificent, long, Coronation procession from a reserved grandstand seat in the East Carriage Road. As explained in the prologue, the story of the eleven months I lived and worked in London, is not included in this book, but can be read in my book *An Aussie Backpacking Londoner* 1952-1953 published by Tale.

CHAPTER 25

THE FIFTH BACKPACKING TOUR

LONDON

Thursday 20th August 1953: When this day eventually came for me to begin my journey home, I did so with the knowledge that I had gained a valuable insight into the English lifestyle, a love of London, England and its people. The months I spent living and working in England and my two years abroad influenced my philosophy of life in so many rewarding and knowledgeable aspects in my journey through life.

iiiiiiiiiiiiiiiiiiiii

LONDON TO NEWHAVEN

With a silent goodbye I was away by 8.30 a.m. closing the door of my boarding house behind me. I took a bus to Victoria station, where I boarded a train to Newhaven. As the train sped through the lovely English countryside, one of the only names I recognised was Lewes, the town nearest to Glyndebourne. I would have loved to have gone there to see an opera performance at this famous venue. Very soon the train pulled into Newhaven.

NEWHAVEN TO DIEPPE

I walked along the wharf to the rather large ferry for Dieppe and I bought my ferry ticket, and again mouthed a silent goodbye as I boarded the ferry, breaking my link with England as I watched the coast of England receding into the misty distance. I consoled myself with the thought that I had lived for eleven months as a Londoner in one of the most important and largest city in the world, the experience of which has enhanced my life of many years, ninety six as I write. I can relate to Queen Elizabeth II, as we are both of the same generation and have lived through much the same trials and tribulations that have beset our world.

Mid-afternoon the ferry reached Dieppe harbour, which still showed signs of war damage. Although it was a rough trip I was pleased that I suffered no ill effects. Dieppe is one of the nearest beach towns to Paris, but from the very little I saw of the beach, and was not impressed.

366

CHAPTER 24
FRANCE

FRANCE

This map shows the location of towns and cities in France and the author's route
through the country. Youth Hotels where the author stayed are shown in bold type

I had no trouble finding the road to take me south to Rouen, the capital city of this region of Normandy, and where there was a YH, 56 km away on the Seine River. I hitchhiked on my 'road to ruin' I hope the only one I ever take! Having no trouble getting lifts in a couple of rickety vehicles through the tree lined, flat, uninteresting countryside, except for the occasional shell hole and other interruptions to the natural ground surface, the result of heavy WWII fighting in this area.

I had a quick look around the large city, which had been in the centre of the invasion fighting. I saw many damaged buildings, exhibiting the ravages of war, and after walking around for a short time to get my bearings, I found the Youth Hostel (YH) on the Rue Diderot. The YH had good washing facilities, but no showers. After a substantial meal of pasta, I wrote up my diary, before settling in for the night in a comfortable bunk, looking forward eagerly to my next destination, Paris.

Friday 21st August 1953: The day dawned cool, but sunny. There

$$\clubsuit$$

DIEPPE TO ROUEN

I quickly found the road to take me south to Rouen the capital city of this region of Normandy, 56 km away on the Seine River. I had no trouble hitch hiking to Rouen getting lifts in a couple of rickety vehicles through the tree lined, flat, uninteresting countryside, except for seeing the occasional shell hole and other interruptions to the natural ground surface, the result of heavy WWII fighting in this area.

ROUEN

I had a quick look around the large city, which had been in the centre of the invasion fighting. I saw many damaged buildings, exhibiting the ravages of war, and after walking around for a short

368

time to get my bearings, I found the Youth Hostel (YH) on the Rue Diderot. The YH had good washing facilities, but no showers. After a substantial meal of pasta, I wrote up my diary before settling in for the night in a comfortable bunk, looking forward eagerly to my next destination, Paris.

Friday 21st August : The day dawned cool, but sunny. There was nothing I wanted to see in Rouen, except to find the market place where a statue of Joan of Arc was erected on the spot where she was burnt at the stake. I soon found the statue and examined its form closely. I thought that the excellent statue did her justice, even if this was not so of those who decreed that she was to end her life in this manner.

♣

ROUEN TO PARIS

Having given some thought to that horrible death, I found my way on to the road to Paris. I managed to get a lift fairly quickly in a rattletrap car all the way to Paris, once again through mostly flat country, along tree lined roads. The leafy trees I thought were poplars. From time to time I saw some war damage in towns along the way. It was a great thrill when I got my first glimpse of the Eiffel Tower, visible quite a long way from the city. I realised as we drove along that I would have to keep my wits about me when I arrived in Paris, because the traffic was driving on the right hand side of the road again.

PARIS

My driver kindly let me off near the YH at the Porte de Chatillon, but the YH was full. The warden directed me to take the Metro to Pigalle and try the Communist hostel in the Rue Victor Masse.

I suppose that I should not have been surprised that the Paris YH was full, considering Paris is one of the top cities in Europe to visit, both for ordinary tourists and YH backpackers. In fact on all my previous tours, this was the one and only YH I found that was full. It threw me out a bit, because I knew very little about the city of Paris, except what I had read about and seen in maps I had studied. I had been in Paris once before when I caught a taxi to take me from the Gare de Lyon to the Gare de Nord, on my way back to England, at the conclusion of my first tour of the Continent, but that was no help at all.

I caught a train to Pigalle on the Metro, as they call the subway. The Metro was not affected by the rail strike thank God that I had heard all about just before I left London, As I travelled along, I noted that the tunnels and platforms of the Paris Metro appeared to be more spacious than the London underground.

Looking at the map, I found the Communist Youth Hostel (CYH) easily and was I was able to book in. The CYH could not have been located in a better place, certainly much better than the YH at the Porte Chatillon, on the south side of the Seine. The CYH was located right next to Pigalle Place, or 'Pig Alley' as the American soldiers called it, in the centre of many of the cabarets and nightclubs, and of course the red light district. The brightly lit windmill of the Moulin Rouge dominated this vibrant area, which was named after the 18th century sculptor Jean Baptiste Pigalle. My first impressions of Paris were that the traffic moved very fast and that the French language was rather pleasant to listen to. I also found that most French people spoke a little English. The currency was also quite different from other countries I had visited. The French franc (Ff) was such a small unit that I thought I was very rich when I changed my first traveller's check for thousands of francs. Not so, I soon discovered 1000 Ff=18 shillings.

Breakfast and an evening meal could be obtained at the CYH, a well appointed building, with large dormitories and a wash room, but without showering facilities. Although adequate in providing cheap accommodation, it was below the standard of most YHs I had stayed in, but it was in an exciting area of Paris, so was I not complaining.

370

In the afternoon I went a walk with a couple of Aussie girls to the district of Montmartre located above and behind Pigalle, the district where many of the artists of Paris live. I climbed to the top of a set of stone stairs, from where I beheld a magnificent church rising up before me. It was the Catholic Church of the Sacred Heart (Baselica Sacre Coeur), which stands on the summit of a high hill, from where the whole city of Paris was visible below me with the huge Eiffel Tower at its centre.

Sacre Coeur is a beautiful white, three domed church, which I instantly likened to the Jungfrau, a mountain above Grindelwald in Switzerland. The similarity to me was not so much in their physical form, but in the virginal beauty of the snow covered north face of the Jungfrau, and this beautiful white church that together with the Eiffel Tower dominates the skyline of Paris. The building of Sacre Coeur in a neo-Romanesque style was commenced in 1873, but was not completed until 1919. The interior is beautiful too. Many of the walls are covered in magnificent mosaics, and there were many beautiful, religious statues and paintings to be seen. Sacre Coeur derives its name from a relic it houses, believed to be a fragment of the heart of Christ.

That completed my first day of sightseeing in Paris and after a nice filling meal of spaghetti in the CYH and a talk with some of the other people there, I retired to my sleeping bag.

Saturday 22nd August: My second day exploring this wonderful city of Paris was to be a very varied and interesting day. First I had a look at the Arc de Triomphe (Arch of Triumph). I walked down from the CYH to the arch, situated slap bang in the centre of the huge roundabout called Etoile (star), from which 12 roads radiated including the famous Avenue de Champs-Elysees. The traffic around this roundabout was well ordered, but very fast. I climbed the stairs to the top of the 50 m high arch, where I was rather taken aback, when asked to pay 50 Ff for the privilege of taking a photo.

371

I took some photos of the view from the top, but it was under protest, because I resented having to pay. There was a very extensive view from the Arc de Triomphe, again with the Eiffel Tower and Sacre Coeur dominating the skyline, while at ground level the long wide Champs-Elysees stretched magnificently away below. The Arch of Triumph was constructed in 1806 for Napoleon to commemorate his victories, but was also used to humiliate the French when the Germans celebrated their capture of Paris.

Leaving the arch, I walked along the Champs-Elysees and window shopped, looking in awe at the beautiful jewellery and clothes displayed, all of which were very expensive.

In the afternoon I met an Aussie called Don at the CYH and we went for a walk together around Paris, but he got bored and left me to myself. He told me he had contracted VD and had to visit a doctor twice a day to have shots of penicillin, so any vague thoughts I may have entertained of being a customer of a girl from the red light area of Paris, were completely quashed. I remembered reading about the 'Ladies of the Evening' in my *American Army Guide Book,* which gave advice to American occupation soldiers visiting Paris.

The book explained how the French government was conducting a testing program for prostitutes. Any prostitute who wished could take a weekly test for VD. If clear, she was issued with a yellow card valid for one week. This was not for being a bad boy as in soccer, but for being a good girl in the brothel. So a customer (if he was not a gentleman), could ask to see the girl's yellow card before he indulged.

The one big problem with this method was that the first customer a girl had immediately after her test, could infect her with VD. Apart from venereal disease, I was lucky to do all of my dating in the age before the scourge of Aids.

I went for a walk with two, rather, attractive girls from New Zealand who were staying at the CYH. We went over the River Seine to the Latin Quarter, situated between the left bank of the

372

Seine River and the Luxembourg Gardens. It was so named, because in early times, the students who attended the university in the district, were required to speak only in Latin to their teachers and professors. It is still a student area, with many schools of learning including two large universities, the Paris University (Sorbonne) and the Cite Universitaire. By reason of the student population, it was a good cheap place to eat as there were many cafes catering to their needs. The City Club was one of these, where we had a beaut meal for 250 Ff., afterwards returning to the CYH by the Metro.

In the evening, we decided to go to the *Romance Club*, a nightclub with bare breasted waitresses, which didn't matter to the girls, they were very broad minded. We had a lovely, busty night, there. I had never had bare breasts so close to me without touching them! The Romance Club had a great band and entertainment, some of which was in English.

Some hostellers warned us before we went that after we paid the admission charge, which included a bottle of beer or wine, we needed to make sure it lasted all night; because if we were to reorder drinks, they would be extremely expensive. We made very sure that the drinks lasted the night, but even so we had a great time, while very slowly, sipping our drinks.

Sunday 23rd August: I went to the Louvre across the Seine, its waters looking a little cleaner than the Yarra and Thames. The Louvre is a huge museum, rectangular in shape with one end opening up to the Jardin des Tuileries (Tuileries Gardens) and the Place de la Concorde, all very imposing and grand. The Louvre was originally a fortress and a palace, prior to becoming a museum in 1793 to house works of art from around the world. The collection has gradually been added to over the centuries. The most interesting museum I had seen so far on my tours, was the technology museum in Munich, a marvellous museum, full of working exhibits and the ski museum at the Holmenkollen, ski jump in Oslo, Norway, with its marvellous collection of skis of all descriptions. I was taken to our Melbourne

Museum as a young lad and the only things I was really interested in were the static, model trains. My other vivid memory of the Melbourne Museum was seeing the room where the Egyptian mummies were kept. I can still remember the musty look and smell of the place.

There were however, two exhibits I wanted to see in the Louvre, the Mona Lisa and Venus de Milo. When I entered the room where the Mona Lisa was being exhibited, I saw that the area around it was roped off. I had no objection to that, but the glass covering the painting reflected light from every direction, no matter which way I looked at it, even though I was in the front row of the people viewing the painting, I couldn't get a clear view of Leonardo Da Vinci's world famous masterpiece, and felt like asking for my admission money back. The Mona Lisa is an oil painting 77 cm by 53 cm. It was painted between 1503 and 1505. It is generally agreed that it is a portrait of the wife of Francesco del Giocondo (hence 'La Gioconda').

In August 1911 the *Mona Lisa* was stolen by someone who just took the painting off the wall and walked out of the Louvre with it. Despite an intensive search and investigation into its whereabouts, it remained a mystery. In November 1913 a letter was sent to an antique dealer. The letter revealed where the painting could be found. It was in fact, in an apartment only a short distance from the Louvre.

Venus de Milo, unlike the Mona Lisa, was not a disappointment. The beautiful smooth statue of Aphrodite of Melos, the Goddess of Love from Roman mythology, was excellently displayed. In 1820 a peasant discovered the damaged statue in a cave on the Aegean Island of Milos. The sculptor was not known, nor was the date. The statue was presented to King Louis XVIII and given the name of Venus de Milo. Having seen the two works of art I most wanted to see, I then wandered around the huge museum and saw many other interesting and beautiful exhibits before I got bored and hungry.

374

I left the Louvre and had an 80 Ff ham roll and a 50 Ff beer, before going to visit the Cathedral of Notre Dame. I walked along the right bank of the Seine, a short distance to the Cathedral of Notre Dame (Our Lady), situated on the Isle de la Cite, an island in the centre the Seine. The cathedral replaced a church that was destroyed by fire in 1194. Notre Dame was constructed in the 13th century in Gothic style and took 30 years to build.

It has two unusual features for a Gothic cathedral, large flying buttresses on the east side. I was not sure if they were a structural necessity, or for decoration. The other unusual feature about Notre Dame, are the many rather hideous gargoyles, which peer down from a ledge on the roof. This famous church is not the most beautiful, but is quite imposing. I was able to have a closer look at the gargoyles when I climbed the stairs on to the roof, from where I had a restricted view of Paris along the banks of the Seine.

The interior of Notre Dame is gigantic, but rather plain, except for all the religious statues and the area around the choir screen and pulpit. The various external portals are decorated with beautiful sculptured patterns, especially the circular rose above the south portal. Although there are many churches in France that carry the name of Notre Dame, this one in Paris is the cathedral where Victor Hugo in his book *Notre Dame de Paris,* wrote about the Hunchback of Notre Dame, Quasimodo, the bell ringer of the cathedral. I didn't have to think too long before I found a mountain, as is my wont, with a similarity to Notre Dame, with its two large 90 m high frontal towers. What could be more appropriate I thought than 'the heavenly twins' Castor and Pollux, a pair of peaks in the Pennine Alps above Zermatt in Switzerland, and the two in the Victorian alps on Mt. Bogong.

On all of my tours including this one, I resisted the not too great temptation, to wear old clothes. Instead I tried to be well dressed within the confines of practicality of being a backpacker, even to the extent of having a white handkerchief showing from the breast pocket of my sports coat. I think this resulted in being offered close contact with people on my backpacking tours. I am saddened when I see many present day backpackers attired in sloppy, dirty clothes and those bloody jeans.

I saw some unusual sights in Paris as I walked around. A man and a girl, kissing passionately in the middle of the road with cars rushing by on either side of them. A family eating and drinking on a pavement cafe with their son, who was about five years old, drinking a bottle of beer with them. There was another novelty I saw and used that day, an outside male urinal, where I stood and had a pee while I watched people go by. There was no screen at the bottom or top, just across the centre.

Monday 24th August: I went with Cecil, an Aussie I met at the CYH, to have a look at the Eiffel Tower, a colossal structure. We approached the tower crossing over the Seine River on the Pont d' Lena Bridge. Looking down, the water was a little cleaner than our Yarra and London's Thames .We didn't go up the tower because it was too expensive. I was not really sorry, it was quite enough for me to admire the immensity of the tower and take a couple of photos from ground level. The Eiffel Tower was built in 1889 to commemorate the centennial of the French Revolution. A competition was held for the design of a tower, which was only to be a temporary structure to be pulled down after 20 years.

The design submitted by Gustav Eiffel won the contest, but it was not Eiffel's design. The engineer Maurice Koechlin, whose design it was, worked for Eiffel's engineering business. He had designed many bridges and viaducts for Eiffel as well as the framework for the Statue of Liberty. Most of these designs used the same building technique of steel girders held together by rivets. The Eiffel Tower is 320 m (1,051 ft), high and weighs 7100 tonnes. Its four legs are mounted on hydraulic dampers, to absorb the movement of the tower caused by high winds.

The statue of Joan of Arc in Reoun

Sacre Coeur a most beautiful church from without and within.

Top section of the Eiffel Tower.

The base of the Eiffel Tower

A view of the Eiffel Tower from the Arc de Triomphe

The tower is held together by 2.5 million rivets. It is repainted every seven years in bronze paint. It was never pulled down, even though the Parisians were initially openly hostile to its construction, but instead was found to be an ideal place to mount broadcasting aerials, as well as an excellent location for carrying out many types of scientific experiments. Now it is Paris's most recognisable icon.

When the Germans captured Paris in World War II, a strange thing happened regarding the Eiffel Tower. The Germans wanted to fly their flag from the top of the tower, but a part of the lift mechanism was broken, rendering all the lifts unworkable. A replacement part could not be procured because the manufacturer was in the enemy's hands. The German soldiers had to climb the 1,780 steps to the top of the tower to unfurl their flag.

Stranger still was the fact that on the day that Paris was liberated from the Germans in 1944, a replacement part was miraculously found and all the lifts began working again. This, however, was not before a team of French men climbed those same steps to remove the German flag and replace it with the tricolour, while fighting was still in progress around the Ecole Militaire, only a short distance away.

The Eiffel Tower stands on the left bank of the Seine and for 40 years it was the highest structure in the world until the Chrysler and Empire State skyscrapers were built in America. On the same side of the Seine a large park, the Parc du Champ de Mars, extends to the Ecole Militaire. The park was originally used as a training ground for cadets from the Military College.

Cecil and I had lunch at the City Club. It was a nice cheap meal, but I found a 25 mm long cockroach in the bottom of my red wine bottle, which gave it a great taste! I showed it to the waiter, but did he offer me another bottle for free? No. Did I ask for one? No, like a fool I didn't. After lunch, we split up and I went back to the arch and then wandered down the Champs Elysees. It is a beautiful avenue lined with expensive looking shops, with tables and chairs outside the cafes. I went into one shop and bought a beautiful, cameo brooch,

378

a present for my mother, after which I returned to the CYH to get ready for a night at the Follies.

When the time came to go, I did not have far to go as the Follies Bergere was just a few streets away on the Rue Richer. The Follies Bergere opened in 1868 and was the major theatrical attraction in Paris, because it also staged opera. The theatre is not particularly large, but it is very cosy. To open the show, a large cage was lowered from the roof containing a beautiful girl in a scanty, but, lovely dress. She danced in the cage and divested herself of items of clothing every now and again during the cabaret acts, which were taking place below her on the stage. The stage acts were all of high standard, can-can dancers, brilliant magicians, comic acts. There were many dance routines, with the dancers clad in feathered gowns.

I thoroughly enjoyed my visit to this world famous theatre, which still lives in my memory. I retained my program, which contained a satchel of perfume. For the next ten years I showed the program to friends and let them marvel at the smell of the alluring, musk perfume, that still permeated the program. Alas I no longer have the program, or the perfume.

I finished my last English cigarette and had to buy French Gauloises, a very strong cigarette. I stopped smoking around 1965, one of the best decisions I ever made, because I believe I would not be writing this narrative if I had not stopped then. At the time, however, I was enjoying smoking a corncob pipe. The CYH was closed so I had a beer and ham sandwich in a cafe in Pigalle Place. This time the cost was 100 Ff, much more expensive for exactly the same beer that I used to wash down the cockroach, flavoured wine, at the City Club.

Tuesday 25th August: Talking with other 'hostellers' in the CYH, I had been told not to miss seeing Napoleon's tomb in the Hotel des Invalides, so that was to be my major visit for the day. Don and Cecil wanted to go to the market area to buy some food and goods, so I went along with them. The market happened to be adjacent to a low class red light area. As we looked around the market a discussion developed among some of the market keepers, with fingers pointed in our direction. The gesticulations and discussions became very heated, so we decided it was time to make a hasty retreat. I believe the argument was about our nationalities, I think they thought we were Americans.

There was still quite a bit of residual animosity towards Americans due to their behaviour during the war and afterwards, a point made to me by my French journalist friend Jacques, while I was in Vienna.

My companions had already visited Napoleon's tomb, so I made my way to the Hotel des Invalides by myself, where Emperor Napoleon's tomb resides, together with many other military relics. I purchased a small booklet at the entrance and entered the high domed Hotel des Invalides, which was built by Louis XIV to house disabled soldiers from the French wars. At the time of my visit they numbered 200, but on some occasions in the past there were as many as 5000. The building was completed in 1735. Since then it has been extended to include the War Ministry, the Army Museum and other government military offices. It has seven chapels in honour of various saints.

Emperor Napoleon's tomb is in a crypt reached by stairs down which I went. There before me I saw, the magnificent, huge, tomb in the centre under the high dome. The sarcophagus was simply breathtakingly beautiful. Red stone porphyry, a rock with crystals embedded, forms the upper part of the tomb, which stands on a green Vosges granite stand. The complete tomb measures 4 m long by 2 m wide and stands a little over 4 m high.

Emperor Napoleon died in May 1821 while in exile on St Helena, where he was first buried. He was exhumed in 1840 and his remains brought to Paris to be buried in this tomb in six coffins, one inside the other, of zinc, mahogany, two of lead, one of ebony and

380

one of oak. The total cost was over six million francs. After admiring his tomb I had a look at the rest of the building and its contents. I saw Napoleon's hat, sword and other relics including his death mask. After a final look around at the chapels and statues, I left this remarkable building with the thought that every visitor to Paris should not fail to visit the Hotel des Invalides. It was one of the highlights of my visit to Paris, alongside the Eiffel Tower.

Returning to the CYH, I passed a stone wall into which were set ten niches. It was a memorial to ten, French, resistance fighters, who had been lined up there and shot by the Germans. I had a bite to eat and wandered around Montmartre, an enchanting locality especially at night, with all the cafes and stalls lit up displaying lots of souvenirs for sale, especially paintings. As I looked at many of the paintings that were for sale, I felt sure that I could paint watercolours better than some of those on view In Montmartre. I vowed that I would to give it a try when I returned to Australia. Before I left Montmartre, I purchased a beautiful painting of Sacre Coeur floodlit at night from within Montmartre for 450 Ff.

Very soon after I returned to Australia, I worked for the State Electricity Commission (SEC) at Mt Beauty in the Victorian Alps, where I was surrounded by scenes that were just begging to be reproduced as watercolours. I bought myself a set of watercolours and went about seeing how good I really was.

Over the course of the next three years I painted many watercolours, with the realisation that I could paint better than many works I had seen on display in Montmartre, and furthermore I sold quite a few.

Until I visited Paris I had come to the conclusion that if I ever returned to Europe and the Continent, which I never did–only by YouTube. I would want to visit Vienna as my first choice. However, since spending the past five days in this wonderful city of Paris, it very nearly eclipsed Vienna as my favourite city. Very soon I will

381

visit the next major city of my tours, Rome, but I doubt if I will find that Rome will be my favourite.

From the standpoint of a tourist like myself, London is a very busy city with loads of tradition, whereas I felt that Paris was a city of historic grandeur without so much of the tradition. Paris is a wide open, clean air city, whereas London is a bit grubby and cramped. Each city has its famous buildings, cathedrals, streets, rivers and transport systems.

There is no doubt in my mind however, that Vienna on the Danube, is my choice for the best city I have visited and lived in on my tours, perhaps because I lived there for two weeks and had time to explore it widely. Vienna with its river the Danube, oozes history, especially musical. The ring road enclosing the inner city of Vienna, is loaded with magnificent, culturally significant buildings, with St Stephens iconic church, near its centre. There are many wonderful buildings too like Schonbrunn and the Vienna Woods close by.

Wednesday 26th August: I was up early ready to begin the next stage of my tour through France to see some of the French mountain country and make my way to the French Riviera and relax in the sun on the beaches of Cannes and Nice. Collecting my belongings, I discovered that my beaut, gabardine raincoat, had been stolen! So much for Communist Youth Hostels. I have left my belongings in many places, mostly youth hostels while I explored the various sights in cities around Europe. It says much for the honesty of all the people in the countries I had visited, that the raincoat was the only article that has been stolen from me up to this time in my tours. I would be interested to know if the same level of honesty applies at the time of writing. My only consolation was that the coat was not stolen from a Youth Hostel, but from the communist hostel where I had to stay because the YH was full.

On the Champs Elysees

The memorial niches to the French resistance fighters

Napoleon's tomb in the Hotel des Invalides

A view from the roof of Notre Dame with the church and the Seine River below

A greyscale image of the oil painting I purchased in Montmatre with Sacre Coeur in the background

The well dressed backpacking author with the church of Notre Dame on an island in the Seine River behind

PARIS TO FORTAINEBLEAU

The weather continued to be fine as I left the hostel, sans raincoat, and caught a coach to Fontainebleau, where I hoped to be able to get a lift to Lyon. Fontainebleau, 60 km to the south of Paris is surrounded by forested country. There was nothing I wanted to see in the city, the third largest in France, so I made my way to the road leading to Lyon. It was about 2 p.m. and almost immediately I got a lift from a bloke in a Renault.

He spoke a little English and said he was going to Lyon, nearly 370 km away. He was a travelling salesman selling stationary.

FORTAINEBLEAU TO LYON

I was extremely lucky to get a lift all the way to Lyon. My driver drove quite fast only stopping for a short time at the towns of Auxerre and Dijon, where we picked up a drink and a bite to eat. The countryside we passed through on the way was alternately flat and undulating. We passed by many vineyards, especially around Dijon, the heart of the Burgundy wine growing district. I noticed that nearly all the churches were rectangular with their sides painted white, and their steeples were high and tapered to a very sharp point.

LYON

We arrived in Lyon in darkness at 8.30 p.m. After thanking my driver for the beaut long lift, I studied my *YHA Pocket Guide to Europe* and found that the YH was quite a way out of the city. I asked a gendarme the best wa7y to get there. He said: "It is getting late. You are most welcome to spend the night in a cell in the police station." "Thanks" I said and off I went with him to the police station, not in handcuffs though. I was shown a cell, that had a single bunk and toilet, all very Spartan, but it was all that I needed for the night. I was very grateful for the private room-er-cell.

I left my rucksack in the cell while I looked for a place to eat. The gendarme directed me to a good, cheap, restaurant nearby, where I had a great meal of pea soup, sausages and mashed potatoes with white wine, a peach, pear, and grapes, all for 600 Ff. It was a very appetising meal. I put the peach and pear away to eat the next day, but ate the grapes.

I thought might like to finish off with a dessert, so I asked the waiter for a *"desert sil vous plait."* Instead of bringing me the dessert menu, he went to the back of the kitchen and after a short time, returned and placed a plate with two fried eggs in front of me! I was astonished and looked across at a German couple on the next table, with whom I had been trying out my German.

I told them what I had asked for, and they both broke out in peals of laughter. They explained to me that the waiter thought I had asked for *'deux oeufs'*, which in French is 'two eggs.' I suppose he imagined I would not want to eat them raw, so he fried them for me. The eggs were very nice. I never tire of telling that story to my friends and others. It is a perfect dining out story, as it always brings plenty of laughs, at my expense of course. I said goodbye to the German couple and thanked them for their help, paid the bill, plus a small amount extra for the eggs. I returned to the cell falling asleep quickly in a comfortable bunk in the cell.

Thursday 27th August: I woke early the next morning in the police station and was given a hot cup of coffee and a slice of jam and toast. I said I wanted to go to Grenoble. The police showed me the way to get out of the city and onto the road to Grenoble. After thanking them for their hospitality, we shook hands and I was off. Lyon I thought must be a very law abiding city, because I was the only one in the cells that night.

Lyon in WWII was one of the largest centres of the French Resistance. It was also the headquarters of the Gestapo Commander Klaus Barbie ('the Butcher of Lyon'), who ordered the death of 4,000 people in Lyon and deported many others.

I had a quick look around Lyon, a city famous for its silk industry and its restaurants, especially the way they serve two beautiful, fried eggs. Then I made my way to the road where I hoped I would get a quick lift to Grenoble, 100 km away. I had to cross over the small Saone River and then over the large, Rhone River, which empties into the Mediterranean Sea in Marseille, over 300 km away. The last time I crossed the Rhone was on my way from Zermatt to Grindelwald, many miles upstream. It is a much larger river in Lyon than I remembered seeing in Switzerland where it was much nearer its source, the Rhone Glacier in the Swiss canton of Valais.

LYON TO GRENOBLE

It was a lovely sunny day out on the road that led to Grenoble and I was absolutely thrilled to see the mountains on the horizon in the direction I wanted to go. Without waiting too long, I got a lift in a 6 cylinder Peugeot. The driver kept up a very high speed on ever rising country arriving at Grenoble at 12.20 p.m. amongst the mountains.

GRENOBLE

Grenoble reminded me of Innsbruck with the high mountains in the background behind the city. I booked into the YH, which had good washing facilities including showers. I had a shower and then I explored the city, populated by gaily dressed, good looking, sun tanned women and well, dressed men, and shops full of attractive clothes and snow and mountain related items.

I liked this city very much, I supposed because it was within sight of the mountains. Grenoble was the nominal venue for the 1968 Winter Olympics; however, most of the events were held a short distance away in the ski village of Chamrousse. The 1996 Winter Olympics were also held in this vicinity at Albertville, about 80 km north of Grenoble. As well as being a centre for mountain related activities, Grenoble has many other places of interest, both in the city and in the surrounding countryside, such as the Forte de Bastille,

386

which overlooks the city. Grenoble also has a university, together with a large student population. Although I liked Grenoble very much, I didn't visit any of its places of interest because my main objective was s to get to Cannes as soon as possible.To this end, I enquired at a travel agency the best way to get to Cannes and Nice and see the alps at the same time? They said to take a coach along the Route Napoleon, so I bought a ticket for 1200 Ff (about £1), on an SNCF coach to take me to Cannes the following morning.

I had been very lucky on the first legs of this tour to get such good, long, car journeys. The rail strike was over, but it did not affect me in any way, because the Metro was still running while I was in Paris. I had a marvellous night at the YH, with a meal of spaghetti washed down with red wine. I talked with a UK communist and told him where I had lost my raincoat. He said there were thieves in every organisation. The one day I spent in Grenoble was very enjoyable, especially with the knowledge that I was on the doorstep of the French Alps. I was looking forward eagerly to the coach journey to Cannes.

GRENOBLE TO CANNES

Friday 28th August: On a beautiful morning, I boarded a large coach to take me on the next exciting stage of my tour. I had been very fortunate, as it had not rained since I set foot in France. The large coach crossed over the Isere River, and joined the Route Napoleon. This 320 km long, mountain highway, follows the route Napoleon took in 1815 on his way to Paris after his escape from Elba. The previous night I felt as though I was getting a cold. Sure enough, this morning my nose was running and I wasn't feeling the best. Why oh why, did I have to catch a horrible cold, just as I was beginning this great coach journey? I had been plagued with colds on my previous tours, so this was nothing new. The first part of the journey was quite hilly. The coach went through the steep sided cuttings of the Infernet Gorges and passed by a large dam that held back the waters of an artificial lake, which I thought was probably a source of hydro-electricity.

As the coach climbed higher, all at once I beheld a spectacular vista of alpine peaks with patches of snow still showing. I was told by a fellow passenger that the highest peak I could see was the Meije, 3,973 m (13,034 ft) high, meaning it just missed out on being classified as a 'Four Thousander'. I felt that this might be my last look at one of the high peaks of the Alps, and sadly it was.

The coach travelled along a high plateau above the Drac River with more views of high mountains, then the coach passed another very long lake before climbing the Bayard Pass, at an altitude of 1.169 m (3,933 ft). The Route Napoleon descended a short distance into a town that I thought was appropriately called Gap, because of its solitary location below the Bayard Pass. It was a very hot, but not a humid day at this altitude.

GAP

I could have imagined I was in the middle of Mexico, because this town and some of the countryside around, was so reminiscent of towns and country I had seen in cowboy movies shot in Mexico. The coach stopped for 45 minutes for lunch. Even the people looked Mexican, with their large hats and clothes.

I went to have a look at the shops, only to find that most of the shops were closed except the cafes. I sat down on a chair at a table outside one of the cafes, and had a ham roll and soft drink and watched the locals pass by. All looked very fit and well dressed in neat summer clothes with sun tans and nearly all sporting large hats. I was told that all the shops were closed from 1 p.m. until 4 p.m. All the shopkeepers went home or wherever at 1p.m. until 4p.m. then worked until 8 p.m. This break called 'siesta time'. It seemed to be a very sensible idea for the type of country and climate here in Gap.

My last look at the spectacular summits of the French Alps. A composite photo of the Dauphine Alps with the Meije just visible on the right

A view along the Isere River in Grenoble to the Forte de la Bastille and the French Alps in the distance

A long lake on the Drac River a scene from the coach along the Route Napoleon

The author right, enjoying a drink and lunch in Gap. Most of the shops were closed for the afternoon siesta

A view of the town of Gap from a postcard I bought in Gap

389

Soon it was time to rejoin the coach after a very pleasant pause in Gap, a smallish, Mexican style, attractive town, on the Rue Napoleon, but I have of course no idea what shopping was like in Gap. I actually imagined that it would have been quite exciting. Many years later, around 1998, when the Tour de France bicycle race was routed through Gap at the finish of a stage, I couldn't believe my eyes. The lazy town I remembered was now transformed into a huge, bustling city with large buildings and suburbs. I wondered if they still had 'siesta time,' but I very much doubted it. This I supposed was one example of the changes that have occurred over 60 or so years to all of the places I visited on my three tours.

Leaving Gap, the coach climbed back up to the pass and descended into a valley to the town of Sisteron, with its old houses and narrow streets that were barely wide enough for the coach to drive along. Sisteron is sometimes referred to as 'The Gateway to Provence' as it is situated between two high ridges in the region of the Provence-Alps-Cot d' Azure.

After Sisteron, the coach entered another valley, arriving at the town of Digne, famous for its thermal springs and lavender. The coach passed a couple of lavender farms where the crops of spindly purple lavender could be seen. Sadly I couldn't smell the lavender because of my bad cold, which was a bit of a pity. Leaving Digne, the coach continued along the Route Napoleon towards Cannes, still about 150 km away.

The coach then entered a region called the 'Prealps of Digne.' This section of the journey was very spectacular, as the Route Napoleon went through many gorges, with cliffs towering above the coach on both sides. Castellane was the next town, and the centre for visiting the canyons of Verdon. We only saw some of the smaller gorges of this region, as we passed by in the coach.

However, at one point high up on the road, the driver stopped the coach for a short time, to allow his passengers to see the spectacular view across the deep Verdon Canyons. These canyons are said in many respects, to rival the Grand Canyon of Colorado, but from the little I saw from the Route Napoleon, I was sure they didn't. Not that I have been to the Grand Canyon in the USA, but I have seen many photos of the huge, long, deep, colourful canyons.

I was fascinated by the socks a well-dressed, middle aged gentleman in the coach was wearing, fawn coloured, sheer nylon the same as worn by ladies. I vowed to buy a pair at the earliest opportunity, because they looked very elegant and cool, and I would see if, when I wore them back in Australia, I would get laughed at. Sadly I never got around to buying any before I boarded the *Orion*. It was very many years, before they became available in Australia. I bought a few pairs, but they were not as sheer as the ones I saw the gentleman wearing in the coach, and when I wore them they never raised any comments, I am sorry to say.

The coach crossed a number of 1.000 m (2,808 ft) passes. On one of these I had my first thrilling glimpse of the, Mediterranean Sea in the distance a very inviting vista. The last town before Cannes was Grasse, on the slopes above Cannes. Grasse is the centre of the perfume industry in France, but once again I was incapable of smelling perfume because of my cold. I believe that in both Grasse and Digne any person with a good nose can smell the perfume in the air.

Sadly, the coach didn't stop at Grasse with its red and orange, roofed houses, but continued on down the final 27 km of winding road, with marvellous views of the very blue Mediterranean. It was late afternoon when the coach arrived in Cannes, on the fabulous, French Riviera, known as 'the playground of the rich and famous'. I am neither rich or famous, but intended to have a really relaxing time time in their playground.

My coach journey of just over 300 km along the Route Napoleon (now the N85), was one of the most spectacular, coach journeys I had ever been on, through a landscape that I didn't believe

391

existed in France. Mexican looking towns, barren country, sage bush, canyons, gorges, bluffs, perfumed plants, and where I saw for the last time the magnificent summits of the French Alps.

CANNES

Cannes I knew was the venue for the yearly Film Festivals, so this was the second film festival venue I had visited, the other one was staged on The Lido, the island beach resort of greater Venice. I knew that Cannes on the French Riviera was a famous region of France on the Mediterranean Sea. As well as Cannes the names of two towns, Jaun le Pine and St Tropez, were stuck in my mind, but why, I was not quite sure? Both very intriguing names conjuring up thoughts of exotic, luxury and beauty.

The French Riviera, or Cote d' Azure (Blue Coast) which I will use in this book, because it is more descriptive of the 200 km long coast of France between Marseilles in the west, and Menton in the east, next to the Italian border. This beautiful coastline includes many fabulous beach resorts, Toulon, Hyeres, Cavalaire and St Tropez, to the west, while continuing along the coastline to the east are most of the well Principality of Monaco and Menton.

Leaving the coach I consulted my YHA guide book and found that the Cannes YH was located in a village called La Bocca about 3 km to the west of Cannes. I walked along a paved path on the side of the Boulevard du Midi, which ran above an inviting, sandy beach. On the opposite side of the Boulevard there was a railway line leading into Cannes and a little further on was the YH in La Bocca,

🏠

LA BOCCA

La Bocca YH was like a camp, with cooking and toilet facilities attached. I booked in and went a walk back along the path to a shop where I bought some spaghetti and tomatoes for my evening meal. I was delighted to see a couple of passenger trains pass by on the other side of the boulevard, but what was most in my mind was getting rid of my cold and going for a swim. Back at the YH I was feeling very

392

hungry, as I hadn't eaten much on the coach, I got stuck into a large plate of spaghetti and tomatoes, before settling down for the night in a bungalow type bunkroom, with the hope that my lousy cold would be better in the morning.

Saturday 29th August: I woke a little later than I intended and my cold seemed to be a little better. Looking at my map, I traced the journey that I had just taken from Grenoble to Cannes. I discovered that the hills behind Cannes were part of the Maritime Alps. Many years later, back in Australia, I purchased a wonderful book called *The Alps in Colour* by Robert Loble and Hugh Merrick. The book contained a host of beautiful colour illustrations of the European Alps from their beginning to the end.

From the book I made the exciting discovery that during my tours in Europe, I had actually traversed the complete 640 km (400 mile) length of the European Alps, crossing and recrossing the Alps by many high passes. I surprisingly learnt that the European Alps commenced with two low mountains called Leopoldberg and Kahlenberg, both around 457m (1,500 ft) high.

These two summits in the Vienna Woods rise above the vineyards beside the Danube River, some 16 km north of Vienna. When I was in Vienna, I went on a tour to the Vienna Woods and travelled around these two low mountains, but I had no idea at the time, that they had such significance with regard to the European Alps. The journey by coach from Grenoble along the Route Napoleon through Gap and the rugged canyons and gorges of the Maritime Alps to Cannes, is where the southern end of the European Alps finally comes to an end, plunging into the Mediterranean Sea around Cannes and Nice.

I walked into Cannes and had a look around the famous resort. I went along a jetty in the harbour admiring all the beautiful yachts. I stopped beside one with a Daimler car parked beside it on the jetty. The name of this large, sleek and very expensive looking yacht was the *Shemara*. I asked a man who appeared to be standing guard.

"Who the car and yacht belonged to?" "Sir Bernard and Lady Docker," he replied proudly. Sir Bernard was the chairman of the Daimler Company. He and his wife were a very wealthy, flamboyant couple who hosted fabulous parties. The *Shemara* weighed just short of 100 tonnes, with a crew of 35. I wandered further along the jetty where I was amazed to see many luxury yachts nearly as large as the *Shemara*.

On the way back to the YH I passed by a low wall on which was written in red paint, the words 'YANKS GO HOME.' Further evidence that some French people do not like the Americans. The writing was quite conspicuous and looked as if it had been there for some time. I returned to La Bocca and had a ham sandwich lunch. Then I sunbathed and lazed on the uncrowded La Bocca beach. I couldn't wait until I felt well enough to have my first swim in the beautiful, blue, Mediterranean Sea, which was so tempting.

I walked back into Cannes and had a further look at all the luxury yachts tied up in the harbour, then wandered further along the promenade admiring the large hotels, shops, swanky cars and elegant women in beautiful clothes. Cannes was everything I had heard about it, a high class, fabulous, seaside resort. Its setting reminded me very much of Lorne, a beach resort in my home state of Victoria, both having beautiful sandy beaches and wooded hills behind. Cannes with the Maritime Alps, and Lorne with the Otway Ranges. The main difference was that the hills above Cannes have many houses built on them, whereas Lorne's hills are heavily timbered, with few houses.

Sunday 30th August: Nearly all the way from Paris, the weather had been fine and sunny and so it was on this morning. Happily, my cold was a little better. After lunch I went to the beach at La Bocca with Paddy, an Irish hosteller I met the night before. We met two lovely French girls, Pauline and Micheline.

We spent a pleasant afternoon with them in Cannes walking along the Boulevard de la Croisette with palm trees lining one side of

The town of Digne in the valley in the Provence region of France with the large Catholic Cathedral in the centre of the photo.

The author's coach in the rugged town of Sisteron

A composite photo looking down into the Verdon Canyons, an unexpected land form seen along the route Napoleon in the Maritime Alps.

Cannes and the Maritime Alps plunging into the Mediterranean Sea

The Boulevard du Midi above the La Bocca beach with Cannes in the distance

395

the promenade and classy hotels on the other. We went to a cafe for a drink, which was very enjoyable. The girls were on holiday and spoke very good English.

Monday 31st August: Today was another beautiful day and at last my cold had nearly gone, thank goodness. I went into Cannes again to have a look around and enquired about catching a train to Nice. I decided I would take a bus instead because it was cheaper.

I had lunch and began walking back to the YH, when I smelled a familiar aroma. I looked around me and discovered that I was surrounded by wonderful, Aussie, gum (eucalypt) trees. For the past few days I had been walking through these gums, to and from the YH, but couldn't smell them because of my cold. When I arrived back at the YH, I met Paddy and we went to the La Bocca beach. At last I felt fit enough to have my first swim in the Mediterranean. The water was a nice invigorating temperature and I had a great time, but there was no surf. Back at the YH I cooked a whacking, great meal of spaghetti and tomatoes, and finished the night with some English blokes over a bottle of white wine.

Even though it was nearly the end of summer and the weather was sunny, the Cannes beaches were not crowded. At the time of writing, I have read that all the beaches of the Cote d' Azure would be packed at this time of the year. Cannes is a very picturesque resort with clean, wide, sandy beaches. The harbour, packed with yachts is quite beautiful, while behind Cannes, the wooded foothills of the Maritime Alps, dotted with orange, red and white, coloured houses amongst the trees, helped to give the coast line of Cannes much of its charm.

While I was in Cannes I had the choice of sunbathing and swimming on the La Bocca beach close to the YH, where not many people bathed and sun baked, or walking 3 km to the Cannes beaches. There was really no difference in the quality, as both beaches were wide, sandy and clean. I preferred the La Bocca beach for sunbathing and swimming, mainly because it was close to the YH

A view across Cannes Harbour to the palms on the Boulevard de la Croisette

Luxury yachts moored in Cannes harbour

'YANKS GO HOME' Graffiti on a wall at the western end Cannes, further evidence that the Americans were not all that popular in France

The Jean Hibert Square named after an English author

Palm trees in Cannes lining the Boulevard de la Croisette and the beach in Cannes

My bathers were completely unfashionable, because the bathers worn by the men were nothing more than a jockstrap tied with a string at the rear. The women were wearing 'bikinis' the very briefest of brief, two piece swimsuits. These came on the market sometime in the forties (but not in Aussie land). Some of them were entrancing and beautiful, but on the other hand, there were some persons of both sexes with certain types of bodies, who should never wear a jockstrap or bikini and be seen on a beach. With those observations about some of the sights I had seen in Cannes, and my bathing attire, I decided it was time to move on to Nice in the morning.

Tuesday 1st September: After breakfast I packed payed my YH fees, and said goodbye to Paddy the Irishman whose company I had enjoyed during my stay in Cannes. I walked into Cannes past the gum trees with their lovely aroma that I would be smelling almost every day in a little over a month. I had my last look around Cannes and caught a bus to take me 27 km to Nice along the picturesque coastline.

CANNES TO NICE

It was only when I got on the bus that I thought while I was in Cannes, I never looked to see where the theatre was that staged the Cannes film festival. In fact, I must have passed it each day I went into Cannes on the Boulevard de la Croisette. In April 1953 *Call Me Madam* (the movie) was featured in the Cannes awards. I saw the stage version of *Call Me Madam* twice in London, but I do not think I would have enjoyed the movie however, I played the 78 r.p.m. records of the show I bought in London many times.

I had a brief look at the each of the towns the bus passed through, and where the bus stopped to set down and pick up local passengers at all the beautiful, seaside resorts. Juan les Pins was one of the towns I had heard about back in Australia, but not St Tropez because it is west of Cannes. The bus rounded many sharp corners as it made its way along the promontory to Cap Antibes. Then back and around to the large and more fashionable resort of Antibes. Quite apart from these fabulous resort towns, there were many multi-coloured dwellings in the small villages to be seen along the way and on the hills above the towns. It was a very scenic journey along the coastline, with the beautiful blue Mediterranean stretching away to the eastern horizon. I certainly saw more of this beautiful promontory, its dwellings and inhabitants than I would have seen from the train, which kept inland not entering Cap Antibes.

⚑
NICE

The bus arrived in Nice about 2 p.m. and without any trouble I found the YH. I booked in, cleaned up a bit, and walked into the city. Nice is a larger city than Cannes, with a long promenade, the Promenade des Anglias, lined with many large hotels and shops. Much grander that the Boulevard de la Croisette in Cannes. Nothing was going to stop me from going for a swim. I returned to the YH, got my togs and a towel, and walked briskly across the wide promenade to the beach where I found that most of the beaches near the centre of the city were private beaches. I continued walking along the promenade past the private beaches to the public beaches, where I went for a refreshing swim.

This was where I discovered another important difference between Cannes and Nice. Cannes has lovely, wide, sandy beaches, whereas the beaches of Nice are not as wide and are composed of light grey shingle, with stones no larger than about 30 mm diameter. The sunbathers lie or sit on wooden benches, towels, or blow up mattresses on the shingle beaches. The transition between sand and pebble beaches begins in Antibes, and from then on they are a mixture of sand and pebble. All the beaches of Nice however, are pebble. A mixture of pebble and sand beaches continues on through Monaco to Menton on the Italian border.

After I had a long swim, one pleasing advantage of a shingle beach revealed itself. When I got out of the water all wet, the shingle didn't stick to me like sand. I found too that it wasn't uncomfortable to walk on in bare feet, as might be expected, as all the stones are quite smooth. The Mediterranean is virtually tideless, with only about 2 cm tidal changes. The sea temperature away from the shoreline maintains a constant 13°C nearly all year, but is much warmer near the shore, a consequence of the small tidal change. I swam and sunbathed most of the afternoon before I returned to the YH, after a wonderful day in one of the world's top resort cities on the Cot d' Azure.

Wednesday 2nd September: I was up early to another fine day. After breakfast I worked out the route I would take down through Italy to Naples to board the *Orion* in 17 days' time. On the way I wanted to see Pisa with its leaning tower, St Peter's and the Sistine Chapel in Rome. When I reached Naples, see Pompeii and Vesuvius. It was about 800 km to Naples and I felt that hitchhiking in Italy might not be as easy as it was in France. To get me to those places I wanted to visit, and be assured of being in Naples in time to board the *Orion* on the 18th of the month, I decided the surest way to travel through Italy, with the least stress, and visit the places I wanted to see, was to take the train if it wasn't too expensive.

I went to the Nice railway station to find out the cost of a train ticket from Nice to Naples, which would allow me to stop off wherever and as many times as I wished. The price was 2,320 Ff (£2/7). It was well within my budget and very reasonable, so I purchased a ticket. I could now relax in Nice, knowing that I had no worries about the final stage of my tour through France and Italy and most importantly, not have to worry about being in time to catch the *Orion* to take me back home to Australia.

I read the *Daily Mail* on the station, while I ate a ham sandwich and watched a couple of electric trains pass through. I returned to the YH and put my ticket in with the rest of my valuables. While I was there I met an American called Hank who was just about to go to the beach, so I went with him. We wandered up and down the

400

Promenade des Anglais looking for a good private beach, because I told Hank that the public beaches were too far out of town.

We selected the Ruhl Plage, owned by the large Ruhl Hotel directly behind the beach across the Promenade des Anglais. Although this private beach was the most expensive, but only by a few Francs out of all of those we had looked at, it appeared to be the best and nearest to the YH, located in the rear of the city.

We paid the very small daily fee of 80 Ff, about two shillings to a uniformed attendant at the entrance. I used the dressing and shower room to change into my togs, but Hank just wanted to sunbake on the beach. We talked with Joan an English girl, who was lying on the beach on a blow up mattress, looking very attractive in a colourful bikini. She had a gorgeous, sun tanned figure. She told us she was working as a Spanish dancer in a nightclub in Nice. After Hank left, I talked with Joan and then had a swim. Joan had to leave, but we arranged to meet on the beach after lunch the next day.

Thursday 3rd September: Another beautiful sunny day. I sunbathed and swam in the morning, together with others, most of whom I thought were probably very wealthy, but when everyone there is in bathers, we all looked alike, except of course that my bathers were rather unfashionable. After lunch I went back to the Ruhl Plage and met Joan. We talked animatedly together until Hank turned up to show us his new motorbike. The three of us talked some more until it was time for Joan to leave. She told us she was not very happy working at the nightclub, because the manager wanted her to fraternise with the clients and accept dates with them. She didn't want to do that, she said, and it was becoming a problem for her.

Hank, a great guy, took me back to the YH on his motorbike. It was only the second time I had ridden pillion, but this time there was no problem, because I didn't have a heavy rucksack on my back, as I had on my previous ride in Germany. It was an exciting experience riding around the streets of Nice, the shining new bike drawing quite a lot of admiring looks. After another large meal of spaghetti, which

I was living on at the moment, we rode back to town and walked around looking at the shops.

Beside us strolling along the promenade were couples, single men and women all beautifully dressed and made up, many complete with suntans. Nice indeed was a city of beauty and elegance. After admiring all this we returned to the YH and went off to our bunks.

Friday 4th September: When I met Joan on the beach again, she told me that she had been sacked! She was great company and I couldn't keep my eyes off her as she lay beside me in her bikini. We had a swim together and when we got out of the water, I told Joan I was on my way to catch the *Orion* in Naples. I said: "I would love to take you to dinner, but I am on a strict budget, and have just paid for a rail ticket to Naples." However, we made a date to meet in the evening outside the Ruhl Hotel.

Back at the YH I met a girl from Sydney who said she knew Leon. She didn't know he had returned to Australia and wasn't able to tell me anything about Leon that I didn't already know. I had another lovely big plate of spaghetti with red wine and then went to meet Joan.

I was outside the hotel early to meet Joan who has short, curly, brown hair, and although not stunningly beautiful, was very attractive. Especially the way she dressed in colourful clothes that showed off her sun tanned face and beautiful figure. I imagined she would be a great Spanish dancer, and I was sorry I would not be able to see her dancing. This was the first time I had seen her in street clothes, and I was very excited to be with her.

As we walked along the Promenade des Anglais, Joan said she had a great idea so that we could be together all the evening. She said to me: "We will go together to the restaurant where I will have my usual meal, and you have a glass of beer while I dine. You pay the bill and I will refund the money to you as soon as we leave". That sounded Ok to me so I said: "Beaut, let's do that." Joan chose a restaurant and we went inside and sat down together at a table.

402

I ordered the meal for Joan and a drink for both of us. While Joan ate, we had a wonderful conversation about our so very different lives. After Joan had finished her dinner, we had another drink and then I paid the bill. We left the restaurant hand in hand and as soon as we were out on the street, Joan refunded the price of her dinner to me. That was really the way to take a lovely girl to dinner, when you're not really taking a lovely girl to dinner. 'A Clayton's dinner, I believe.'

It was all very romantic as we strolled around Nice hand in hand. I was intending to leave Nice the next day, and was quite thrilled when Joan asked me to stay another day. I said I would love to. Where oh where was my so called inferiority complex? Late at night I took her back to her lodging where I kissed her goodnight and returned to the YH very happy, climbing into my sleeping bag full of contentment.

Saturday 5th September: Regrettably, this was my last day in Nice with Joan. I met her on the beach and after a swim we lay on the beach and again talked our heads off. I noticed that water skis could be hired for a cost of about 10/–for five minutes to be towed behind a boat, but I wasn't tempted. This was the first time I had ever seen water skiing. The second time was when I was at the beach at Rosebud after I came back to Australia. My Uncle Reg had a powerboat and skis. He invited me to have a go, knowing that I was a good snow skier. He said there was not much difference. It took me two tries to get up on the surface of the water, but I had no problem staying on the skis after that, even though he drove the boat in such a way as to try to get me to fall off.

There was a Nice to Nice car race getting ready to drive off on the Promenade des Anglais. The cars were nearly all French production cars, Citroens, Peugeots and Renaults. Joan and I left the beach to watch the start, not as exciting however, as a Formula One race start. There were about fifty cars competing, driving along a route on the mountain roads behind Nice and Cannes, before returning to the start.

Late in the afternoon I left Joan sunbathing on the beach, while I went back to the YH. On the way I purchased a beautifully, coloured, roll-out panoramic view of the Promenade des Anglais. It was nearly three feet long by six inches wide, but sadly it disappeared sometime after I arrived back in Melbourne. I had my usual large plate of spaghetti, tomatoes and wine, and then tidied up before going into Nice to meet Joan in the evening.

I met Joan and we greeted each other with a kiss, before hand in hand, following the same dining procedure as the night before, going to a restaurant of Joan's choice, a different one than last night. I had a beer while Joan had her dinner. Before we left the restaurant Joan wrote out her address in England on a piece of paper for me:

This made me wish I was going west not east. I paid the bill and Joan paid me back as soon as we were outside. We then walked down the gaily lit Promenade des Anglais. As usual it was a lovely warm night and Joan looked gorgeous in another colourful dress. We strolled along window shopping, amongst the other beautiful people, which I reckoned we were too. I thought to myself: 'if only this could go on forever.'

I said to Joan that I wished I could stay longer, but I had to keep moving. Joan said that she too would have to move on tomorrow, and look for another job in Cannes, or another resort along the coast. It was getting very late so I took her back to her lodging. We stopped at her front door and I took her in my arms and kissed her, telling her how much I had enjoyed being with her the last few days.

Joan looked up at me and said: "Gordon, I don't know whether I should take you up to bed with me or not?" I didn't know what to say. I was tongue-tied. I said something to the effect that I thought it might spoil the lovely short, but exciting time I had spent with her. We parted with a lingering kiss and wished each other good luck.

My final day in Nice finished in quite an unexpected way, when

404

I did not accept Joan's very tempting invitation to come to bed with her. To this day I don't know why I didn't. Maybe subconsciously, I felt that the brief, but exciting, romantic time I spent with Joan, in the fabulous city of Nice, which exuded romance might have been tarnished by a more physical experience. Or maybe, this was a manifestation of the inferiority complex that Netta accuses me of having. Nevertheless my romantic interlude on the Cote d' Azur remains as one of my most treasured memories of my time abroad

After having spent nine days on the Cote d' Azure in Cannes and Nice, I thought that Nice was a more beautiful resort than Cannes. Comparing the two main promenades, the Boulevard de la Croisette of Cannes did not have the same grandeur as the Promenade De Anglais. The inhabitants, tourist or otherwise, were I thought, dressed more elegantly in Nice.

It had been just perfect for me to be swimming, sunbaking and relaxing on the private, Rhule Plage beach in Nice. Strangely too, the pebble beaches of Nice gave the city a more ordered and clean appearance. I suppose for children the sandy beaches of Cannes were better, but I loved not having to get rid of all the sand when I climbed out of the water after a swim. Cannes has the sandy beaches and the film festival, but Nice is by far the better resort, and I was very fortunate in having such a relaxing, economical and exciting time there.

!!!!!!!!!!!!!!!!!!!!!!!

NICE TO MONTE CARLO

MONARCO

Sunday 6th September: I was up early ready to catch the train to Monte Carlo the capital of the Principality of Monaco, 17 km east of Nice. It was a quick journey along the sun, soaked coast. I was thrilled when the train pulled up at the rather plain, Monti Carlo railway station, where I got off to spend a few hours in this unique place that I had heard so much about, especially the gambling at the casino. Monaco's area is only 1.59 square km. It has no taxes, but receives all of its operating revenue from the casino and the tourist trade. Monaco rises from the sea in a series of steps with grand buildings of all colours and designs, built on the terraces. Monaco is not only famous for its casino, but also for the rich and famous people who live and visit there. Monaco was neutral during WWII, and a favourite place for high ranking Nazi officers to visit and gamble at the casino, where, it was said, a lot of money was laundered by the Germans. The year of my visit was also the year that Aristotle Onassis, the Greek shipping magnate, purchased a share in the casino, which was very helpful because the principality was experiencing financial problems at the time.

Monaco became even more famous when Grace Kelly, the beautiful American actress, married Prince Rainier III to become Princess Grace of Monaco in 1956. It was most important that the union produce a son, which it did, to ward off the possibility that Monaco would revert to French territory, if no heir was born. Prince Albert was born in 1958. Tragically Princess Grace was killed in the car she was driving in Monaco in 1982.

I walked up a hill from the station to the casino along the Rue Grimaldi, Prince Rainier's family name. There were no admission charges or dress rules to enter the casino. The interior, like the two story, rugged, exterior of the building, was magnificent. The gaming room has gold decorations on the roof, supported by large, grey columns, from which beautiful chandeliers hang. The gaming tables and chairs were upholstered in 'billiard table green,' the whole effect being rather subdued.

I wanted to see what really happened on the gaming tables. I saw all manner of different betting games taking place. I noticed some persons were keeping score of the numbers coming up on each table. A person very like Pablo Picasso, was slowly building up some good winnings. A man plonked oodles of francs down on a table, won and left the room. A lady made a point of touching wood and

The private Ruhl Plage Beach

The author centre on the balcony of the Ruhl Plage dressing room

Joan sun bathing on the shingle beach at Nice

Water skiing at Nice

The front of the casino in Monaco

The gaming room in the casino in Monaco

finally a man lost £500 in five minutes. Thinking about it afterwards, I was sure that it was the artist Picasso I saw. His face was very familiar to me, because he was in the news quite a lot at the time. I could have had a bet, as the lowest acceptable bet was a quite low, 100 Ff, because it was Sunday, but after leaving the casino, I had a bottle of beer instead.

Having spent about an hour and a half in the casino, I left having seen enough of the world's most famous, gambling venue. Although I only saw one gaming room I was sure there were more. My lasting impression of the casino was of its elegant furnishings and interior decorations that gave the casino a quiet relaxing ambience, although I was not sure that this was so of the gamblers. So different to the glaring, gaming casinos, I see on TV now in my home country and around the world.

I made my way back down the hill to the railway station and as I did, I was able to look down on the Monaco harbour and the surrounding coast, a beautiful sight with many luxury yachts at anchor in the harbour. I was also able to pick out part of the route of the Grand Prix racing circuit, which the Formula One racing cars use when they race in Monaco each year. While I waited for the train, I made notes about the actions of all the people I had seen around the gaming tables. My next destination was Bordighera in Italy where there was a YH.

iiiiiiiiiiiiiiiiiiii

MONTE CARLO TO BORDIGHERA

The train journey from Monte Carlo took me along the coast and after stopping at Menton, the last large town on the Cot d Azure in France, the train crossed the border into Italy.

408

CHAPTER 25
ITALY

This map shows tne route the author took through Italy and the towns and cities the author visited. Youth Hostels he stayed in are shown in bald type

The first station the train stopped at in Italy was Vitminglia just over the border, the train then travelled about 10 km further along the coast to Bordighera where there was a rather perfunctory customs check.

A

BORDIGHERA

I left the train here and followed the directions in my Italian YH guide book to the YH some distance above the large, bustling town. I booked in and had a meal of meat and potatoes, a nice change from spaghetti. Bordighera's only claim to fame seemed to be that it has the contract to supply the Vatican with palm fronds for Palm Sunday, and other Holy occasions. As evidence of this there was an abundance of palm trees growing in palm farms on the slopes that rose steeply from the sea around the town.

I talked to a couple of hostellers, one an English hosteller who told me to make sure I visited the YH in the castle at La Spezia, down the east coast. From the glowing description he gave me of the hostel and its surroundings, I said I most certainly would.

BORDGHERA TO SAN REMO

Monday 7th September: I left Bordighera early in the morning, because there was nothing more I really wanted to see there. The next place on my list to visit was San Remo. There was no YH in San Remo, I just wanted time to have a look around this Italian resort with the same name as a town in my home state of Victoria, which is also by the seaside. There wasn't a train until 12.15 p.m. so I caught a bus, which was quite cheap. It was a pleasant bus ride of just 20 minutes along the beautiful Italian coast to San Remo

SAN REMO

Arriving in San Remo, I left the bus and walked through the town and found a place to change my left over French francs and a traveller's check into Italian lira, which was still all flimsy, paper money. I walked to a sandy beach just out of town, where I sat down, propped my head on my rucksack and soaked up the sun. Most

410

interesting was the bathing attire. What a difference. There were no bikinis here. Most of the swimsuits worn by both men and women were black and one piece. The bathers too all seemed to be on the large side. I didn't see any beautiful bodies like I had seen on the beaches in France.

San Remo is a large beach resort and fishing town on the so-called 'Italian Riviera.' I used the word 'uninteresting' in my diary, as San Remo is nothing like Nice or Cannes, except for the way the land rises behind the town, It is very different from the little seaside town of San Remo in Victoria, with its few shops, guest and residential houses. It too has rising ground behind the town.

San Remo in Victoria is said to be 'the gateway to Phillip Island' as it is at the entrance to a long bridge that connects the mainland to Phillip Island, a popular tourist destination. In Chapter 13 I have written about my short, but very interesting and enjoyable holiday on the Isle of Wight, which in size and land features, has a very striking, similarity to Phillip Island, which also has towns named after those on the Isle of Wight.

After relaxing on the beach for about an hour or so, I looked at my map and found my way back to the railway station, where I had a ham roll for lunch.

‖‖‖‖‖‖‖‖‖‖‖‖‖‖‖‖‖

SAN REMO TO GENOA

I didn't have too long to wait before a train came along, to take me to Genoa 130 km to the west. It was a very scenic railway journey, because the railway line ran close by the seashore providing beautiful coastline views. A short time into the journey, I was standing in the corridor looking through an open window at the Mediterranean, when all of a sudden an American, who I had been talking to by the window yelled: "Look out!" Quickly pulling me away from the window, as I saw a large piece of bent wire go by, and the train came to a grinding halt. I got a hell of a fright. It was quickly evident what had occurred.

411

Our train, hauled by an electric locomotive, had pulled down the overhead catenary system above the train, from which the locomotive picked up its power. I realised that our train would not be capable of moving for a long time, but as a railway man, I was very interested in the procedure adopted, to solve the problem and get us on our way again. The Italian train staff helped us down from the train and many of us walked down to the beach, only about 30 m away. Most of the passengers sat on the beach and relaxed in the sunshine. I sat with the American, and we continued our interrupted talk. I thanked him for quickly pulling me away from the window.

We had wait of about two hours before a diesel electric locomotive came along with a work wagon, and the wire was quickly cleared away. The diesel locomotive was then coupled on to our train and hauled us into the Genoa railway station, better late than never.

GENOA

I sat on the station and watched the trains in Genoa being shunted, but I never saw much of Christopher Columbus's city, except what was visible from the station and from our disabled train coming into the city.

|||||||||||||||||||||||||

GENOA TO LA SPEZIA

About 4.30 p.m. a train came along going to La Spezia and Rome. I realised that I still had time to get to La Spezia, only 80 km to the south so I climbed aboard. The train was comfortably full and leaving the Genoa the single track railway cut a path through the town and suburbs with houses and high buildings rising on both sides with level crossings every now and again. I moved to my favourite spot in the corridor and opened a window, just as the train moved across to the seaboard, where it began burrowing through tunnel after tunnel, most bored precipitously into the rock high above the sea. A couple of the tunnels were so close together that at times the front of the long train was in a tunnel with the middle carriages in the open air hanging above a shear drop to the sea, and the rear of the train in another tunnel. From the corridor window in between tunnels I was afforded glimpses of the blue Mediterranean Sea a long way below. After a few more tunnels the country flattened out and the train arrived at La Spezia.

LA SPEZIA

Stepping down from that thrilling train journey, I found myself in the rather picturesque fishing town of La Spezia, but I wasn't sure where the YH was, because I couldn't understand the directions given in my Italian language YH handbook. (*Guida Ostelli Italiani per la Gioventu*). I showed it to a shopkeeper who spoke a little English. He said the YH was not in La Spezia, but in a castle in Lerici 10 km south along the coast.

LA SPEZIA TO LERICI

The shopkeeper pointed to the bus stop for the bus to take me to Lerici. It was getting dark, so I decided not to try to hitchhike, and after a short wait a bus came along and took me across to the coast at Lerici.

⛰

LERICI

The YH I discovered was in a castle located on a small headland, and in no time I had booked in. The warden directed me to a cheap cafe in the fishing village close by.

It was a great surprise to discover that the cafe was run by an Australian bloke from Sydney, who said he had come to Lerici for a short holiday, and had fallen in love with the place. He opened up the cafe, which he said was doing very well catering to hostellers like me. "Wait till you see Lerici in daylight, you will love it too". In a short time he made me a up a meal of soup and some sort of very tasty stew.

I thanked him and went back to the YH, where I found it was full of young people of all nationalities and they all got together for a marvellous night of spontaneous singing and dancing in the kitchen.

I joined in the conviviality, eventually climbing into my sleeping bag around 11 p.m. very tired, but happy. It had been such an eventful day.

Tuesday 8th September: I woke to another beautiful day. Doesn't it ever rain in Europe I wondered, only snow. I loafed all day on the beach, punctuated from time to time by walking around the seashore in both directions, watching fishermen at work, talking, smoking and mending their nets. Lerici is a charming fishing town on the Gulf of Spezia. The old castle that housed the YH was built between the 13th and 15th centuries and is said to be 'a worthy species of late medieval architecture.' The view of the fishing village and harbour of Lerici from the parapet of the castle was one of peace and tranquillity.

Wednesday 9th September: I loafed on the beach again, this time with two girls from Vienna. They were able to talk English, so we had a great time together talking about ourselves and helping me with my *Deutsch*. I spent the evening with them in the town, dining at the cafe owned by the Aussie, who said to me in his Aussie twang: "I told you Lerici was a bonza place, didn't I?" Of course I had to agree.

Again in the YH after dinner, there was another hearty sing song in the kitchen and I joined in. I was really sad that I would have to move on in the morning; because the two days and nights I spent in this idyllic town was one of the most joyous I had spent so far on my tours in any YH. It was so different from the joy I had being with Joan in Nice, which was a personal, idyllic experience.

My special memories of Lerici were of the harbour surrounded by shops, fishermen's houses and small cafes, the cafe run by the Aussie and the beautiful sunsets I saw across the harbour. I could have spent many more days there. This little seaside town was every thing I had been told about it, except it is in Lerici not La Spezia. All visitors to Italy, hostellers or otherwise, should make a point of spending some time in Lerici, a really beautiful spot, as is La Spezia.

414

Thursday 10th September: I woke to another sunny day and after a porridge breakfast, I bade farewell to the happy YH hostellers in the rugged, old Lerici castle.

LERICI TO LA SPEZIA

Sorry to leave Lerici, I caught the bus back to La Spezia

LA SPEZIA

La Spezia was subjected to heavy bombing by the Allies during the war, because it has been an Italian naval base since Napoleon's time. However, the present site of the naval base is in a bay to the west of the Lerici YH, but it was not visible from the YH castle or the beach.

‖‖‖‖‖‖‖‖‖‖‖‖‖‖‖‖‖

LA SPEZIA TO PIZA

The weather changed and there were a few showers as I boarded a slow, stopping train, for the 80 km journey to Pisa. My train ticket was not valid for an express or 'Rapide' train as they are called. This however, was the way I wanted to travel, because I was able to see more of the country and have close contact with its people.

Last year, when I travelled from Venice to Milan in the train, the conversation between the Italians who were with me in the compartment was quite intriguing. I could not understand what they were saying, but I understood more or less what they were talking about. On this journey to Pisa no such interesting dialogue occurred, and from that point of view it was rather dull. Nobody was very interested in me and my rucksack with the small, triangular, Aussie flag, sewn on to the flap.

Maybe this was evidence of the cultural difference between the southern and northern inhabitants of Italy that I had been told about, a difference stemming from the more industrialised and sophisticated north, compared to the more rural south. The Tuscany countryside I saw from the train however, was not dull. The railway line ran down the west coast of Italy a short way inland, while out to the east I

415

could see a large range of mountains interspersed with high peaks. These were the Apennine Mountains that run down the middle of the leg of Italy. Mt Cimone, 2.170 m (6,090 ft) high, was one of the high peaks shown on my map.

This region of Italy is rich in limestone and marble. The train passed many masonry yards where the marble was being cut. Many of the streets I saw from the train were lined with cypress trees and the hills were covered with vineyards.

PIZA

When the train pulled into the Pisa railway station, I set out to find the Leaning Tower of Pisa. I crossed over the Arno River and walked along streets lined with churches, museums and other historic buildings, all of which were *closed.* Why, I didn't know, or bothered to ask.

The weather was very dull and overcast, quite depressing in fact after the good weather I had been enjoying. For about 20 minutes of walking around, I turned a corner and there it was. The Leaning Tower of Pisa, leaning over to welcome me. I took a couple of photos and read some history of the tower on a notice board. Galileo, who was born in Pisa, used the tower's lean to demonstrate that: 'acceleration due to gravity is independent of the mass of an object.' He did this by dropping three different sized balls from the top of the tower.

The construction of the tower, which leaned over a little more than I had imagined, was commenced in 1174. When the tower reached three storeys, it began to develop a lean. Construction was halted for a further 90 years. In 1350 however the tower was extended to eight storeys with a bell tower on top, and 204 steps up a spiral staircase to reach the belfry, which has seven bells, each one sounding a note of the musical scale.

Just like the bell tower of Big Ben, special permission was required to get into the leaning tower's bell tower, and that was not possible for the ordinary tourist like me.

The torn down catenary wire

The disabled train by the beach

The Lerici Castle and YH above the harbour

View of Lerici from the parapet of the YH castle

The Leaning Tower of Pisa

The lean of the tower continued to increase a little each year and in 1990 it was 6 degrees, or 4 metres from the vertical at the top. It was realised then that something had to be done before the tower fell over, so engineers devised a method of stabilising the tower. After the work on the tower was complete, the lean of the tower was halted, and even reversed by about 40 cm.

iiiiiiiiiiiiiiiiiiiii

PISA TO ROME

Thursday 10th September: The town of Pisa depressed me, so without looking around the old town any more, I caught the 3.24 p.m. stopping train to Rome. The next stage of this great railway journey of 330 km to Rome was down through the province of Lasio. Not very long after the train left Pisa, the railway line ran a short way inland from the coast for a while, and I believe I got a glimpse of the island of Elba about 30 km to the west.

The landscape on the way to Rome was mostly undulating, wooded country, with open fields, alternating with flat, dry, but cultivated countryside, very similar to that between La Spezia and Pisa. There was plenty of lively and loud discussions between the mostly male passengers, who changed sometimes when the train stopped at stations along the way. Not once however, during the whole journey was any interest shown in me. Rather strange, I thought. Although I was on a stopping train, between stations the train roared along at quite a fast clip, approaching Rome through densely populated suburbs.

ROME

At 7.30 p.m. the train pulled into the very modern Rome railway station, which Mussolini had built while he was in power. After the long journey on the train, just short of four hours, I was very tired and longing to find the Rome YH, have something to eat, and collapse into my sleeping bag. It was not to be however, because when at last I found the YH, it was *closed*. I looked again in my

418

Italian YH guidebook and managed to follow the directions to another YH, only to find that it too, was *closed*. What was so special about Thursday 10th September, I wondered? To this day I do not know.

I met two Dutch blokes outside the YH who were in the same predicament as me. We tramped, tramped, tramped, around Rome looking for a cheap hotel, finally discovering one that was open for 350 lira a night. We booked in and then had a meal together at a cafe nearby. At last I was able to climb dog tired, into bed between sheets, which at least was some consolation. What a day. It was really a disappointing blow to find the youth hostels closed. There had been no mention of a public holiday anywhere in Rome or in Pisa.

Friday 11th September: I left the hotel early to find my way to St Peter's Baselica. I walked through a maze of streets, crossing over the not very imposing Tiber River on the way. Finally, I turned around the corner of a building and there confronting me was St Peter's, the largest Cathedral in the world, which I approached across the large expanse of St Peter's Square (Piazza San Pietro). The piazza is enclosed on two sides by Bernini's colonnade consisting of 284 columns and 140 statues. In the centre of the piazza, the high Egyptian obelisk from Nero's Circus stands tall. The piazza is where St Peter was executed in 67 AD. It can hold 30,000 people, as it does when the Pope wishes to speak to an audience.

St. Peters was not closed. I entered the famous cathedral and just inside the door I saw the large, beautifully sculpted, bronze statue of St Peter. I was amazed as I watched people crossing themselves and kissing the feet of the statue. I observed how St Peter's toes had been worn away over the years by the millions of people who had performed this ritual.

I then walked inside the huge cathedral and admired many of the art works in gold, marble, and the mosaics along with the usual icons seen in Catholic churches. The cathedral is a mixture of Renaissance and Baroque styles and was built in the period from

419

1506 to 1626. The belief is that it was built over St Peter's tomb. With my wont for comparing churches and cathedrals with mountains and because St Peter's is the largest cathedral in the world, it was only logical for me to choose Mt Everest, the highest mountain in the world as its counterpart. Mount Everest and St Peter's cathedral are immense, the largest of their kind. Mt. Everest for me is ethereal, but St. Peter's is not.

I have never seen Mt Everest with my own eyes, but I have read and seen many photographs of this wonderful mountain from numerous angles and in different snow conditions. The sight of Mt Everest always gives me a feeling of reverence, but St Peter's does not evoke those same feelings in me. Especially so, is Mt Everest's Tibetan name Chomolungma (Goddess Mother of the World), which at times, can bring a tear to my eye. Mt Everest has never been conquered–only climbed–nor has any other mountain in this, our world.

I left St Peter's and walked a short distance to the Vatican City guarded by soldiers in their colourful uniforms. The Vatican Palace and the Vatican Museum are inside Vatican City. I paid 200 lire to look over the Vatican City Museum, which has one of the largest, diverse variety of collections of objects from around the world. It also houses the Sistine Chapel, which I knew about from an early age, with its ceiling painted by Michelangelo.

The Sistine Chapel is like a large warehouse. It was built between 1475 and 1483 and is 40.9 m long, 13.4 m wide and 20.7 m high. The frescos on the roof (water colour paintings done on a surface before the plaster is dry) were painted by Michelangelo between 1508 and 1512.

The roof was originally painted with gold stars on a sky blue background, but Michelangelo painted over these with scenes from the Old Testament. Michelangelo also painted the end wall in 1536, with a fresco of the Last Judgement. Michelangelo was certainly a genius to be able to paint all those pictures working above his head.

The side walls were also painted, but not by Michelangelo. It was all very breathtaking and magnificent.

Leaving the corporate head office and marvellous buildings of the Catholic Church behind me, I bought and posted a Vatican card and stamps to my father. I had been told that there was a place called the Piazza del Siena in Rome, where outdoor operas were sometimes staged in the summer. It sounded interesting, so I took a tram there to have a look. It did not look as though anything had happened there for quite a while, as the site was all rocky and overgrown.

I decided to walk to the Coliseum, where I met a couple from Ceylon. The Sinhalese lady was very beautiful and the Sinhalese man with her could have passed as a modern gladiator, such was his physique. We paid a guide to show us through the massive structure. He explained its history to us. Its construction was started in 72 AD. When completed could seat around 80,000 people, only 20,000 less than the Melbourne Cricket Ground. I tried to picture it as it was when the gladiators fought with the tigers in front of a huge crowd, but it was beyond my powers of imagination. The partly ruined structure is a marvellous and thought provoking example of the work of architects and builders of past centuries.

I then took a tram that circled the city, which allowed me to have a good look at many areas and buildings of the city of Rome. I saw many sights of interest to me, especially a beautiful, white, marble church, which I thought was the Church of Victor Emanuel. It was so magnificent that got off the tram and took a photo, climbing aboard the next tram that came along.

During the remainder of the tram trip I never really saw anything that took my interest, but the 'church' was definitely the highlight of my tram ride around the streets of Rome. I should have visited this most elegant church, but I didn't, a decision which I regret.

Soon after, I discovered that this beautiful building was not a church, but the Victor Emanuel Monument, completed in 1911 to honour the first king of unified Italy. It was nicknamed the 'wedding cake' and was derided by architects as being a monstrosity. So much for my appreciation of the merits of architectural buildings.

I was satisfied that I had seen the major historical sights of Rome and there was nothing more I wanted to see in this curious city of antiquity. I suppose that if I were a Catholic, I would have stayed longer, finding many more things of interest to me. Netta I believe spent nearly a week in Rome, but Rome was not the kind of foreign city that had much of an appeal for me, Philistine and Protestant that I am. Rome is in fact no rival for Vienna as my favourite city, and doesn't feature in my best ten.

To complete the day, I went to a restaurant where I had a succulent meal of Italian spaghetti that was infinitely better than the spaghetti, I cooked. I then returned to my pension to write up my diary and notebook ready to catch the train in the morning to Naples, the last, large city on my tour before boarding the *Orion*. I was becoming a little excited.

Sometime later in a guidebook I read the following statement: 'Anyone who has been to Rome and hasn't walked at least once up and down the Spanish Steps hasn't really been to Rome.' In that case I haven't been to Rome, but I am sure that even if I had walked up and down the Spanish Steps, it would not have altered my view of the city.

iiiiiiiiiiiiiiiiiiiii

ROME TO NAPLES

Saturday 12th September: I had my last look around Rome on the way to the Rome railway station, which I admired for its modern, simple, architectural style. I left Rome for Naples, 217 km south at 12.20 p.m. On this journey I was able to travel on an electrically hauled express train, because it was not classified as a *Rapide*. I sat back to enjoy my last train ride on foreign soil, reflecting on my wise decision to purchase a ticket in Nice to take me all the way to Naples

My train entering the modern Rome railway station

St Peter's Basilica

A Vatican Guard

The Victor Emmanuel Monument the most beautiful building in Rome

The Sinhalese couple and guide

The modern Rome railway station

a distance of over 600 km. It had allowed me to plan where and how long I would stay in each location I visited, one of the benefits of travelling alone, which I have done without any regrets from the day Leon left me in Bad Ischl in January 1952. It also gave me the advantage of knowing exactly where and when I would arrive at any particular location. That is, except for such unplanned incidents such as my train pulling down the overhead wires.

Greater Italy is nominally divided into two parts, northern and southern, the south being considered the poorer agricultural half. Most of Italy is shaped like a leg. The upper or northern part of the leg above Rome is located just above the knee and is the more industrialised region. The southern or lower part of the leg is where Naples is located, about halfway between the knee and the ankle.

The railway line to Naples through the Province of Campania took me along mile upon mile of open fields, vineyards and cultivated land with crops of various kinds. The train stopped at a number of stations and one I noted was Latina, 54 km from Rome. The carriages as usual were the corridor type, and as the train sped along the weather cleared and the sun came out.

I moved to the corridor and opened a window, with my camera ready to take a photo of anything particularly interesting that may have appeared. As I write, taking photos from most main line trains operating in Europe is not now possible as the trains are air conditioned and the windows are permanently closed. It would not have been possible for me to take the photos of the Simplon Tunnel portals, but this is by no means a criticism of Europe's fabulous modern, main line trains of both types, single and double decker, resplendent in their very, colourful liveries,.

Further on in the journey, the train approached a range of low mountain peaks about 300 m high and after skirting around these, suddenly the Mediterranean Ocean came into view, which was really thrilling. The train then travelled around a large inlet with low hills in the background, and came to a stop in Formia, a large seaside

424

resort town. It was really great to be seeing the beautiful blue Mediterranean Ocean up close again. Leaving Formia the train continued on around the inlet before moving back inland amidst farmland and scattered vineyards. Further on there were a few short tunnels to burrow through before the next stop Minturno, a big rural town. The landscape became hilly again as the train approached the town of Villa Literno, where it stopped and took on many passengers.

The last 25 km to Naples was double track through an area of low mountains and a tunnel, which soon gave way to many dwellings that grew in number as the train reached the outer suburbs of Naples, taking on more passengers when it stopped at suburban stations. The now comfortably, full train entered Naples railway station at 3.30 p.m. Bringing to a close my journeys of *Backpacking By Train,* but not the end of my backpacking travels in Europe.

It had been an uneventful, three hour journey to Naples and once again, little interest was shown in me, or my rucksack. How different is the south of Italy from the north? I asked myself, a little piqued that I had been ignored.

A

NAPLES

I found the YH located a short distance outside the city in a huge, multi storey hotel, called the Hotel Grille. The hotel was full of Americans, because as well as housing the YH, it was occupied by the US Occupation Forces offices, and once again on this journey I come in contact with another division of this great force. The YH was accommodated on the top floor.

I booked in and deposited my rucksack ready to go and explore Naples. Just as I was about to leave, I met an Aussie wearing a Geelong Grammar School blazer. This quite nice Grammar boy, asked me to lend him some money until he changed a traveller's cheque. I obliged, loaning him the equivalent of £5 in Italian lira. I walked into the city to the Orient Line offices, but they were not open, and of course I was quite used to important places being closed in Italy by now. I wanted to find out if the *Orion* was on schedule. I had a look around Naples, had a meal and a few beers and returned to the YH, where the Geelong Grammar lad gave me back the money he had borrowed, thanking me profusely. I retired to my sleeping bag with the thought that in only six days, if the *Orion* is on time, I would be on my way home. I was beginning to get really excited at last.

The Hotel Grille is a big hotel and at one end a large, spiral ramp, giving cars access to the car park on the roof. From the roof there was a great view of Naples and the surrounding countryside, including Vesuvius, the Bay of Naples and a mountainous island across the bay. This I discovered was the Island of Capri that I had heard about from a song my mother used to sing about Capri: *'It was on the Isle of Capri that I found her,'* was the first line. I decided I must visit the island. Tired after a long journey I had a good meal in the YH, and having written up my diary and notes I retired to my bunk.

NAPLES TO POMPEII AND RETURN

Sunday 13th September: It was another sunny day and to see the city of Pompeii was my first objective. I decided to hitchhike along the road to Pompeii, 24 km south of Naples. I managed to get a lift almost immediately, right to the gates of Pompeii.

POMPEII

I paid a small admission fee and joined a guided party to escort me through the unique city. In 79 AD Pompeii was buried beneath ash and pumice when Mt Vesuvius, 1.277 m (4,190 ft) high, erupted. There were in fact two major cities buried, Pompeii and Herculaneum. Pompeii at the time had a population of 20,000, 2,000 of whom were killed in the eruption.

I saw the ruins of the buildings and the remains of the inhabitants, as a quick death overcame them from the ash and

426

pumice, burying them alive, and turning their bodies into solid, fascinating forms. The bodies and the places where they were found assisted archaeologists in establishing the way of life of the citizens of Pompeii at the moment when the disaster overtook them. Excavation to uncover these relics commenced in the middle of the 18th century. As digging progressed, the layout of Pompeii, its houses, places of entertainment, worship, and the modes of travel of the time were gradually uncovered.

The guide told us the names of the various houses, the 'House of Mystery', the 'House of the Faun' and many others, all of which contained fascinating frescos, statues and many other relics pertaining to the name of the house.

About halfway through the tour, the guide said that there was a room in which the wall frescos and other relics were only suitable for male eyes. The men left the ladies, while the guide took us to a room in a house that had erotic paintings around the walls. The best of all of them was of a man with a huge, erect penis, which was laid out horizontally on the pan, being weighed on a set of scales. It was absolutely hilarious. There were more sexy murals besides that one.

I spent over an hour with the guide, enthralled by what I saw in the unique old city, and when the guided tour came to an end, I wandered around having a further look for an hour or so. Walking around Pompeii, I was always conscious of Mt Vesuvius in the background and as I was leaving Pompeii I noticed that there were houses and some vineyards on the lower slopes of the mountain. The people who lived there must be aware that they were taking a risk, because ever since Vesuvius first erupted, there have been further small eruptions every now and again. In 1631 there was a large eruption resulting in the deaths of 3,000 people. The last eruption was a small event in 1944. I hitchhiked back to the YH, which was closed during the day.

I had to wait about an hour for the YH to open, so I went up on to the roof car park to admire the view. I met an attractive, English girl there also admiring the view of Vesuvius, the Bay of Naples and the Isle of Capri. We talked for a long time about ourselves and what we had been doing. We stayed on the roof talking together, well after the YH opened. It was a great pity that she wasn't in Naples to join the *Orion,* but was leaving in the morning to go south to Sorrento.

I told her all about Lerici, where it was, and said to make sure she went there. We wished each other good luck and parted with a hug, before we went back down to the YH, where I met a man, his wife and a girl there, all New Zealanders, who like me, were in Naples to join the *Orion.*

Monday 14th September: I went into Naples to the Orient Line office, where I received some letters from my mother, telling me how much she was looking forward to seeing me. This was a beaut surprise to see again that my mother was keeping up with me along the way. I also got my boarding pass and found that the *Orion* was on time. That was really great news. I was told too, that when the *Orion* came in, I could board her between 10 a.m. and 12 noon. I window shopped most of the rest of the day in the busy, attractive city of Naples with its lovely arcades, before returning to the YH, which was closed each day from 9 a.m. to 4 p.m.

In the evening I went on an unplanned walk with a NZ girl that took us through the filthy streets of the slums of Naples, the worst and only slums I had seen during my whole time abroad. I could not help but compare these slums with the splendour I had seen at St Peter's and the Vatican a couple of days ago. Then we saw a very entertaining open air Neapolitan song festival. We had a drink together before returning to the YH. I had three days to fill in before boarding the *Orion* on the 18th, plenty of time to visit the Island of Capri in the Bay of Naples. When I told the warden at the Naples YH that I was going to Capri in the morning, he told me there was a YH on the island. This was excellent news. He said that Fanny Aprise, the warden, was a wonderful old lady who had been running the YH

The seaside resort of Formia as seen from the train on the way to Naples

The train passing through an area of low mountains as it nears Naples

The Hotel Grille in Naples that housed both the YH and the USA Occupation forces

A magnificent shopping arcade in Naples

Some of the ruined buildings of Pompeii where the author went on a guided tour

A young boy in the slums of Naples smoking a cigarette

in Capri for many years. He said she was a bit of a legend on the island. So with that in mind for the morrow, a visit to the island my mother used to sing about I went off happily to my sleeping bag.

NAPLES TO CAPRI

Tuesday 15th September: I left the YH early in the morning for Capri boarding a large ferry that took an hour to cross the Bay of Naples to the island, with its steep cliffs, reaching right down to the water's edge.

CAPRI

The ferry pulled into the wharf of the Marina Grandi, on the north side of the island, and I climbed up the steep road to the Capri YH. Fanny Aprise an old lovely, looking lady I reckoned to be about 70 years of age welcomed me warmly and booked me into the sparse, but clean and comfortable YH.

I left my rucksack at the YH and walked a short way down to Capri's small, but delightful Piazza Umberto surrounded by shops displaying all manner of souvenirs. I sat down in the square and had a ham sandwich and a beer, while I looked at my map. The Isle of Capri is only 6 km long and just under 3 km wide, with Monti Solaro the highest point at 589 m on the western end of the island. There are only two towns on the island, Capri in a low saddle between Monti Solaro in the west and Monti Tuoro, 266 m, in the east. The other town is Annacapri located on the slopes of Monti Solaro.

Looking at my map I decided to explore the island and have a swim at the Marina Piccola. I knew that Gracie Fields, the English singer, 'The Lassie from Lancashire,' lived on the island with her husband. I did not expect to see her, nor did I have any intention of trying to find out where she lived.

Walking down the sealed road to the beach, I passed a villa with two people frolicking in the pool. I would probably have paused for a moment to look at the lovely pool in the villa, and then moved on, but just at that moment the lady in the pool laughed as the man with her dived off the board and did a huge 'belly-whacker.'

430

I straightway recognised the laugh that I had heard so many times on the radio, and in newsreels during the war years. It was a loud, raucous laugh and its owner was none other than Gracie Fields. It was her husband Boris, who had dived off the board and did the big belly-wacker. I stopped and took a couple of photographs of Gracie in the pool about 80 m away. My only regret was that I did not yell out: "Good on you Gracie" because from all that I have read about her since, I believe that there was a possibility that she might have left the pool and come over to speak to me, because I was the only person nearby. During the war years, Gracie Fields helped to maintain the morale of the British people by singing patriotic and other songs, in a wonderfully positive and happy manner.

When I returned to Australia I learned that Boris was born in Russia. He had lived on Capri for many years. He was not a plumber, as was widely reported, but a well-known resident on the island, who circulated among the wealthy and important people of Capri. Gracie was introduced to him after the death of her second husband. Gracie Fields was awarded many honours during her life and died in 1979 as Dame Gracie Fields. Was this another case of serendipity, actually seeing Gracie Fields in this way? Yes It was.

Moving on I walked down a steep path to the Marina Piccola below rocky cliffs, where I had a deliciously, refreshing swim in the clear, warm water, of this very small and secluded beach. Leaving this gem of a beach, I returned to the YH for lunch, where I met an English bloke called Brian. We went for a walk exploring the eastern end of the island around Monti Tuoro.

At one point, we had a great view across the houses and villas of Capri. These residences were built among the many trees on the terraces, which sloped down to the beautiful blue Bay of Naples. In the other direction we could see Naples and Vesuvius in the distance. From this viewpoint we also looked over Capri to Annacapri nestled below the high cliffs of Monti Solaro in the west. Capri to my mind is indeed an island with few rivals for rugged beauty.

431

Back at the YH after consuming a large plate of delicious stew, I had a look at the shops in Capri. One article I admired amongst all the other souvenirs was a special kind of table lamp. When the lamp was turned on, silhouettes of a variety of fish, flowers and other objects slowly rotated behind the light of the lamp shade the effect was quite fascinating. I had never seen any like them elsewhere, nor have I seen them anywhere else since. I had a detailed look to see how they were made. I didn't want to cash another traveller's cheque into Italian lira, otherwise I would have bought one, another decision that I have regretted to this day. I planned to make one when I got back to Australia, but I never did.

On a beautiful, balmy evening I joined Daphne, an English girl for a drink and talk in the picturesque Piazza Umberto, bringing to an end a very pleasant and exciting day. The Isle of Capri, we agreed, was just wonderful and beautiful.

Wednesday 16th September: I rose early again to sunny day. There were a couple places I wanted to see before I left this enchanted island, the Blue Grotto and San Michele. I could have taken a coach to the Blue Grotto, but I elected to walk and save a bit of money. The Blue Grotto is located below the cliffs of Annacapri on the northern side of the island. It was a quite a long walk on the sealed road downhill to the jetty, where I boarded a boat holding about 20 people.

The Blue Grotto was discovered in 1826. Most of the cave is about 2 m below sea level. It is completely enclosed except for an opening of about 1.3 m above the water. The opening remains constant due to the fortunate lack of high tidal change in the Mediterranean Sea. It is just large enough to allow a small boat to pass through, except in bad weather. We were rowed a short distance around the high cliffs, which dropped steeply into the sea, until we came to where four small boats with oarsmen were waiting for us.

We were helped to transfer into the smaller boats, which could only hold six people. When we were all settled, the oarsman rowed a

The ferry wharf to Capri in Naples with Vesuvius in the background

Looking down on the Marina Grandi in Capri

The secluded Marina Piccola beach

Gracie Fields and Boris in the pool at their villa

Fanny Aprise the warden of the Capri YH

A view of Capri and the cliffs of Monti Solaro beyond

433

little way toward the cliff face, where we saw the small entrance to the Blue Grotto. We were lucky there was only a small swell. As we approached the opening, the oarsman said: When he called out: "heads down," to lower our heads. He rowed near to the entrance and on the cry of "heads down," he skilfully chose the distance between the swells to take the boat into the cave.

The scene inside the aptly named Blue Grotto was overwhelmingly beautiful. The water in the cave became an indescribable, brilliant, translucent blue and the grotto walls shimmered with the reflection from the ripples of the seawater in the cave. The oarsman said the cave went in about 18 m. We were in the Grotto for about five minutes, and then we had to leave (lowering our heads when told) to allow the other small boats to enter. Once all the people had been inside the grotto, we were safely transferred back into the main boat and rowed back to the jetty. I will never forget that experience. I was very lucky that I had a bright, sunny, calm day to visit the Blue Grotto, which I experienced at its best, with the effect of the sunlight in the cave. The magnificent blue lighting effect was the result of the sun's rays entering the cave, below the waterline and being refracted (bent), which produced the blue colour, together with the effect of the light, reflected from the white, sand floor.

Leaving the boat at the jetty I walked up the hill toward Annacapri, as there was still another interesting sight to be seen on this end of the island. I walked past a small village, then made my way up towards the villa called San Michele, enjoying wide views from the road as I approached the villa. I paid a small entrance fee and went inside the villa, which is actually a museum and was the home of the Swedish doctor Axel Munthe.

The museum has statues and other artefacts placed tastefully around the rooms that he had collected over many years from excavations around the villa and nearby. I had a good look at all these very varied exhibits, small statues, vases and the like, then

434

walked around the extensive grounds and gardens in which there were many more statues and other sculptured works of Roman art.

Axel Munthe wrote a book called *The Story of San Michele*. I read his book some years later and found it extremely interesting and enthralling, more so because I had visited his villa. The book is a fascinating autobiography. It tells the story of his life as a doctor and how he built San Michele on the site of the villa of Emperor Tiberius, who lived on Capri some 2,000 years ago. Axel Munthe was born in Sweden and spent much of his life in various European cities, where he had many loyal and rich patients, who paid him well. This allowed him to tend to the medical needs of the poor in Naples and many other cities. The name of his villa, San Michele, came from a small ruined chapel he found near Annacapri, when he climbed up the slopes of Monti Solaro on a visit to Capri, when he was about 18 years old. Axel Munthe died in 1949.

I walked back to the YH admiring the great views of a beautiful landscape of wooded hills, steep cliffs and spectacular coastlines that is the Isle of Capri. I thanked Fanny the warden, paid the fees and crossed the square and walked down the steep road to the Marina Grandi, where I boarded the ferry to take me back to Naples.

CAPRI TO NAPLES

I fell in love with Isola, Isola Capri, a beautiful, enchanting being. She revealed many of her charms to me. As the boat made its way to Naples, I looked back and saw a cloud building up over Isola Capri's lovely form. Below is a verse from my mother's song.

Summer days are nearly over,
Blue Italian skies above,
I said: "Lady I'm a rover,
Can you spare a sweet word of love?"
She whispered softly; "It's best not to linger,"
Then, as I kissed her hand I could see,
She wore a plain, golden ring, on her finger,
It was goodbye on the Isle of Capri.

NAPLES

Thursday 17th September 1953: Back at the YH in Naples I thought that my visit to Capri was another highlight of this, my fifth and last tour. It was a perfect place to spend the last few days of my travels abroad.

I went into Naples to buy presents, and once again I entered the magnificent, long, high roofed arcade, of grand architecture, with a high arch supporting the roof. I purchased two fashionable, Italian, silk scarves, one for my father and one for my brother Donald. Naples is a large rambling city, located at the head of the Bay of Naples. It is a city of contrasts, from the squalid slums to the beautiful shopping arcades. Naples was bombed heavily during the war and evidence of the damage could still be seen on some of the old buildings and statues around the city.

The traffic made the city quite noisy with its trams, trucks and cars, but strangely not many scooters like I had seen in Milan on my first tour. Was this further evidence of the difference between the peoples of the north and south of Italy? The rich north and the poor south. Italian men's fashions were very attractive, pointed shoes and wonderfully tailored suits, mostly of dark material. The women's clothes, too, tended to be on the dark side, and there were many most attractive, olive skinned brunettes, to be seen.

I returned to the YH, where I saw a couple of Yanks talking with an Aussie girl, who I discovered, was trying to stow away on the *Orion!* How very interesting, I thought. Then I met a dinkum, Aussie girl and we went to a small local restaurant, where we had a great meal of spaghetti and minestrone, finishing the meal with quite a few beers, both of us ending up very merry indeed. She, sadly, was not joining the *Orion,* but was on her way to Rome and then Austria, so I gave her a few tips and wished her good luck.

Before I got into my sleeping bag for the last time in Europe, I wrote up my diary and notebook, reflecting on the events of my tour after leaving Cannes. Meeting Joan in Nice and spending three very

Boats waiting to take visitors into the Blue Grotto

'Heads down' as a boat enters the cave of the beautiful, Blue Grotto

The front door of the museum of San Michele

Outside Axel Munthe's San Michele museum in Annacapri

On the ferry returning to Naples looking back cloud had formed over Isola Capri

The TSS Orion the ship that the author will board on 18th September to take him home to Australia

exciting days with her. The short day I spent in Monaco visiting the Casino allowed me to get a feel for the unique principality, which brought to a conclusion my visit to probably the most well known of and famous area of the whole long coastline o the Cote d' Azur.

When I crossed the border into Italy and stopped in San Remo for just a day, I realised that I was in a vastly different culture from the one I had left in France. Pisa and Rome were of little interest to me, except of course for the major historical architectural tourist attractions of each city about which I had learned in my primary school days. By contrast Lerici and Capri were two, absolutely enchanting, beautiful gems of places, which I believe no visitor to Italy, be they ordinary tourist, or in particular YHA backpackers, should miss.

To mimic somewhat the comment made about Rome and the Spanish Steps, I would say that: 'Any visitor to Italy who has not been to Lerici and Capri has not seen Italy.' I was not 'seeing Naples and dying.' I was seeing Naples and going home to Australia, after a fantastic time as an Aussie backpacker abroad. I climbed into my sleeping bag for my last night in a Youth Hostel abroad.

BACK TO AUSTRALIA

Friday 18th September 1953: I was up awake and out of my sleeping bag early and down to the wharf to see the *Orion* enter the harbour at 7 a.m. The ship, its hull painted a light yellow, looked a little larger than the *Moreton Bay*, and it is. Straightway after breakfast, I paid the small YH bill and signed out of the YH. With my boarding pass, passport and rucksack on my back I made my way down to the wharf and passed through the boarding gates. I walked along the wharf and climbed up a gangway on to the *Orion* and made my way to the pursers office.

I was welcomed aboard and given my cabin and bunk number. I asked the purser if he had any printed matter to explain about the ship and the voyage. He said that the *Orion* would be raising anchor at 5 p.m., and any other information I required was on the ship's

438

noticeboards. A very short welcome I thought. I found my bunk, one in a cabin of four bunks.

Leaving my rucksack on my bunk, I went back into Naples and shopped for odds and ends to get rid of all the Italian money I had left. I returned to the ship in time for lunch and was directed to a table where there were some young people about my age. After the introductions, I settled down to enjoy an excellent cold lunch, so different from my usual ham rolls and sandwiches. After lunch I had a few beers and a swim in the ship's pool.

At exactly 5 p.m. with the sounding of the ship's horn the *Orion* pulled up anchor and I was off back to Australia. As we steamed out of the Bay of Naples I took one last look at Naples and Vesuvius. I noticed that Mt Solaro on the Isle of Capri had again generated an impressive cumulus cloud, just like the day before. It reminded me of the cloud on the Matterhorn on my last skiing day in Zermatt. Before I retired to my cabin I watched the sun dropping behind the cloud over Capri in a blaze of glorious red and orange, my last continental sunset. The *TSS Orion* arrived in Port Melbourne on my mother's birthday, 15th October which could not have been planned better. Just another case of serendipity

EPILOGUE

I enjoyed writing *Backpacking By Train* because I am a rail fan and was able to travel on, and see first hand, trains, locomotives and railways that I had read about in my books about trains in my youth. Especially being able to travel behind, and see many of the last remaining steam trains in the UK and Europe, which were being replaced by diesel and electric traction.

My five backpacking tours, two in England and three in Europe were all successful backpacking journeys. They were very economical thanks to Youth Hostel accommodation, and the many hundreds of miles I was able to hitchhike without any problems using various forms of transport. This book is a valuable TRAVEL GUIDE for the present day backpacker and tourist

As mentiond in the introduction the two companion books. *Come on Board* published by Tale and *An Aussie Backpacking Londoner,* also published by Tale, complete the story of my two years abroad, and my time in London, during the year of the Coronation of Queen Elizabeth II on June 2nd 1953.

I have wondered what my life would have been like if I had not made the big decision to go abroad. I am sure my life would not have been so fully charged with knowledge of the world that has made my life so interesting. Of all the events and experiences I enjoyed during my time abroad, none was so unexpected as to be in London and be part of the Coronation celebrations for Queen Elizabeth II, together with the news, received in London on the morning of the Coronation that Mt Everest had been climbed by Hillary and Tenzing.

The years I was abroad were very exciting and significant with regard to events that occurred not only in the UK, but in the world six years after the end of WWII, and there was still much evidence of the war to be seen.

I believe that every young person over 18 years of age should aim to travel abroad, to get our wonderful country in perspective. This perspective cannot be gained through the media or books, it can only be attained by leaving Australia and travelling abroad. Life and world events, including those in Australia, can then be seen from a more enlightened viewpoint.

As I write and complete this book, I am 96 years of age and have lived an exciting life full of interest. I have been married to my beautiful wife Dilys, also 96 years of age. We have been married for 69 wonderful years and together we have achieved much. Dilys has been a great help to me with my writing that began in 2001. This is my last book, but I have many other interests to keep my brain active and keep me alive.

A quoatation that my wife Dilys showed me is very appropriate to complete this book

A man's real possession is his memory
In nothing else is he rich, in nothing else is he poor
Alexander Smith

441

TRAVEL GUIDE INDEX
LEGEND
⁞⁞⁞⁞⁞⁞⁞⁞⁞⁞⁞⁞⁞⁞	TRAVEL BY TRAIN TO DESTINATION
⚲	YOUTH HOSTEL ACCOMMODATION
⌂	OTHER FORMS OF ACCOMODATION
👍	HITCH HIKING TO DESTINATION

INTRODUCTION	1
CHAPTER 1	7
ENGLAND	7
SOUTHAMPTON TO LONDON	7
LONDON	8
LONDON TO HITCHIN	9
HITCHIN	9
HITCHIN TO LONDON	11
LONDON	11
CHAPTER 2	24
THE FIRST BACKPACKING TOUR	24
HITCHIN	24
ENGLAND	.24
HITCHIN TO DOVER	24
DOVER TO CALAIS	24
CHAPTER 3	25
FRANCE	.25
CALAIS TO BASEL	25
CHAPTER 4	26
SWITZERLAND	.26
LES VERRIERES	26
BASEL	26
BASEL TO SALZBURG	.27
CHAPTER 5	29
AUSTRIA	29
SALZBURG	32
SALZBURG TO BAD ISCHL	35
ATTNANG	35
BAD ISCHL	36

FERRY

	BAD ISCHL	41
	BAD ISCHL TO BAD AUSSIE	46
	BAD AUSSIE	49
	BAD AUSSIE TO BAD ISCHL	49
	BAD ISCHL	50
	BAD ISCHL TO SALZBURG	51
	SALZBURG	52
	SALZBURG TO BERCHTESGADEN	55
	AUSTRIA–GERMAN BORDER	55
	A–G BORDER TO SALZBURG	55
	SALZBURG	56
BUS	SALZBURG TO BERCHTESGADEN	56
	CHAPTER 6	57
	GERMANY	57
	BERCHTESGADEN	57
	STRUB	57
BUS	BERCHTESGADEN TO SALZBURG	62
	CHAPTER 7	65
	AUSTRIA	65
	SALZBURG	65
	SALZBURG TO KLAGENFURT	66
	VILLACH	67
	KLAGENFURT	69
	KLAGENFURT TO VIENNA	71
	VIENNA	74
	VIENNA TO KLAGENFURT	96
	KLAGENFURT	98
.I AND BUS	KLANGENFURT TO VOLKERMARKT	98
	VOLKERMARKT	100
	VOLKERMARKT TO KLAGENFURT	101
	KLAGENFURT	101
	KLAGENFURT TO TARVISIO	101
	CHAPTER 8	103
	ITALY	103
	TARVISIO	103

‖‖‖‖‖‖‖‖‖‖‖‖	TARVISIO TO VENICE	103
⚠	**VENICE**	106
‖‖‖‖‖‖‖‖‖‖‖‖	VENICE TO MILAN	112
⚠	**MILAN**	113
‖‖‖‖‖‖‖‖‖‖‖‖	MILAN TO BRIG	117
	CHAPTER 9	120
	SWITZERLAND	120
	BRIG	120
‖‖‖‖‖‖‖‖‖‖‖‖	BRIG TO ZERMATT	121
🏠	**ZERMATT**	124
‖‖‖‖‖‖‖‖‖‖‖‖	ZERMATT TO THE GORNERGRAT	126
	GORNERGRAT	127
SKI	SKI TOUR TO THEODULE PASS	135
‖‖‖‖‖‖‖‖‖‖‖‖	ZERMATT TO BRIG	144
	BRIG	144
‖‖‖‖‖‖‖‖‖‖‖‖	BRIG TO SPIEZ	146
‖‖‖‖‖‖‖‖‖‖‖‖	SPIEZ TO GRINDELWALD	149
🏠	**GRINDELWALD**	150
‖‖‖‖‖‖‖‖‖‖‖‖	GRINDELWALD TO KLEINER SCHEIDEGG	152
	KLEINER SCHEIDEGG	152
‖‖‖‖‖‖‖‖‖‖‖‖	GRINDELWALD TO BERN	164
‖‖‖‖‖‖‖‖‖‖‖‖	BERN TO PARIS	164
	CHAPTER 10	166
	FRANCE	166
	PARIS	166
‖‖‖‖‖‖‖‖‖‖‖‖	PARIS TO CALAIS	166
	CALAIS	167
	CALAIS TO FOLKSTONE	168
	CHAPTER 11	169
	ENGLAND	169
FERRY	CALAIS TO FOLKSTONE	169
‖‖‖‖‖‖‖‖‖‖‖‖	FOLKSTONE TO HITCHIN	169
🏠	**HITCHIN**	170
🏠	**STEVENAGE**	174
‖‖‖‖‖‖‖‖‖‖‖‖	STEVENAGE TO LONDON	177

⌂	**NOTTING HILL GATE**	177
	CHAPTER 12	179
	THE SECOND BACKPACING TOUR	179
COACH	LONDON TO MINEHEAD	179
⛺	**MINEHEAD**	180
BUS	MINEHEAD TO LYNTON	180
⌂	**LYNTON**	181
	LYNMOUTH	181
BUS	LYNTON TO BARNSTAPLE	182
|||||||||||||||||||	BARNSTAPLE TO EXETER	182
	EXETER	183
BUS	EXETER TO LYNTON	184
	LYNTON	184
BUS/TRAIN	LYNTON TO STEVENAGE	184
⌂	**STEVENAGE**	186
	CHAPTER 13	211
	THE THIRD BACKPACKING TOUR	211
|||||||||||||||||||	STEVENAGE TO LONDON	212
|||||||||||||||||||	LONDON TO PORTSMOUTH	212
FERRY	PORTSMOUTH TO RYDE	212
	RYDE ISLE OF WIGHT	212
|||||||||||||||||||	RYDE TO VENTNOR	212
⌂	**VENTNOR**	213
COACH	**SOUTH OF ISLAND COACH TOUR**	213
COACH	**VENTNOR TO RYDE COACH TOUR**	215
|||||||||||||||||||	PORTSMOUTH TO STEVENAGE	218
⌂	**STEVENAGE**	218
|||||||||||||||||||	STEVENAGE TO CAMBRIDGE	233
	CAMBRIDGE	233
CAR	STEVENAGE TO LONDON	242
⌂	**LONDON**	242
	CHAPTER 14	246
	THE FOURTH BACKPACKING TOUR	246
COACH	LONDON TO GLASGOW	246
	CHAPTER 15	248

	SCOTLAND	248
🏠	**GLASGOW**	250
‖‖‖‖‖‖‖‖‖‖‖‖‖	GLASGOW TO ARDROSSAN	252
	BRODICK	252
COACH	**ISLE OF ARRAN COACH TOUR**	253
‖‖‖‖‖‖‖‖‖‖‖‖‖	ARDROSSAN TO GLASGOW	254
COACH	**THREE LOCHS COACH TOUR**	257
CRUISE SHIP	**LOCK LOMOND CRUISE**	259
‖‖‖‖‖‖‖‖‖‖‖‖‖	GLASGOW TO FORT WILLIAM	263
	FORT WILLIAM	265
BUS	FORT WILLIAM TO OBAN	266
🏠	**OBAN**	268
CRUISE SHIP	**CRUISE TO IONA AND STAFFA**	268
	IONA	268
	STAFFA AND FINGALS CAVE	269
	TOBERMORY	270
‖‖‖‖‖‖‖‖‖‖‖‖‖	OBAN TO GLASGOW	270
	GLASGOW	272
BUS	GLASGOW TO EDINBURGH	272
🏠	**EDINBURGH**	273
‖‖‖‖‖‖‖‖‖‖‖‖‖	**THE FIRTH OF FORTH BRIDGE**	274
	DUNFIRMLINE	274
BUS	DUNFIRMLINE TO NORTH QUEENSFERRY	274
BUS	NTH. QUEENSFERRY ACROSS THE FIRTH	275
BUS	EDINBURGH TO GLASGOW	276
	GLASGOW	276
TRAM/BUS	GLASGOW TO PRESTWICK AIRPORT	276
	PRESTWICK AIRPORT	278
AIRCRAFT	**PRESTWICK AIRPORT TO NORWAY**	278
	CHAPTER 16	280
	NORWAY	280
🏠	**STAVANGER**	280
SHIP	STAVANGER TO BERGEN	282
🏠	**BERGEN**	284
‖‖‖‖‖‖‖‖‖‖‖‖‖	BERGEN TO VOSS	285

🏕	**VOSS**	287
👍	VOSS TO GUDVANGEN	287
FERRY	GUTVANGEN TO AURLAND	288
🏕	**AURLAND**	289
BUS	AURLAND TO FLAM	289
⫯⫯⫯⫯⫯⫯⫯⫯⫯⫯	FLAM TO MYRDAL	289
⫯⫯⫯⫯⫯⫯⫯⫯⫯⫯	MYRDAL TO FINSE	290
🏕	**FINSE**	292
⫯⫯⫯⫯⫯⫯⫯⫯⫯⫯	FINSE TO GEILO	293
👍 TRUCK	GEILO TO GOL	294
🏕	**GOL**	294
👍 TRUCK	GOL TO NESBYEN	294
⫯⫯⫯⫯⫯⫯⫯⫯⫯⫯	NESBYEN TO OSLO	294
🏕	**OSLO**	295
⫯⫯⫯⫯⫯⫯⫯⫯⫯⫯	OSLO TO STOCKHOLM	298
	CHAPTER 17	301
	SWEDEN	301
🏠	**STOCKHOLM**	302
👍 CAR	STOCKHOLM TO COPENHAGEN	306
👍 CAR🏠	**JOHNKOPING**	309
👍 CAR	**HALMSTAD**	309
👍 CAR	**HELSINGBORG**	309
FERRY	HELSINBORG TO HELSINGOR	309
	CHAPTER 18	310
	DENMARK	310
🏕	**COPENHAGEN**	310
⫯⫯⫯⫯⫯⫯⫯⫯⫯⫯	COPENHAGEN TO GLOSTRAP	314
	GLOSTRAP	314
CAR	GLOSTRAP TO KONSOR	314
FERRY	KONSOR TO NYBORG	316
⫯⫯⫯⫯⫯⫯⫯⫯⫯⫯	NYBORG TO OBENSE	316
🏕	**ODENSE**	316
👍 CAR	ODENSE TO ABENRA	317
👍 CAR	ABENRA TO FLENSBURG	317
	CHAPTER 19	319

	GERMANY	319
TRUCK	FLENSBURG TO KIEL	320
	KIEL	320
	KIEL TO HAMBURG	321
	HAMBURG	321
CAR	HAMBURG TO CELLE	324
	CELLE TO HANNOVER	324
	HANNOVER	325
MOTORBIKE	HANNOVER TO GOTTINGEN	326
	GOTTINGEN	327
CAR	GOTTINGEN TO HEIDELBERG	327
	HEIDELBERG	328
COACH	HEIDELBERG TO MUNICH	332
	MUNICH	333
CAR	MUNICH TO STARNBERG	336
	STARNBERG TO INNSBRUCK	338
	MITTLEWALD	338
	CHAPTER 20	339
	AUSTRIA	339
	INNSBRUCK	339
	INNSBRUCK TO HAFELEKAR	341
VAN	*INNSBRUCK TO ZURICH*	344
	LIECHENSTEIN	346
	CHAPTER 21	348
	SWITZERLAND	348
	ZURICH	348
	ZURICH TO BASEL	348
	BASEL	349
	BASEL TO FRANKFURT	350
	CHAPTER 22	351
	GERMANY	351
	FRANKFURT	352
	FRANKFURT TO MAINZ	352
	MAINZ	352
	MAINZ TO COLOGNE	353

	COLOGNE	355
🏕	COLOGNE TO AMSTERDAM	356
⫴⫴⫴⫴⫴⫴⫴⫴⫴	**CHAPTER 23**	357
	HOLLAND	357
🏕	**AMSTERDAM**	357
	🏠	359
⫴⫴⫴⫴⫴⫴⫴⫴⫴	AMSTERDAM TO THE HOOK OF HOLLAND	360
CC FERRY	HOOK OF HOLLAND TO HARWICH	362
	CHAPTER 24	363
	ENGLAND	363
⫴⫴⫴⫴⫴⫴⫴⫴⫴	HARWICH TO LONDON	363
🏠	**LONDON**	363
	LIVING AND WORKING IN LONDON	363
	THE FIFTH BACKPAKING TOUR	364
🏠	**LONDON**	364
⫴⫴⫴⫴⫴⫴⫴⫴⫴	LONDON TO NEWHAVEN	364
FERRY	NEWHAVEN TO DIEPPE	364
	CHAPTER 24	366
	FRANCE	366
👍 CAR	DIEPPE TO ROUEN	366
🏕	**ROUEN**	367
👍 CAR	ROUEN TO PARIS	367
🏠	**PARIS**	368
BUS	PARIS TO FONTAINEBLEAU	383
👍 CAR	FONTAINBLEAU TO LYON	383
🏠	**LYON**	383
👍 CAR	LYON TO GRENOBLE	385
🏕	**GRENOBLE**	385
COACH	GRENOBLE TO CANNES	386
COACH	**GAP**	387
🏕	**LA BOCCA**	391
	CANNES	391
BUS	CANNES TO NICE	397
🏕	**NICE**	398
⫴⫴⫴⫴⫴⫴⫴⫴⫴	NICE TO MONTE CARLO	404

	MONACO	404
iiiiiiiiiiiiiiiiiiii	MONTE CARLO TO BORDIGHERA	407
	CHAPTER 25	408
	ITALY	408
🛖	**BODRDIGHERA**	409
iiiiiiiiiiiiiiiiiiii	BORDIGHERA TO SAN REMO	409
	SAN REMO	409
iiiiiiiiiiiiiiiiiiii	SAN REMO TO GENOA	410
	GENOA	411
iiiiiiiiiiiiiiiiiiii	GENOA TO LA SPEZIA	411
	LA SPEZIA	412
	LA SPEZIA TO LERICI	412
🛖	**LERICI**	412
	LERICI TO LA SPEZIA	414
iiiiiiiiiiiiiiiiiiii	LA SPEZA TO PISA	414
	PISA	415
iiiiiiiiiiiiiiiiiiii	PISA TO ROME	417
	ROME	417
iiiiiiiiiiiiiiiiiiii	ROME TO NAPLES	421
🛖	**NAPLES**	424
🛥 CAR	NAPLES TO POMPEII AND RETURN	425
	POMPEII	425
FERRY	NAPLES TO CAPRI	429
🛖	**CAPRI**	429
FERRY	CAPRI TO NAPLES	434
🛖	**NAPLES**	435
SS ORIONs	**BACK TO AUSTRALIA**	437
	EPILOGUE	439
	ABOUT THE AUTHOR	450

ABOUT THE AUTHOR

The author 24 years

Gordon James Robert Smith. Author, historian and artist was born in 1927 in Victoria. He went to the Heidelberg State School and the Preston Technical School, and became a tradesman fitter and turner with the Victorian Railways (VR) in 1949. He was a member of the Boy Scouts, Rover Scouts and the Youth Hostels Association (YHA). Together with another YHA member he left Australia in 1951 to travel by ship to the UK on a working and backpacking holiday for two years. He returned to Australia in 1953. Soon after, in December 1953, he joined the SEC Kiewa Hydro-Electric Scheme and began water colouring. In 1954 he married Dilys Terry and during his ten years on the Scheme, they raised a family of a girl and two boys.

In 1963 he and his family left the SEC and shifted to Melbourne where he worked for Australian General Electric (AGE) as a facilities engineer until AGE closed down in 1983. He then taught pneumatic and hydraulics at the Royal Melbourne Technical College (RMIT) until he retired in 1993 He played golf and skied for much of his life. After he retired he began writing many books about his life. He is now 96 and lives with his wife in Box Hill North.

The author 94 years

BOOKS BY THE AUTHOR

Co-authored Pneumatic Control for Industrial Automation, published by John Wiley. *Come on Board,* and *An Aussie Backpacking Londoner* both published by Tale.: Self published-*An Australian Backpacker Abroad 1951-1953-Mountains of My Youth-Working and Raising a Family On The Kiewa Scheme* and *Learning a Trade 1944 to 1949-20 Watercolours of the Kiewa Scheme.* He has published the following Ebooks on Smashwords. *Two Voyages-My Journey Through Occupied Austria 1952-To the Swiss Alps via Venice-The Assimilation Of An Aussie Backpacker-Backpacking in 1952-An Aussie Backpacking Londoner-Back to Australia via France and Italy-Concrete Hard Rock Earth and Snow-The High Plains Patrol.* His last two books completed and to be offered for publication. *Backpacking by Train* and *Skiing In Zermatt 1952.*

www.ingramcontent.com/pod-product-compliance
Ingram Content Group UK Ltd.
Pitfield, Milton Keynes, MK11 3LW, UK
UKHW020818171224
452405UK00018B/107